D0213713

English Literature:

THE BEGINNINGS TO 1800

Third Edition

Arthur H. Bell, Ph.D., and Bernard D. N. Grebanier, Ph.D.

BARRON'S

Copyright © 1994 by Barron's Educational Series, Inc.

Prior editions copyright © 1948 and 1959 by Barron's Educational Series, Inc.

All rights reserved.
No part of this book may be reproduced in any form by photostat, microfilm, xerography, or any other means, or incorporated into any information retrieval system, electronic or mechanical, without the written permission of the copyright owner.

All inquiries should be addressed to:
Barron's Educational Series, Inc.
250 Wireless Boulevard
Hauppauge, New York 11788

Library of Congress Catalog Card No. 94-13990
International Standard Book No. 0-8120-1775-7

Library of Congress Cataloging-in-Publication Data

Bell, Arthur H. (Arthur Henry), 1946–
    English literature: the beginnings to 1800 / Arthur H. Bell and
Bernard D. N. Grebanier. —3rd ed.
        p.   cm. — (College review series)
    ISBN 0-8120-1775-7
    1. English literature—Outlines, syllabi, etc.   2. English
literature—Examinations—Study guides.   I. Grebanier, Bernard D.
N., 1903–   .   II. Series.
PR87.B44   1994
820.9—dc20   94-13990
                                                                                CIP

Printed in United States of America
4567 9770 987654321

PREFACE

The one thousand years of English literature under consideration in this book contain, in Chaucer's apt phrase, "all God's plenty." Here are the towering geniuses of English literature (or any literature, for that matter): Chaucer, Shakespeare, Spenser, Milton, and others. Here are important women authors such as Aphra Behn, who wrote eloquently against the slave trade; Ann Radcliffe, the mother of the Gothic novel; and Suzanna Centlivre, a shrewd dramatic anatomist of love relations. In this millennium of literature we can observe the interrelations of literature and politics, literature and art, literature and religion, literature and philosophy, and, perhaps above all, literature and day-to-day life.

A one-volume literary tour of the approximate period 800 to 1800 must guard against the tendency to "see England from 30,000 feet." Broad generalizations about periods, authors, and works (while sometimes useful) are less memorable and interesting than the plots, characters, and events that filled these years. Therefore, after brief period summaries, we turn directly to the highlights and selected minor details of our authors' works and lives. Plot summaries are provided for major works not as a substitute for reading the original but instead as a reader's guide. Even the most famous Shakespearean scholars have, in private moments, admitted an inability to keep all the Bard's plots and characters clearly in mind. A succinct summary can perform the same useful service that program notes provide at the opera or ballet. We end up seeing more in the work itself for the brief time we have invested in such notes.

Readers should note that this edition has been revised considerably, not only in content, but by the addition of new features. For example, at the end of each of the five Parts in this volume appear Review Questions, with answers. Students of literature can use these questions to check comprehension and, perhaps, to prepare for literature examinations. Attention to the relative minutiae of literary facts (dates, authors, works, genres) in these questions is inescapable for the serious reader or student. Literature cannot be fruitfully discussed in only general terms; discussion must be grounded in particulars—who wrote what, why, when, how, and where. The Review Questions provided here can be helpful in securing this level of literary knowledge. Also, we have added other new features—Works at a Glance and the Chronology of English Historical and Literary Events—as well as expanded the Suggested Readings and Glossary.

San Francisco, California   *Arthur H. Bell*
February 1994   *University of San Francisco*

PREFACE TO THE FIRST EDITION

For the understanding and appreciation of so rich a literature as England's some idea of the history of that literature is necessary. Only when a given work is apprehended in correct perspective can its maximum of meaning be extracted. And that perspective involves an acquaintance with the temper and tendencies of the times as well as a conception of the position the work occupies in literary tradition. It is these needs which the present book undertakes to supply. In addition, the author feels that some basic information of the historical events of the time must be in the possession of the sincere student—and this too is herein provided. Moreover the summaries of major works found in these pages should smooth the road for the reader who goes directly to the work itself. Naturally, the most extensive consideration is accorded to the most important writers. The careers of Shakespeare, Milton, Chaucer, Spenser, Dryden, and Pope, for instance, are given more particular attention than those of lesser poets.

In short, [this series] is intended to act as a reliable and sufficiently complete guide to reading the major as well as the minor writers who have made English Literature. The information which anthologies too often omit it proposes to make available.

Naturally, a history of literature can justify itself only to the extent that it succeeds in inviting its readers to study and enjoy the literature described. Nothing said in this volume can be a substitute for the actual reading of English poetry and prose. The author has little sympathy with that company of "scholars" which is familiar with literature by date and title only. On the other hand, he hopes that the student of English Literature will find in this book much of the assistance required for sound reading, as well as enough pregnant suggestion to encourage the formation of individual judgment and opinion. The only way to develop literary taste is to read the best that has been written, and to know what to look for in what is read. Above all, it is hoped that these ensuing pages will make quite clear which writings, amidst all the bewildering variety of English Literature, are essential to read.

The author wishes to express his profound gratitude to Professor Vincent F. Hopper of New York University. Professor Hopper went through every line of the manuscript before it was published, and made many invaluable suggestions.

Brooklyn, New York   *Bernard D. N. Grebanier*
May 15, 1948   *Brooklyn College*

CONTENTS

PART 3
THE RENAISSANCE, THE REFORMATION, AND THE ELIZABETHANS

Part 4
THE SEVENTEENTH CENTURY

Part 5
THE EIGHTEENTH CENTURY

CHRONOLOGY OF ENGLISH HISTORICAL

ENGLISH HISTORICAL EVENTS

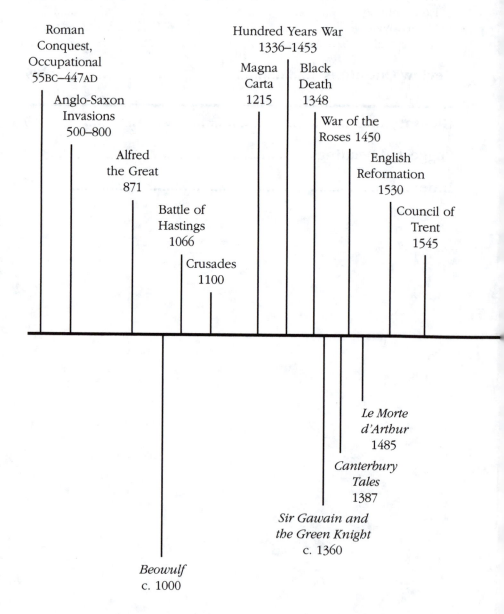

Roman Conquest, Occupational 55BC–447AD

Anglo-Saxon Invasions 500–800

Alfred the Great 871

Battle of Hastings 1066

Crusades 1100

Hundred Years War 1336–1453

Magna Carta 1215

Black Death 1348

War of the Roses 1450

English Reformation 1530

Council of Trent 1545

Le Morte d'Arthur 1485

Canterbury Tales 1387

Sir Gawain and the Green Knight c. 1360

Beowulf c. 1000

ENGLISH LITERARY EVENTS

AND LITERARY EVENTS

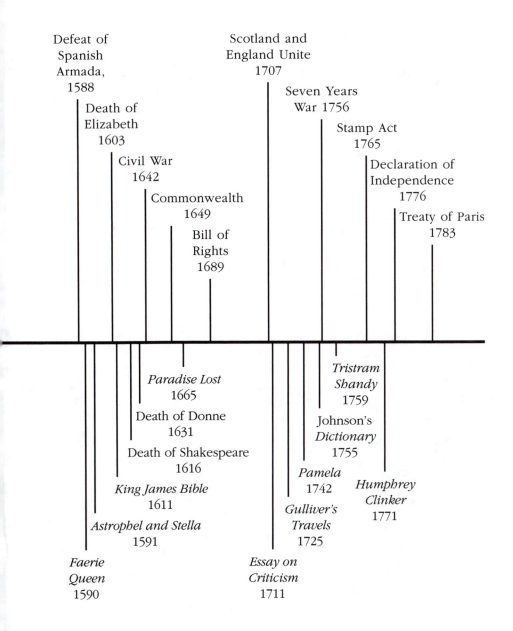

Defeat of
Spanish
Armada,
1588

Death of
Elizabeth
1603

Civil War
1642

Commonwealth
1649

Bill of
Rights
1689

Scotland and
England Unite
1707

Seven Years
War 1756

Stamp Act
1765

Declaration of
Independence
1776

Treaty of Paris
1783

Paradise Lost
1665

Death of Donne
1631

Death of Shakespeare
1616

King James Bible
1611

Astrophel and Stella
1591

*Faerie
Queen*
1590

*Tristram
Shandy*
1759

Johnson's
Dictionary
1755

Pamela
1742

*Gulliver's
Travels*
1725

*Essay on
Criticism*
1711

*Humphrey
Clinker*
1771

Part 1

THE OLD ENGLISH PERIOD

WORKS AT A GLANCE

Anonymous

c. 750   *Beowulf* composed   c. 1000   Existing *Beowulf* manuscript
                                                 transcribed

The Venerable Bede

731   *Ecclesiastical History of the
        English People* completed

Cynewulf

c. 760–800   *The Christ
               Elene
               Juliana
               The Phoenix
               The Fates of the
                 Apostles*

Alfred

892   *The Anglo-Saxon Chronicle*
        begun

1
HISTORY, LANGUAGE, AND FOLK EPIC

EARLY INHABITANTS AND INVADERS

The earliest inhabitants of Britain recorded in history were a Celtic people, the Britons. A few geographic names (*Avon,* river; *Pen,* mountain; *Ox,* water—Avon, Penzance, and Oxford in modern England) are all that survive of their ancient tongue. The modern Welsh are the only direct descendants of these ancient Britons; besides Welsh, modern languages close to the tongue of the Britons are Manx, native Irish, and the Gaelic dialect of the Scottish highlands.

Roman Invasion (55 B.C.–A.D. 410)

In 55 B.C., Julius Caesar conquered the island, and placed it under Roman sway as far as St. Albans. In A.D. 43, the Romans recommenced a siege of Britain, lasting forty years, which terminated in their conquering as far as the Tyne. At the end of another fifty years they had established their domination to the Clyde. They built forts, elegant buildings, good roads; the Britons seemed to have been willing enough to become Romanized. Besides structural remains of Roman civilization still to be seen in England, these conquerors also left their mark on the language by surviving place names (*Castra,* camp; *Strata,* street; *Portus,* port). By A.D. 410, Rome, falling herself before barbarian invaders, had recalled all her legions.

Anglo-Saxon Invasion (5th–6th centuries)

The Britons, thus left helpless to inroads from their neighbors, were particularly at the mercy of the most fearful of their enemies, a Germanic people coming from those parts of the continent now called Schleswig-Holstein and the Jutland peninsula. In A.D. 449, Hengist, chief of the Jutes, was established in Kent. Learning of his success, Angles (from Schleswig), Saxons (from Holstein) and other Jutes (from South Jutland) came over too. For 150 years the Britons were victimized by a campaign of ruthless destruction at the hands of these Teutons, who so far as subsequent history is concerned turn out to be the first Englishmen. When the devastation was over, little remained of Celtic or Roman civilization on the island. The Angles, Saxons, and Jutes set up kingdoms throughout the country. Having moved from a harsh land defying cultivation to a pleasant, arable soil, these barbarians began to move up the scale of civilization by the more peaceful pursuits of agriculture. Their island came to be known as the land of the Angles, or England.

ANGLO-SAXON CIVILIZATION

From the continent the Anglo-Saxons had brought with them their terrible Teutonic deities: *Tiu*, the God of War (Tuesday); *Woden*, Father of the Gods (Wednesday); *Thor*, God of Thunder (Thursday); and the all-controlling *Wyrd*, Goddess of Fate. The Anglo-Saxons were a stalwart, fierce, and gloomy people. Their profession having been for so long piracy on the sea, it is no wonder that their literature abounds in enthusiastic reference to the sea and to battle. Nothing stirred their poets' imaginations more than a ship or a sword. More than anything else this race worshiped glory and fame in battle. They had, moreover, a well-developed sense of community justice, and their laws show them already making punishment and the meting out of justice a public, not a private, matter.

In 597, Pope Gregory sent Augustine, a Benedictine monk, to convert the English to Christianity. Ethelbert, king of Kent, accepted the new religion, and soon after the faith spread throughout the land. Ireland, already Christianized, also sent missionaries to the north of England, where Christianity began to flourish in literature. The monasteries, which soon grew up, became the centers of culture, so that it is not strange that the first recorded English literature should have a heavy religious cast. The new religion brought with it a new philosophy, and the Anglo-Saxons, once a ferocious race, were soon burning with religious exaltation. The Christian religion also taught them to look upon life as a discipline in preparation for a Hereafter. It proved, as well, the occasion for introducing new words into the language (*altar, candle, creed,* and so on).

Old English

The language in which the first English literature was written is known as *Old English*, or *Anglo-Saxon*, a derivative of Low German, and closest to Dutch among modern languages. Old English was an inflected language with three genders and four cases in the nouns, and a fifth case for some pronouns and adjectives. It was a powerful language, given to explosive consonants and combinations of consonants, such as *sc, sp, st, str, hr, th, thr*. The vocabulary provided the basic and indispensable part of modern English—all the household words, and the words of elemental experience—for example, *night, day, star, wind, he, she, it, house, brother, sister, hot*.

BEOWULF

The most imposing piece of literature that has been handed down to us from the Anglo-Saxons is the folk-epic *Beowulf*. (A *folk-epic* is a long narrative poem relating the exploits of a hero who celebrates the ideals of his race in his deeds). The manuscript (now in the Cottonian Collection of the British Museum) that has transmitted *Beowulf* to us was written in the Wessex dialect, and dates from about 1000. It has been conjectured that the poem was actually composed around 750 in Mercia or Northumberland, and that the anonymous author was a man familiar with court life, a Christian who was addressing himself to a royal audience. It is something of a mystery why the hero of an Anglo-Saxon poem should be a Scandanavian whose great exploits take place in Denmark and Sweden. Perhaps the author was deliberately writing about an older time where his imagination could have free play. A certain historical thread may be perceived in this epic: Hygelac, Beowulf's uncle, is known to us in history as Chochilaicus, who raided the Frisian coast around A.D. 516.

There are three episodes related in the career of the hero: the fight with the monster, Grendel; the fight with Grendel's mother; and the return of Beowulf to his native kingdom where, fifty years later, he engages in mortal combat with the Fire Dragon.

The Fight with Grendel: Heorot Hall is the home of Hrothgar, lord of the Danes, widely known for his generosity. Life at Heorot is agreeably spent by the king and his thanes drinking mead and listening to the tales sung by the court poets, until one night this happiness is ended by the unexpected appearance of a hideous Fen-Dragon, Grendel. Overcome by drink, the sleeping thanes offer no resistance, and Grendel slays thirty of them, carrying off their remains to the marshlands. Grendel continues thereafter his nightly depredations, and not only decimates Hrothgar's court but also outrages the splendors of Heorot Hall. This demoralizing state of affairs continues for many years until news of it reaches across the sea into Sweden, where the hero Beowulf lives with his uncle the king, Hygelac. The tale of Grendel's infamy so incenses Beowulf that he departs from his native land with fourteen warrior-friends to save Hrothgar's thanes from the monster. One day after embarking, they come into sight of Denmark, and soon landing, they behold in the valley gold-bedecked and richly ornamented Heorot Hall. King Hrothgar, old, gray, and disconsolate, welcomes the young Geats in their shining coats of mail. Beowulf asks the privilege of ridding the land of the monster, and since boasting is the mood of the feast, promises to kill the demon without a weapon. The queen, Wealtheow, offers the ale-cup to all assembled, and goes throughout the Hall distributing gifts. The night watch for the demon begins, the king, queen, and courtiers retiring to an adjacent building. Beowulf alone remains awake, angrily awaiting his foe. At last out of the moors Grendel stalks to the Hall, bursts open the bars of the door, treads the many-colored floor with a dreadful light blazing from his eyes. He seizes a sleeping warrior, bites into his joints and drinks his blood. Soon he approaches Beowulf, who seizes Grendel with the grip of thirty men. The monster cannot escape and his cries awake the other men. Grendel is forced to wrench free his arm out of its socket, and flees the hall to die in the Fens, the haunt of the Nicors (sea-beasts), and plunges beneath the waves to the cave of his mother. Meanwhile Grendel's arm is nailed to Heorot's door as a grim trophy. In the morning, on the return of the court, there is great feasting in the Hall and giving of gifts. The harp is struck and the gleeman (singer) chants a heroic song.

The Fight with Grendel's Mother: After an evening of feasting, the revelers in Heorot Hall are inclined to sleep. Grendel's dam appears, bent on avenging her son's death. She kills and carries off Æschere, counsellor to Hrothgar. With Beowulf, his followers, and Hrothgar in pursuit, she escapes to her underwater lair, overhung by sharp rocks and shaggy trees in the midst of a "joyless" wood. Beowulf prepares to descend into the bloody boiling waters. Even the warrior Unferth, who had challenged Beowulf's boasts on his arrival, is impressed by the hero's courage and gives Beowulf his sword, Hrunting. It takes Beowulf a full hour to reach the bottom of the flood. The battle with Grendel's mother ensues. The fight is carried into a subterranean waterless cave. When Beowulf would employ his sword, he finds it only melts against her hideous body. At one moment she throws him to the ground, squats on his body, and draws her short sword to kill him. (All would have been over with him then if his coat of mail had not saved him!) He leaps to his feet, spies an ancient sword forged by the giants, and seizes it from the pile where it lies. With one stroke he cuts off her head. In the cave he finds the dead Grendel, and decapitates him too. The giant's blood is so venomous that it melts the sword up to the hilt. He returns with the evidences of his great victory to his thanes who are still keeping watch beside the pool's embankment; the Danes have given him up for dead and returned to Heorot. When Beowulf arrives there with four of his own men bearing Grendel's monstrous head, joy is unbounded throughout the Hall. The hero recounts his adventure. More feasting and more bestowing of gifts follow. And now it is time for the killer of Grendel, the hero Beowulf, to return to his own land and his own lord, Hygelac.

Beowulf's Last Fight: Before the last episode of the poem, a long time is supposed to have elapsed. Hygelac, king of the Geats, has died, and his nephew Beowulf has succeeded him. As our story reopens, Beowulf has been king of the Geats in Sweden for fifty successful years. After so long a period of unalloyed fame and glory, the old monarch is sorrowed because a fire-breathing dragon is now ravaging the land in revenge for a golden goblet that had been stolen from the dragon's treasures by one of the Geats. Beowulf's hall itself is burned by the night-flying beast. The old hero-king goes forth to fight the dragon. Before the combat he makes his last boast to his companions and insists on fighting alone. But against the Fire-Breather, Beowulf's sword proves of no avail. All the King's followers, save Wiglaf, flee. The Fire-Breather pounces on Beowulf and bites a deep wound in the hero's neck. Wiglaf comes to the rescue with his sword, and Beowulf is able to deal the dragon a deathblow. The hero himself, however, is mortally wounded. Dying, Beowulf asks Wiglaf to seize upon the dragon's treasure of gold and jewels, still lying in the lair, so that approaching death may seem sweeter to the King, seeing the wealth he will bestow upon the Geats displayed before his expiring eyes. Wiglaf enters the cave and finds all manner of dishes, vessels, old armor, and countless ornaments. When the hoard is brought out, the dying monarch bestows a gold collar on Wiglaf, and asks that his thanes "build on the foreland a far-seen barrow" after his body shall have been cremated, a mound that shall tower high "over the headland of whales," and which shall stand as a memorial to him among his people. So the old hero dies. A herald announces his death to the people. Beowulf's body is carried to the funeral pyre and the body of the fifty-foot dragon is cast into the sea. Amid loud lamentations the hero's remains are burned. His people build a wall round the pyre to be known as Beowulf's Barrow, and fill the enclosure with the dead King's treasure-hoard. The sturdy poem concludes with a description of the mourning ceremonies:

> *Thus joined the men of the Geats in mourning*
> *Their hero's end. His hearth-companions*
> *Called him the best among the kings of the earth,*
> *Mildest of men, and most beloved,*
> *Kindest to kinsmen, and keenest for fame.*

IMPORTANCE

Pagan and Christian elements exist side by side in *Beowulf*. The presence of Wyrd (Fate), omens, blood revenge, and cremation are all pre-Christian Teutonic concepts; but we also find one God ruling over the world, Heaven, Hell, the Devil, and a Last Judgment. Though the basic part of *Beowulf* is undeniably Christian, older Teutonic memories still survive in it.

2
EARLY POETRY AND PROSE

ANGLO-SAXON POETRY

Anglo-Saxon poetry is full of the Teutonic love of battle, boastfulness, pride in glory, and blood-thirstiness, and the poet is never more inspired than when describing a sword, a battle scene, or the terrors of the sea. The Anglo-Saxon imagination was dark and gloomy; characteristically, the poets measure the passage of time by nights, moons, and winters, rather than by days, suns, or summers. But there is a spiritedness in their verse because of their respect for bravery and loyalty.

The original authors of poems were the *scops*; the *gleemen* traveled from place to place singing the songs of the scops.

The versification of *Beowulf* is typical of all Anglo-Saxon poetry: there are four beats or accents in every line, with no fixed number of unaccented syllables; each line is divided into two parts, each containing two accents, separated by a *caesura* (break); there is an alliteration on the accented syllables on each side of the caesura, and there may be two or three accented syllables in alliteration in any line:

> Deeds of renown　　that were *done* by the heroes

and

> The *sor*row they *suf*fered　　He *saw* full well
>
> (from the translation of *Beowulf* by Spaeth)

The third accented syllable in the line is the key to the alliteration since it is always in alliteration with the first or second accent or both. Sometimes, when the third accented syllable is in alliteration with only one of the first two syllables, the fourth accented syllable may be in alliteration with the other. For example:

> Lest *h*arrying FOE　　with *h*ostile FLeet.

Other traits of Anglo-Saxon poetry include the use of *kennings*, hyphenated expressions that make metaphors (the king is called *ring-giver*; the sea is the *whale-road*; a ship is a *wave-traveler*.) These metaphors exhibit the Anglo-Saxon predilection for somber imagery, love of glory, and enthusiasm for battle and the sea.

Lyric and Gnomic Poetry

Other Anglo-Saxon poems that bear the marks of a pre-Christian time are *Widsith* (the far-traveler), which tells how a scop traveled over Europe and Asia, visiting many peoples, singing for them, and receiving rich gifts from their lords; *The Fight at Finnsburg*, which tells of the treachery of Finn, King of the North Frisians, when he attacked his brother-in-law, Hnaef, although the latter was his invited guest; and *Waldhere* (Walther), whose hero as a child was given as a hostage to the King of the Huns and who, in manhood, was a great warrior against that Attila—the fragments that make this poem recount his sweetheart's preparing Waldhere for battle and the exchange of challenges between the hero and his opponent.

There exist also some quasi-lyrical Anglo-Saxon poems: *The Lover's Message*, in which an absent lover sends a carved wooden tablet to his love asking her to come south to him when spring begins; *The Wife's Complaint*, the lament of a wife who has been falsely slandered; *The Seafarer*, which sings of its author's love of the sea for all its dangers; *The Wanderer*, in which the author dreams of his lost glory and awakes to find himself wandering a wintry sea; *Deor's Lament*, the complaint of a scop who has lost his lord's favor to a rival; and *The Ruin*, a lament over the ruins of a once-flourishing Roman site.

There are, finally, Anglo-Saxon *Charms*, *Riddles*, and *Gnomic Verses*. The Riddles are obscure, intended to test the cleverness of the audience and are on all kinds of subjects from a hurricane to a nightingale. The Charms were intended as cures for disease or prayers to Higher Powers. The Gnomic Verses are maxims and proverbs.

CHRISTIAN ANGLO-SAXON LITERATURE

The Venerable Bede (673–735) was England's first scholar and historian. In his *Ecclesiastical History of the English People*, written in Latin at the Benedictine Monastery at Jarrow, we find some of our most valuable information about Anglo-Saxon history. It is in the book of this fervent Christian that we read of the "first English poet," Caedmon. Bede tells us how Caedmon, an inarticulate layman who kept the monastery stables, was commanded in a dream to sing the beginning of things; Caedmon began to sing, and with so divine a gift that he was received among the brothers as a monk and spent his days composing verses on the Scriptures.

In the tradition of Caedmon, other anonymous poets versified the Bible and its commentaries in *Genesis*, *Exodus*, *Daniel*, *Judith*, and *The Fall of the Angels*.

Some of the finest of the Christian poems are a group attributed to Cynewulf, who may have been the Bishop of Lindisfarne of that name (died about 783). The most admired is *The Christ*, a poem dealing with the Birth and Ascension of Christ and the Last Judgment. The others, all containing Cynewulf's name in acrostic, are *Elene*, the life of St. Helena and the Vision of the Cross experienced by the Emperor Constantine; *Juliana*, the life of a martyr-saint; and *The Fates of the Apostles*. To Cynewulf have also been ascribed *The Phoenix*, on the Death and Resurrection of Christ; *Andreas* and *Guthlac*, the lives of two saints; and *The Dream of the Rood*, an imaginative history of the Cross on which Christ was crucified. Two other poems of this epoch worthy of mention are *The Discourse of the Soul to its Body*, celebrating the triumph of the immortal soul over the decaying body; and *The Bestiary*, which summarizes popular notions of natural history.

DANISH INVASION

Nearly all of Anglo-Saxon literature up to this time came from the north, in Northumbria. But all this literary activity was suddenly ended by the Danish invasion. The Danes, kinsmen of the Anglo-Saxons, brought the old pagan gods with them from the continent, and ruthlessly destroyed the monasteries of Jarrow and Whitby, and with them the treasures of learning housed in them.

The threat of Danish domination brought about unity among the Anglo-Saxon kingdoms against the common enemy. The King of Wessex in 828 united the central nations in an "English Kingdom." But the great hero of the era was King Alfred the Great (849–901). It was he who kept the Danes in the north by his heroic fighting. (Their assimilation there gave our language new Danish words like *sky*, *fellow*, *ugly*, and so on.)

ALFRED

When Alfred came to the West Saxon throne in 871, he had already visited the brilliant French court, and was anxious to make his country a center of culture. It is to him that we owe the preservation of older Anglo-Saxon literature.

He was a scholar, a writer himself, and gathered scholars around him to aid him in his historic work. Together they translated Bede's *Ecclesastical History*, Pope Gregory's *Pastoral Care*, Boethius' *Consolation of Philosophy*, and many other works for the guidance of the clergy and the people. It was he who preserved for us *Beowulf*, the poems attributed to Cynewulf, and other pieces. Equally important to us, he inaugurated the *Anglo-Saxon Chronicle*, an historical register of national events from the dim past through his own day; this work was continued by monks long after Alfred's death. After Alfred's death, Anglo-Saxon culture began to disintegrate under the siege of invaders. Two battle poems celebrate fights between the English and the invading Danes: *The Battle of Brunanburh*, an enthusiastic account of an English victory; and *The Battle of Maldon*, a gloomy story of English defeat.

REVIEW QUESTIONS

THE OLD ENGLISH PERIOD

Multiple Choice

1. _____ The earliest inhabitants of Britain recorded in history were
   a. the Romans
   b. the Britons
   c. the Saxons
   d. the Gaels

2. _____ The names of many English days of the week derive from
   a. Teutonic dieties
   b. English place names
   c. Roman heroes
   d. Celtic gods

3. _____ Another term for Old English is
   a. Middle English
   b. Anglo-Saxon
   c. Deutsche
   d. Welsh

4. _____ Some of the events that take place in *Beowulf*, although heavily distorted by mythic materials,
   a. were the additions of fifteenth century translators
   b. stem from Roman history
   c. did have historical roots
   d. originally took place on Italian soil

5. _____ Heorot Hall is the home of
   a. Grendel
   b. Hrothgar
   c. Grendel's mother
   d. Wyrd

6. _____ Anglo-Saxon poetry can best be characterized as
   a. dark and gloomy
   b. light and optimistic
   c. humorous
   d. sermonic

7. _____ Anglo-Saxon Riddles were intended to
   a. convey secret political messages
   b. act as a form of prayer
   c. test the cleverness of the audience
   d. replace heroic tales

8. _____ The Venerable Bede wrote
   a. *Beowulf*
   b. *Ecclesiastical History of the English People*
   c. *Juliana*
   d. *The Phoenix*

9. _____ One of the translators of the Venerable Bede's work was
   a. Caedmon
   b. Cynewulf
   c. Constantine
   d. Alfred

10. _____ Alfred inaugurated
   a. *The Anglo-Saxon Chronicle*
   b. *The Bestiary*
   c. the first English Bible
   d. the struggle to eradicate Anglo-Saxon literature

True or False

11. _____ English towns or cities whose names end in -chester or -caster were probably founded by the Celts.
12. _____ Anglo-Saxon heroes were most honored for their honesty.
13. _____ Words of Latin derivation entered the English language during the Roman occupation of Britain.
14. _____ Augustine of Canterbury was the missionary sent by the Pope to convert the people of Britain to Christianity.
15. _____ *Little, house,* and *home* are all words of Anglo-Saxon derivation.
16. _____ *Beowulf* was written in Middle English.
17. _____ Grendel, Grendel's mother, and the Fire Dragon are actually the same beast in various disguises.
18. _____ *Beowulf* was originally composed around the year 1000.
19. _____ Grendel's mother attempts to avenge her son's death.
20. _____ The most notable characteristic of the verse of *Beowulf* is the regular end-rhyme scheme.

Fill-in

21. In the verse of *Beowulf*, the poet uses _____ to associate the accented syllables in a poetic line.
22. The Britons were ethnically a _____ people.
23. Julius Caesar invaded Britain in _____ A.D.
24. Woden, Tiu, and Thor are all _____ dieties.
25. *Beowulf* was written in the _____ dialect.
26. *Beowulf* concludes with the hero's fight against _____ .
27. *Beowulf* contains both pagan and _____ elements.

28. The term for a rhythmic break in a poetic line is _____ .
29. Hyphenated expressions forming metaphors are known as
_____ .
30. The Venerable Bede tells the story of _____ , an early religious poet.

Matching

31. _____ Venerable Bede		a. maxims and proverbs	
32. _____ Alfred		b. Beowulf's uncle	
33. _____ Charms		c. Anglo-Saxon god of fate	
34. _____ Geats		d. Scholarly king	
35. _____ Welsh		e. poets	
36. _____ Wyrd		f. Britons	
37. _____ Scops		g. Beowulf's people	
38. _____ Gnomic Verses		h. Words for healing	
39. _____ Celts		i. Wrote of Caedmon	
40. _____ Hygelac		j. Descendants of Britons	

Answers

1. b	15. t	28. caesura	
2. a	16. f	29. kennings	
3. b	17. f	30. Caedmon	
4. c	18. f	31. i	
5. b	19. t	32. d	
6. a	20. f	33. h	
7. c	21. alliteration	34. g	
8. b	22. Celtic	35. j	
9. d	23. 55	36. c	
10. a	24. Anglo-Saxon or	37. e	
11. f	Teutonic	38. a	
12. f	25. Wessex	39. f	
13. f	26. the Fire Dragon	40. b	
14. t	27. Christian		

Part 2

THE MIDDLE ENGLISH PERIOD

NORMAN INVASION

In 1066, William, Duke of Normandy, claiming title to the English crown, fought and overcame Harold at Hastings. That victory altered the entire complexion of English culture for several centuries. The bulk of the populace continued to speak the Old English tongue; their rulers and the clergy spoke and wrote French. Since it was to the rulers that literature was addressed, the literary output of the twelfth century and much of the thirteenth, in England is not part of English literature. In course of time, the two cultures were bound to merge. When they did, a new language emerged, which embraced both Old English and the Norman French. The basic part of the language remained Old English; the intellectual, artistic, and theologic came from the French. This new tongue was already rich. It still possessed much of the power of its Teutonic origins, but had acquired a grace and charm.

With the Norman French came powerful changes in many aspects of English culture. The years preceding the Conquest had been a period of gradual decay for the Anglo-Saxon order. The Norman French brought with them a feudal system, which William was able to impose upon the country. He confiscated the land, and redistributed it in the form of large estates to his most powerful nobles. These gifts, coming from the hand of the king, placed the lords of the land in direct subjection to him. When, in turn, the estates were divided among tenants, the tenants were similarly bound in service to their lords. In this way the king was able to centralize English society in his own person. Feudalism was soon the order of society in England.

English literature inevitably felt the influence of the Norman French. In poetry, for example, the Anglo-Saxon versification gave way to regular meter and the pleasures of rhyme. In subject matter too, the alteration was great. The French had developed the chivalric system to a point of brilliance and elaboration heretofore unknown in England. Their own narrative poetry was a storehouse of chivalric exploit: "The Matter of France," dealing with the deeds of Charlemagne and his knights; "The Matter of Britain," treating of Celtic legends and the Arthurian stories; and "The Matter of Rome," reinterpreting the great stories of classical antiquity. The French also brought with them a new lyric poetry, originated in Provence by the Troubadours. Then, in 1095, began the first of several Crusades, bringing into Europe's horizon Oriental luxury and color. From this many-sided contact with new cultural experiences, literature, when it again emerged in English, was bound to have a new character.

WORKS AT A GLANCE*

Anonymous

c. 1350–1400   *Sir Gawain and the Green Knight*

Geoffrey Chaucer

1369	*The Book of the Duchess*	1387–1400	*The Canterbury Tales*
1377–1382	*The Parliament of Fowls*	1384–1386	*The Legend of Good Women*
1379–1384	*The House of Fame*	1399	*The Complaint of Chaucer to His Empty Purse*
1382–1385	*Troilus and Criseyde*		

Anonymous

c. 1370   *The Pearl*

William Langland

c. 1362   *The Vision of Piers Plowman*

John Gower

c. 1386	*Confessio Amantis* *Speculum Meditantis*	after 1381	*Vox Clamantis*

Sir Thomas Malory

1469   *Le Morte d'Arthur*

*Dates are approximate dates of composition.

3
EARLY MIDDLE ENGLISH LITERATURE

HISTORICAL BACKGROUND

Towards 1200, the earliest pieces of Middle English literature began to appear; they were chiefly sermons, prayers, lives of saints, and homilies. The *Poema Morale* (around 1170) is written in rhymed couplets that urge the devout life. *The Ormulum* (around 1200), written by the monk Orm, is a metrical translation of the Gospel. *The Ancien Riwle* (around 1237) is a good piece of prose, instructing women for life in a convent. A strong poem of the next century, *Handlyng Synne* (around 1300), incorporates homilies and stories attacking the clergy and the world of fashion. A very popular work was the *Cursor Mundi* (1320), a poetic retelling of Biblical tales. Of these religious authors, the identity of only one has come down to us with any detail—Richard Rolle of Hampole, whose long poem, *The Pricke of Conscience*, is a vivid picture of the world's misery, the good life, and the horrors of hell. (Some scholars question his authorship of this work.)

The most beautiful of the mystic poems of the period is Thomas de Hales' *Love Rune*, which tells with tender rapture of a nun's mystic union with the Heavenly Bridegroom.

Somewhat later than the religious writers, the English secular poets began to appear. No figure attracted their imagination more than that of King Arthur, an ancient British hero. Arthur first appears in literature in the Latin *History of the British Kings* (around 1147), a chronicle of the Welshman Geoffrey of Monmouth. Writing what is largely a fictional history of Britain, beginning with its mythical settlement by one Brutus, a descendant of Aeneas, Geoffrey makes his book chiefly an excuse to elaborate on the astounding doings of his people's great hero, Arthur. Various French poets seized upon this material and soon a whole legend began to grow up around Arthur's person. In the meantime, the English-Norman Robert Wace adapted Geoffrey into French in the *Roman de Brut* (around 1155). It was a paraphrasing of Wace into English by Layamon in his *Brut* (around 1205) that provided the first example of Middle English in a secular poem.

After *The Brut*, a considerable number of English narrative poems, imitated from the French and dealing with knightly adventure, were composed; these are known as *metrical romances*. *King Horn* (around 1250) is a tale of faithful and untiring love; *Havelok the Dane* (around 1300) has a hero who, fighting against his treacherous guardian, avenges himself and wins the crown of England; *Guy of Warwick* (around 1300) carries us to adventures in the Holy Land and back to England, in both of which places Guy slays giants; and *Sir Bevis of Hampton* (around 1300) tells an incident-filled story of knightly prowess in the Orient.

SIR GAWAIN AND THE GREEN KNIGHT

IMPORTANCE

Of all the metrical romances none approaches in beauty the anonymous *Sir Gawain and the Green Knight*, a poem of the mid-fourteenth century, one of the most exquisite pieces of medieval literature extant. It is also an allegory, the purpose of which is to exemplify chastity, courage, and honor as the qualities belonging to the perfect knight.

The Green Knight appears at Arthur's court at Camelot on New Year's Day, amid the feasting of brave knights and fair ladies. He challenges the knights to strike off his giant head, provided one of them is willing to receive the same treatment from him after a year and a day. Gawain accepts, and with one blow of his axe severs the Green Knight's head. The Green Knight picks up his head, reminds Gawain of the pact, and departs. Gawain sets forth on his mission to keep his tryst. A year later, on Christmas Eve, Gawain comes upon a beautiful castle in a great wood. He is welcomed by the lord and lady. The lord and Gawain agree to exchange whatever they should acquire during the day when they meet again at night. The lord goes hunting, and from the lady Gawain accepts one kiss the first day, two kisses the second, and three kisses and a green girdle on the third day. The girdle is to make him invulnerable. At the Green Chapel, on New Year's Day, Gawain meets the Green Knight, bends his head to the axe, but receives only a surface cut. The Green Knight then reveals that he was the lord of the castle, that his wife was a sorceress, and that both were in a plot to disrupt the Round Table of King Arthur. Gawain's only sin having been his concealing of the girdle, he therefore was dealt only a slight wound. Indeed, because he was chaste, had kept his word, and was courageous, he would have been safe without the girdle. Thereafter, the Court of Camelot all wear green in commemoration of Gawain's adventure.

LYRICS

Middle English literature also contains a store of lyrics that show the French influence in their developing the theme of love, their sensitiveness to natural beauty, and their use of rhyme. These anonymous little poems are full of charm. *"The Cuckoo Song"* (around 1240) welcomes the season of growth prophesied every spring by the song of the bird; *"The Spring Song"* (around 1300) describes the softening effect of the season on all things; *Alysoun* (around 1300) describes the beauties of the poet's sweetheart; *Lenten Is Come With Love To Towne* (around 1300) also tells of the joy of spring; *Ubi Sunt Qui Ante Nos Fuerant* (around 1350) typifies a number of religious poems that warn against taking too many pleasures in this life.

GEOFFREY CHAUCER (c. 1340–1400)

The greatest poet of the Middle English period was the son of a wealthy wine merchant of powerful connections. As a boy he was a page to the Countess of Ulster, and later was employed as a valet in the royal household. In 1359, serving with the army in France, he was taken prisoner and ransomed. Thereafter he spent many years in the service of his king. In 1372–1373 he was sent to Genoa on a commercial mission; in 1374 he was appointed comptroller of the customs for the Port of London; in 1376 and in 1377 he was on the continent again, and possibly again in France and in Milan the next year; in 1385 he was appointed justice of the peace for Kent; and in 1386 he was elected member of parliament. His last years were spent at Greenwich, where he died in 1400. He is buried in the Poet's Corner at Westminster Abbey.

Chaucer's public career must have greatly enriched his observation and his stock of ideas. His travels to Italy and France brought him into close contact with literatures far excelling the English in quality and polish. In Italy, in particular, his imagination must have been stirred when he found himself in the midst of the flourishing Renaissance. Thus, in a manner of speaking, he developed into a pre-Renaissance writer addressing a medieval English audience.

His works are conventionally divided into three chronological groups; his French period (to 1372), his Italian period (1372 to 1385), and his English period (1385 to 1400).

French Period

In his French period, which exhibits the French love of skill and artifice, he wrote *The Book of the Duchess* (1369) and translated a large fragment of the French *Romance of the Rose.*

The Book of the Duchess: This dream-allegory is a lament over the death of the Duchess of Lancaster, John of Gaunt's first wife. Reading the old tale of Alcyone, Chaucer falls asleep. In his dream he is in a room painted with pictures of Troy and the Romance of the Rose. Soon he has joined the Emperor Octavian in a hunting party. He wanders into a forest where he finds a black knight lamenting the death of his lady. The knight expands on his lost love's beauty and on his inconsolable sorrow. A bell tolls the midnight hour, and the poet wakes to find his book in his hand.

Romance of the Rose: The poet falls asleep in a pleasant field of flowers and dreams that he has come to a high wall enclosing a garden. He finds his way within and dances in the garden with Beauty, Riches, Largesse, Franchise, Courtesy, Fair Idleness, and Youth. Continuing on his way, and followed by the God of Love, he comes to the fountain where Narcissus died, around which hundreds of roses grow. The first fragment of this work closes when the dreamer attempts to pluck a rose lovelier than all the rest.

Italian Period

In his Italian period, when Chaucer exhibits the influence of the great Italian writers Dante, Petrach and Boccaccio, he wrote *The House of Fame* (1379–84), *The Parliament of Fowls* (1377–1382), *Troilus and Criseyde* (1382–5), and *The Legend of Good Women* (1384?–1386?).

The House of Fame: In this dream-allegory, Chaucer dreams that he is in the Temple of Venus, whose glass walls are inscribed with the story of the *Aeneid.* Aeneas' betrayal of Dido reminds him of other betrayals by unfaithful lovers—Achilles' betrayal of Briseis, Paris' betrayal of Oenone, Jason's betrayal of Medea. The poet is then carried by a golden eagle aloft to the House of Fame, where the presiding goddess's instability is made plain to him; those who deserve most receive least at her hands, whereas fame is granted to the undeserving. He now enters the House of Rumor, filled with pilgrims, pardoners, messengers—all carrying baggages of lies. Then the poet sees a man of great authority. At this point the unfinished poem breaks off.

The Parliament of Fowls: A long dream-allegory in which all the birds of the earth meet in conference to decide who shall marry the noble female eagle. In his dream Chaucer is led by Scipio Africanus to a garden where this Parliament of Birds is in session. The Goddess Nature sits enthroned with the noble eagle on her hand. Various suitors among the eagles advance their claims as mate. Other fowl, including the duck and the cuckoo, give their views. At last the Goddess orders the hubbub to subside and herself announces that the female eagle will choose her own mate, though the Royal Tercel is particularly recommended. The female eagle asks for a year to decide. Nature grants her this request and a song is sung in honor of the Goddess. The din raised by the birds awakens the poet.

Troilus and Criseyde: This chivalric poem is often called Chaucer's finest complete literary achievement. His longest poem, its nearly eight thousand lines are written in stanzas of rime royale (a stanza of seven iambic pentameter lines rhyming ababbcc). Chaucer's inspiration and influence for this work was the poem *Filostrato* by Boccaccio, which, in addtion to creating the characters of Troilus, Criseyde, and Pandarus, also established the basic outline of the plot. Chaucer for his part, changed the basic character of Pandarus, greatly enriched the plot of the poem, and explored in much finer detail several of the themes hinted at by Boccaccio, including a very developed, almost psychological presentation of the character of Criseyde.

Troilus and Criseyde is both a medieval romance and an exposition of the courtly love traditions. In three books, it tells of the love of Troilus for Criseyde, of her sincere love for him, of their three-year union, and finally of her deception of Troilus and the latter's death. The story begins with Troilus, a young Trojan who falls in love with the beautiful young widow Criseyde. Troilus, with the aid of his friend Pandarus (Criseyde's uncle), wins her love. The two live together for three joyous years until, with all the forebodings of a tragic conclusion, Criseyde leaves to join her father in the Greek camp. Though she swears devotion and undying love to Troilus, promising to return in ten days, she soon decides, partly through the influence of her Greek escort Diomede, to stay with the Greeks. Within several months she has given Diomede the broach that Troilus had given her as a parting gift, and Troilus himself is dead.

Beautiful and mysterious, Criseyde is in many ways the embodiment of the ideal woman of the courtly love tradition. But her actions are by no means transparent, and although her affection for Troilus is clearly genuine, she abandons him in a moment of weakness and lacks the courage to return to a love whose loss she nonetheless regrets. At the same time, Chaucer is sympathetic to her character, and by no means does he show her to be of a low moral character. Instead, the poet expresses sorrow at her weakness and tells the reader to judge her not too harshly.

The Legend of Good Women: Another dream vision, in which Chaucer playfully announces his intention to atone for his defaming the character of women by his portrait of Criseyde. The charming prologue, one of the freshest poems Chaucer ever wrote, shows us Chaucer leaving his books to enjoy the flowers of the spring, and falling asleep during his contemplation of the flowers. The God of Love comes to him in his dream to chide him for his unfairness to women, and Chaucer undertakes to atone by telling the stories of Cupid's saints. There follow the stories of women faithful in the service of the God of Love: Cleopatra, Thisbe, Medea, Lucretia, Phyllis, Dido, and Ariadne. Of the twenty lives intended to form the Legend, Chaucer completed only eight and one half. His sources for these stories include Boccaccio, Virgil, Ovid and Plutarch.

English Period: *The Canterbury Tales*

The Canterbury Tales (1387–1400) and a few shorter poems comprise Chaucer's English period. For the first time, he was addressing himself not to the Court but to a wider reading public. Living in comparative seclusion at Greenwich, he was no longer obliged to please the tastes of his royal patrons. *The Canterbury Tales* is his most ambitious work, and though unfinished will probably always be his most widely read and admired poem.

The Canterbury Tales: Chaucer finds a group of twenty-eight pilgrims at the Tabard Inn in Southwark, just across the Thames from London. They are on their way to the shrine of Thomas à Becket in Canterbury. The host of the inn and the poet agree to join them. It is suggested by the host that each pilgrim tell two tales on the way to Canterbury to entertain the company, and two on the way home. (Only 22 of the 120 planned tales were completed.)

The Prologue: In April, when the earth quickens, people long to go on pilgrimages. In England they specially wend their way to Canterbury. While Chaucer is stopping at the Tabard Inn in Southwark, he finds a company of twenty-nine. Soon he has spoken to every one of them. He gives us their portraits, a complete panorama of typical English society of his day. The Knight, valiant and honored, modest and prudent, has fought against the heathen in distant lands; his horses are good, but he himself is soberly dressed. The Squire, his son, about twenty, is a lusty young soldier who has already done well in campaigns at Flanders; he is as fresh as May, always singing or playing the flute; he loves the ladies so ardently that he sleeps no more at night than a nightingale. The Yeoman, their servant, dressed in green, handles his gear well, and completely understands woodcraft. A Prioress, Madame Eglantine, whose greatest oath is by St. Loy, speaks French as it is spoken at Stratford-le-Bow; she is expert and dainty in her table-manners, and imitates the manners of court-life; she is all warm feeling and tender heart, and hence weeps when one of her dogs is beaten off by anyone; she is accompanied by a nun and three priests. The Monk is imposing, a lover of hunting, who has a full stable. The begging Friar, who is wanton, jolly, skilled in flattering talk, and has married off many a young woman at his own cost, is familiar among women of the town because of his papal license as confessor; his absolution is pleasant and his penance easy; he knows the taverns; he knows when to be courteous to his advantage, for begging yields him a good income; he speaks in an affected lisp and his name is Hubert. The pompous Merchant with a forked beard is cunning in multiplying his own profits.

An Oxford Clerk, lean as his own horse, spends everything on books; a threadbare philosopher, he speaks well and modestly, and all he says tends toward moral virtue. A Sergeant of the Law, who can recall every judgment of the courts, is a frequenter of St. Paul's porch. The Franklin, traveling with him, is an epicure of sauces and viands. The Haberdasher, Carpenter, Weaver, and Upholsterer, all fresh in new gear, dignified representatives of their guilds, travel with a Cook. The sun-bronzed Shipman, bold, shrewd, and conscienceless, is fearless on the sea. The Doctor of Physic, well-grounded in astrology, works hand in hand with apothecaries. The gap-toothed Wife of Bath, somewhat deaf, gaily attired despite her advanced years, is skilled in making cloth; she has had five husbands, not counting youthful lovers, is an authority on love, and has been thrice to Jerusalem. The poor Parson, truly holy and modest, generous to sinners, is fearless to correct the stubborn though they be rich; his life is an example to his flock. His brother, the Ploughman, is a faithful toiler who loves God, and lives with charity.

The Miller, a brawny fellow and bawdy prater, a prize wrestler with a beard as red as a sow, knows how to cheat at his mill; he plays the bag-pipes. A Manciple of an Inn of Court, whose craft exceeds that of attorneys, hoodwinks everybody. The Reeve, slender and bilious, is in charge of his Lord's estates; he is able to please his Lord while swelling his own purse; he wears a rusty sword. The fiery Sumner, cherub-faced, pimply, with slits for eyes, as hot and lecherous as a sparrow, when drunk mutters a few Latin terms; for a quart of wine he would hand over his paramour; he is chief adviser of the town's youth. With him rides the yellow-haired Pardoner, with a wallet full of pardons hot from Rome, and worthless relics which he sells to gullible folk; his smooth tongue masks his avarice and vice.

The Tales then follow. But not the least interesting part of *The Canterbury Tales* is the links with which Chaucer connects the different stories. These passages between tales have been called by one critic, "the most original of all his contributions." They fill out the characters of the Pilgrims and enrich what we already know of them through the Prologue. And the spirited dia-logue that is carried on among them in these connecting passages is one of the most life-like and fascinating interests of the work.

The Knight's Tale: The longest and one of the best, a tale of chivalric romance adapted from Boccaccio. Theseus, returning in victory to Athens with his new queen Hippolyta and her sister Emilia, is met by a company of black-clad women. King Creon of Thebes will not allow their dead husbands decent burial. Theseus battles Creon and slays him. Among his prisoners are two wounded Theban knights, Arcite and Palamon, cousins, sentenced to perpetual imprisonment. Years later, Emilia is seen by the two prisoners from their tower, and both fall in love with her. They quarrel fiercely and face bit-terly the future of having to be imprisoned together forever. Pirithous, a close friend of Theseus and of Arcite, persuades Theseus to release the latter. Theseus complies on the condition that Arcite is never to come near Athens. Palamon is anguished that Arcite is free to woo Emilia; Arcite mourns his inability to see Emilia again, and goes to Thebes. Two years of suffering so much alter Arcite's face that he determines to return to Athens in disguise. He takes service under Emilia's chamberlain and assumes the name of Philostrate. Theseus makes him a squire, and he soon becomes the King's trusted aide. Five years pass. Palamon drugs the jailer and escapes. Hiding in the woods till nightfall, he overhears Arcite lamenting. Palamon reveals him-self. They quarrel in jealous rage, promising to meet on the same spot to battle it out next day; Arcite will bring the other food and armor. Theseus, out hunting with his court, comes upon the two fighting. The ladies move his pity, and he forgives the two men. They are to return in fifty weeks with a hundred knights each, and joust for the hand of Emilia.

Theseus meanwhile builds a theater a mile in circumference for the event. Before the battle Palamon prays to Venus and receives a sign foretelling his victory. Emilia prays to Diana and asks peace for the rivals, since she wishes to marry neither; Diana reveals that Emilia must marry one. Arcite prays to Mars, who grants him a sign of victory. Thus there is strife in Heaven; but Saturn hits on a compromise. At the tournament Palamon is wounded and Arcite declared victor. But a Fury bursts forth out of the earth and Arcite is hurled to the ground. Theseus declares both sides victorious. Dying, Arcite yields to Palamon and urges Emilia to wed. Theseus declares a hero's funeral for Arcite. After a period of mourning, Theseus seals the bond between Emilia and Palamon. They marry and live happily.

The Miller's Tale: A naughty but well-written piece of ribaldry. A rich Oxford carpenter has lately married a wild, wanton young wife, Alison; a poor scholar, Nicholas, boards with them. Nicholas woos Alison in her husband's absence, and speaks so well that she agrees to give her love if he can contrive to fool her jealous husband. At church one day, the parish clerk, Absalom, is smitten by her too, and that night serenades her; but she loves only Nicholas. Nicholas has a plan: With provender he locks himself in his room for days. When the carpenter questions him, Nicholas seems immersed in studies of astrology, and tells the former that soon a flood greater than Noah's will drown the earth. He urges the carpenter to get three tubs and suspend them by ropes from the ceiling, so they can be prepared to float away in safety. The carpenter does as bidden. The three climb ladders to their tubs, and Nicholas cautions the carpenter to be silent and pray. The husband falls into a deep sleep; Nicholas and Alison descend and take their pleasure. Absalom, who has been told that the carpenter is off in London, goes again to Alison's window. When he pleads for a kiss, she puts her backside out the window, and he kisses that.

Absalom hears himself mocked. From a smithy he procures a hot coulter and returns, promising a gold ring for another kiss. In sport, Nicholas leans out the window and is struck with the coulter. He shouts out in pain for water. The carpenter hearing the cry, thinks the floods have come, releases the tub, and drops to the floor. The hue and cry bring the townsfolk. When the carpenter tells his story, he is pronounced mad by his wife and Nicholas, and the townsfolk believe he must be.

The Reeve's Tale: Another clever bawdy story. Near Cambridge lives a sly miller named Bully Simkin, a thief of corn and meal. His wife, a parson's daughter reared in a nunnery, is full of disdainful airs. They have a twenty-year-old daughter and a six-month-old infant. The miller is prospering, grinding the wheat from all about, his chief source being the great college at Cambridge, King's Hall. Two young clerks, Alan and John, bring their wheat to the miller, determined he shall steal nothing from them. But the wily miller unhitches their horses, and the clerks pursue it into the fen while Simon steals half a bushel of flour and his wife kneads it into a loaf. The weary clerks return late and ask for lodgings for the night. While the miller and his wife are snoring, Alan creeps into the daughter's bed, and is welcomed there. John takes the cradle from the foot of the miller's bed to his own. The wife, getting up to answer a call of nature, mistakes John's bed for her own because of the cradle. He leaps on her and gives her a merry time. At dawn the girl tells Alan where to find the loaf made of his meal. He creeps back by mistake to the miller's bed, and wakens him. They fight furiously. The wife by error hits her husband on the head with a staff. The clerks escape with the flour and bread.

The Cook's Tale: A merry apprentice of the guild of victuallers, Perkin, uses his master's money to dice with. His master finally discharges him, and goes to a friend whose wife keeps a shop for show but makes her living otherwise. (Here the tale stops.)

The Man of Law's Tale: This tale is written in rime royal. The Soldan of Syria, hearing reports of the beauty, courtesy, and virtue of the Roman Emperor's daughter Constance, falls in love with her and pines for her. He and his barons and subjects are therefore all christened; the Emperor thereupon agrees to the marriage, and Constance, after mournful farewells, journeys to her promised husband. But the Soldan's mother and her co-conspirators swear to defend their old faith. Treacherously, she pretends to accept Christianity, and at the wedding-feast the evil woman has all the Christians and converts murdered, except Constance, who is set adrift on a ship without a rudder. God protects her for more than three years, when at last the seas cast her ship on the shores of Northumberland, near where resides the Constable of the castle and his wife, Hermengild. The latter pities the girl, who by her example wins over to Christianity first Hermengild and then the Constable. But Satan is jealous of her success. He causes a young knight to lust for her. When Constance repels his advances, he cuts Hermengild's throat and lays the bloody knife at Constance's side, for Constance has been sharing the lady's bed in the Constable's absence. The Constable returns with Aella, king of the land. None believes Constance guilty, but the false knight accuses her, swearing with his hand on the Gospels. Thereupon a hand strikes him on the neck; he falls down and his eyes burst from his head. The knight is executed, and many, including the king, are converted. Aella marries Constance. While he is away at battle, Constance bears him a son. Aella's mother, Donegild, intercepts a messenger carrying news of the birth of Maurice. She gets the man drunk, substituting a letter saying the child is a fiend and the mother an elf. The King weeps, but accepts the news with patience, and directs that mother and child be well looked after. Donegild intercepts this letter too, and her counterfeit letter orders the Constable to set Constance afloat with the child in the rudderless ship. In this way she floats on the sea for five years. The King, returning, discovers the plot and slays his mother, and sorrows for his lost wife and child. Meantime, the Roman Emperor has sent an avenging army to Syria. On their return, they come upon Constance's ship, and bring the pair to Rome, where she lives unknown. In expiation for his mother's death, Aella makes a pilgrimage to Rome. At a feast there he beholds his son, Maurice, and is struck by the boy's resemblance to Constance, whom he seeks out. Aella protests his innocence, and they are reunited. Aella invites her father to a feast, and Constance discovers herself to the Emperor, to the latter's great joy. In later years the Pope makes Maurice Emperor. Aella and Constance return to England, but Aella dies a year later. Constance returns to Rome and lives with her father, keeping herself busy with noble works.

The Shipman's Tale: A rich merchant and his lovely, extravagant wife love company and revelry. Among their many guests is one to whom the merchant has pledged close ties of brotherhood, a monk called Brother John, who always comes bearing gifts for all. Before taking a business-trip to Bruges, the merchant invites Brother John for a brief visit. On the third day, while the merchant is in his counting-house, the wife inveighs against her husband's stinginess to Brother John, begs him to lend her a hundred francs for a gown, and promises in return to render whatever service he will exact. After dinner, the priest borrows the money from the merchant. The latter leaves for Flanders. Brother John gives the wife the money in return for her love. Meanwhile, the merchant is worrying about his diminishing finances, goes to Paris to make a loan, and en route stops by to see the priest, who tells him the hundred francs have been returned to the wife. When the merchant is home again, he chides his wife for not telling him the loan was repaid. Defiantly, she says that she thought the monk had given her the money in a cousinly way to spend on herself, and that she has spent it all on clothes. Seeing he cannot change her, her husband forgives her with the exhortation to be less lavish henceforth.

The Prioress's Tale: One of the most exquisite and flawlessly written of the tales. In a great city in Asia, a little Christian boy passes through the Jewish quarter on his way to and from school. He always sings *O alma redemptoris*. Satan incites the Jews to murder the child and cast his body into a pit. His anxious mother, a widow, seeks her son the next day and discovers him with his throat cut. She weeps. Suddenly the boy begins to sing the song he loved so much. Passing Christians marvel at the event, and send for the Provost, who tortures and executes the guilty Jews. The boy is placed upon a bier, and when holy water is sprinkled on him, he sings again. The abbott questions him and the boy says that Christ's mother mercifully appeared to him as he lay dying, placed a grain upon his tongue, and bade him sing. When the grain is taken away, She will fetch him. The abbott takes off the grain, and the child dies, and is buried in a tomb of marble.

The Rime of Sir Thopas: Told by Chaucer himself, this is a burlesque on the chivalric romance. Sir Thopas, a fair and noble knight, is described in great detail; many a maid mourns for him in vain. Riding in a forest, he falls to longing, and dreams that an elf-queen alone of women would be a worthy mate for him. He rides in quest of her, but meets instead a huge giant, who challenges him. He prepares himself in fine array, and rides forth to meet Sir Elephant . . . Here the Host stops Chaucer, disparaging his verse, and bids him try something in prose. Chaucer, thereupon launches into the *Tale of Melibeus.*

The Tale of Melibeus: Perhaps by comic design, a dull affair. Melibeus, young and rich, one day goes to his fields, leaving his wife and daughter at home. Three old enemies beat his wife and dangerously wound the daughter. Returning, he is overcome by hate and grief, and would wreak vengeance on the men. But he is dissuaded by his wife, with many quotations from the classics and the Scriptures, and decides to temper justice with mercy. (This tale is a translation from a French condensation of a Latin original.)

The Monk's Tale: A series of instances of the fall of illustrious men, taken largely from Boccaccio and *The Romance of the Rose.* The accounts vary from a few lines (as in the stories of Lucifer and Adam) to a few hundred (as in the stories of Samson and Zenobia). Other tales are those of Hercules, Nebuchadnezzar, Belshazzar, King Peter of Cyprus, Nero, Alexander, Caesar, and Croesus.

The Nun's Priest's Tale: A masterpiece of humor, lively dialogue, and intelligence. It is a beast's fable, influenced by such works as *Reynard the Fox.* A poor widow lives with her two daughters in a little cottage. In her yard is a fine cock, Chanticleer, a trusty, merry crower with a harem of seven hens. His favorite is Partlet. One night he dreams he is being attacked by an ugly beast, and awakens Partlet with his groans. He tells her his dream, and she chides him for his cowardice. Chanticleer counters with the tale of a man who disbelieved a warning dream and in consequence his friend was killed; in a second dream a man was told where to find the body, and thus the murder was discovered. Another man refused to sail because of a dream; his companion paid no heed and was drowned. Chanticleer tells other tales—of Joseph, of Andromache. But the sight of Partlet gives him such joy that he defies all dreams. But women's counsel is baneful. One March morning, Chanticleer sees a fox, who has been lying in wait for him. The sly beast keeps him from fleeing by flattering him: he is enchanted by Chanticleer's exquisite voice, and begs him to sing. Chanticleer stands on his toes, stretches his neck, and closing his eyes, begins to crow. Russel, the fox, seizes him by the throat, and carries him off to the woods. The seven hens set up a loud lamentation, louder than those that were heard at the sack of Troy. The widow and her daughters run out in time to see the fox's escape. They raise the neighbors, and all give chase. Frightened Chanticleer suggests to the fox, now that he has come to the edge of the woods, to defy the pursuers. The fox opens his mouth to answer, and the cock flies high up into a tree. Once more the fox seeks to capture him with flattery, but Chanticleer has learned his lesson.

The Physician's Tale: The knight Virginius, of whom Titus Livius tells, has a beautiful chaste daughter. One day an evil judge, Appius, sees her and determines to have her. He hires a cunning churl, Claudius, to bring suit against Virginius, accusing him of stealing the girl from his household. Without giving Virginius a chance to plead, Appius gives judgment to Claudius: the girl is to be put in Appius' keeping. Rather than see his daughter forced to live in shame, Virginius cuts off her head and brings it to court. Appius orders him hanged. But a thousand people, hearing of the false accusation, burst in to save the knight. Appius is thrown into prison, where he kills himself. Claudius is condemned to be hanged, but at Virginius' intercession is exiled.

The Pardoner's Tale: In the prologue, the Pardoner quite candidly tells the tricks of his trade, and how he manages to cheat simple people into buying indulgences. The tale itself is a brilliant narrative, swiftly told, with lively dialogue and vivid characterization. The tale moves to Flanders, where a company of young folk indulges in riotous living, all laughing at one another's sins. Three revelers are drinking in a tavern, when they hear the tinkling of a bell that is carried before a corpse. They learn that the body is that of an old comrade, slain suddenly as he sat drunk upon a bench. The trio (intoxicated themselves) pledge brotherhood to one another and swear revenge against Death. They leave the tavern to seek him. On their journey they meet an old man who directs them to an oak where Death is. They run there and find instead eight bushels of gold florins, which make them forget their mission. But they cannot, without arousing suspicion, carry the gold in daylight; therefore two of them stand guard till night falls, while the third returns to town for food and wine. The pair agree to kill the youngest when he returns with refreshments. But he has his own ideas, and buys poison to put into two of the three bottles of wine. When he returns they kill him. Before burying his body, they drink the wine and die too. They have all found Death. The Pardoner now exclaims against sin and tries to sell some pardons.

The Wife of Bath's Tale: The important prologue is written with raciness and brilliant satire at the expense of marriage. She speaks from experience, having had five husbands, but is willing to have a sixth; but any husband, in her view, must be prepared to be her slave. Three of her husbands were good, rich, and old, but she cared little for them though she managed them easily by chiding and whining and trickery. Her fourth husband had a mistress; her fifth, her favorite, was the most villainous of all, slighting and beating her; but he was so fresh and merry! Though half her age, she had chosen him while her fourth was still alive. She gave him all her land and money; they had many quarrels, one of which she relates at full, but in the end she won dominion over him, and after that there was peace. The Tale she proceeds to tell is laid at the court of King Arthur. One of Arthur's knights ravished a maid and for the deed was condemned to death. But the Queen and her ladies beseech the King to spare him, and the knight's life is put in her hands. The Queen will grant him life if in a year and a day he can provide the answer to the question: What is it that women desire most? He travels far and wide for the solution, but can find no two creatures who agree on the answer. Still ignorant, he is sorrowfully journeying back to the Court when he meets a company of dancing ladies in the forest. Thinking to question them, he approaches but the dancers disappear. Instead, an ugly old crone is there sitting on the grass. He states his problem. She agrees to furnish the answer if he will swear to do the first thing she requires of him. She whispers in his ear, and the knight leaves for the Court. Before the full assembly there he announces that what women wish most is to have sovereignty over their husbands and lovers. All the women are compelled to accept that as the correct answer, and agree he has won his freedom. Whereupon, the old lady jumps up and demands justice: the knight must marry her. He tries to offer other payment for her help, but she insists. They are married. When they are alone, she asks the reason for his misery; he tells her it is due to her being so old, ugly, and lowly. She reminds him that Jesus was poor; if she is old, she ought to be the more respected; moreover, he need not fear she will ever deceive him with another man. He may now choose whether he will have her old, ugly, and faithful; or young, fair, and wanton. Sighing, he decides to put himself in her hands. Suddenly she is transformed into a young beautiful woman, who swears (because of his trust in her) ever to be faithful. They live in perfect joy to the end of their days. The Wife of Bath concludes with a wish that women may have young, meek husbands. May those who will not be ruled, die before their wives!

The Friar's Tale: Told with comic effect. A certain archdeacon was unrelenting in his punishment of sins and offenses, especially those of lechers. In his employ was the slyest of Summoners, who could well spare two lechers if they led to two dozen; he often plots with bawds to extort money from their clients. One day, riding to summon a widow, he meets a gay yeoman, who reveals himself to be a fiend from hell, after they have sworn brotherhood. They travel on, agreeing to share their pickings. They come upon a carter cursing his horses; but the fiend cannot take him because the curse wasn't really meant. They find an old widow; the Summoner demands twelve pence of her even though he knows of no fault in her. He accuses her of having cuckolded her husband. She curses him in earnest: "May the devil take him ere he die unless he repent." Since he will not repent, the fiend carries the Summoner off.

The Sumner's Tale: A certain begging monk travels in Yorkshire with a fellow who writes down what they receive from people to pray for them; a sturdy ruffian is their treasurer. When they leave a house, they scratch the name off the tablet. At last the friar reaches a house where he expects particularly superior refreshment, while his fellows have gone off to the hostelry in town. The goodman is ill. The friar tells goodman Thomas how he has prayed for him, and kisses the wife in welcome, flattering her. She complains of her husband's temper. The friar chides him. She then asks the monk what he would like for dinner, and reveals that her child died two weeks ago. He professes to have known this sad event by revelation, and tells her that he and his brothers have sung a *Te Deum*. Praising his order, he exclaims against wealth, and observes that the prayers of friars are always effective, Thomas declares that he has given most of his wealth to friars. Why spread the gift so thin? the friar asks. Let Thomas give all his money to the friar's convent for potent prayers, and not fight with his wife any more. Thomas agrees to give something if he will share it with his brothers equally. He tells the friar to reach beneath his buttock; the former does so, whereupon Thomas lets out a blast of wind. The friar is then driven from the house, and in anger goes to the lord of the village. The friar tells the lord and his lady, whom he is used to confessing, how his holy convent has been blasphemed by Thomas. They react calmly; the lady describing it as a churl's deed, and the lord wondering where Thomas received the inspiration. The lord's squire offers, in exchange for a new gown, to tell how the gift of Thomas can be divided equally. When the air is clear, let a cartwheel with twelve spokes be brought; twelve brothers are to have their noses at each end, and the friar is to have his nose at the nave. Thomas can then be set by the nave with a taut belly. The stink will spread, and each of the brothers will get his share.

The Clerk's Tale: The old story of Patient Griselda, told first by Boccaccio in the *Decameron* and later by Petrarch. Walter, the Marquis of Saluzzo is favored by birth, an able and honored monarch. His greatest fault is thinking only of present delights like hawking and hunting, and he has given no thought to marriage. A delegation of his subjects begs him to choose a wife and continue the family line. Moved by their plea, he agrees on condition they give all honor to his wife, nor grumble at whoever shall be his choice. They assent, and prepare for a great marriage feast. Near his palace lives the poorest man in the village, Janicula, and his daughter Griselda, a fair and virtuous maid, patient and reverent to her father. The Marquis has noted her qualities, and decides to wed her. The wedding day arrives. The Marquis has had made rings and clothing to her measure, though Griselda little dreams she is the chosen one. The Marquis goes to her cottage with his retinue, where she is waiting for a glimpse of the new Marchioness, and asks for the girl's father. Though astonished at the Marquis' request, the old man consents. The Marquis asks Griselda whether she will be governed in all her moods by his pleasure. She promises never to disobey him in deed or in thought, even though death threaten. They bring her to the palace where, transformed into a richly garbed noblewoman, she is hardly recognized by the people. God is kind, and in time she acquires all the manners of one to the manner born. She is a perfect wife, and is celebrated for her charity and good works. Presently, she bears her husband a little girl. Now the Marquis decides to test her loyalty. He pretends that there have been complaints against the disparity of their rank since the child's birth, and sends a trusted officer to take the girl to his sister in Bologna. Griselda, informed that her infant is to be killed, endures the agony with patience, requesting but that the little body be given decent burial. She remains a good wife, never mentioning her daughter. Four years later a boy is born to them. Two years after that Walter again submits Griselda to the same test; again she is docile. When the daughter is twelve, Walter procures from Rome, which knows his plans, a counterfeit papal bull granting him the right to abandon Griselda and take another wife. Though grieved, Griselda still wishes only her lord's happiness. In the meantime he has asked his brother-in-law, the Earl of Panigo, to bring home the daughter and son with great pomp, the girl to be arrayed as if she were his bride-to-be. Walter makes as his excuse the dissatisfaction of the people, and tells Griselda to return to her father's hut. She goes there to live in widowhood. The royal retinue presently arrives, and Griselda is sent for, as the only one who knows how to arrange things for the Marquis' pleasure. When the girl is seen, the common folk think that Walter is making a good choice in this second wife. Griselda is asked by Walter for her opinion of the new bride; she prays for the girl's prosperity and begs Walter not to torment her, for the girl was not nurtured in a way to endure adversity. He now confesses the whole truth, amid fountains of tears. The feast of celebration is far more splendid than their marriage feast was. The Marquis marries off his daughter well, and his son succeeds him. The Clerk remarks that Petrarch told this story not to preach humility of wives, an intolerable idea, but the need of firmness in adversity.

The Merchant's Tale: A satire on married life. An aging knight of Lombardy, after a life of pleasure, yearns to marry a young, beautiful maid, someone he can mold and live with in perfect joy. His brother, Justinus, who is married, warns him in vain of the folly of such a union. January finds a young and beautiful May, and weds her midst much feasting. He can hardly wait for night to come. His squire, Damian, is entranced by May, but she pays him no attention. God knows what May thinks of her husband the next morning. Damian inscribes a letter of anguish and lays it next his heart. Four days after the wedding, Damian's absence at the table is noted. Informed that his squire is ill, January asks May to visit him. Accompanied by her women, she goes, and Damian secretly gives her the letter. She is moved to pity for him, and writes him a letter granting him her favor; all that lacks now is the time and place. Damian instantly recovers. January makes a garden walled with stone, wherein to be merry with May. But Fortune strikes him with blindness in the midst of his joy. He begins to brood in fits of jealousy, and makes her swear that should he die she will remain a widow. She and Damian are burning with desire for each other, and he has a duplicate key to the garden made when she lets him have a wax impression. One day in the garden, while January is imploring her to be true and she is weeping at the idea that she could be thought capable of infidelity, she beckons Damian to climb a peartree. Pluto and Proserpina, watching the scene, take sides; Pluto wishes to restore January's sight, while Proserpina declares she will make May equal to the emergency. May expresses her longing for some pears; in her condition she will die unless she have them. January stoops; she uses him as a stool to climb the tree, where Damian receives her. Pluto restores January's sight; the husband sees the lovers in the tree, and loudly demands an explanation. Proserpina then affords May the answer: May declares that she was taught to stand in the tree with a man in order to restore her husband's sight. He cries that he has seen a worse sight than her merely standing; she assures him his sight is still imperfect. Lightly she leaps down; January embraces her, and leads her back to the palace.

The Squire's Tale: An unfinished romance, often referred to by later poets. A noble, excellent king, Cambuscan of Tartary had by his wife Elpheta two sons, Algarsyf and Cambal, and a beautiful daughter, Canacee. Each year on his birthday he holds festivities. In the twentieth year of his reign, during the feast on the Ides of March, a strange knight appears, bearing gifts from the King of Araby. Cambuscan is presented with a wonderful brass horse that will bear him safely and swiftly wherever he wishes to go. A mirror, a gift to Canacee, will reveal who is friend and who is foe, and foretell adversity to the realm or king. The ring, also a gift for the princess, will teach the wearer to understand the voice of the birds and the herbs and grass. Cambuscan is given, too, a magic sword that can cut through all armor, and that can restore to health any man cut by its blade when the flat side is laid across the wound. The next morning Canacee arises early for a walk with some of her women. They come upon a white falcon, weeping and lamenting, tearing at her bloody breast with her beak. The princess understands the bird's lament, which tells how she was betrayed in love by a tercelet to whom she has yielded her honor, and who has deserted her for a kite. The falcon shrieks and swoons into Canacee's lap. The princess takes her home to nurse her. Chaucer says he will tell now of the deeds of Cambuscan. But the tale is unfinished.

The Franklin's Tale: An elegant story of courtly love and magic. In Armorica (Brittany), Arveragus, a noble knight, has won as his wife by his noble deeds the lady he loves. For a year they live in joy until he departs for England for two years to seek honor in arms. Dorigen, his wife, mourns his departure and broods in sorrow. Her friends devise amusements to restore her cheer. At a festive gathering, the squire Aurelius, long in love with her, speaks with her, confesses his adoration, begging for her love lest he die. She vows she will never be an unfaithful wife, and jestingly adds that she could yield her love only when the sombre rocks that line Brittany's coast have disappeared. Arveragus returns to his joyful wife, and he and Dorigen take up their happy life together. Aurelius meanwhile languishes in torment. After two years, his brother remembers something of the magic arts of the clerks at Orleans, where he has studied. Knowing Aurelius' plight, he goes off with him there. A magician promises to create the illusion of the removal of the rocks if paid a thousand pounds. Aurelius agrees. With astrological aid, the miracle is accomplished. Aurelius reminds Dorigen of her promise. She is determined to die rather than be disloyal to her husband. He, seeing her weep, questions her, and she tells him all. Rather than see her betray her word, Arveragus tells her she must keep it, no matter what misery it cost him. She tells Aurelius of her husband's decision. Impressed by their nobility and honor, Aurelius releases her from her promise. But he must still pay the magician. He begs the latter to allow him to pay in installments. The magician, hearing the whole story, releases the squire from the debt. Which, we are asked, is the most generous?

The Second Nun's Tale: The story of St. Cecilia (Cecily) related with pious simplicity. Cecily, born of a noble Roman family, has been raised as a Christian. On her wedding night, she tells her new husband, Valerian, that an angel has been guarding her and has threatened to slay the man who will attempt her virginity. She adds that Valerian must be baptized before she can offer him proof of this. After being baptized by Urban, Valerian sees the angel, who gives a crown of lilies to Cecily and one of roses to Valerian, both garlands fresh from Paradise. Valerian asks that his brother Tiburtius be allowed grace, and he is also persuaded to become a Christian. Later both brothers are sent to their death as Christian martyrs. Almachius, the prefect, summons Cecily to sacrifice before Jupiter and renounce Christianity. When she refuses, he orders her to be set in a bath with a great fire beneath it, but she does not sweat even a drop. The executioner hacks at her neck three times in vain; the law forbids a fourth stroke. For three days she lives with her neck cut, preaching and instructing. Then she dies, Urban and his deacons burying her.

The Canon's Yeoman's Tale: A clever attack on alchemy. One day a canon approaches a priest who lives in the house of a goodwife at her expense, for he is a very pleasant priest. The canon borrows a mark, which he returns as promptly as promised. For the priest's courtesy, the canon offers to show him how to work in alchemy. First he makes silver out of quicksilver by putting some real silver in the hollow of a coal, stuffing it with wax, which quickly melts. He repeats his magic by putting some silver in a hollow stirring-stick in the same manner. A goldsmith examines the silver and finds it pure, much to the priest's delight. In exchange for the recipe, the canon exacts forty pounds in nobles from the priest, and then disappears. The moral is to beware of alchemists.

The Manciple's Tale: A warning not to meddle in the love affairs of anyone else. Phoebus, flower of knighthood and a fine musician as well, has a snow-white crow in a cage at his house, and which he has taught to speak as well as a man and sing as sweetly as a nightingale. Phoebus also has a wife whom he loves dearly and guards jealously. But it is a waste of labor to watch a wife. While Phoebus is away, his wife sends for her lover and they enjoy themselves while the crow watches in silence. But when Phoebus returns home, the crow sings, "Cuckoo!" and tells how a man of small reputation has supplanted the noble Phoebus in his wife's favors. In rash ire Phoebus slays his wife with his celebrated bow. But as she lies dead before him, he doubts the crow's truth, and begins to hate him. Furiously he tears out the bird's white feathers and makes him black, bereaving him of song as well as of speech. For this cause all crows are now black and have harsh voices. Conclusion: Never tell a man of his wife's frailty.

The Parson's Tale: The longest and dullest of all the tales, and is heavily weighed down by moralizing. Beginning with a discussion on the nature of penance, it proceeds to a weary sermon on the seven deadly sins, the captains of all other sins, and on their related vices, and the cures available. Pride is the root of all evil, and Meekness the chief remedy.

Critical Commentary on *The Canterbury Tales*

Groups Within *The Canterbury Tales*: The relation between tales, including their intended ordering, has been the subject of much scholarship and dispute. The Tales begin with a clear relation among the first storytellers. Harry Bailey, the host, supervises the drawing of lots and the Knight thereby becomes the first to tell a tale. After the pilgrims have expressed their approval of the Knight's tale, the host invites the Monk to continue. The Miller, however, drunkenly insists on telling his indecent tale about a carpenter—to which the Reeve responds by telling a tale about a miller. With the following tale, the incomplete Cook's Tale, the mystery is posed: Did Chaucer intend each tale, often in subtle ways, to continue the thrust and parry sequence developed thus far? Scholars have attempted to resolve this question not only by reference to narrative and thematic elements within the tales themselves but also by allusion to time, day, and place along the route.

To date, no single arrangement other than that found in the Ellesmere manuscript (the earliest and most complete text of the Tales) has won general acceptance.

One apparent subgroup has attracted the attention of many readers and scholars since it was first proposed by Professor Lyman Kittredge in 1912. The so-called "Marriage Group" consists of tales told by the Wife of Bath, the Friar, the Summoner, the Clerk, and the Franklin. Each tale treats in one way or another the topic of marital relationships. The Wife of Bath opens the argument by bragging about her sovereignty over five husbands and her requirements for a sixth. After the topic is explored, often in elaborate ways, by the intervening tales, the Franklin concludes with a story about the harmonious married life of Arviragus and Dorigen. On this note Chaucer leaves readers free to draw their own conclusions.

The Question of Chaucer's Retraction: *The Canterbury Tales* end with a perplexing retraction in which Chaucer repents of any offense he may have given by his bawdier tales. Scholars have attempted to undercut the apparent content of this statement by interpreting it as sarcasm or irony, or as the late emendation of meddling monk-scribe. The Princeton school of Chaucerian scholarship argues, however, that such a retraction is not unexpected from a man deeply influenced by the Church—that is to say, a man of his time.

Chaucer is also the author of a number of charming short poems, all in complicated French style. The most admired of them is one of his last compositions, *The Complaint of Chaucer to his Empty Purse* (1399), in which he addresses his purse as his dearest lady, complains of her lightness, and begs that she will be heavy again.

IMPORTANCE

It was not until modern scholarship uncovered the secret of reading Middle English that we could understand that Chaucer, far from being a rude versifier, was a perfectly accomplished technician, and that his verse is rich in music and elegant to the highest degree. Chaucer's own urbane personality is a delight to encounter in his books. He is avowedly a bookworm, yet few poets observe nature with more freshness and delight. He is a master of genial satire, but can sympathize with true piety and goodness with as much pleasure as he attacks the hypocritical.

It is not an uncommon estimate of Chaucer that he must be counted among the few greatest of English poets. In range of interest he is surpassed only by Shakespeare. He was recognized already in the Renaissance, when it came to England, as the Father of English Poetry. He was a man of wide learning, and wrote with ease on religion, philosophy, ethics, science, rhetoric. No man has more completely summed up an age than Chaucer has his, yet the people of his great poems are revealed as men and women for all times.

Master of verse as Chaucer was, he introduced into English poetry many verse forms: the *heroic couplet,* (in which form most of *The Canterbury Tales* is written), verse written in iambic pentameter, rhyming *aa, bb, cc,* etc.—a form that was to be very important in the eighteenth century; the *rime royal,* a seven-line stanza in iambic pentameters, rhyming *ababbcc,* (*Troilus and Criseyde*); the *terza rima,* three-line stanzas, rhyming *aba, bcb, cdc,* etc. (which Chaucer imitated from Dante, and used in some of his minor poems); and the eight-line iambic pentameter stanza, rhyming *ababbcbc* (the *Monk's Tale.*)

4
LATE MIDDLE ENGLISH LITERATURE

Besides *Sir Gawain and the Green Knight*, and the writings of Chaucer, there are a number of fourteenth-century works of interest and importance.

THE PEARL

The Pearl (around 1370), is thought by some scholars to have the same author as *Sir Gawain and the Green Knight*. It is a beautiful elegy, a lament on the death of a little girl, and is cast in the form of a dream-allegory employing both alliteration and rhyme. In his sleep the poet sees his lost child across the stream, enthroned as a queen in Heaven. She grants him a vision of the New Jerusalem. Eager to join her, he is about to plunge into the stream when he awakes and finds himself by her grave.

THE VISION OF PIERS PLOWMAN

The Vision of Piers Plowman (around 1362) has been attributed to William Langland, who died in 1400. The existence of some sixty manuscripts of this poem indicates its great popularity. There are three different texts of the work: the "A" text, written around 1362; the "B" text, which shows considerable revision and contains 10 more cantos (around 1377); and the "C" text, which shows even greater revision (around 1394). Opinion is varied as to whether these three texts are the work of one man. Although a contemporary of Chaucer, the author seems to come from another civilization. His vocabulary is the lively speech of the countryside, his style blunt and unpolished. Chaucer has infinite tolerance; this author is a burning reformer. Chaucer is a self-conscious artist; the author of *Piers* is interested chiefly in his message. The poem is an attack on the corruptions of the rich and the wickedness of the clergy. Pity, fury, and enthusiasm run through the lines, and there are vivid scenes of poverty, luxury, vice, and strife. Everywhere the author sees idleness destroying the foundations of life, and little of Christ's teachings in a Christian society. For him the only salvation is work, and Christ Himself is pictured as a humble tiller of the soil. The verse employed is essentially that of Anglo-Saxon poetry, accentual and alliterative.

JOHN GOWER (c. 1325–1408)

John Gower, the poet, was a friend of Chaucer. His work is perhaps more valuable as a measure of Chaucer's greatness than for any merit of its own. He writes pleasantly and skillfully, but he lacks the scope, narra1tive power, and originality of Chaucer. He was perhaps too much the moralist to delight us. His most important works are *Speculum Meditantis,* a French poem sermonizing on the immorality of the age; *Vox Clamantis*, a dream-allegory recounting the Peasant's Revolt of 1381 and the career of the rebel Wat Tyler, and concluding with a prayer to the King to reform social evils; and *Confessio Amantis,* a poem of uneven quality containing a number of stories that illustrate various states of love.

In the fifteenth century, formal poetry fell into a great decline. The only poets worthy of mention, John Lydgate (1370?–1450?) and Thomas Occleve (1368?–1450?), were imitators of Chaucer without his genius. Though once considered almost equal to his, their works are no longer read. But in Scotland, a royal disciple of Chaucer, King James I of Scotland, (1394–1437), wrote a charming, tender allegory in Chaucer's rime royal, *The King's Quair* (The King's Book).

The fifteenth century, however, is not without its own literary importance. Three groups of works are of consummate interest: the writings of Sir Thomas Malory, the popular Ballads, and the Drama.

SIR THOMAS MALORY (c. 1400–1741)

The dates and details of the life of Sir Thomas Malory, as is the case for many of his contemporaries, are obscure at best. Malory is a bit of a special case simply because of the number of possible life stories long attached to him (at least four). However, the discovery of a manuscript of Malory's *Le Morte d'Arthur* in 1934 more or less substantiates that Malory was in fact the thief, rapist, traitor, and general scoundrel he was long purported to be. It remains a matter of some debate, however, whether this historical Malory was the author of *Le Morte d'Arthur.*

A knight from a family in Warwickshire, Malory served at least twenty years of his life, starting in the 1460s, in jail for his crimes. It was during this time the Malory supposedly broadened his knowledge of the legend of Arthur through one or more French Arthurian romances. If France was Malory's main literary source, he clearly did leave much to his own imagination, and his text is both concise and lyrical. His writing of the legend of Arthur is today the primary source for our knowledge of this story.

Le Morte d'Arthur

Malory's best-known work, transcribed in 1469 and printed in 1485 by Williaim Caxton, presents the complete legends of Arthur and his knights of the Round Table in English. The legends surrounding the great knight Arthur have their origins in Celtic folklore, but they were long told and developed in France, first in Britanny and later in other regions of the *langue d'oil*, the medieval language of northern France.

The chivalric romance begins prior to Arthur's birth, when King Uther battles the King of Cornwall for the love of his beautiful wife, Igraine. Igraine is found to have been magically impregnated by King Uther, and the two are married and have a son, Arthur. After the death of his father, Arthur secures his right to the throne by wrenching a sword from an anvil in a rock, and he receives the sword, Excalibur.

Arthur marries Guinevere, and receives from her father, King Leodegrance, a wedding gift: the Round Table and one hundred knights. Meanwhile, the reader learns that one of the Ladies of the Lake, who had previously bestowed Excalibur upon Arthur, has imprisoned Merlin the magician under a rock. Arthur's political adventures continue through a series of battles, and he is eventually crowned Emperor of Rome. Thus his glory spreads across the European continent. This glory is only augmented by the vast sum of brave deeds performed by Sir Lancelot, the first knight of all Cristendom and Guinevere's personal favorite.

The narrative takes a turn at this point and incorporates a large part of another medieval romance, the story of Tristram and Isolde. Tristram, after accidentally drinking a love potion with Isolde, falls hopelessly in love with her. Unfortunately, she is the bride-to-be of his uncle, Mark, and Tristram is put in the difficult situation of watching his only love marry his patron and uncle, whom he greatly respects. Tristram's sadness forces him into the forest. He is brought back to the castle, banished by Mark, and flees to Camelot. Gaining great renown in Camelot, Tristram has soon also won the respect of Arthur and Launcelot, and when Mark appears with a plot to murder Tristram, Launcelot discovers him. Mark is ordered by Arthur to let Tristram return to his kingdom, where he successfully avoids all of Mark's traps and escapes to England with Isolde.

Next begins the quest for the Holy Grail. A prophesy of an ancient hermit is realized when a young knight by the name of Galahad pulls the magic sword from the rock, thus proving his worthiness to accompany his father, Sir Launcelot, on the quest for the Grail. This great adventure concludes with the death of Sir Galahad, who, after receiving communion from the Grail and performing a miracle, had been imprisoned and subsequently chosen king of an unnamed city in the near East.

Trouble brews beneath the celebration of the victorious Grail-seekers, for Launcelot is in love with Guinevere. He rescues her from an evil knight, at which point he is engaged by Arthur's troops. A great battle ensues, which

Launcelot wins, and after Arthur attacks Launcelot's castle, the queen and Launcelot escape to France. But this is no safe haven, for Arthur is soon waging war against France, and he suffers yet another disloyalty when his son, Mordred, tries to take the queen, who has been returned to Arthur, for his bride. A final great battle ensues in which Sir Mordred is killed and Arthur is mortally wounded. On his deathbed, Arthur asks Sir Belvedere to return Excalibur to the Lady of the Lake, which he does. As Excalibur slowly is drawn by a hand into the icy lake, so Arthur is drawn to his death. Merlin's warning that Arthur not pursue wandering fires thus goes unheeded. Launcelot learns that Guinevere, after her return to Arthur, has become a nun, and he too takes holy orders, leaving the throne to Sir Constantine of Cornwall.

BALLADS

Ballads (literally, *dance songs*) were the literature of the common people. It was not until the eighteenth century that any organized attempt was made to collect the ballads in print; Bishop Thomas Percy's *Reliques of Ancient English Poetry* (1765) was the first important book to arouse interest in them, and with it a serious search and study of them began. Naturally the ballads, being a literature of the folk, lingered longest where urban civilization was slowest to penetrate. For this reason most of the ballads come to us from the neighborhood of the Scottish border.

There is no agreement among scholars as to how these folk-narrative songs might have been composed. Some students of the ballad believe that any given ballad is the work of an individual now anonymous. Others argue that the ballad was composed communally at village gatherings in the manner in which African-American spirituals have been made in more recent times. In any event, the ballads are unquestionably the possession of a people; they were composed often around topics of local interest and passed on from generation to generation. The manner of their transference inevitably resulted in changes, so that for the 305 or so extant ballads there are more than a thousand versions. Some of these must be very ancient indeed, even though the language of very few antedates the fifteenth century.

The ballads exhibit a variety of subject matter and mood. Some are stories of simple domestic tragedy (*Edward, The Douglas Tragedy, Babylon, The Twa Corbies*); some of the supernatural (*Thomas Rymer, The Demon Lover, The Wife of Usher's Well*); some of historical events (*Chevy Chase, Sir Patrick Spens*); some of humor (*Get up and Bar the Door, Our Goodman, The Crafty Farmer*); and some of the adventures of Robin Hood. The Robin Hood ballads would seem to be the raw material for an epic; had some genius of the people appeared to string them together into one flowing narrative, we might have had another English epic on a truly English hero.

The ballads are written in a number of verse forms. The most common of these are rhyming couplets and the *ballad stanza*—four line stanzas, the second and fourth lines rhyming. Fairly often old musical effects survive in words that have no meaning, such as *fal lal lal, eh vow bonnie, hey down a down a down*, and so on. The ballads have been much admired for their strange mixture of crudity, directness, and unexpected subtlety.

Edward tells the story of a young man who has murdered his father at the instigation of his mother, and who curses her for her counsel.

Babylon is the story of an outlaw who comes upon three sisters, kills two of them for rejecting his advances, only to discover from the third that they are his sisters. He thereupon commits suicide.

The Douglas Tragedy tells of the abduction of Lady Margaret by Lord William, how they are pursued by her father and brothers, and how all involved come to death in the ensuing fight.

The Twa Corbies tells of two crows who are discussing the fate of a newly slain knight and how his wife has already taken another mate.

Thomas Rymer tells of a man who falls in love with a fairy and how he is taken away from the world of men by her into fairyland.

The Demon Lover tells the story of a woman who forsakes her husband and children to follow a lover who turns out to be a demon and bears her off to Hell.

The Wife of Usher's Well recounts how a woman has lost three sons at sea and is visited by their ghosts.

Chevy Chase celebrates the great fight in which the heroes Percy and Douglas meet their death.

Sir Patrick Spens is the account of how a brave sea captain is ordered by the King to sail in weather he mistrusts and how all the crew and passengers are drowned.

Get Up and Bar the Door tells how a good citizen loses a bet to his wife by being the first to speak during their pact of silence when some burglars break in.

Our Goodman tells how an over-credulous husband confronts his wife with the proof that a favored lover is making constant visits and how she convinces him that what he observes has another meaning.

Robin Hood Rescuing the Widow's Three Sons tells how the outlaw and his men save three squires condemned to be hanged for poaching on the King's preserves and how they hang the Sheriff instead.

MEDIEVAL DRAMA

The great drama of the classical world had virtually ceased to exist after the fall of Rome. To the Middle Ages, the classical drama of Greece and Rome was a closed book. Drama was reborn in the early medieval period as though it had never existed before. Its origins in the Middle Ages seem to be connected with the Easter Mass in churches. Tiny pieces of musical dialogue, probably accompanied by some symbolic action, were thrust into the body of the Mass to catch the interest of churchgoers not skilled in Latin. Thereafter the Christmas and Easter stories were dramatized into little plays in Latin for church presentation, the actors being monks and priests. The next step obviously was to dramatize stories from the Bible. Various parts of the church were used as stage setting. (The pulpit, for instance, could be used as Herod's throne; the church aisles as roads to Bethlehem, and so on.). As interest in these playlets developed, the inside of the church became too small to house the spectators, and the performances were moved to the churchyard.

Once outside the church, the drama was well on the way to passing into the hands of the laity. The trade guilds presently took over the performance of plays, and soon various regions had their own cycles of plays. Each guild would choose a biblical story appropriate to its trade; thus, the shipwrights would present the *Building of the Ark*; the fishermen would give *Noah and the Flood*; the bakers, *The Last Supper*. The various cycles of plays include *The Cornish Cycle* (1300–1400), containing fifty episodes dealing with the origin of the world, the Passion of Christ, and the Resurrection; *The York Cycle* (1350–1440), containing, originally, fifty-four parts of which forty-eight survive; *The Chester Cycle* (1475–1500), containing twenty-five plays, highly religious, didactic, and sometimes humorous; *The Wakefield Cycle* (1425–1475), containing thirty-two plays, not all complete, roughly humorous and with considerably superior dramatic composition. The *Wakefield Cycle* is sometimes known as the *Towneley Cycle* (after the family that once owned the manuscript) and contains the celebrated *Second Shepherds' Play*.

These plays whose plots are taken from the Bible and the lives of the saints are known as *mystery* or *miracle* plays, the names often being used interchangeably. (Some make a distinction, using the term *mystery plays* to refer to plays based on Biblical narratives, and *miracle plays* to refer to those based on lives of the saints.) The actors were of course amateurs. Each play was presented on a wagon, usually in a square of the town. The characters of these dramas, derived from biblical lore and the lives of the saints, were soon simplified into types. Herod became the cruel tyrant, for instance, and Noah's wife the shrew. The Devil was a familiar person of these dramas. Generally the miracle plays tend to exalt Providence, and to show the punishment visited on those who are disobedient to God.

The miracle plays sometimes allowed elements of comedy to intrude upon the religious stories. In the *Second Shepherds' Play* already mentioned, dealing with the Birth of Christ, there is a subplot connected with the theft of a sheep; again in *The Deluge* of the *Chester Cycle*, Noah's wife refuses to enter the Ark without her cronies and Noah is forced to push her into the Ark just in time. Perhaps the best-known of the miracle plays are the *Abraham and Isaac* and the *Second Shepherds' Play*.

In the fourteenth century a new type of popular play appeared, the *morality play*, a play representing allegorically as its characters such moral abstractions as Vice, Charity, Faith, Good Deeds, and so on. The typical plot was the contest between Evil and Good, with victory, of course, for Good. Technically these plays show a considerable advance over the miracle plays in affording an opportunity for original plot construction and depicting character traits. The most celebrated of the morality plays is *Everyman* (printed around 1525).

Everyman is written largely in rhyming couplets. The story tells how God, dissatisfied with the worldliness of his creatures, sends Death to summon Everyman to a pilgrimage. In his need, Everyman is forsaken by Fellowship, Kindred, Goods, Knowledge, Beauty, Strength, and Five-Wits. Only Good Deeds accompanies him when he goes to meet God's judgment. All earthly things are thus proved to be vanity.

The last type of play to develop in the late Middle Ages is the *interlude*, a short play intended for amusement as much as for instruction, to be presented at banquets or occasions of festivity. Most of them were written after 1500. The name of one writer of interludes, John Heywood, has come down to us. His best known interlude is *The Four P's*.

The Four P's, more of a debate than a play, according to modern tastes, presents a contest between a Palmer, a Pardoner, a Peddler, and a Poticary (apothecary) to see who can tell the biggest lie. The Palmer wins when he declares that he never saw a woman lose her temper.

Certain plays are intermediary between the morality play and the interlude. Such is John Skelton's *Magnyfycence* (around 1520) in which Good Hope saves Mankind, with the aid of other good qualities, from the domination of Vice. In this work there is a certain amount of satire though the characterization is weak. The play called *Mind, Will and Understanding* (around 1460), which has been attributed to Henry Medwall, is a well-constructed but heavily didactic piece. Medwall is the author of the plays *Nature* (around 1495), a morality play without a devil, and with spirited dialogue in the interlude manner, and *Fulgens Et Lucres* (around 1497), with a prominent element of comedy in the subplot.

REVIEW QUESTIONS

THE MIDDLE ENGLISH PERIOD

Multiple Choice

1. _____ At the Battle of Hastings
   a. an English king conquered a French opponent
   b. a French duke conquered an English king
   c. the Romans conquered native British people
   d. the English and French united against the Danes

2. _____ The Norman Conquest brought with it
   a. the establishment of Anglo-Saxon as the intellectual language of England
   b. a new wave of alliterative verse
   c. the feudal system
   d. complete independence for English lords

3. _____ Which of the following is NOT an allegory?
   a. *The Parliament of Fowls*
   b. *Piers Plowman*
   c. *Sir Gawain and the Green Knight*
   d. *Troilus and Creseyde*

4. _____ The troubadours were the source of
   a. a new lyric poetry
   b. the Anglo-Saxon epics
   c. the Matter of Rome
   d. the alliterative system of rhyme

5. _____ The author of *Sir Gawain and the Green Knight* is
   a. unknown
   b. Guy of Warwick
   c. Chaucer
   d. Langland

6. _____ Chaucer held all of the following positions except
   a. customs official
   b. valet
   c. justice of the peace
   d. priest

7. _____ *The House of Fame* is a
   a. tale of adventure
   b. Greek epic
   c. dream allegory
   d. letter

8. _____ In *Troilus and Criseyde*, Chaucer borrows freely from
   a. the Venerable Bede
   b. Malory
   c. Boccaccio
   d. Dante

9. _____ *The Canterbury Tales* includes stories by
   a. each of the pilgrims
   b. some of the pilgrims
   c. Chaucer in the role of a pilgrim
   d. religious figures only

10. _____ *Piers Plowman* is
    a. an agricultural instruction book
    b. an attack on the corruptions of the rich and the clergy
    c. a translation from Boccaccio's *Decameron*
    d. one of *The Canterbury Tales*

True or False

11. _____ Sir Thomas Malory added nothing original to his retelling of the French tales of King Arthur.

12. _____ Bishop Percy wrote all of the ballads contained in his *Reliques of Ancient English Poetry*.

13. _____ Medieval drama builds upon and extends the great classic traditions of drama from Greece and Rome.

14. _____ Early English plays focused on Christmas and Easter events.

15. _____ Loosely associated plays were organized into "cycles."

16. _____ The miracle plays never allowed elements of comedy to intrude upon their otherwise serious matter.

17. _____ Following the Norman Invasion, the bulk of the English populace quickly began to speak French as their first language.

18. _____ Chaucer's versification is based strictly on English models.

19. _____ Much middle English literature used French themes and imitated French forms.

20. _____ *Piers Plowman* idealizes the social attitudes of the Norman court.

Fill-in

21. The final revolt against King Arthur is led by _____ .

22. Chaucer's most prestigious public position was as _____ .

23. In *Troilus and Criseyde*, Chaucer is simultaneously judgmental and sympathetic toward _____ .

24. Chaucer says that he wants to atone for earlier slights against women by writing _____ .

25. The General Prologue opens in the month of _____ .

26. Chaucer's pilgrims are on their way to _____ .
27. A ribald tale about a carpenter and his wanton young wife is
_____ .
28. *The Nun's Priest* tells a tale about two chickens, Chanticleer and
_____ .
29. Chaucer offers an apology for any offense he may have given in an
addition to *The Canterbury Tales* known as his _____ .
30. *The Pearl* is thought to have been written by the same author as
_____ .

Matching

31. _____ Langland   a. Looking for a new husband
32. _____ Chaucer   b. Based on Biblical material
33. _____ Wife of Bath   c. A knight at King Arthur's court
34. _____ Gower   d. Greatest middle English poet
35. _____ Boccaccio   e. Source for Chaucer
36. _____ Malory   f. Probable author of *Piers Plowman*
37. _____ Mystery plays   g. One of Chaucer's male pilgrims
38. _____ Summoner   h. A dream allegory
39. _____ Gawain   i. Wrote of the Arthurian legends
40. _____ *Book of the Duchess* j. Wrote *Confessio Amantis*

Answers

1. b	16. f	29. *Retraction*
2. c	17. f	30. *Sir Gawain and*
3. d	18. f	*the Green Knight*
4. a	19. t	31. f
5. a	20. f	32. d
6. d	21. Modred	33. a
7. c	22. Member of	34. j
8. c	Parliament	35. e
9. b	23. Criseyde	36. i
10. b	24. *The Legend of*	37. b
11. f	*Good Women*	38. g
12. f	25. April	39. c
13. f	26. Canterbury	40. h
14. t	27. *The Miller's Tale*	
15. t	28. Partlet	

Part 3

THE RENAISSANCE, THE REFORMATION, AND THE ELIZABETHANS

WORKS AT A GLANCE*

John Lyly

1578	*Euphues*
1580	*Euphues and his England*
c. 1584	*The Woman in the Moon*
	Alexander and Campaspe

c. 1588	*Endimion*

George Peele

1584	*The Arraignment of Paris*
1593	*The Old Wives' Tale*
	Edward I

Robert Greene

1588	*Pandosto*
1589	*Menaphon*
c. 1591	*Friar Bacon and Friar Bungay*
	James IV

1591	"Sweet Are the Thoughts That Savour of Content"
1592	*A Groatsworth of Wit Bought With a Million of Repentance*

Thomas Lodge

1594	*Marius and Sylla*

Thomas Kyd

1589	*The Spanish Tragedy*

Christopher Marlowe

c. 1587	*Tamburlaine*
c. 1588	*Doctor Faustus*
c. 1589	*The Jew of Malta*
c. 1593	*Edward II*

1598	"Hero and Leander"
1599	"The Passionate Shepherd to His Love"

William Shakespeare

1589–1592	*Henry VI, Part 1*
	Henry VI, Part 2
	Henry VI, Part 3
1592	*Venus and Adonis*
1592–1593	*Richard III, The Comedy of Errors*

1593–1594	*Titus Andronicus*
	The Taming of the Shrew
	The Rape of Lucrece

*Dates are dates of first performance or publication.

William Shakespeare *(continued)*

1594–1595	*The Two Gentlemen of Verona*	1601–1602	*Twelfth Night*
			Troilus and Cressida
	Love's Labour's Lost	1602–1603	*All's Well That Ends Well*
	Romeo and Juliet		
1594–1596	*Richard II*	1604–1605	*Measure for Measure*
	A Midsummer Night's Dream		*Othello*
		1605–1606	*King Lear*
1596–1597	*King John*		*Macbeth*
	The Merchant of Venice	1606–1607	*Antony and Cleopatra*
		1607–1608	*Coriolanus*
1597–1598	*Henry IV, Part 1*		*Timon of Athens*
	Henry IV, Part 2	1608–1609	*Pericles*
1598–1599	*Much Ado About Nothing*	1609–1610	*Cymbeline*
		1610–1611	*Winter's Tale*
	Henry V	1611–1612	*The Tempest*
1599–1600	*Julius Caesar*	1612–1613	*Henry VIII*
	As You Like It		*The Two Noble Kinsmen*
1600–1601	*Hamlet*		
	The Merry Wives of Windsor		

Ben Jonson

1598	*Every Man in His Humour*	1609	*Epicoene*
1599	*Every Man Out of His Humour*	1610	*The Alchemist*
		1611	*Catiline*
1603	*Sejanus*	1614	*Bartholomew Fair*
1606	*Volpone*	1623	"To the Memory of My Beloved Master, William Shakespeare"
1608	*The Hue and Cry After Cupid*		

Francis Beaumont and John Fletcher

c. 1608	*The Knight of the Burning Pestle*
c. 1611	*The Maid's Tragedy*
	A King and No King
	Philaster

John Fletcher

c. 1609	*The Faithful Shepherdess*	1621	*The Wild Goose Chase*

Thomas Heywood

1603	*A Woman Killed With Kindness*

*Dates are dates of first performance or publication.

Phillip Massinger

c. 1625 *A New Way to Pay Old Debts*

Thomas Dekker

1599	*Old Fortunatus*	1604	*The Honest Whore*
1600	*The Shoemaker's Holiday*	1608	*The Belman of London*
1603	*The Wonderful Year*	1609	*The Gull's Hornbook*

George Chapman

1605	*All Fools*	1607	*Bussy D'Ambois*
	Eastward Ho!	1613	*The Revenge of Bussy*
1606	*The Gentleman Usher*		*D'Ambois*

Thomas Middleton

1608	*A Trick to Catch the Old One*	1615	*The Witch*
1611	*The Roaring Girl*	1623	*The Changeling* (with
1612	*A Chaste Maid in Cheapside*		Rowley)
	Women Beware Women		

John Marston

1598	*The Metamorphosis of*	1599	*The History of Antonio and*
	Pygmalion's Image		*Mellida*
		1604	*The Malcontent*

Cyril Tourneur

1607	*The Atheist's Tragedy*	1611	*The Revenger's Tragedy*

John Webster

1611	*The White Devil*	1613	*The Duchess of Malfi*

John Ford

1633	*'Tis Pity She's a Whore*	1634	*Perkin Warbeck*
	The Broken Heart		

James Shirley

1626	*The Maid's Revenge*	1635	*The Lady of Pleasure*
1631	*Love's Cruelty*	1641	*The Cardinal*
1632	*Hyde Park*		

---

*Dates are dates of first performance or publication.

Thomas Campion

1601–1617	*Airs*	1617	"Cherry Ripe"
1601	"My Sweetest Lesbia"		
	"When to Her Lute Corinna Sings"		
	"When Thou Must Home"		

Sir Philip Sidney

1590	*Arcadia*	1595	*A Defence of Poesie*
1591	*Astrophel and Stella*		

Edmund Spenser

1579	*The Shepherd's Calendar*	1596	"Prothelamion"
1590–1596	*The Faerie Queene*		*View of the Present State of Ireland*
1595	*Colin Clout's Come Home Again*		
	Amoretti		
	"Epithalamion"		

Sir Walter Ralegh

1591	*A Report of the Truth of the Fight About the Isle of Azores*	1596	*The Discovery of Guiana*
		1614	*History of the World*

Thomas Nashe

1594	*The Unfortunate Traveller*

Richard Hooker

1593	*The Laws of Ecclesiastical Polity*

---

*Dates are dates of first performance or publication.

5
HISTORY AND HUMANISM

RENAISSANCE

The Renaissance (rebirth) came to England much later than in Italy, its cradle, or Spain or France. Its origins can be traced to the growth of trade and commerce with the consequent development of towns, as a result of the new contact with the East after the Crusades. As a class of wealthy merchants began to appear in Europe, the prohibition against the making of profits, which the Church insisted upon, began to be challenged. Members of the great Italian merchant families found it wise to be represented in the Papacy; the Church began to take on a very worldly character, and its influence to crumble. Coincident with these great changes in the economic order was a series of extensive voyages and explorations by Vasco da Gama, Columbus, Magellan, the Cabots, and others, opening new horizons on the earth and for the mind. People began to be interested in learning more about the world which they inhabited as well as about themselves. Commercial rivalries resulted in a growing consciousness of nationality, and with that consciousness a pride in the native tongue as a vehicle for expression. The influence of Latin over writers diminished rapidly.

Paradoxically it was Latin that particularly fostered the Renaissance, though not the Latin of the Middle Ages. The classic Latin of Rome's Golden Age (the days of Virgil and Cicero) was rediscovered by an enthusiastic group of Italian scholars led by Petrarch. An organized search for forgotten manuscripts of the antique classics uncovered many valuable and long-slumbering works. From this fresh contact with the life of the pagan world, a new zest for the values of this world rather than those of the next took hold of writers, painters, and scholars. This revival of learning, which we know as *Humanism*, sought to discover *human* wisdom rather than the *divine* wisdom of the Middle Ages. Petrarch (1304–1374) and his friend Boccaccio (1313–1375) rediscovered Homer (in Latin), Cicero, and other Latin classic writers, and studiously wrote under their influence. Later, in order to escape the persecution of the Turks, many Greek scholars came to live in Italy, and by degrees the literature of ancient Greece was rediscovered too, though Greek never had the importance of Classical Latin to the Renaissance. The invention of printing, too, accelerated the movement by increasing vastly the number of available books and reducing their price from something prohibitive to a sum within the resources of a greater number of people.

REFORMATION

In England, the Renaissance began to be effective at about the same time as the Reformation. Corruption in the Church had caused the revolt of Luther and Calvin; and in 1534 King Henry VIII of England, for many reasons (few of which were religious), renounced the sovereignty of the Pope and declared himself the head of the English Church. Thus, Protestantism became official in England. Between 1536 and 1542 all the religious institutions were seized and their possessions confiscated by the Crown. By degrees the English language, instead of Church Latin, became the language for religious offices. The Coverdale *Bible* and Cranmer's *Book of Common Prayer* carried the break with Rome even further among the people. During the short reign of Edward VI, the English Reformation moved closer to the Protestantism of the Continent. Edward's sister Mary tried vainly to reestablish Catholicism in England. After her death the reign of Elizabeth sealed and ratified the Protestant victory.

EARLY ENGLISH HUMANISTS

Sir Thomas More (1478–1535) was one of the most important Humanists under Henry VIII. Unwilling to support Henry in his break with Rome, he was beheaded; in 1935 he was elevated to the sainthood. His chief work is the *Utopia*, written in Latin (1516), an imaginative description of an ideal commonwealth based upon the common possession of goods.

Roger Ascham (1515–1568) was the first lecturer on Plato in Cambridge, tutor to Princess Elizabeth, and her Latin Secretary after she became queen. In common with many Englishmen, he resented the Italianate excesses of some of his contemporaries. His works on education make him the first important English writer on that subject. The *Toxophilus* (1545) is a treatise on archery, full of patriotism and recommending the value of English for the purposes of scholarship. His most influential book is *The Scholemaster* (1570), a treatise on education, which manages to show the superiority of virtue as practiced in London to vice as found in Italy.

This period also produced several poets worthy of mention, two of them (Wyatt and Surrey) of importance. John Skelton (c. 1460–1529) was the last of the Chaucerians, and though what he wrote is little better than doggerel, there is much verve and vivacity in his lines.

Sir Thomas Wyatt (1503–1542) held various positions at Henry VIII's Court. In 1527 he was sent to Italy on an embassy and there was a witness to the worship of Petrarch's writings. He caught the enthusiasm and began to write sonnets in imitation of the great Italian poet. His poems, circulated in manuscript among friends, were first published after his death by the printer Richard Tottel in his *Miscellany* (1557).

Henry Howard, Earl of Surrey (c. 1517–1547), was a friend and disciple of Wyatt. He made two extraordinarily unusual contributions to the future of English poetry: He invented the "English" form of the sonnet and blank verse—both of which were to have a glorious future in English poetry. His work was also published in Tottel's *Miscellany*.

A *sonnet* is a lyrical poem in fourteen lines of iambic pentameter, arranged according to one of two forms: The *Italian sonnet* (or Petrarchan sonnet) consists of an octave (a section of 8 lines) and a sextet (a section of six), rhyming *abbaabba cdecde* (or, *abbaabba cdeedc*; or, *abbaabba cdcdcd*).

The *English sonnet*, (or Shakespearean sonnet) consists of 12 lines and a couplet, rhyming *ababcdcdefef gg*.

There is a division in thought between the two sections of a sonnet.

Blank verse is iambic pentameter, unrhymed. It is a form that has been used in some of the loftiest poetry in English—for example, Shakespeare's plays and Milton's *Paradise Lost*.

ELIZABETHAN HISTORY

The historical tapestry of the Elizabethan period is as rich in many ways as its literary fabric. Its background lay in the lifelong attempts of the previous monarch, Mary Tudor, to restore Catholicism to England. Mary died in 1558 amidst not only the failure of her religious reforms but also in a period of unprecedented crop failures, unpopular taxation, and economic downturn. To this England came the young queen, Elizabeth. A Protestant, she began her reign by preventing a European Catholic coalition against England by personal diplomacy, flirtation, and secret support of anti-Catholic revolts in the Netherlands. Her underlying priority was more economic than spiritual: Elizabeth believed that England could attain prosperity only by avoiding wars.

At Elizabeth's urging, Parliament in 1559 repealed the heresy acts and passed the Act of Supremacy. This law formally renounced England's ties to the Pope and established Elizabeth herself as the head of the Church of England. To avoid offending or alienating the many English citizens who favored Lutheranism or Catholicism, the creed of the Church of England was kept purposely vague in the Thirty-Nine Articles (passed in 1563).

On the political front, Elizabeth faced ongoing struggles with Scotland. After the death of her husband, Francis II of France, Mary Stuart (a Catholic and Elizabeth's cousin) returned to rule Scotland in 1561. In a bloody civil war, Mary was captured and forced to abdicate the throne to her infant son, James VI. After a brief escape and rebellion, she and her followers were defeated and Mary fled to England. There she became the center of a whirlwind of plots attempting to put her in Elizabeth's place as ruler. Even the Pope played a role in these intrigues by excommunicating Elizabeth in 1570.

After the discovery of a plot by Babington and others to put Mary on the throne, Elizabeth had the Scottish queen beheaded in 1587.

England's greatest commercial rival during the period was Spain, a Catholic country. After the death of Mary Stuart, Philip II of Spain, who had been married to Mary Tudor, claimed the English throne for himself and sent a large fleet (the Invincible Armada) to enforce his will. But a combination of foul weather and clever naval tactics on the part of the British fleet turned back the Spanish fleet. That epic battle united England under Elizabeth and ended the Catholic threat within England's borders.

After an eventful reign of forty-five years, Elizabeth died in 1603, passing the throne to Mary Stuart's son, who became James I of England.

6
ELIZABETHAN DRAMA AND THEATER

ELIZABETHAN DRAMA

Historical Background

Popular taste for drama during the later Middle Ages had so increased that the performances that the guilds could give proved insufficient for public demand. Acting companies were formed. The actors, whose social status was that of servants in the household of some powerful lord, gave public exhibitions of their art in inn yards on improvised wooden stages.

On the other hand, at the universities another tradition was developing. As the result of the new enthusiasm over Latin classics, the Roman plays of Plautus and Terence (comedy) and Seneca (tragedy) were studied, acted, and imitated. These university plays educated future dramatists in making plays well-knit and more polished than popular drama had been. The most celebrated English plays written for the universities are *Ralph Roister Doister* (1551) by Nicholas Udall, and *Gammer Gurton's Needle* (1553) by a Mr. S. of Cambridge—both comedies. For the delectation of the law students at the Inns of Court, the first English tragedy, *Ferrex and Porrex, or Gorboduc* (1561), was written in imitation of Seneca.

Ralph Roister Doister: Dame Christian Custance is a wealthy widow engaged to marry Gavin Goodluck, but is pressed by the attentions of Ralph, a boaster. Matthew Merrygreek acts as go-between and provides much of the comedy. Goodluck at first believes his sweetheart inconstant, but learns that she is true, and marries her.

Gammer Gurton's Needle: Gammer Gurton had lost her one and only needle. She is led to believe by Diccon that Dame Chat has taken possession of it. However, the needle literally turns up in the breeches of her servant Hodge, which she had been mending.

Gorboduc: The Kingdom of Gorboduc is divided between his two sons, Ferrex and Porrex. Porrex slays his mother's favorite, Ferrex. In revenge she murders him. *Gorboduc* is written in blank verse.

Popular traditions and university traditions in the drama met at last when James Burbage in 1576 built *The Theatre*, the first playhouse in England, just outside the limits of the City of London. Among the first dramatists to write for this theater and the many new theaters that soon opened (Curtain, Rose, Swan, Fortune, and Globe) was a group of young men, called the *University Wits*, graduates of Oxford and Cambridge: Robert Greene, Thomas Lodge, John Lyly, Thomas Nashe, George Peele, and Christopher Marlowe. These men were trained in the Latin classics and their training was brought to bear on what they wrote. But they wrote for a public used to the traditions of medieval drama. These two traditions then met in their works, created a drama not unfit for the theater, and prepared the way for Shakespeare.

John Lyly (c. 1554–1606)

John Lyly is the writer of charming, witty plays that were often performed at Court by children. The subject matter is usually drawn from mythology, with allegorical interpretations. His prose is good, and his comedy is best when witty. His plays are interspersed with charming songs. The best of them are *The Woman in the Moon*, a compliment to Elizabeth; *Alexander and Campaspe*, in which the great conqueror generously gives up his sweetheart to the artist; and *Endimion*, a court-allegory on Elizabeth.

George Peele (c. 1557–1596)

George Peele is a writer of much delicate imagination, with a lively interest in folklore. His best plays are *The Arraignment of Paris*, in which the story of the judgment of Paris is used as an elaborate compliment to Elizabeth; *Edward I*, a history play; and *The Old Wives' Tale*, his masterpiece, a satire on the extravagances of his contemporaries, written with considerable charm.

Robert Greene (c. 1560–1592)

Robert Greene is a writer who approaches closer to realism than his colleagues, and is the first able portraitist of women in the drama. His best plays are *Friar Bacon and Friar Bungay*, in which the magic of the legendary Roger Bacon is mixed with a well-written love story; and *James IV*, a history play in which the plot of an Italian tale is introduced.

Thomas Lodge (c. 1558–1625)

Thomas Lodge is an imitator of Lyly, though his surviving play is Marlowesque: *Marius and Sylla*, a dramatization of Roman history.

Thomas Kyd (1558–1594)

Thomas Kyd though sometimes grouped among the University Wits, was never a university student. He is the author of *The Spanish Tragedy*, one of the most popular and influential plays of the time. It established the *tragedy of blood* (or *blood and thunder tragedy*) as the most popular type of Elizabethan tragedy. In such a play there is much violence of action, and ghosts are likely to appear. Shakespeare's tragedies, though marvelously transforming the type, are written in this tradition.

The Spanish Tragedy: Hieronimo, Marshal of Spain, finds his son Horatio hanged on a tree in an arbor. Horatio had been killed while in the company of Princess Belimperia by her brother Lorenzo and by Balthazar, whose suit for her hand is encouraged by her parents. Hieronimo, driven mad by grief, arranges a play at Court; in this drama all the characters involved are made to act, and Balthazar and Lorenzo are killed. The Princess and Hieronimo commit suicide.

Christopher Marlowe (1564–1593)

Christopher Marlowe was the greatest dramatist before Shakespeare. A great poet and daring innovator in the drama, his career was cut short by a dagger when he was only twenty-nine. He was the first man to put blank verse to great use on the London stage ("Marlowe's mighty line"). His plays are also the first to center about the career of a hero. He was born at Canterbury, the son of a shoemaker, went on a scholarship to Cambridge, came to London, and with his first play took the theatrical world by storm. Besides an unfinished narrative poem of great brilliance, *Hero and Leander*, and the celebrated lyric, *The Passionate Shepherd to His Love*, Marlowe is the author of the following plays: the 2 parts of *Tamburlaine, Dr. Faustus, The Jew of Malta,* and *Edward II.*

Tamburlaine: A Scythian shepherd, Tamburlaine, by the sheer force of his personality wins captains and generals to fight under his banner until he has conquered kingdoms and then empires. He also wins by his beautiful rhetoric the Princess Zenocrate while she is en route to marry the Sultan. They prove a loyal and devoted couple. Before he is through, he has kings drawing his chariot and drags about his enemies in cages like wild beasts. He kills his own son when he finds him too cowardly to fight. The play ends with his own death. This was the first play to employ blank verse on the London stage.

Dr. Faustus: We find the learned Doctor Faustus in his study at Wittenburg, rehearsing for himself his vast achievements in knowledge. What is the use of logic? Only to teach one to dispute well. Medicine? Drugs cannot make men live eternally or wake them to life when they are dead. Law? "A pretty case of paltry legacies!" Religion? The Bible teaches us that we are all sinners, and that the reward of sin is death. No, all that he knows, Faustus decides, is futile, useless. He will now venture into the newer field of magic. At this point a Good Angel and an Evil Angel each strives to win mastery over Faustus' soul. His friends Valdes and Cornelius encourage his dark ambitions. Alone, Faustus reads from a forbidden volume a mystic passage, makes the necessary signs, and Mephistopheles appears, vanishes as bidden, and reappears in the garb of a friar. Faustus questions him and learns that Mephistopheles serves Lucifer, the Prince of Devils, who was once the angel "most dearly loved of God," and who conspired against God and so was thrust into Hell.

Faustus offers his soul to Lucifer in exchange for twenty-four years of having his every wish fulfilled. At midnight Faustus awaits Lucifer's answer in his study. The Good and Evil Angels once more strive to influence him. Mephistopheles enters to bring word that he himself is to be Faustus' servant once the contract is signed in Faustus' blood. Faustus stabs his arm to draw the blood in which he is to write, but the blood congeals; Mephistopheles applies a live coal and the blood flows. Faustus' first desire is for a wife. A devil dressed like a woman and equipped with fireworks soon cures him of that desire. Mephistopheles promises him all the beautiful women in the world for his bedfellows, and shows him how to make whirlwinds and lightning, and how to summon an army to his need. The Good Angel again tries to make Faustus repent but he finds he cannot.

Lucifer himself appears before Faustus and warns him never to think of Heaven. The Seven Deadly Sins now enter and Faustus interrogates each: Pride, Covetousness, Wrath, Envy, Gluttony, Sloth, and Lechery. Faustus begins to tour the world. At Rome he becomes invisible so that he may annoy the Pope by snatching away His Holiness' food and drink; he and Mephistopheles also beat up some friars and fling firecrackers at them. He visits next the Holy Roman Emperor, and to please His Majesty evokes the spirits of Alexander the Great and his paramour. At the court of a Duke and a Duchess he fetches grapes in the dead of winter to please the lady. The years are running out, and now Faustus has a desire to see the most beautiful woman of history, Helen of Troy. An Old Man tries to awaken Faustus' conscience to repent, but in vain. Faustus craves to embrace the vision of Helen that he was allowed to see but momentarily. Mephistopheles obliges, and as she enters, Faustus cries rapturously:

> *Was this the face that launched a thousand ships*
> *And burnt the topless towers of Ilium? . . .*
> *O, thou art fairer than the evening air*
> *Clad in the beauty of a thousand stars*

Faustus' time is now up, and we find him with but "one bare hour" to live. He tries now to repent:

> *See, see where Christ's blood streams in the firmament!*
> *One drop would save my soul—half a drop!*

It is too late. Faustus would now gladly hide in the bowels of the earth, or be dissolved in mist, if only his soul might still ascend to Heaven. He would even be willing to endure a hundred thousand years of Hell, if at the end he might be saved. But "no end is limited to damned souls." Amidst thunder and lightning, the Devils carry him off.

The Jew of Malta: The governor of Malta seizes half of the wealthy Jew Barabas' wealth to help pay the tribute demanded by Turkey. Barabas' daughter Abigail is converted to Christianity by some lechers. In revenge, the

Jew causes the death of his own daughter, her lover, and the Governor of Malta. In the end he meets his own death when he is hurled into a caldron of boiling water, which he had prepared as a trap for the Turkish Commander. The first two acts of this play are among the best Marlowe ever wrote.

Some critics have professed to find a source of Shakespeare's *The Merchant of Venice* in *The Jew of Malta,* but outside of a wealthy Jew and a young daughter there is little resemblance between the two. They differ totally in spirit.

Edward II: Defying the hostility of his courtiers and Queen, Edward elevates to great honor the low-born Gaveston, of whom he is enamoured. Courtiers plot to kill Gaveston and succeed. In revenge Edward makes new favorites of the Spencers. The neglected Queen Isabella agrees to conspire with young Mortimer against the King. They arrange his assassination at Berkeley Castle. This is Marlowe's best-written play, the finest historical play before Shakespeare. It is his most human work, and shows a softening in his attitude towards life.

Two other plays have been attributed to Marlowe: *The Massacre of Paris,* on the St. Bartholomew Massacre; and *Dido of Carthage,* which dramatizes the Dido-Aeneas story from the *Aeneid.*

The latter play has derived some special interest from the fact that in Shakespeare's *Hamlet* the First Player quotes what seems like a paraphrase of a long passage from the work.

It is curious to reflect that although there was no predecessor of Shakespeare who had anything like the influence on subsequent English drama which Marlowe exerted, we today admire him far less as a dramatist than as a great poet. For his plays are burdened with what we feel to be absurdities, but his verse is as radiant as any in our language.

ELIZABETHAN THEATER

It was not uncommon in the Elizabethan period for traveling troops of actors to perform in an inn yard, often with a balcony above and the audience standing in the yard or looking out of windows from neighboring houses. The design of such Elizabethan theaters as The Swan and The Globe followed this general design. Actors performed on a raised stage within a house of sorts, with audience members watching from the yard and tiered balconies.

In this regard, Elizabethan theaters appeared not unlike meeting houses for more gross public entertainments such as bear-baiting, in which bears, tied to stakes, were attacked by dogs. Octagonal or round in overall design, the theaters were constructed of wood and thatch—and consequently particularly vulnerable to fires. About half the area above the stage was roofed and often painted to imitate the sky. Doors to the rear and sides of the stage were used for entrances and exits. Scenery was minimal, though costumes and special effects were as elaborate as the acting troupe could manage. There was no curtain for the main stage, so scenery—and "dead" bodies— had to be carried off.

Elizabethan theater-goers typically paid a penny (about $5 in contemporary buying power) to stand or sit in the yard and twice that amount for an upper gallery seat. People of widely ranging tastes, backgrounds, and economic level attended the theater together. This may explain in part the necessity for Shakespeare's wide range and the comic material that appears even in the tragedies.

7
SHAKESPEARE'S LIFE AND EARLY WORKS

INTRODUCTION

William Shakespeare (1564–1616), the world's greatest dramatist-poet, was born at Stratford-on-Avon, the son of a wealthy tradesman of political influence. He attended a very good grammar school. Sometime around his fourteenth year, his education must have ceased for his father seems to have lost his holdings. At eighteen he was married (apparently by compulsion) to Anne Hathaway, eight years his senior. Six months later, their first child, Susanna, was born. Twins, Hamnet and Judith, were born in 1585. Soon after that Shakespeare left his native town for reasons unknown to us. The rather silly story that he fled to escape the wrath of Sir Thomas Lucy, on whose estate he had been caught poaching, is almost certainly apocryphal. By 1588 he was in London, where he had attached himself to a company of actors. We know that he was associated as actor and playwright from 1594 to the time of his retirement with Lord Strange's Company (whose name was later changed to The Lord Chamberlain's Men and still later to The King's Men). The first record of Shakespeare's presence in London is Robert Greene's reference to him as an upstart dramatist (1592), indicating that he must have been writing for several years. During the temporary closing of the theatres in 1592 because of the plague, Shakespeare began the composition of several nondramatic works dedicated to the youthful Earl of Southampton, whose patronage he thereby gained. Rapidly Shakespeare became the most popular and successful dramatist of his time. In 1597 he was able to purchase New Place, one of the finest estates in Stratford. Two years later he was granted a request for a coat of arms, and in the same year (1599) became part owner of the Globe Theatre. After 1608 he began to spend more and more time at Stratford. During the last few years of his life he seems to have been there most of the time. He died there on April 23 (which was also probably his birthday), 1616. His son had died in childhood; both his daughters were married but left no issue. To his daughters he left the bulk of his estate, made many small bequests to his friends and fellow-actors, and to his wife he left his second-best bed. The First Folio of his collected plays was published in 1623 by two of his former fellow-actors, Heminges and Condell.

Shakespeare is the greatest figure in literature, both as poet and dramatist. During his lifetime a number of his plays, because of their popularity, were published piratically. Though these publications (Quartos) indicate the dates by which such plays must have been written, there is little agreement among scholars as to the date of composition of many of his plays. They are, however, generally arranged into four groups: his experimental period (1590–1594); the period of the comedies and histories (1594–1600); the period of the tragedies and the vitriolic comedies (1600–1608); and the period of the dramatic romances (1609–1611).

DATING OF SHAKESPEARE'S PLAYS

In the majority of cases, it is not possible to date the plays exactly. The list of first performances that follows is based on general scholarly consensus derived from both internal and external evidence.

1589–92	*Henry VI Part I, Henry VI Part 2, Henry VI Part 3*
1592–93	*Richard III, The Comedy of Errors*
1593–94	*Titus Andronicus, The Taming of the Shrew*
1594–95	*The Two Gentlemen of Verona, Love's Labour's Lost, Romeo and Juliet*
1594–96	*Richard II, A Midsummer Night's Dream*
1596–97	*King John, The Merchant of Venice*
1597–98	*Henry IV Part 1, Henry IV Part 2*
1598–99	*Much Ado About Nothing, Henry V*
1599–1600	*Julius Caesar, As You Like It*
1600–01	*Hamlet, The Merry Wives of Windsor*
1601–02	*Twelfth Night, Troilus and Cressida*
1602–03	*All's Well That Ends Well*
1604–05	*Measure for Measure, Othello*
1605–06	*King Lear, Macbeth*
1606–07	*Antony and Cleopatra*
1607–08	*Coriolanus, Timon of Athens*
1608–09	*Pericles*
1609–10	*Cymbeline*
1610–11	*Winter's Tale*
1611–12	*The Tempest*
1612–13	*Henry VIII, The Two Noble Kinsmen*

Venus and Adonis and *The Rape of Lucrece*, Shakespeare's two narrative poems, can be dated 1592 and 1593–94 respectively, a period when the plague halted dramatic performances in London. The sonnets were written at various times between 1593 and 1600.

QUESTION OF AUTHORSHIP

By the end of the eighteenth century, Shakespeare had been positioned more as a literary god than as a mortal poet and playwright. This movement, often called "Shakespeare idolatry," contributed in large part to a backlash. Working alone or in confederation, a few scholars and critics throughout the nineteenth and twentieth century have announced their skepticism about the tradition that a villager of inauspicious origins should be capable of such sustained and varied literary genius. Much more likely, they argue, that Shakespeare's plays were written secretly by a more educated Elizabethan—Sir Francis Bacon, for example, or one of various earls such as the Earl of Oxford—than by theater manager and sometime actor, William Shakespeare. In fact, the first letters of some lines from the plays have been taken as a code "proving" Bacon or someone else wrote these works.

It is unfair to dismiss such theories as absurd, but neither are they compelling. Recent computer analyses of the playwright's diction play to play do not substantiate the Baconian theory of that of any other nominated author. Although unanimity of opinion hardly is conclusive in these matters, it is a fair estimate that the great majority of Elizabethan and Shakespeare scholars think that Shakespeare's plays, except for a few collaborations, were in fact written by William Shakespeare.

EXPERIMENTAL PERIOD

Henry VI, Parts 1, 2 and 3

(by 1592) A trilogy, Shakespeare's first attempts at the history play. He is part author of these, and probably revised old plays as an introduction to and preparation for his own *Richard III*. The subject matter is the quarrel between the houses of York and Lancaster, the breaking out of the civil war (War of the Roses), and the collapse of Henry VI's throne. Part 3 is the most interesting for in it the character of young Richard, later Richard III, emerges.

The Comedy of Errors

(1592) An extremely deft slapstick comedy in a plot derived from Plautus, much improving on the original. Two sets of twins, separated in boyhood, by accident are in the same town. The play deals with the ever-mounting excitement that results from the confusion of identities. The end, very dexterous, solves all the apparent mishaps and errors. There is little characterization here, and the emphasis, as in all classic comedy, is on complication of the plot.

Richard III

(1593) Shakespeare's first original history play, based on Hall's and Holinshed's *Chronicles*. It follows the career of Richard, Duke of Gloucester, through a series of murders and betrayals to the throne as Richard III. Once he is apparently safely seated, however, the structure he has raised on villainy begins to crumble. In the end he is defeated by Richmond (crowned Henry VII), founder of the Tudor dynasty, who by a marriage with the rival house ends the War of the Roses. Richard is a brilliant villain whose moves are sudden and violent; it is his character that holds the play together. Everyone is familiar with his cry, in the midst of his last battle: *"A horse! a horse! my kingdom for a horse!"*—the last words he utters.

Titus Andronicus

(by 1593) Shakespeare's first tragedy, and his greatest failure as a writer. It is a dreadful blood-and-thunder tragedy imitated from Kyd, but leaving him far behind in its accumulation of horrors: a tongue is cut out, an arm is lopped off, a rape is committed, a father at table is served up his children baked in a pastry, and in the end there is a general slaughter. The only value of this play is as a measurement for the greatness of Shakespeare's best tragedies, for, amazingly enough, *Hamlet, Macbeth, King Lear,* and *Othello* belong, technically, to the same school of drama.

Love's Labour's Lost

(1594) An artificial comedy of satire on the theme of love versus learning. It contains some amusing ridicule of bombast pedantry, and the artifice of contemporary life. It is Shakespeare's most stylized play, but excellent for a beginner. It tells the story of a group of young courtiers who cannot keep their oath any more than can their King to avoid the company of women for a year and devote themselves to study. It takes only the appearance of the same number of lovely girls in the company of a princess to end all their good resolutions. The play concludes with a wonderful song full of the most natural descriptions of winter in the country: *"When icicles hang by the wall . . ."*

The Two Gentlemen of Verona

(1594) Shakespeare's earliest romantic comedy. Its subject matter, as in the sonnets, is love versus friendship. The story is taken from the Spanish, Montemayor's *Diana Enamorada.* Proteus and Valentine are very close friends. Valentine loves the beautiful Silvia and plans to elope with her. Proteus, falling in love with Silvia too, reveals Valentine's plans to Silvia's father, who banishes Valentine from the kingdom. In Valentine's absence his false friend seeks to further his own desires and woos Silvia for himself. His perfidy is foiled by Valentine who, somewhat amazingly, forgives Proteus. Valentine is pardoned by Silvia's father, and Proteus marries Julia, a girl he had neglected. The ending of this play ruins an otherwise charming romantic comedy. The fourth act contains the exquisite song "Who Is Sylvia?" for which Schubert later wrote wonderful music.

King John

(by 1597) A highly patriotic play adapted from an old chronicle play on the same subject. John is made the courageous defender of England, politically and religiously. The real hero of the play is Faulconbridge, the bastard son of Richard the Lionhearted. Curiously, the Magna Carta scene is not presented.

The high points in the play, dramatically, are the lamentations of Constance, John's sister-in-law, and the touching innocence of her boy, Arthur, who is killed attempting to fly from his uncle's malice. Famous is Faulconbridge's

Naught shall make us rue,
If England to itself do rest but true.

Poems

It should also be noted that during these years Shakespeare composed his two narrative poems and began his sonnets. *Venus and Adonis* (1593), written in a very florid, voluptuous manner, went through eight editions in its author's lifetime. It is the story of the goddess' unreturned love for the beautiful youth who loved only hunting. It shows the wonderful technical resources of Shakespeare as a poet. *The Rape of Lucrece* (1594) tells the story of Tarquin's rape of the modest Roman matron, and of her death by her own hand when she cannot face the shame of the consequences. The style, similar to that of *Venus and Adonis,* shows more maturity.

The *Sonnets*, written at intervals between 1591 and 1603, were published without the author's consent in 1609. The manner of their publication raises every kind of question as to their possible autobiographical significance, the identity of the persons referred to, and even the correct order in which they should be printed. The best opinion rejects any personal intention on Shakespeare's part. At most it can be stated that nothing can be affirmed with any certainty about the sonnets beyond the fact that the collection contains some of the greatest sonnets in the English language, and that others are too artificial to merit the same high praise. The poet may have been merely following the fashion, as he did in his plays, in writing in a popular form. Many of the sonnets have to do with ideas employed by other sonnet writers of the time: the beauty of the loved one, the promise of the poet to confer immortality on the object of his adoration, the pain of separation, the cruelty of the loved one, and so on. The finest sonnets are perhaps numbers 12, 15, 17, 18, 25, 29, 30, 33, 55, 60, 66, 71, 73, 97, 98, 99, 106, 107, 116 and 146.

8
SHAKESPEARE'S PERIOD OF COMEDIES AND HISTORIES

A NOTE ON SHAKESPEARE'S LITERARY PERIODS

To say that Shakespeare entered a "period" of comedies and histories is not to suggest that every work written during these years falls within these genres. *Romeo and Juliet*, for example, is clearly a tragedy. Shakespeare did not restrict himself narrowly to one or two genres for prolonged periods of his writing. In a practical sense, the demands of Shakespeare's theatre for new and various plays would have made such a restriction to particular genres inadvisable. What can be said, however, is that Shakespeare emphasized particular genres during relatively distinct periods in his life. It is most useful to see even the exceptions to this pattern of emphasis in the context of Shakespeare's art during the period at hand and against the backdrop of Elizabethan history. For this reason, we have followed the traditional organization of Shakespeare's plays by period rather than grouping them out of context and chronology by genre.

A MIDSUMMER NIGHT'S DREAM

(by 1596) A romantic dream play, it takes hints for the plot taken from Chaucer's *Knight's Tale,* Plutarch's *Life of Theseus*, and Montemayor's *Diana,* among other sources. Bathed in moonlight, it is an exquisite mixture of folklore, vivid rusticity, and fairy magic. Hermia, a lively little brunette, is in love with Lysander; Helena, a tall blonde, is in love with Demetrius. Hermia's father insists that she must marry Demetrius or suffer death. Lysander and Hennia agree to escape to the wood; but Helena, to win the waning love of Demetrius, unfolds the plot to him. The wood, however, is haunted by fairies who have come to bless the wedding of Theseus and Hippolyta. The fairies, too, have their difficulties: King Oberon and Queen Titania are having a jealous quarrel. Oberon sends mischievous Puck to punish Titania by causing her to fall in love with a monster through the magic juice of a flower dropped on her eyelids. Oberon, observing the unhappy state of the Athenian mortals, commissions Puck to set matters right with the same flower. The result of the fairies' intervention is to create only greater confusion among the lovers. In the meantime, some country bumpkins have been rehearsing a play for Theseus' nuptials; sly Puck fixes an ass's head on the greatest of these simpletons, Bottom. Titania falls in love with this uncouth monster. In the end, out of pity, Oberon removes the enchantment from Titania's eyes and makes all right between the lovers. Oberon and Titania make up their quarrel; Demetrius wants Helena; and Lysander's claims to Hermia are unchallenged. At the wedding festivities of Theseus and Hippolyta and the two pairs of lovers, the "most lamentable comedy of Pyramus and Thisby" is presented by the rustics in hilarious awkwardness. The play ends with singing and dancing and an epilogue by Puck. Everyone knows Puck's outburst: "Lord, what fools these mortals be!" The following lines are also celebrated:

> *The lunatic, the lover, and the poet*
> *Are of imagination all compact.*

ROMEO AND JULIET

(by 1595) Shakespeare's only tragedy of this period introduced a new type to the English stage, the romantic tragedy. Shakespeare's source was a long narrative poem by Arthur Brooke, which had been adapted from the tale of the Italian Bandello. Shakespeare's play contains some of his most inspired, lyrical passages, but the work is marred in parts by some youthful extravagances and artificialities of language and style. But it is perhaps Shakespeare's earliest masterpiece, and begins the cycle of his great creations. The first two acts open with prologues of little interest beyond the description in the first of the central characters as "a pair of star-crossed lovers," and the reference to the fact that a performance of this play, which is of average length for an Elizabethan play, took two hours.

I, i: Sampson and Gregory, two servants of the Capulets, indulge in some unamusing puns. Abraham and Balthasar, servants of the Montagues, enter. They half-heartedly try to pick a quarrel among themselves, but dare not until the Capulet men see Tybalt approaching, when they begin to quarrel in earnest. Benvolio, always a friend of moderation, enters at the same moment and tries to stop the fray, but the hotheaded Tybalt insists on fighting with him. Soon the whole town is up in arms, Capulet and Lady Capulet, Montague and Lady Montague coming in too. The Prince enters, stops the fight, and threatens death to anyone who is found fighting again in the streets of Verona. He and the mob leave. Montague questions Benvolio about the former's son Romeo, who spends his time in melancholy moping. Seeing Romeo approach, Montague leaves. Romeo enters, and after a considerable display of insincerity and being in love with his misery, he confesses being smitten by the beauty of Rosaline, who does not return his affection.

I, ii: Young Paris, kinsman of the Prince, is speaking with Capulet, who admits that it is time the Montagues and Capulets stopped quarreling. Paris asks for the hand of Capulet's daughter Juliet. Although she is only fourteen, Capulet answers that he consents if the girl herself accepts Paris. He invites Paris to a feast this night, and hands a list of guests to be invited to the stupid servant Peter. When Paris and Capulet go out, Peter finds himself in difficulties because he does not know how to read; Romeo entering with Benvolio, Peter asks Romeo to read off the list for him, and discloses the fact that the Capulets are feasting tonight. Benvolio suggests that they go too, though not invited, for Rosaline will be there. Romeo agrees.

I, iii: Lady Capulet tells Juliet of Paris' proposal and urges her to accept it, aided by the garrulous Nurse, who not only speaks glowingly of him but also enlarges on Juliet's brilliance when a child, Juliet, who is utterly obedient, will try to love Paris.

I, iv: Romeo, Benvolio, and their hot-tempered, witty friend Mercutio come in before going to the Capulet feast. Mercutio jeers at Romeo for being a slave to love. Romeo, still carrying out his role of wounded lover, decides he will not be dancing, and in a sudden burst of sincerity speaks of a premonition that some tragic occurrence will begin tonight.

I, v: Romeo, Benvolio and Mercutio, masked, join other masked dancers at the Capulet feast. Romeo and Juliet see each other and fall in love at first sight. Fiery Tybalt recognizes Romeo by his voice and wants to fight with him for daring to come uninvited, but Capulet, who has heard that Romeo is a fine young man, refuses to spoil the party by allowing any contention. Tybalt vows that he will demand satisfaction of Romeo later. Romeo manages to talk to Juliet and receives a kiss from her. As the party is breaking up, Romeo and Juliet each learns through the Nurse of the other's identity. Juliet decides that she will die unwed unless she be married to him.

II, i: Romeo, unable to leave without seeing Juliet again, leaps the orchard wall into the Capulet garden. Mercutio, accompanied by Benvolio, yells for Romeo in the dark; unanswered, he leaves disgusted for his own lodgings.

II, ii: Standing in the garden, Romeo beholds Juliet come out on her balcony, and hears her quietly confess to the stars her love for him. He answers her, assuring her of his love. She promises to send the Nurse to him tomorrow to arrange where and when they are to be married. Romeo leaves in rapture.

II, iii: He goes to see his friend and confessor, Friar Lawrence, who is astonished to see him up so early. When the good friar wonders whether Romeo has been spending the night with Rosaline, Romeo behaves as though he had never heard the name before. He confides his hopes to marry Juliet and asks for the friar's assistance. The old man agrees to help them, for the union might end the old hate between the families.

II, iv: Mercutio admits to Benvolio that, no matter how much he may rib Romeo, he is worried about what Rosaline is doing to their young friend. He knows that Tybalt, whom he loathes, has sent a challenge to Romeo. Romeo enters, well-dressed and for the first time in excellent spirits (such being the alchemy of true love!), and is so swift in exchanging pleasantries with Mercutio that the latter cries: "Come between us, good Benvolio; my wits faint." The Nurse enters, wishing to speak with Romeo alone. Mercutio insults her by pretending to think she is a bawd who has come to arrange a meeting with one of her clients. Alone with Romeo, the Nurse reads Romeo a lecture on his future treatment of her beloved Juliet. He arranges to meet his love at Friar Lawrence's cell this afternoon, there to be married to her.

II, v: Juliet impatiently awaits the Nurse's return. When she arrives, the old woman teases the eager girl by pretending to be too tired to talk, but at last, to the accompaniment of low jests, reveals the meeting place at Friar Lawrence's cell.

II, vi: The Friar marries Romeo and Juliet.

III, i: It is a hot day, and Benvolio is for quitting the streets to avoid a fight, "for now these hot days is the mad blood stirring." Mercutio, in a dangerous mood, will not leave. When Tybalt comes in looking for Romeo, Mercutio does all he can to provoke Tybalt into a fight. But the hot-tempered Capulet, the soul of method, manages to smooth his own fury until he has settled with Romeo. The latter enters, but to everyone's astonishment, instead of drawing his sword at once at Tybalt's challenge, he assures Tybalt of his warm feelings for him. Mercutio, outraged at what seems like his friend's cowardice before the detested Tybalt, forces the latter to duel with him. As Romeo tries frantically to stop the fight, Tybalt mortally wounds Mercutio under Romeo's interceding arm, and flees. Mercutio, dying, upbraids Romeo for his interference, and is carried out by Benvolio, who soon comes back with the news of their friend's death. Romeo, feeling responsible, is all rage now; when Tybalt reenters, he fights with him and kills him. Benvolio urges Romeo, whose life is now forfeit because of the Prince's edict against street fights, to flee, which he does as the townsmen come crowding in. Benvolio gives the Prince an account, highly partial to Romeo, of the slaying of Mercutio (kinsman to the Prince) and Tybalt. The Prince dooms Romeo to exile on pain of death.

III, ii: Juliet awaits Romeo at night for the consummation of their marriage. The Nurse enters, melodramatically in tears over Tybalt's death, but tells the tale so badly that at first Juliet thinks it is Romeo who is dead. When she learns of her husband's exile and its cause, she exclaims against him, until the Nurse agrees with her; whereupon she turns on the Nurse in defense of Romeo. His banishment is a worse blow to her than the death of her entire family would be. To comfort her, the Nurse volunteers to find Romeo for her, and to bring Juliet's ring to him.

III, iii: At his cell, Friar Lawrence brings Romeo news of the Prince's verdict. At the thought of being parted from Juliet, Romeo falls to the floor in grief. The Nurse enters and gives so graphic an account of Juliet's sorrowing that Romeo is sure his wife must hate him, and tries to stab himself. The friar seizes the weapon and gives him a sound scolding for his suicidal attempt.

Then he reminds Romeo how much he has to be grateful for—his death might have been ordered according to the Prince's earlier decree. The Nurse enjoys the sermon thoroughly. The friar bids the Nurse inform Juliet that her husband will come to say farewell, and arranges for Romeo to go to Mantua, where he will keep him informed of the news.

III, iv: Because his daughter seems too much stricken by Tybalt's death, Capulet decides that Paris shall marry her in three days.

III, v: After a single night of love, Romeo takes leave of Juliet, leaving her lost and frightened. Lady Capulet enters, and interprets her daughter's tears as owing to Tybalt's death. She brings joyful tidings: the hastening of the date of the marriage to Paris. Taken off guard, Juliet angrily declares she will not marry Paris. Seeing both women weeping, the entering Capulet speaks with male superiority over this prolonged weeping over Tybalt, until his wife informs him that Juliet has suddenly decided that she will not have Paris. Infuriated, he denounces his daughter as a wilful child and threatens to disown her unless she goes through with the ceremony. He leaves before she can speak, followed by his wife. In despair, Juliet asks the Nurse for guidance. The Nurse, utterly worldly, counsels marrying Paris, since Romeo in exile is as good as dead. Horrified at such advice, Juliet pretends to agree; when left alone she divorces herself forever henceforth from the Nurse's love.

IV, i: At Friar Lawrence's cell, Paris encounters Juliet and speaks to her with love and concern. She is very curt with him, and makes it plain that she wishes to be alone with the friar. To the latter she tells her fears. His plan is to give her a potion that will produce in her the effect of death; she will then be borne to the Capulet vault; in the meantime he will send for Romeo, and the two will be able to flee together. She agrees to the scheme.

IV, ii: Preparations are made in the Capulet household for the approaching wedding. Juliet pretends that she is sorry for her rebellion, and will marry Paris.

IV, iii: Juliet says goodnight to the Nurse and her mother. Left alone, she must now take the potion. If it does not work, she will kill herself in the morning. But what if the potion is really a poison the friar tempered to be rid of his own complicity in the marriage to Romeo? What if she awakens too soon in the vault and is stifled by the close air? Or driven mad by the sights of the sepulchre? Knowing no answers to these terrors, she drains the drink in reckless frenzy, and falls upon her bed.

IV, iv: Preparations are made for the marriage feast.

IV, v: The Nurse enters Juliet's chamber to awaken her on this marriage morning, and finds her apparently dead. She shrieks. Lady Capulet, then Capulet come running in, and are bowed down with grief. Paris and Friar Lawrence enter, and Paris is overcome with grief at the death of his betrothed. The friar counsels obedience to the will of Heaven.

V, i: In Mantua, Romeo has been dreaming of Juliet. His servant Balthasar enters in haste to tell him the terrible news of Juliet's death. He orders the boy to procure some horses, and decides to come back to Verona and die at Juliet's side. Knocking at the shop of an impoverished apothecary, Romeo bribes him to sell him a powerful poison.

V, ii: Friar John comes to Friar Lawrence to inform him that he has been unable to deliver the letter he was charged with to Romeo; he was quarantined in a house because of the plague. Friar Lawrence, full of fears as to the possible consequences of this unfortunate accident, hurries to the Capulet vault, intending to keep Juliet in his cell until he can reach Romeo.

V, iii: Paris comes to the churchyard before the Capulet vault with flowers and perfume to pay his obsequies to Juliet's remains, as he means to do every night. Romeo and his man enter; he pretends his purpose is to force his way into the vault to procure from Juliet's finger a ring; he tells the boy to go away, but the latter merely conceals himself in the dark. As Romeo approaches the vault with a crowbar, Paris by his torch recognizes him and thinks he has come to do some shame to the vault of the enemy family. He seizes him, and the two fight, Romeo unwillingly. Romeo kills Paris, who asks to be laid by the side of his betrothed. Romeo peruses the face of the dead man, and finds that he has slain Mercutio's kinsman, Count Paris. He now remembers Balthasar's words, on their mad ride from Mantua, about Paris' betrothal to Juliet. Pitying Paris as a victim of luckless Fate, he carries him into Juliet's tomb to bury him in "a triumphant grave." Romeo looks about him, can hardly believe that Juliet, still so beautiful, can truly be dead, and cries:

> *Death, that hath sucked the honey of thy breath,*
> *Hath had no power yet upon thy beauty:*
> *Thou art not conquered; beauty's ensign yet*
> *Is crimson in thy lips and in thy cheeks,*
> *And death's pale flag is not advanced there.*

He gives his bride a farewell kiss, and drinks of his poison with the toast, "Here's to my love!" The drugs acts at once, and he falls dead upon her breast. Friar Lawrence now enters the cemetery, learns from Balthasar where Romeo is, runs unhappily to the tomb, notes the sword and the blood at the threshold, and sees Romeo dead in the tomb. Juliet awakes, sees the friar, then the dead Romeo. The friar tries to get her to come away with him. She will not go, so he leaves to save himself. Swiftly she seizes Romeo's dagger, and with the cry, "This is thy sheath!" stabs herself to death. The two families, arriving too late, learn of the mischief their hate has caused, vow friendship, and undertake to build a memorial to the lost lovers.

The play abounds in magnificent lyrical poetry. Juliet ponders:

> *What's in a name? That which we call a rose*
> *By any other name would smell as sweet.*

Romeo's description of the dawn is famous:

> *Night's candles are burnt out, and jocund day*
> *Stands tiptoe on a misty mountain top.*

as is Mercutio's speech on Mab, Queen of the Fairies:

> *She is the fairies' midwife, and she comes*
> *In shape no bigger than an agate-stone*
> *On a forefinger of an alderman.*

RICHARD II

(1596) Probably inspired by Marlowe's *Edward II,* and based on Holinshed's *Chronicles,* it recounts the trials of the weak, unstable Richard and of his downfall at the hands of Bolingbroke, who became Henry IV. The play abounds in patriotic speeches, the most celebrated of which is John of Gaunt's:

> *This royal throne of kings, this sceptred isle,*
> *This earth of majesty, this seat of Mars,*
> *This other Eden, demi-paradise,*
> *This fortress built by Nature for herself*
> *Against infection and the hand of war,*
> *This happy breed of men, this little world,*
> *This precious stone set in a silver sea . . .*
> *This blessed plot, this earth, this realm, this England,*
> *This nurse, this teeming womb of royal kings*

The character of Richard, a victim of his own rapid imagination, is the focus of interest in the play.

THE MERCHANT OF VENICE

(1597) One of Shakespeare's great comedies. The Shylock-Antonio story comes from the Italian collection of tales *Il Pecorone*; the casket story is a motif common in folklore. The gallery of portraits in this play is in itself a brilliant achievement. Not less so is the dramatist's ability to steer close to tragedy and yet remain safely within the bounds of comedy. Antonio, a wealthy merchant of Venice, in order to supply his friend Bassanio with means to go in style to Belmont to win Portia's hand, is forced to borrow a sum from his only enemy, Shylock, the moneylender. Shylock, who bitterly hates Antonio, disguises his evil intentions by refusing to take interest and instead asks merely for the signing of a "merry bond" in which Antonio will forfeit a pound of his flesh if the sum is not paid back on the date due. At Belmont, the beauteous and gifted Portia is besieged by suitors. Her father's will, however, requires them all to make a choice among three caskets (one of gold, one of silver, and one of lead); she may marry only the man who chooses the right casket. The Prince of Morocco and the Duke of Arragon choose the wrong caskets. But Bassanio, whom Portia favors, chooses the right one (of lead). Just as both lovers are overjoyed at the kindness of fate, word comes that Antonio has been unable to repay Shylock because of the apparent loss of his ventures at sea, and that Shylock is demanding the terms of the bond. After a hasty wedding ceremony, Bassanio leaves for Venice. Portia and her maid Nerissa, disguised as men, go to Venice too, for Portia is determined to save Antonio's life. Appearing in the court as a lawyer, she teaches Shylock how dreadful the letter of the law can be when mercy is abandoned, and saves Antonio by threatening Shylock with death if one drop of blood is spilled in the cutting of the pound of flesh. Shylock is heavily fined and forced to become a Christian. Roguishly Portia will accept only the ring on Bassanio's finger (a ring she had given him on his oath never to part with it) as payment for her services. Back in Belmont there is much merriment over the ring until Portia is disclosed to have been the lawyer. The subplots also tell us of the romantic love and elopement of Jessica, Shylock's daughter, and of Lorenzo's love for Jessica; the fortunes of the clown Launcelot Gobbo; and the love affair of Gratiano and Nerissa, paralleling the love of their friends Bassanio and Portia. The play is brilliantly constructed and full of beautiful poetry. The last act contains some of the most exalted poetry in our language. The most celebrated passage, however, is Portia's:

> *The quality of mercy is not strained.*
> *It droppeth as the gentle rain from Heaven*
> *Upon the place beneath* . . . .

HENRY IV, PART 1

(1597) Based upon Holinshed's *Chronicles* and parts of an old play, *The Famous Victories of Henry V.* The main plot deals with the rebellion of Percy, nicknamed Hotspur, whose family had helped Henry to the throne and was now cast off by the King. Henry's son, Prince Hal, long a wastrel, rises to the occasion and proves himself a hero in action on the battlefield, where he slays Percy. The chief interest in the play, however, centers about the person of Falstaff, Shakespeare's most superb comic creation. Falstaff, old, fat, a liar, knave, and cheat, but with an incomparable sense of humor, is depicted as the leader of the gang of knaves that has led the young prince astray.

I, i: King Henry IV, after speaking of his year-old purpose to go on a crusade to the Holy Land, hears from the Earl of Westmoreland that that purpose must be postponed. Wild Glendower, the Welshman, has captured Mortimer; Douglas, the Scot, and Henry Percy, called Hotspur, are clashing; but the King already knows of Hotspur's victory over the Scots at Holmedon. The King wishes his own son were like Hotspur, and reveals that he has sent for Percy, who has refused to give up the prisoners.

I, ii: After an exchange of merry insults between Falstaff and Prince Hal, Poins, a member of Falstaff's gang, comes to tell of the robbery they are planning to commit on the highway. When Falstaff leaves, the Prince, who has been reluctant to join in the deed, is persuaded by Poins to come along for a prank. He and the Prince will disguise themselves and rob the robbers, just to hear what fantastic tale Falstaff will have to tell of the day's doings later.

I, iii: The King, feeling oppressed by a sense of gratitude towards Percy's family, begins to assert his independence. When Worcester reminds him of his debt, he is dismissed at once. Hotspur explains that it was a fool who commanded him to give up prisoners, that he intended no challenge to the King when he refused. But when the King declares that he will not ransom Mortimer because he is a traitor, Hotspur flares up to defend his brother-in-law. The King demands Hotspur's prisoners now, and goes out. The other nobles try to calm Hotspur, reminding him that Richard II had declared Mortimer to be his heir—a good reason why Henry will not ransom him. They determine to plot against the King for his ingratitude: Percy will release Douglas and make him an ally; Northumberland will procure the aid of the Archbishop of York; Worcester will bring in Glendower and Mortimer.

II, i: At four in the morning we see Gadshill, of Falstaff's gang, conferring at the inn with the chamberlain, who is supplying needed information on the departing travelers.

II, ii: Poins hides Falstaff's horse at the scene of the proposed robbery; he and the Prince quietly withdraw at the crucial moment. The four other thieves rob the travelers. Then Poins and Hal, disguised, come in and rob the robbers, all of whom flee, with the exception of Falstaff; he strikes a blow or two, then, seeing the case hopeless, flees too.

II, iii: At his castle, Hotspur reads the letter of a coward who now backs out of the conspiracy. Hotspur swears at the idea of such knaves, and cries: "Hang him! Let him tell the King!" There follows a great scene between him and his wife, in which we see the close love between them; after teasing her, he promises that where he goes she will come with him.

II, iv: At the Boar's Head Tavern in Eastcheap, the Prince makes merry with the drawer. Falstaff, who has torn his clothes and hacked his sword to make himself look like a hero, comes in with the gang. Falstaff tells his exaggerated version of the robbery—the vast numbers he fought against single-handed; he is especially graphic in his account of the men who robbed them, and how he braved them. The Prince, with Poins' backing, punctures the fantasy, and exposes Falstaff as an egregious liar. Not at all put out, the old rogue declares that he knew the Prince for what he was, despite the disguise, and asks whether he was to be expected to kill the heir apparent. "I was a coward on instinct." News arrives of the Hotspur rebellion. Falstaff undertakes to demonstrate how the King will upbraid his son when they next meet; not being applauded, he next takes on the role of the Prince in that coming interview—managing both times to deliver himself of a panegyric in Falstaff's praise. (In these passages Shakespeare, through Falstaff's lips, satirizes the artificial prose made fashionable by Lyly's *Euphues*.) Heavy with drink, Falstaff falls asleep behind the arras. The Prince plucks a memorandum out of the old scoundrel's pocket, showing that most of his money goes to buy wine. Hal decides to procure Falstaff a command in the army.

III, i: At Bangor, Hotspur cannot tolerate Glendower's boasting and superstition, and mocks him. He insists on a meticulous division of the spoils when they all win. Glendower's daughter sings, during some teasing byplay between Hotspur and his wife Kate. He and Mortimer set off; Glendower and the ladies are to follow.

III, ii: The King lectures Hal, telling him of all his bitter struggles to win to the crown. Hal is sincerely repentant, and promises to prove his worth against Hotspur. The King is willing to trust him with command. Blunt arrives with the news of the rebel gathering at Shrewsbury.

III, iii: At the Boar's Head, Falstaff has some fun with Bardolph at the expense of his ruddy nose, and with the stupid Hostess. The Prince arrives to tell Falstaff that the stolen money has been restored, and that he has procured a charge of foot soldiers for his old friend, who is less than enthusiastic at the idea of going off to war.

IV, i: Hotspur and Douglas exchange expressions of mutual regard. The news arrives that Northumberland, Hotspur's father, is ill; Glendower is not coming when needed either. Worcester thinks Northumberland's absence will breed questions on the justice of their cause. Hotspur's verdict is "Die all, die merrily."

IV, ii: Falstaff discourses on the miserable unfitness of the ragtag men he has plucked for his troops. The Prince and Westmoreland view them; Falstaff's excuse for them is that "they'll fill a pit as well as better."

IV, iii: At the rebel camp, Hotspur and Douglas are for an immediate engagement with the enemy; Worcester and Vernon are for waiting for reinforcements. Blunt arrives with a message from the King offering redress for their griefs and absolute pardon. Hotspur remembers how Henry became King through broken promises, and reviews their recent wrongs and provocations. In the morning Worcester will speak with the King.

IV, iv: The Archbishop of York sends out various letters to prepare a power to face the King should he defeat Percy. He says that Northumberland has the greatest strength, and thinks that Percy's force is too weak for present trial against the King.

V, i: Worcester speaks with the King, reminding him how he once broke his staff of office in Richard II's time, and how Henry pretended to claim only his rightful dukedom back, and how his ingratitude has forced the rebels to their present action. The Prince offers to settle the contention by single combat with Hotspur. The King tells Worcester that they may have his friendship again if the rebels will return to the fold. Falstaff, left alone, discourses on military honor, finding it only a word, empty, useless to the dead, and never accorded to the living. "Therefore," he decides, "I'll none of it."

V, ii: Worcester persuades Vernon that they must not tell Hotspur of the King's offer of peace; he does not trust the King's word and is sure vengeance will be visited upon them if they give up their arms. Hotspur would have accepted the challenge to single combat with Hal, but he has not the time to read the letters that come for him.

V, iii: The battle begins. Douglas kills Strafford and Blunt, both of whom were dressed as the King. Falstaff stands idly by, avoiding the fight. The Prince enters angrily, having lost his sword and demanding Falstaff's, who professes unwillingness to part with his weapon in the midst of so much danger. When Hal reaches into the old villain's pistol-case, he draws out a bottle of wine, and flings it in fury at Falstaff. Alone, Falstaff declares that he has no intention of pursuing honor, when honor means death.

V, iv: Fortune at first favors the rebels. Despite his wounds the Prince will not withdraw from battle. When his father is about to fall before Douglas' onslaught, Hal saves the King's life. Hal and Hotspur at last meet. Falstaff looks on, cheering his friend. Douglas enters and Falstaff falls down as if killed by the Scot, who goes out. Hal kills Hotspur, and pays tribute to his bravery. Then he sees Falstaff apparently dead on the ground; he is grieved, and laments the passing of his old companion. He goes out, and Falstaff gets up. Pleased that his ruse has saved his life, he wounds Percy again, to make sure he is dead; "the better part of valor is discretion." He takes Percy on his back, when Hal enters again, at the conclusion of the battle, with his brother John. He is astounded to see Falstaff alive, and good-humoredly allows Falstaff to claim credit for Percy's death.

V, v: The King condemns Worcester and Vernon to death. The Prince asks for the disposal of Douglas; his request is granted. John and Westmoreland are to march to meet Northumberland and the prelate Scoop. The King and Hal are to engage Glendower and the Earl of March.

HENRY IV, PART 2

(1598) Based upon Holinshed and *The Famous Victories of Henry V*. The plot deals with the rebellion of Northumberland in the North, the failing health of the King, the King's reconciliation with Prince Hal, the King's death, and the crowning of Hal as Henry V. In this play Falstaff luxuriates in the country at the expense of Justice Shallow, to whom he promises great rewards when Hal is crowned. At the end, however, the new King repudiates Falstaff and the roguish life he stands for.

Induction: Rumor, painted full of tongues, noises abroad the misinformation that Hotspur has killed Hal, and Douglas the King. These false comforts come to Northumberland who lies craftily ill.

I, i: To Northumberland Lord Bardolph brings "certain news" (procured at second hand) that Hotspur's forces have been victorious. The servant

Morton, who was at Shrewsbury, brings a true account of what has occurred. In a rage of passion, Northumberland rouses himself to vengeance for his son. The gentle Archbishop of York is in arms, turning insurrection into religion.

I, ii: In a London street Falstaff justifies himself: "I am not only witty in myself, but the cause that wit is in other men." The Prince has given him a diminutive page only to provoke mirth at the disparity of their sizes. The Chief Justice, who committed the Prince once for striking him in a quarrel, speaks to Falstaff, whom he had sent for because of his offences. But since the military is not subject to civil authority, the old rogue has been safe against prosecution. Besides, his "service" at Shrewsbury has gilded over Falstaff's participation in the robbery. Falstaff is to march with Lancaster.

I, iii: The Archbishop, Hastings, and Mowbray weigh their chances. They decide that even without Northumberland they have sufficient strength, for the King's powers are divided: one against the French, one against Glendower, and one against them. The country is sick of its choice, they feel.

II, i: The Hostess, Dame Quickly, has pressed charges against Falstaff; Fang and Snare are to arrest him. They know he will resist. Mistress Quickly does amusing violence to the English language in her misuse of words. Falstaff and Bardolph get into a quarrel. The Chief Justice comes upon the scene, and orders Falstaff to satisfy the Hostess for the sum he owes her. He has also promised to marry her and make her Lady Falstaff. Falstaff insists that he cannot be held, for he is busy about the King's affairs. Gower brings news of the King's return, and Falstaff ingratiates himself with Dame Quickly all over again.

II, ii: The Prince seeks out his old companions. He is too much worried about his father, and desires some distraction. If he wept, as he feels he must do, the world would think him a hypocrite.

II, iii: Lady Percy, after a magnificent tribute to her dead husband, persuades Northumberland, her father-in-law, to wait for the outcome of the battle; if the nobles win over the King, then let Northumberland join them. He goes to Scotland.

II, iv: The mouthing, swaggering Pistol comes into the Boar's Head Tavern dead drunk. Falstaff is compelled to drive him out at the point of a sword. The fat rogue is the darling of both Dame Quickly and Doll Tearsheet, the prostitute. With Doll on his lap, he rakes Poins and the Prince over the coals, not recognizing them in their disguises. When they are revealed, Falstaff declares that he has dispraised the Prince before the wicked so that the wicked might not fall in love with him. Peto comes in with the news that the King is at Westminster, that posts are coming from the North, and that a dozen captains are looking for Falstaff. The Prince now blames himself for idling and profaning time, and leaves. Falstaff, too, must leave. Doll and Mistress Quickly are overcome with grief at his departure.

III, i: The King soliloquizes: his poorest subjects sleep in peace, even sailors do in stormy seas; he himself is tortured by wakefulness because of his bad conscience:

Then happy low, lie down!
Uneasy lies the head that wears a crown.

He speaks to Warwick and Surrey, and reflects on the bitterness of his life, remembering Richard II's prophesy that all would crumble before his successor's unscrupulous ambition. But Henry still insists he became king for the country's sake. The King knows that York and Northumberland are five thousand strong. Warwick disparges the figure, and assures the King that he will win, and that Glendower is dead. The King purposes to go to Jerusalem, as he had hopes, once the war is over.

III, ii: We meet Shallow and Silence, country justices, both tremendously impressed with Falstaff's importance. The latter reviews his conscripts. He rejects Wart after one look at his weak physique, but later presses him into service when Mouldy and Bullcalf bribe their way out. Falstaff decides to make profit out of simple-minded Shallow.

IV, i: In Gaultree Forest, Yorkshire, the Archbishop of York receives a letter from Northumberland, who has gone to Scotland to levy forces. The enemy has thirty thousand men. The rebels are ready to march when Westmoreland comes in. His news is crucial: he declares that John of Lancaster has commission to give audience to their demands; York presents their articles of grievances. Mowbray has a foreboding of treachery, but Hastings and the Archbishop persuade him that they will have nothing to fear.

IV, ii: The leaders of the opposition meet. When Lancaster upbraids the Archbishop for counterfeited zeal of God against God's anointed, the King, the Archbishop reminds him that their petitions were scorned in court. Lancaster declares his father's purposes were mistaken by those about him, and promises redress of grievances. They agree to peace and to discharge their armies. The Northern army breaks up at once, but Lancaster's army will not until expressly commanded by him. Westmoreland declares Hastings, the Archbishop, and Mowbray under arrest for high treason. Lancaster's treachery is to redress grievances by hanging the rebels.

IV, iii: Coleville surrenders to Falstaff. Falstaff cannot make the humorless Lancaster laugh, but the King's son promises to speak better of him than he deserves. "I would you had the wit," Falstaff mutters to himself. He is disgusted with Lancaster, but what can one expect, he asks, from a man who drinks no wine?

IV, iv: In the Palace chamber known as "Jerusalem," the King is ready for the crusade, waiting his own recovery to health and news of the defeat of the rebels. He tells Thomas of Clarence to cultivate Hal, who likes him better than any other, so that he may be a hoop of gold to bind the brothers together. The King shows appreciation of Hal's qualities, and Warwick prophesies that Hal will in time cast off his low companions. Westmoreland brings news of the putting down of the northern rebels. Word is then brought of the defeat of Northumberland by the Sheriff of Yorkshire. The King is suddenly stricken with another attack of illness.

IV, v: The King, carried to his bed, falls asleep. Hal enters, thinks his father dead, and laments bitterly. With dignity he takes the crown, which he now believes his, from the pillow, and goes out with it. The King wakens, calls for his attendants, learns Hal was in the room, sees the crown gone, and feels sure his son is anxious to bury him before he is dead. Warwick goes to look for the Prince, and returns with the report that he found Hal weeping. The Prince enters, exclaiming, "I never thought to hear you speak again." His father counters, "Thy wish was father, Harry, to that thought." Hal defends his intentions sincerely and with such real grief that his father credits him. The King admits the devious means he has employed to reach the throne, reminds Hal that many are still hostile to his family, and avers that he planned the crusade to take the nobles' minds off the crown. He urges his son to keep the country busy with foreign quarrel. He is taken back to the Jerusalem chamber to die.

V, i: Shallow and Silence are kept busy entertaining Falstaff.

V, ii: Henry is dead, and the Chief Justice voices the general opinion when he fears that "all will be overturned;" he also fears the worst for himself because of his arrest of Hal long ago. Hal, now Henry V, enters, and reminds the Chief Justice of his grievance against him. The Justice defends himself, saying that at the time he represented the "image of the king" himself. Hal admires the man's courage and integrity, and at once appoints him Councillor, sets everyone at ease by his show of wisdom and moderation, and summons a parliament of "noble counsel" to direct the affairs of state.

V, iii: Pistol brings to Falstaff in Gloucestershire the news of Henry IV's death. Falstaff is sure that any post in the kingdom will be his for the asking. He promises Shallow the choosing "of what office thou wilt," and Pistol with the weight of all kinds of new dignities. He knows that the young king is "sick" for sight of him, and cries: "Let us take any man's horses; the laws of England are at my commandment."

V, iv: Mistress Quickly and Doll Tearsheet are arrested for beating a man to death.

V, v: In a public square near Westminster, Falstaff, Shallow, Pistol, and Bardolph place themselves prominently among the crowd to watch the new king pass by on his way to the coronation. Falstaff is promising rich plums to all, and vows to have Dame Quickly and Doll released from prison. The procession enters. Falstaff greets Hal with vulgar familiarity. The King replies:

> I know thee not, old man. Fall to thy prayers.
> How ill white hairs become a fool and jester!
> I have long dreamed of such a kind of man, . . .
> But, being awake, I do despise my dream . . .
> Reply not to me with a fool-born jest!

> *Presume not that I am the thing I was,*
> *For God doth know, so shall the world perceive,*
> *That I have turned away my former self,*
> *So will I those that kept me company.*

He provides Falstaff with a competence so that the old rogue may give up a life of vice. If he reforms, they may meet again. If not, Falstaff, on pain of death, is to keep ten miles between them. The King passes on, and Falstaff says brokenly: "Master Shallow, I owe you a thousand pound." Shallow would like to have his money now, and no longer believes his fat guest when the latter assures him that the King was behaving thus only publicly. The Chief Justice enters and orders Falstaff and the gang to prison. The play ends with talk of war with France.

Epilogue: The author promises to continue the story with Falstaff in the sequel.

HENRY V

(1599) Based on Holinshed and *The Famous Victories.* The play is epic rather than dramatic, the entire interest centering on Henry, England's beloved warrior-king, and abounds in Shakespeare's greatest patriotic poetry. It is worthy of note that with this work Shakespeare completed the dramatic representation of a cycle of English history. The events beginning with *Richard II* and continuing with *Henry IV, Parts 1, 2, Henry V, Henry VI, Parts 1, 2, 3,* form an uninterrupted sequence terminating in *Richard III. Henry V* shows us the hero of Agincourt as well as the bluff, democratic soldier-lover. The history sequences are enlivened by the comic utterances of Pistol and the Welshman Fluellen, and the broken English of the French princess. Falstaff, instead of reappearing, comes in only by report—the report of his death. Shakespeare must have realized that he had made it impossible to use the fat knight unless he showed him reformed, and Falstaff reformed would no longer be Falstaff.

Prologue: The author apologizes for having to represent vast events within the confines of the miserable little "wooden O" that forms the theatre. He calls on his audience to allow their imaginations to supply the deficiencies of what their eyes behold.

I, i: The bill to disendow the Church came up in the reign of Henry IV, and would have been passed had the times been less unquiet. The Archbishop of Canterbury speaks to the Bishop of Ely, giving all praise to the new King, who seems partial to the Church; he has offered the monarch a larger sum than has ever been given by the clergy to his predecessors. Henry was much interested in what Canterbury had to say about the claims of his throne to France, derived from Edward III, but the French ambassador had cut off that interview.

I, ii: In the Presence Chamber, Henry asks Canterbury to speak further about his claims, demanding strictest truth since war means terrible bloodshed. The King wishes to know whether his claim would be just; the clergymen spur him on to war. Canterbury suggests Henry take one fourth of the army to France, and Henry agrees to the expedition. He gives leave to the French ambassador, who now enters, to speak. The latter brings an insulting message from the Dauphin, who sends Henry the slighting gift of tennis balls as a symbol of the King's greater fitness to indulge in sports than in fighting. With dignity Henry answers, promising to strike the crown off the head of the French monarch.

II, Prologue: We are informed that Henry has set out for France.

II, i: In London, our old friend Bardolph (of Falstaff's gang), now a lieutenant, arbitrates a quarrel between Corporal Nym and the braggart Pistol. Mistress Quickly announces that Falstaff is dying; "the King has killed his heart."

II, ii: In the Council Chamber, Cambridge, Scoop, and Grey, traitors, demand the death of one who railed against the King, and thereby pass judgment on themselves. The King delivers them to the law of the land for the kingdom's safety.

II, iii: Mistress Quickly, now Mrs. Pistol, announces Falstaff's death. The rogues set out for the wars.

II, iv: At the French King's palace, the Dauphin still thinks of Henry as vain, giddy, and shallow. The Constable recognizes the English monarch's greatness and has a true perspective of his earlier life. Exeter, Henry's messenger, comes in to demand the French crown, and return Henry's scorn and defiance of the Dauphin. The French promise an answer on the morrow.

III, Prologue: We are informed that the French King has offered the Princess Katherine's hand to Henry to settle the contention, in addition to certain dukedoms.

III, i: Before the town of Harfleur Henry delivers an inspiring address to his men.

III, ii: The Boy, in attendance of the ex-thieves, gives a penetrating portrait of Nym, Bardolph, and Pistol. He wishes he were safely back in London. Fluellen, the Welshman, speaks with Gower; he admires Captain Jamy but despises Captain Macmorris for his ignorance of military theory. A parley is sounded, and cuts off the argument between Fluellen and Macmorris.

III, iii: Henry, in the plains before Harfleur, warns the town's Governor that as he is a soldier—a name that in his thoughts becomes him best—and he will utterly destroy the place if it does not yield; nor will he be able to restrain the soldiers from violent deeds once they are in the heat of a siege. Since the Dauphin is not sending reinforcements, the town decides to surrender. Exeter is left in command; Henry will take his sick ranks to Calais for the winter.

III, iv: Katherine begins to learn English from her attendant Alice, who is none too well equipped to teach her. She learns to say "De hand, de fingers, de nails, de arma, de bilbow" (elbow).

III, v: The French nobles still scorn Henry, and send Montjoy to demand a ransom for his army, which they feel is bound to fall.

III, vi: Fluellen, who believes that the braggart Pistol did noble service at the bridge, is asked by him to intercede for Bardolph, who is condemned to die for robbery of a church. When Fluellen refuses, Pistol insults him. Fluellen promises, when time permits, to fight it out with him. Gower sets him straight on Pistol's cowardice. Fluellen tells the King that the only man lost in the action of the bridge was Bardolph, who was to be executed anyway for his stealing of the pyx. Montjoy comes; the King confesses that his army is indeed ill, but he will not shun a battle.

III, vii: In the French camp, the morning before the battle, the French are much too overconfident.

IV, Prologue: The contending armies are described; Henry, wakeful, walks about the camp among his men, cheering them with his example.

IV, i: With humor Henry confesses the gravity of the battle before him. He meets Pistol, who does not know who he is, and listens to Fluellen and Gower speaking, and then to three men, who discuss the King with him, without realizing their companion is their monarch. Harry vindicates the King to them. One (Williams) quarrels with him; they exchange gloves; another (Bates) tells them that they have enough quarrelling to do with the French, without inventing more mischief. Alone, Henry soliloquizes: the peasant sleeps while the King must watch; the pomp of rank is hollow. He prays God not to think of his father's wrongs in winning the crown; he has done penance, though he well knows that nothing can undo his father's treachery.

IV, ii-iii: The French, six thousand strong, prepare for battle. The odds against the English are five to one. When Westmoreland wishes they had one ten-thousandth of the idle now in England, Henry gives his famous St. Crispin's Day speech: if they are to die, then it is enough for their numbers to perish; if they are to win at such odds, the greater glory will be theirs. Montjoy enters; Henry tells him to come no more for ransom.

IV, iv: Pistol captures a Frenchman; the Boy acts as translator. The latter tells us that Bardolph and Nym have been hanged.

IV, v-vi: The first repulse of the French causes them to lose their heads and forget military order. When Henry hears a French alarum reinforcing their scattered men, he orders that the prisoners be killed.

IV, vii: Gower tells Fluellen of the massacre of the English boys by the French, which was Henry's reason for killing his prisoners. Fluellen reflects on Henry's greatness by remarking on his rejection of Falstaff. After the massacre of the boys, Henry is really angry. Montjoy enters; he wishes to bury the French dead and concede victory to the English. Henry calls the soldier Williams, and bids Fluellen be his champion. But the King accepts the soldier's defence: Had Henry been in his own person, the offense would never have been committed. The King fills the soldier's glove with crowns, and graciously forgives him.

V, Prologue: We are wafted to England again, where Henry is described as receiving a greater welcome than Essex would now receive on his return from Ireland. The Emperor himself comes to England in behalf of the fallen France.

V, i: Fluellen now has time to take up the quarrel Pistol provoked. The latter's cowardice is at once made manifest and he is put to the humiliation of eating a leek, the symbol of Wales, to satisfy the Welshman's wrath. Pistol tells us that Doll Tearsheet is dead; he will now turn pimp himself.

V, ii: In the French palace, while the French King is considering the terms of peace, Henry is wooing Princess Katherine in his own rough-and-ready way. He cannot woo her in courtly terms, nor can he do it in a dance, for he is no good at these things. "Take a soldier, take a King," is his offer. She accepts. The French King hopes that their issue will know no more wars.

THE TAMING OF THE SHREW

(by 1594) A farce adapted from an old anonymous play *The Taming of a Shrew*. The story deals with the shrew Katherina, who is unmarried because of her terrifying temper. Petruchio's imagination is captivated by the challenge of taming her. He marries her, apparently against her will, and leads her a taxing life for a few days, during which he almost starves her. In the end she becomes a more obedient and tractable wife than her sweet sister Bianca.

MUCH ADO ABOUT NOTHING

(1598) One of Shakespeare's best romantic comedies—certainly his wittiest. The main plot deals with the love affair of Claudio and Hero, but the chief interest in the play will ever lie in the "war of words" between her incomparably witty cousin, Beatrice, and the equally clever Benedick, and in the process whereby their friends disarm them of their slashing words until they admit their love for each other. Hardly less delightful are the vagaries of the Constable Dogberry, a typical ignoramus in a position of petty officialdom, whose abuse of the English language is almost magnificent ("comparisons are odorous").

I, i: The scene is Messina, at the house of Leonato, the governor. Peace has just been concluded between Don Pedro, Prince of Arragon and his evil bastard-brother Don John, who had started a revolt against the Prince. The victorious Prince has forgiven his wicked kinsman. A messenger arrives to tell these tidings to Leonato. Beatrice, Leonato's niece, listens impatiently to hear how Benedick, friend to the Prince, has fared in battle. She is compelled to inquire about him, even though she dislikes giving anyone the impression that she has the least interest in him. Relieved to hear he is safe, she speaks mockingly of him. Don Pedro, Don John, Benedick, and the handsome Claudio, a brave soldier, arrive. Leonato greets them all. In a moment Beatrice has managed to pick a quarrel with Benedick, into which he plunges with zest. It is obvious to us, though not to their friends, that this "war" between them is less the product of dislike than of powerful mutual attraction. Left alone with Benedick, Claudio confesses his love for Leonato's modest daughter, Hero. Benedick, in his professed role of woman hater, is amazed that any man can waste a sigh over a woman. Don Pedro comes back, and Benedick mocks Claudio for falling in love. The other two are sure, nevertheless, that they will yet see Benedick "looking pale" for love. Benedick swears he will always be a bachelor; if ever he falls from this vow, he is willing to have a sign hung on him: "Here you may see Benedick the married man." He goes out. There is to be a masked ball that night, and Don Pedro offers to propose to Hero in Claudio's guise, since the latter is too shy to speak for himself. Claudio is grateful.

I, ii: Leonato tells his brother Antonio that he understands Claudio will propose marriage to Hero tonight. He is happy at the prospect.

I, iii: Don John is bitter over his late defeat. He still hates his brother and all his brother's friends. Borachio brings word that he has overheard the Prince offer to speak up for Claudio. Don John, seeing a chance for mischief, enlists his men to aid him in whatever villainy they can effectually contrive.

II, i: It is the night of the ball. Leonato and Antonio are disturbed by the example of excessive freedom which Beatrice may set for the well-tamed Hero. They warn her that her ways will never get her a husband. She professes a disdain for all men. She will avoid marriage: "I have a good eye, uncle; I can see a church by daylight!" The others come in, and the masked ball begins. Beatrice and Benedick manage to annoy each other by pretending to be other people and recounting tales to the disparagement of each other. Beatrice tells him that everyone considers Benedick nothing more than a dull-witted clown. He tells her that everyone says Beatrice procures all of her witticisms out of a popular joke book. Don John, recognizing Claudio, approaches him with the pretense that he thinks he is Benedick, and urges him to tell his friend Claudio that the Prince is stealing Hero for himself. Claudio, ever quick to take offense, despite the Prince's generous offer, chooses to believe the worst, and is out of temper with Benedick when the latter (who does not know of the Prince's suing for Claudio's sake) approaches with the same news. Benedick is astounded that Claudio gives up so easily. When Pedro comes in, Benedick satirically upbraids him, but happily learns that Pedro has been speaking only for Claudio. When Beatrice enters, Benedick quits the room with an insult to her. Pedro tells the wretched Claudio that Hero has accepted the latter, and the ungracious young man's happy spirits return. Beatrice is so happy to see her cousin's joy, that unwittingly she sighs out her lack of hope of ever marrying herself. Pedro laughingly offers to be her husband, but she declines: "No, my lord, unless I might have another for workingdays; your Grace is too costly to wear every day." She goes out. Then the rest plan to make Beatrice and Benedick fall in love with each other. They little know that it will not take much to effect this plan—they take too literally "the war of words" between these two brilliant people.

II, ii: To further Don John's hopes for mischief, Borachio offers to arrange a scene in which he will be heard wooing the maid Margaret in the guise of Hero in the middle of the night; if Don John can contrive to have Claudio witness the interview, the love match can be blasted, and Don John thus have some revenge against an enemy.

II, iii: Benedick, alone, is pondering the reason men marry, but his thoughts show that he is not unsmitten by Beatrice. Seeing him in the orchard, Don Pedro, Claudio, and Leonato talk, in tones which he cannot help overhearing, of Beatrice and the frustrated love which they "know" she has for Benedick; she has vowed to die rather than indicate that love since she is sure of being rebuffed by him. Alone again, Benedick decides that he may have been too cruel. And, after all, "the world must be peopled. When I said I would die a bachelor, I did not think I should live till I were married." When Beatrice is sent to ask him to come into dinner, he is sure her face and words speak love—though she is as rude as ever.

III, i: Beatrice is given the same treatment. Hero and the maid Ursula cause her to hear how Benedick is pining with love for her. They are of the opinion that she is not good enough for him. She decides to reciprocate his affection.

III, ii: Benedick, transformed by love, appears before his friends with his beard shaved; he is well-scrubbed, fashionably dressed. His friends make him uncomfortable by hinting that the change must be due to love. He leaves, embarrassed, to talk to Leonato about Beatrice. Don John enters and assures Claudio and the Prince that Hero is unchaste, and that he can offer the proof of it this very night. Claudio, too prone to feel injured, vows to disgrace her in the church where he is to marry her, if the evidence damns her.

III, iii: We meet the stupid Constable Dogberry and his yes-man, old Verges. In confused style he gives orders to the night watch, and leaves with the admonition: "Be vigitant!" Conrade and Borachio enter, under the influence of liquor, and the latter informs his friend how he has wooed the servant Margaret at her mistress' chamber window, calling her "Hero," while Claudio overheard his fiancée's apparent treachery. The illiterate watch overhear the story without understanding, but, believing they have surprised two desperadoes, arrest them.

III, iv: As Hero is preparing for the ceremony in church, Beatrice is sick at heart to think how impossible it seems that her love for Benedick can ever be consummated. She is teased for her moodiness.

III, v: Leonato, about to leave for church, is visited by Dogberry and Verges, who interfere with each other in trying to report the story of the arrest of "two aspicious persons." Could they talk sense they might avert the catastrophe in the church. As it is, they cannot spill out their message, and Leonato impatiently bids Dogberry take down the examination of the prisoners himself. He is gratified by such responsibility.

IV, i: In the church, as the friar is about to marry him to Hero, Claudio accuses her before everyone of unchastity. When he announces that he heard her making love to Borachio, and adduces the Prince as witness, Hero becomes confused and faints. Claudio, Don Pedro, and Don John leave. Leonato is convinced by the fact that Hero has not defended herself that his daughter is guilty. Beatrice alone, despite the evidence, is certain that the girl is incapable of such conduct. The friar, too, inclines to believe in her innocence. Hero recovers and protests that she has no guilt. The friar suggests that the best procedure is to spread the rumor of Hero's death; she can be hidden in a convent. And Claudio, when he hears of her dying, will repent his accusation, and perhaps then the real truth will come to light. Leonato unwillingly agrees. All leave but Benedick and Beatrice. She is weeping quietly because of the wrong to her cousin. To ingratiate himself with her, he pretends he believes in her cousin's innocence too, and offers to do whatever she suggests to prove his "friendship." Caught off guard, Beatrice forgets to say something ironic to him. Before he knows it, he is saying: "I do love nothing in the world so well as you; is not that strange?" And she, in her complicated style, answers with her admission of love for him. He is so happy that he bids her command him any task. She takes up his offer at once: "Kill Claudio." At that he balks—the man is his friend. But seeing her hurt by his refusal, he promises to fight with him.

IV, ii: Dogberry makes new confusion in taking down the testimony of the two arrested men. Despite his scatter-brained illiteracy, Dogberry, however, does not prevent the Sexton from getting the basic facts straight. We learn that Don John has mysteriously stolen away this morning. The Sexton leaves with the testimony, and Conrade, out of patience with the constable's idiocy, calls him an ass. Dogberry is incensed: "Dost thou not suspect my place? dost thou not suspect my years" (my ears)? He is furious that this insult has not been recorded by the Sexton: "O that he were here to write me down an ass!"

V, i: Leonato, convinced at last of his daughter's guiltlessness, is tormented with grief at the injustice to her. When Claudio and the Prince come in, he upbraids them for their ignoble deed, but they defend what they have done. Though feeble, Antonio, as Leonato's older brother, takes up the quarrel, and tries to spur Claudio to duel with him, but the latter will not fight with an old man. The two aged brothers leave in impotent rage. Benedick enters to challenge Claudio to a duel. At first the Prince and Claudio think he is jesting as usual. When he does not smile and, leaving, flings at their heads the fact of Don John's stealing away, they realize he is in deadly earnest, and that he has provoked the fight out of love for Beatrice. At this point Dogberry enters with the prisoners without any idea of their offense. But Borachio himself confesses his crime. Leonato comes in again with Antonio. Claudio is now all penitence. He will do anything that Leonato suggests by way of atonement.

The old man asks him to marry a niece of his, now that Hero is dead. Claudio agrees, calling the opportunity a great kindness, and tonight will mourn over Hero's grave.

V, ii: Benedick and Beatrice have a love scene during which, in their fantastic way, they make plain their love for each other. They love each other, they avow, in despite of themselves. But Benedick concludes: "I will live in thy heart, die in thy lap, and be buried in thy eyes."

V, iii: Claudio and Don Pedro pay tribute to Hero before her supposed tomb with funeral songs.

V, iv: With some embarrassment Benedick asks Leonato for Beatrice's hand. First the Prince and Claudio, then the two girls, masked, come in. Claudio, as is the agreement, swears before the friar to marry the masked girl who is presented as Hero's cousin. She unmasks and proves to Claudio's joy and astonishment to be the living Hero. Benedick now asks if the other fair masked one be not Beatrice. She unmasks, and he asks her to admit publicly that she loves him. Not too sure of him yet, she answers guardedly until he shall have confessed his love first. For similar reasons, he is equally only half-committal. They are on the verge of a quarrel again. But their friends come to the rescue with certain manuscripts which show that they have been secretly writing love poems to each other. Happily they laugh at themselves. Benedick says: "I will have thee; but, by this light, I take thee for pity." And she answers: "I yield upon great persuasion; and partly to save your life, for I was told you were in a consumption." The play ends in a dance before the double wedding.

The drama contains the charming song:

> Sigh no more, ladies, sigh no more,
> Men were deceivers ever;
> One foot in sea and one on shore;
> To one thing constant never.

SHAKESPEARE'S HEROINES

Beatrice is one of the many enchanting women Shakespeare created. Beatrice and her sister-heroines, Portia, Rosalind, Viola, Desdemona, Isabella, Cordelia, Helena (of All's Well That Ends Well), Cleopatra, Imogen, Perdita, and Miranda form what is undoubtedly the most remarkable gallery of alluring women and girls in the annals of literature—remarkable not only for their charm and winning ways, but also for the extent to which each of them is individualized. For although they are all women of deep feeling, personal beauty, quick sympathies, wit, and intelligence, each of them is exclusively herself and no one else. Portia, despite her gaiety, is essentially of a philosophic cast of mind. Beatrice, capable of fierce loyalty, is running over with excessive animal spirits and merriment—a girl with no patience for fools or the slow-witted. Rosalind is gaiety itself, a girl who can summon her highest spirits in the midst of discouraging circumstances and hardship. Viola is all compassion and understanding for the suffering of others. Desdemona is a creature of exquisite refinement and courage too. Cleopatra is perhaps all things—a new woman at every moment, the eternal enchantress. If we were to continue our list—and we could add others (Juliet, Hermione, Brutus's Portia) we should find that somewhere in his works Shakespeare has depicted every kind of woman that exists. In the comedies the play tends to focus about the heroine, rather than the hero, and in consequence the comedy tends to take on the tone of the heroine's character. For this reason, *Much Ado* is perhaps the most brilliant comedy in English. Some carping critics object that a woman like Beatrice would be too difficult to live with. Benedick wins her, but will he not wish a divorce in a year? We doubt it. His life with her may not prove easy, but he certainly never will be bored!

THE MERRY WIVES OF WINDSOR

(1600) Said to have been written to satisfy Queen Elizabeth's desire to see Falstaff in love. But the Falstaff in this play is everyone's dupe, and seems more like another man by the same name, except for his physical characteristics. This play is a comedy of plot rather than character, with a good-humored depiction of life among the solid burghers of Elizabeth's day. The old lecher Falstaff makes love to two married ladies at once, Mrs. Ford and Mrs. Page. The good wives, comparing his love letters, decide to be revenged upon him. They both pretend to encourage his attentions. In the end Falstaff is made the butt of everyone and is put through some very humiliating experiences. The love affair of young Anne Page with Fenton forms the subplot.

AS YOU LIKE IT

(1599–1600) The gayest of Shakespeare's romantic comedies, based upon Thomas Lodge's romance *Rosalynde*. Orlando, whose older brother, Oliver, will do nothing for him, evokes the love of Rosalind, daughter of the banished Duke, at a wrestling match where he tries his skill as an amateur. He falls in love with her. The usurping Duke Frederick banishes her. In the company of Frederick's daughter Celia, her devoted friend, she goes to find her father in the Forest of Arden. To be safe, Rosalind disguises herself as a boy and takes along Touchstone, the court jester. To escape his brother's enmity, Orlando flees to Arden too with his faithful old servant Adam. There he meets Ganymede (the disguised Rosalind), who promises to cure him of his love for Rosalind if he will pretend that Ganymede is his sweetheart. He plays the game until he begins to weary of it. In the end she reveals herself to him; the wicked brother and the usurping Duke both reform. Rosalind marries Orlando, Oliver marries Celia, and the Duke is restored to his throne. The play gains much from the disenchantment of the cynic Jaques, a courtier of the banished Duke's, as well as from the clever sardonic thrusts of Touchstone. The feeling of the forest is very strong, and there is even some satire at the expense of pastoral artificialities.

Jaques' soliloquy is celebrated:

> *All the world's a stage,*
> *And all the men and women merely players.*
> *They have their exits and their entrances;*
> *And one man in his time plays many parts.*

The play contains several beautiful songs:

> *Blow, blow, thou winter wind*
> *Thou art not so unkind*
> *As man's ingratitude.*

and,

> *Under the greenwood tree*
> *Who loves to lie with me,*
> *And turn his merry note*
> *Unto the sweet bird's throat.*

and,

> *It was a lover and his lass,*
> *With a hey, and a ho, and a hey nonino.*

TWELFTH NIGHT OR WHAT YOU WILL

(1601) The most perfectly balanced and sweetest of the romantic comedies, based on Barnaby Riche's tale *Apolonius and Silla*, itself taken from a tale of Bandello; the story had also appeared in an old Italian play *Gl'Ingannati*, which had been translated all over Europe. The title implies that the play may have been first produced on January 6th (the twelfth night after Christmas). Viola, shipwrecked in Illyria, disguises herself as Cesario, and enters the service of the lovesick Duke Orsino. He is suing in vain for the hand of Olivia, who lives in retirement mourning for her brother. Olivia's household contains the melancholy Puritan, Malvolio, who is overbearing towards everyone else; her irresponsible uncle, Sir Toby Belch, who is always drunk; and the charming witty clown, Feste. To line his pockets, Sir Toby is encouraging the suit of a stupid old knight, Sir Andrew Aguecheek. Cesario (Viola) although in love with Orsino, is sent as an ambassador of love to Olivia, who herself falls in love with the youth. Olivia is put in the humiliating position of proposing to the boy. Tactfully Cesario rejects her advances and recommends Orsino's suit, although the woman in Cesario's garments is heartsick at the task. Sebastian, Viola's twin brother, whom she imagines drowned in the shipwreck, arrives in Illyria. Olivia, meeting him, and mistaking him for Cesario, seizes the moment when the youth seems to be compliant, and is married to Sebastian, who is astounded at his sudden good fortune. Of course, the mistaken identities are cleared up. Orsino, realizing that Cesario is a girl, discovers that he has been falling in love with her and marries her. One of the most amusing aspects of the subplot is the elaborate revenge of Olivia's household, when its members deceive Malvolio into thinking Olivia is in love with him. The play is rich in beautiful speeches and witty lines, and is interspersed with some of Shakespeare's most beautiful songs: "O mistress mine," "When that I was and a little tiny boy," "Come away, come away death."

9
SHAKESPEARE'S PERIOD
OF TRAGEDIES

JULIUS CAESAR

(1599–1600) Based upon Sir Thomas North's translation of Plutarch. This noble and stately tragedy centers about the career of Brutus, philosopher-patriot, who is torn between his love for Caesar the man and his love for the freedom of Rome. Convinced that Caesar is about to put an end to the ancient Roman liberty, he enters into a conspiracy to assassinate him. Cassius, his fellow-leader, is less idealistic but more practical than Brutus. Against Cassius' advice, after the assassination of Caesar, Brutus allows Mark Antony to speak to the people. Antony turns the crowd, which had just given Brutus its support, into a vengeful, blood-thirsty mob crying for the blood of the conspirators. After the battles that ensue between the armies of the conspirators and those of the Triumvirate (Antony, Octavius, and Lepidus), Brutus commits suicide on the sword of a friend, and Cassius orders his servant to kill him. The tone of this play is intellectual rather than deeply emotional; the dignity of Brutus and, the passion of Antony form the focus of interest in the play. Among the celebrated lines in the play may be quoted Cassius':

> The fault, dear Brutus, is not in our stars,
> But in ourselves, that we are underlings.

HAMLET

(1600–1601) With *Othello*, *King Lear*, and *Macbeth*, this is one of the four greatest tragedies of Shakespeare. Based on a lost play, probably written by Kyd, which in turn was based upon the story as told in French by Belleforest, the origin of the story is the *Danish History of Saxo Grammaticus*. *Hamlet* is the most widely read, performed, and discussed of Shakespeare's plays. Countless critiques have been written on merely two aspects of the hero's character and behavior: Was Hamlet mad or sane? Why does he procrastinate in killing the King? In answer to the first question, opinion ranges from considering Hamlet a deranged person through labelling him a neurotic bordering on insanity, to declaring him a perfectly sane man pretending madness. In answer to the second, some critics have averred that Hamlet postpones his revenge because he is too sensitive a man, too much the thinker, too much the Christian, too much devoted to his mother, or too much devoted to his father; some hold that revenge was postponed because of circumstances over which Hamlet had no control, and the security of the King's position. In a work such as this outline, it is impossible to examine all these views. Whatever the correct interpretation may be, *Hamlet* continues to be the delight of audiences and the aspiration of leading actors.

I, i: It is midnight on a platform before the castle at Elsinore. Bernardo comes to relieve Francisco, who has been on guard. Horatio and Marcellus enter and begin to discuss the apparition that has twice appeared before this; Horatio is skeptical that ghosts exist. Suddenly the Ghost appears in the exact figure of the late King. Horatio addresses it, but it refuses to answer him and vanishes. Horatio relates how the dead King had overcome the old King of Norway, and how the latter's son, Fortinbras, is collecting an army to win back the lands his father lost. The Ghost comes in again, seems about to speak, but disappears at the crowing of the cock. The men decide to tell Hamlet of what they have seen.

I, ii: Before the Danish court, King Claudius expresses grief for the death of his brother, explains his hasty marriage to his brother's wife, Gertrude, as owing to the pressure of state affairs, delegates two envoys to deal for him in the Fortinbras affair, and grants Laertes, son to his counsellor Polonius, the permission to return to France. He then addresses himself with elaborate affection to his nephew Hamlet, and gently upbraids him for still wearing mourning for his dead father, and urges him to look on himself as his father. Hamlet insultingly repulses the offer, ignores the King, and ironically assures his mother that *his* mourning goes beyond black dress and momentary tears. The King informs Hamlet that he wishes him to stay at court. Left alone, Hamlet expresses his revulsion at his mother's marriage so soon after her late husband's death, and to the man Hamlet hates most of all men. Horatio and Marcellus come in and tell Hamlet of the appearance of the Ghost. Hamlet, very much excited, promises to join them at the platform that night in hopes to see the Ghost too.

I, iii: At Polonius' house, Laertes takes leave of his sister Ophelia, and warns her to have nothing to do with Hamlet; he is convinced that the Prince's love is not honorable and is sure he would never marry her because she is a commoner. Polonius comes in, gives his son a farewell blessing, and reinforces Laertes' warnings about Hamlet. He commands the girl to have no further communication with the Prince.

I, iv: It is the second night, and Hamlet is awaiting the Ghost with Horatio and Marcellus. The Ghost appears. Hamlet addresses it, but instead of speaking, it indicates that he is to follow it. When Hamlet begins to do so, the other two try to pin him back. They are afraid that the spirit may mean mischief. Hamlet throws them off and follows the Ghost.

I, v: Hamlet affirming that he will follow no further, the Ghost identifies itself as the spirit of Hamlet's father, reveals that the latter had been secretly killed by Claudius, the late King's own brother, who had first seduced the Queen to adultery. The Ghost lays the burden of ravenging this murder upon Hamlet's shoulders, with the injunction that he is not to taint his mind or contrive anything against the Queen. Dawn begins, and the Ghost disappears. Horatio and Marcellus now catch up with Hamlet, who swears them to complete secrecy on what they have seen.

II, i: Some two months have elapsed. Polonius sends his servant Reynaldo after Laertes to Paris, to spy on the young man and find out how he has been behaving himself. Ophelia comes in very much upset; Hamlet has broken into her room and frightened her by the disorder of his garments and the way he studied her face. She insists that she has all this while refused to see Hamlet, as her father has commanded. Polonius decides that the Prince has become mad out of love for Ophelia.

II, ii: The King has sent for Rosencrantz and Guildenstern, two old friends of Hamlet, and tells them that Hamlet is behaving very oddly. He begs of them to find out what is troubling the Prince, and to do what they can to revive Hamlet's spirits. The ambassadors from Norway return with the good news that the King of Norway has forbidden Fortinbras to war against Denmark, and asks only that the latter be allowed to pass with his troops through the country on their expedition against Poland. Polonius now, at great length, informs the King and Queen that he knows the cause of Hamlet's madness: a frustrated love for Ophelia. The Queen hopes that this may be the case; she would be happy to see Ophelia married to her son. Polonius promises to prove the point by having the King overhear the encounter he will arrange between Hamlet and Ophelia. Hamlet enters and is soon joined by Rosencrantz and Guildenstern, whom he first greets with great joy. Soon he suspects, however, that they are acting as spies for the King, and he treats them with scorn. They are glad to change the subject by informing him that a company of players is in town. Hamlet is delighted at the news. The Players enter, and Hamlet asks them to recite a passage from a play he admires. During the recitation, Hamlet is struck by one of the lines, and conceives a plan. He informs one of the Players that he wishes *The Murder of Gonzago* staged before the Court tomorrow night; this play contains a plot similar to the events of the murder of Hamlet's father. Hamlet hopes that the performance will force the King publicly to confess his guilt; at the very least, Hamlet will be certain from the King's reactions whether he is guilty as the Ghost has charged.

III, i: The next day, Ophelia is placed where Hamlet is bound to meet her, a prayer book is thrust into her hands, and Polonius and the King hide to observe. Hamlet enters and delivers his famous "To be or not to be" soliloquy; it is the fear of what lies in wait for us after death that makes men put up with the catastrophies of life; we prefer to bear those burdens we know than hasten to assume those hidden from our knowledge. Hamlet now sees Ophelia, who surprisingly wishes to return his gifts to her with the accusation that he no longer loves her. Unable to believe his ears, he bitterly urges her, while she weeps, to flee the world and enter a nunnery. (Some scholars interpret the nunnery to be a whorehouse.) Suddenly, Hamlet is aware that they are being overheard, insults Ophelia as a hypocrite, and leaves in a fury. The King, emerging with Polonius, is convinced of neither Hamlet's madness nor his love for Ophelia.

III, ii: Hamlet urges upon the players a natural, convincing performance of his play, and engages Horatio to watch the King's reactions carefully. The Court enters, Hamlet taking a position near Ophelia, where he can study the King well. The play is offered first in pantomime, and as it proceeds the King is mightily alarmed. But he is a strong man and does not break. Noting the King's agitation, Polonius dismisses the Players and the Court, as the King staggers out. Hamlet is overjoyed: the Ghost has plainly told the truth; Horatio certifies his own observation of the King. Rosencrantz and Guildenstern come back to say that the Queen wishes to see her son.

III, iii: In the King's room, Claudius informs Guildenstern and Rosencrantz that Hamlet must be sent to England. Polonius enters and tells the King that he is going to overhear the Queen's talk with Hamlet in her room. Alone, Claudius tries to pray but cannot. Hamlet, en route to the Queen's closet, finds the King on his knees, is tempted to kill him, but postpones the act to a time when the murderer's soul will be sure to go to Hell.

III, iv: In the Queen's room, Polonius urges her to be severe with Hamlet, then hides behind the tapestry. Hamlet enters and pours out a torrent of accusation on her head. Terrified, she calls for help. Polonius loses his wits and calls out too. Hearing his cries, Hamlet whips out his sword and runs the old man through, crying: "Is it the King?" When he sees whom he has killed, he has no remorse and continues to upbraid his mother until the Ghost enters to quiet him. Gertrude, not seeing the Ghost, is convinced that Hamlet is insanely talking to the air.

IV, i: Gertrude informs Claudius of Polonius' death. The King decides Hamlet must leave for England at once under the conduct of Rosencrantz and Guildenstern.

IV, ii: The latter find Hamlet and bring him away to the King.

IV, iii: The King tells Hamlet he must go to England. Alone, the King tells us that England's sovereign has been commanded to put Hamlet to death.

IV, iv: Fortinbras is passing through Denmark. Hamlet, seeing the former's army, is stirred by the example of his bravery, and resolves to hasten his revenge.

IV, v: A week later, the Queen witnesses the madness of Ophelia, whose mind is broken by her father's death and Hamlet's exile. A messenger announces that Laertes, back from France, has collected a rabble that is storming the palace. Laertes enters, threatens Claudius, but is soon placated by him, and is overwhelmed at the sight of Ophelia's madness.

IV, vi : A sailor brings Horatio a letter from Hamlet recounting how coming on a pirate at sea, Hamlet has boarded the pirate ship alone, won over the crew, and been brought back to Denmark by them. Hamlet asks Horatio to meet him.

IV, vii: Claudius tells Laertes that Hamlet is Polonius' murderer. A letter arrives from Hamlet announcing the latter's return. Claudius plots with Laertes to challenge Hamlet to a fencing match; Laertes is to use a poisoned unbuttoned sword; the King will also have a poisoned drink prepared for Hamlet in case the other plot fails. Gertrude enters with the news of Ophelia's death by drowning.

V, i: Two men are preparing Ophelia's grave. Hamlet and Horatio speak with the elder gravedigger. The funeral procession enters. Grief-stricken to learn of Ophelia's death, Hamlet is disgusted at Laertes' public display of grief, and jumps into the grave after him. Laertes grapples him and they are forcibly parted.

V, ii: Hamlet tells Horatio of his discovery aboard ship of a letter to the King of England ordering his death, and how he substituted another letter demanding the execution of Guildenstern and Rosencrantz. Osric, a fop, brings Hamlet Laertes' challenge to the duel; Hamlet accepts. The Court enters; the duel begins. Hamlet is lightly wounded, but does not guess the sword was envenomed. Infuriated at the treachery of an unbuttoned sword, he picks it up himself and runs Laertes through. Before dying, Laertes reveals the plot against Hamlet's life. The Queen, meanwhile, has drunk the poisoned drink unknowingly, and dies. With Claudius' treachery unfolded, Hamlet stabs the King with the poisoned sword and forces the rest of the poisoned drink down Claudius' throat. Hamlet's last words are a prayer to Horatio to tell the world the facts of his story. He dies. Fortinbras enters, claims the throne as now rightfully his, praises Hamlet, and orders a military funeral for him. Though all the persons are painted by Shakespeare with great vividness, no play of Shakespeare's revolves more completely around the hero than does *Hamlet*. Hamlet is Shakespeare's noblest and most brilliant creation.

As it is the most discussed of Shakespeare's plays, so *Hamlet* is also the most frequently quoted. The following are only a handful of many famous passages:

> *Frailty, thy name is woman! . . .*

> *Be thou familiar, but by no means vulgar . . .*

> *Give every man thy ear, but few thy voice . . .*

> *Neither a borrower nor a lender be . . .*

> *But to my mind, tho' I am native here*
> *And to the manor born,—it is a custom*
> *More honored in the breach than in the observance.*

> *Something is rotten in the state of Denmark . . .*

> *There are more things in heaven and earth, Horatio,*
> *Than are dreamt of in your philosophy . . .*

Brevity is the soul of wit . . .

Use every man after his desert, and who should 'scape whipping . . .

The play's the thing
Wherein I'll catch the conscience of the King . . .

To be, or not to be: that is the question:
Whether 'tis nobler in the mind to suffer
The slings and arrows of outrageous fortune,
Or to take arms against a sea of troubles
And by opposing end them . . .

Thus conscience does make cowards of us all . . .

The rest is silence . . .

TROILUS AND CRESSIDA

(1602) Though included among the tragedies, it is actually a bitter satire, based on Chaucer's *Troilus and Criseyde*. Shakespeare's picture of the Trojan War is painted with sympathy for the Trojans. Hector is probably the only admirable character; the other Homeric heroes are all fools or knaves. The story deals with Cressida's betrayal of Troilus' love and her giving herself to Diomedes. Though unsatisfactory as a play, this work abounds in magnificent poetic passages.

OTHELLO

(1604–1605) Based upon a tale of Cinthio in the Italian *Hecatommithi,* this is Shakespeare's most perfectly contrived play and contains a plot closer than is his custom to everyday experience ("domestic tragedy"). It is the most intense of the tragedies. The exquisite Desdemona, daughter of a Venetian senator, braves her father's wrath and public opinion by marrying the valiant Moorish General, Othello. When he is sent to Cyprus to fight the Turk she joins him, escorted there by Othello's ancient (ensign) Iago. Iago, incensed at having been bypassed when Cassio was promoted, and chafing, moreover, at having to serve under a Moor, decides to poison Othello's peace by making him suspect his wife's fidelity. Employing the aid of a young fool, Roderigo, the contents of whose purse he is forever emptying into his own, Iago manages to make Cassio drunk while on duty. In the brawl that ensues, terminated only by Othello's appearance, Cassio is publicly demoted by Othello, even though Othello loves him dearly. Iago urges Cassio to sue for Desdemona's help in procuring his reinstatement. This she gladly promises.

Seizing upon Cassio's shamefaced withdrawal on Othello's entry, Iago uses the incident to undermine Othello's belief in his wife. Iago, luckily for his plans, manages to get his wife Emilia to filch a valuable handkerchief the Moor had given Desdemona. Iago pretends to Othello that Desdemona has made a present of it to Cassio, and recounts what seems to be proof of intimacies between Cassio and Desdemona. He even arranges to have Othello overhear Cassio's boasts and contempt for his light-of-love; although Cassio is actually talking of a courtesan who dotes on him, the enraged Othello supposes the woman to be Desdemona. Convinced of Desdemona's adultery, Othello asks Iago to kill Cassio while he himself will avenge his honor on his wife. He smothers Desdemona in her bed. But Iago succeeds only in wounding Cassio. When Othello declares to the world the reason for killing his wife, Emilia, shocked that her own husband has been the cause of this mischief, blurts out the truth. Struck down by this revelation, Othello kills himself with his own dagger by the side of his innocent wife. The fall of noble Othello from the great calm of his beautiful soul to the depths of agonizing jealousy is one of the most terrifying spectacles in drama. Few of Shakespeare's heroes speak lines of greater beauty than he.

> She loved me for the dangers I had passed
> And I loved her that she did pity them

> I had rather be a toad,
> And live upon the vapor of a dungeon,
> Than keep a corner in the thing I love
> For others' uses

> O! now, for ever
> Farewell the tranquil mind; farewell content! . . .
> Farewell the neighing steed, and the shrill trump,
> The spirit-stirring drum, the ear-piercing fife,
> The royal banner, and all quality,
> Pride, pomp, and circumstance of glorious war . . .

> Put out the light, and then put out the light.

> One that loved not wisely but too well.

Iago's speech is also famous:

> Good name in man and woman, dear my lord,
> Is the immediate jewel of their souls:
> Who steals my purse steals trash; 'Tis something, nothing;
> 'Twas mine, 'tis his, and has been slave to thousands;
> But he that filches from me my good name
> Robs me of that which not enriches him,
> And makes me poor indeed.

MEASURE FOR MEASURE

(1604–1605) Based upon George Whetstone's play *Promos and Cassandra,* which in turn was taken from a tale of Cinthio, this vitriolic comedy, in which there is no amusement, contains the most appalling picture of humanity Shakespeare ever painted. We see degradation in the lowest and highest places. But the work is saved from cynicism by the shining integrity of the heroine Isabella. The play also contains passages of poetry equal to the best of anything Shakespeare ever wrote. Angelo, who has deceived himself and everyone else into believing he is a man of incorruptible virtue, takes over the reins of government of Vienna at the request of the Duke, who feels that Angelo can reform the vice rampant in the state. One of Angelo's first decrees is to make adultery punishable by death. The first victim under the law is young Claudio, who is only technically guilty; Juliet, the girl involved, and he have been planning to marry as soon as finances permit. Claudio's sister, Isabella, about to enter a nunnery, comes to Angelo to plead for her brother's life. Angelo, noting her innocence, is overwhelmed with lustful desire for her. At first, embarrassed as she is by the nature of her plea, she does not understand his proposal to spare Claudio's life if she will surrender her body to Angelo's uses. When she at last understands the foul bargain, she leaves indignantly and bids her brother prepare for death. Meanwhile, the Duke, disguised as a Friar in order to investigate the true state of his dukedom, learns of Angelo's hypocrisy, and urges Isabella to fall in with his plans. She pretends to agree to the wretched offer, but instead of her, Mariana, a girl abandoned by Angelo, is substituted in Angelo's bed. Angelo reveals the full depth of his iniquity by ordering Claudio's death after all. In the end, having saved Claudio's life, the Duke reappears in his own right, forces Angelo to marry Mariana, and himself asks for Isabella's hand.

KING LEAR

(1605–1606) Based upon an old play, *The True Chronicle History of King Leir,* still extant, also on the story as told in the Chronicles of Geoffrey of Monmouth and Holinshed; the subplot of Gloucester and his sons, from a story in Sidney's *Arcadia.* This is generally conceded to be Shakespeare's greatest expression of the tragic spirit, though *Othello* is more perfect as a play. Certainly the whole cosmos seems in this work to be groaning at man's inhumanity to man, and no theme could more powerfully illustrate that inhumanity than the theme of filial ingratitude.

I, i: The courtiers are discussing Lear's decision to divide the kingdom among his daughters. Gloucester introduces his illegitimate son Edmund to Kent, making some unpleasant jests at the expense of the boy's mother. King

Lear enters with his court. He points out on the map how he intends to divide his kingdom in three parts, and asks his three daughters in turn to say "Which of you shall we say doth love us [the King] most." Goneril, the eldest, assures him that she loves him more than all the wealth, liberty in the world—more than her eyesight. She is given her third of the kingdom. Regan, next, not only agrees with her sister but vows that her love for her father is even greater than that. She is given her share. Lear now turns to his best-loved, his youngest, Cordelia, whose hand the King of France and Duke of Burgundy both seek. But she, angered at her sisters' hypocrisy, in answer to his "What can you say to draw a third more opulent than your sisters?" murmurs, "Nothing." Astounded, he asks again, but she flings in her father's face, "Sure, I shall never marry like my sisters to love my father all." Incensed at her apparent lack of love, Lear, who should know her better, disinherits her. Kent tries to intervene, and begs Lear to revoke his pronouncement, but only enrages Lear the more. When the loyal earl refuses to be silent ("Be Kent unmannerly when Lear is mad," he says), Lear banishes him, giving him ten days to quit the kingdom. Lear now informs the suitors of Cordelia, Burgundy and France, that she is now dowerless. Burgundy, under these conditions, withdraws his suit; but the King of France is now more enamored of Cordelia because of her honesty than ever, and she accepts him. She takes leave of her sisters, bidding them use their father well. Lear has divided Cordelia's share between Goneril and Regan, reserving for himself the title and a hundred knights to attend on him; he will stay alternately with Goneril and Regan. Left alone, the two older sisters agree that Lear's behavior to Cordelia and Kent prove that he is becoming infirm in mind. They shall have to check his innate rashness.

I, ii: Edmund soliloquizes on his state, and determines to unseat his legitimate brother Edgar from his inheritance. As his father enters, he pretends to be trying to conceal a letter. Edmund, under protest, shows his father the paper when the latter demands to see it. It is a letter Edmund has forged in his brother's handwriting, hinting at a desire to murder Gloucester with Edmund's aid. Edmund promises Gloucester to find out more about Edgar's purposes. When the old man goes out, Edgar enters. Edmund now tells Edgar that their father is full of hate for Edgar, the cause unknown, and counsels the latter not to go out unarmed.

I, iii: Goneril orders her Steward, Oswald, to tell her servants to be slack in their service to Lear. She is anxious to make an issue of it with her father, whose brief stay at her castle is already irksome to her.

I, iv: Kent, shaved of his beard and disguised, enters Goneril's castle, and asks Lear, who does not recognize him, to employ him in any capacity. Oswald enters and ignores Lear's summons. One of the King's knights reflects on the slights recently being visited upon Lear at Goneril's. Oswald reenters and is insolent with Lear. Kent trips up the Steward in punishment, and endears himself to the King. The Fool enters and assures Lear that he is the greater fool for having parted with his kingdom. Goneril comes in to give her father a tongue-lashing for the disorder of his knights, of which there is no evidence, and the freedom of speech exercised by his Fool. Lear is at once aroused to wrath, and calls for his horses. He will go off to Regan. Albany, Goneril's well-meaning but weak husband comes in, and stands helplessly by while his wife further provokes Lear into a rage with her demand that he discharge some of his attendants. Lear rushes out but soon comes back with the infuriated discovery that she has already sent away fifty of his men. Lear departs with a threat to recover from her all he has given her. Goneril silences her worried husband, and sends Oswald to Regan to warn her that their father has become dangerous.

I, v: Lear sends Kent with a message to Regan of his coming to her. The Fool continues to torture Lear with his quips on the King's folly.

II, i: Edmund learns that Regan and her husband, Cornwall, are on their way to visit Gloucester. He feels it a propitious day to act. He calls in Edgar, and before his brother knows what it is all about, tells him they must pretend to fight since he has been ordered to take Edgar in charge. He pushes his brother out, telling him to flee for his life. Edmund wounds himself to make it appear he has been defending himself against Edgar, and calls for his father. Gloucester runs in, and is told by Edmund that Edgar tried to force him to help him murder Gloucester. Gloucester sends men after Edgar to apprehend him, and promises to bequeath everything to Edmund. Cornwall and Regan arrive. She tries to connect Edgar's apparent perfidy with the "riotous behavior" of her father's knights. Cornwall is taken with Edmund and promises him his patronage.

II, ii: Before the castle, Oswald and Kent meet. Kent beats Oswald. Hearing the noise, the others come out and, as an affront to the King, Cornwall and Regan order Kent, Lear's messenger, put in the stocks. Gloucester is sorry for Kent, but is unable to help him.

II, iii: Edgar, to save himself, decides to masquerade as a lunatic, a Tom o' Bedlam, covering himself with filth and going almost naked.

II, iv: Lear arrives and is indignant to find his messenger in the stocks. Kent informs the King that when he delivered Lear's letters to Regan, Oswald arrived with his from Goneril, and that Regan and her husband at once took horse to leave their palace, since Lear was expected. Gloucester tells Lear that Regan and Cornwall cannot yet be seen; they are weary from travel. At length the two deign to appear. Lear begins to relate Goneril's cruelty to him, but is cut short by Regan, who sides with her sister, and reminds Lear that he is an indigent old man. Kent is released from the stocks. At this juncture Goneril arrives. Lear is shocked to see Regan greet her cordially. Regan urges her father to return to Goneril's; it is not now convenient to have him at her castle. Between the two, the sisters begin to bate Lear, announcing that he has no need of a hundred knights. Regan decides that her sister is too generous to allow fifty; she will tolerate no more than twenty-five. Goneril asks why he needs twenty-five, ten, or even five? Regan adds, "What need one?" Despite himself, Lear begins to weep bitterly at the perfidy of these daughters, and threatens them impotently. The sounds of a growing storm are heard. Lear leaves, followed by Kent, the Fool, and Gloucester. Gloucester returns, worried about Lear, but is ordered by Regan to shut his doors against the storm. Lear will have to learn the hard way to obey his betters, she tells him.

III, i: Kent meets a gentleman in the open country, and bids him hasten to Dover, where Cordelia has landed with a French force to save her father, and he asks the good man to report Lear's plight.

III, ii: The elements are now raging. Amidst sheets of lightning, volleys of thunder, and cascades of rain, Lear wanders on the heath in the company of his Fool. Kent comes upon them; he has found a hovel for shelter against the night. Lear fears his mind is cracking, but bravely tries to maintain his sanity.

III, iii: Gloucester confides to Edmund that he has received a letter assuring him that Lear's wrongs will soon be righted, and that they must support the King. He also is sure that Albany and Cornwall will soon be in contention.

III, iv: Kent leads Lear and the shivering Fool to the hovel. Here Edgar has taken refuge. But Lear prefers to expose himself to the fury of the weather By degrees, in the cataclysm of rain and lightning, and amidst the mad cries of Tom o' Bedlam (Edgar), Lear's mind becomes unhinged. Gloucester, solicitous for the King, comes to warn him that the two daughters are plotting against Lear's life. At length Lear is persuaded to enter the hovel.

III, v: Edmund dutifully reveals to Cornwall his father's treason in siding with Cordelia and the French forces, and delivers the telltale letter, which he has stolen, to the Duke. Cornwall promises to make him Earl of Gloucester.

III, vi: Lear, now mad, thinks he is bringing his daughters before a court of justice. Exhausted, he is prevailed upon to rest in the hovel. As he sleeps, Gloucester comes with dread tidings: the plot against Lear's life is about to be executed. Kent must convey Lear at once, despite his condition and need of sleep, to Dover, where he will find Cordelia and her forces.

III, vii: Oswald informs Goneril and Regan of Gloucester's succor of Lear. They will punish him. Goneril leaves to prepare her army against the French invasion; to spare Edmund the unpleasantness of seeing his father punished, Cornwall sends him along with Goneril. Gloucester comes in, and is immediately pinioned, though in his own house. Regan insults him by plucking at his beard, and forces him to admit his sympathy with Cordelia's forces, and demands to know where he has sent the King. Careless of his own safety, Gloucester upbraids her for her treatment of Lear, and expresses the hope to see him avenged. "See it shalt thou never!" cries Cornwall, and stamps out one of Gloucester's eyes with his foot. Impatiently, Regan puts out the other. A servant who tries to stop this fiendishness is stabbed from behind by Regan. Regan now informs the blind old man that it was Edmund who revealed the truth about him, Edmund who hates him. Too late Gloucester guesses his folly and cruelty towards Edgar. Cornwall, who has been wounded by the servant, is bleeding freely.

IV, i: Tom o' Bedlam meets the blinded Gloucester on the heath. Grief-stricken, he agrees to lead the old man to the cliffs of Dover.

IV, ii: Edmund brings Goneril to her palace. As they take leave, it is clear that she is violently in love with him. Albany enters and upbraids his wife for her fiendish conduct towards Lear. She answers him with contempt. A messenger arrives with the news of Gloucester's blinding and Cornwall's death. Goneril is not pleased that her sister would now be free to marry Edmund.

IV, iii: Kent learns that the King of France has returned to his country, leaving Cordelia in charge of the troops. Cordelia has received word of her father's treatment, and is anxious to help him, but Lear is ashamed to see her.

IV, iv: Cordelia sends to find her father. The British army approaches.

IV, v: Oswald arrives with a letter from Goneril to Edmund; Regan tells him to warn her sister that Edmund is not for her.

IV, vi: Edgar leads his father to a field, which he pretends is a cliff, and retires. Gloucester hurls himself forward, and falls safely on the ground. In another voice Edgar speaks to him again, assuring him he was saved after so precipitous a fall by sheer miracle. Lear enters completely mad; Cordelia's men take him in charge. Oswald enters and wants to apprehend Gloucester, hoping for a reward. Edgar fights him and slays him, and reads the letter to Edmund in which Goneril asks the former to rid her of Albany.

IV, vii: Lear, newly clothed in kingly garb and asleep, after treatment by Cordelia's doctor, is brought before her. As he awakens, she kneels before him in love. He wishes to kneel to ask her forgiveness, but she will not allow her King to do that. She warms him with her love, and he is sane again.

V, i: Before the battle Edgar hands Goneril's letter to Albany, and promises to bring a champion to prove the truth of the contents.

V, ii: The British win the battle.

V, iii: Lear and Cordelia are led in as prisoners, but Lear is supremely happy because he is with her again. They are taken out and Edmund orders a captain to execute them. Albany, who has read Goneril's letter, would arrest Edmund. Regan defends her husband-to-be, but suddenly becomes mortally ill because her sister has poisoned her. Edgar appears in armor, fights Edmund, and deals him a deathblow. The whole truth is revealed. In a rage, Goneril stabs herself to death. Dying, Edmund repents and tries to save Lear and Cordelia. It is too late. Cordelia is already hanged. Lear comes in with her body and, weeping over it, dies of a broken heart. Gloucester, too, has died when Edgar at last revealed himself.

Despite the complexity of this plot, the greatness of the art with which it has been told creates amazingly the impression of unity and simplicity.

Among the celebrated lines in the play are:

> *How sharper than a serpent's tooth it is*
> *To have a thankless child . . .*

> *Blow winds and crack your cheeks!*

I am a man
More sinned against than sinning . . .

O! that way madness lies . . .

The worst is not
So long as we can say, 'This is the worst.'

Every inch a King . . .

Men must endure
Their going hence, even as their coming hither.

ALL'S WELL THAT ENDS WELL

(1602–1603) Based on a story in the *Decameron* of Boccaccio as it was translated into English by William Painter in his *Palace of Pleasure*. This is another bitter comedy without amusement. It shows signs of belonging in part to Shakespeare's early career, while other portions distinctly indicate composition of the tragic period. It may be that it is a reworking of a play ascribed to Shakespeare as having been written before 1598, *Love's Labour's Won*. The story is one of the unpleasantest in Shakespeare, but maintains its dramatic interest chiefly because of the beautiful character of its heroine, Helena. Helena, daughter of a famous physician, cures the King of an apparently incurable disease. As her reward, she asks to be married to Bertram, Count of Rousillon, with whose mother she has been living. The young count protests against the marriage on the grounds of Helena's inferior rank. Helena is willing to withdraw her request, but the King will not permit it. Immediately after the marriage ceremony, without even a kiss, Bertram leaves with his follower, Parolles, to fight for the Duke of Florence. Returning to the home of the old Countess, Helena receives a letter from Bertram which tells her that he will never be her husband until she can procure the ring on his finger and show him a child born to her by him. He intends, of course, that these things shall never be. Grieved that she has caused his exile, Helena leaves the kind Countess secretly, and allows the old lady to accept the rumor that she is dead. Helena reaches Florence as Bertram returns victoriously from the wars. She learns from the widow with whom she lodges that Bertram has been trying to seduce the widow's daughter, Diana. Revealing herself as Bertram's wife, she persuades the girl to pretend to agree to a midnight meeting. Helena takes the girl's place and procures Bertram's ring. Bertram, hearing from his mother that his wife is dead, returns home. While the King is visiting the old Countess, the widow, Diana, and Helena appear, and prove that Bertram's conditions have been fulfilled. Abashed by Helena's loyalty, Bertram declares that he will love her forever.

MACBETH

(1605–1606) Based on Holinshed's *Chronicles*. A few passages in the play (III, v; IV, 1, 39–43, 125–132) dealing with the character of Hecate were probably added later by Middleton. *Macbeth* is conceded to be Shakespeare's greatest poem; no other work in the world contains such poetic riches. The hero of this play might indeed have seemed a terrible villain if Shakespeare had not managed to convince us that Macbeth was essentially a man capable of great goodness. He loses his virtue through the power of ambition, and is hurried from crime to crime in his wearied search for peace of mind. His wife, hardly less magnificent in herself, despite her terrible complicity, never loses her womanliness.

Macbeth and Banquo, brave generals in the service of King Duncan, meet three witches on a heath, who prophesy that Macbeth will be King, and that Banquo's sons will be king thereafter. The King, as reward for Macbeth's services, elevates Macbeth to the Thanedom of Cawdor. Lady Macbeth, hearing of her husband's good fortune and what has been promised by the witches, is fired with ambition for Macbeth and goads him to undertake the murder of Duncan. There is a deep love between Macbeth and his wife—too deep to need expression. But their characters are different. Her desire to see her husband elevated in life is so intense that she steels herself against every womanly impulse of tenderness, and imagines that she has the fortitude to take the consequences of Duncan's murder. Macbeth, however, who possesses a powerful imagination, foresees the penalties of having to live with oneself after such a crime. Not understanding his imagination, Lady Macbeth thinks her husband too weak, and feverishly spurs him on to what she considers a needful task.

Duncan visits Macbeth's castle, and in his sleep is murdered by Macbeth. Lady Macbeth, overwhelmed by her husband's inability to carry out the whole of their plan, herself enters the King's apartments and smears the drunken grooms with Duncan's blood. The murder is discovered the next morning, and Macbeth kills the grooms under the pretense that his passion over the deed spurred him to the act. In fear for their lives, the King's sons, Malcom and Donalbain, flee the country. Macbeth is crowned King. Certain that Banquo suspects him, Macbeth arranges to have him and his son waylaid by murderers while he is pretending to give a banquet in Banquo's honor. Banquo is slain but his son escapes. At the banquet, Macbeth deplores Banquo's absence; Banquo's ghost appears and causes Macbeth to quake with terror. The Queen dismisses the company with the excuse that her husband is ill.

Macbeth seeks out the witches again to learn his future. They show him a series of apparitions that warn him to beware of Macduff, a powerful lord; to fear no harm from anyone born of woman; and to expect to be safe until Birnam Wood moves to Dunsinane. Macduff has gone to England to offer his services to Malcolm; in his absence Macbeth has ordered Macduff's wife and children to be slaughtered.

Lady Macbeth, no longer partner to her husband's plans, is sinking rapidly under the heavy weight of conscience. She is aware that dreadful crimes are being committed by Macbeth, but is too sick at heart even to desire to know what they are. After Duncan's murder she has been in a state of collapse. The punishment of her own thoughts, which she had not been able to expect in advance, gradually breaks her. Macbeth, who had understood the consequences from the beginning, is better able to live with his conscience. Lady Macbeth's breakdown becomes fully evident when we watch her walking in her sleep, going through the motions of trying to wash her hands of imaginary blood, and reliving the dreadful moment of Duncan's murder.

The English forces arrive at Birnam Wood, and conceal their numbers behind trees they carry before them. Birnam Wood is moving to Dunsinane. Macbeth learns that his Queen has committed suicide; he is determined to put up a brave fight, no matter what the consequence. As the invaders storm his castle, he fights well until he is face to face with Macduff. Macduff informs him before they fight that he was not born of woman but ripped prematurely from his mother's womb. Macduff kills Macbeth and cuts off his head. Malcolm is crowned King.

Among the many magnificent lines in the play are:

> Nothing in his life
> Became him like the leaving it . . .

> There's no art
> To find the mind's construction in the face

> Look like the innocent flower
> But be the serpent under it.

> And pity, like a naked new-born babe,
> Striding the blast, or heaven's cherubim, horsed
> Upon the sightless couriers of the air.
> Shall blow the horrid deed in every eye,
> That tears shall drown the wind. I have no spur
> To prick the sides of my intent, but only
> Vaulting ambition, which o'erleaps itself
> And falls on the other

> Tomorrow, and tomorrow, and tomorrow,
> Creeps in this petty pace, from day to day,
> To the last syllable of recorded time;
> And all our yesterdays have lighted fools
> The way to dusty death. Out, out, brief candle!
> Life's but a walking shadow, a poor player
> That struts and frets his hour upon the stage
> And then is heard no more: it is a tale
> Told by an idiot, full of sound and fury,
> Signifying nothing

TIMON OF ATHENS

(1607–1608) Based on Plutarch's *Life of Antony* and Lucian's *Timon the Misanthrope*. Only parts of this play are by Shakespeare. Although the play is not a success, there are some wonderful passages. The story deals with Timon, who while wealthy is a lavish entertainer of his friends, a generous master, a liberal patron. Too late he discovers that he has spent more than he owned. He tries to borrow without success. All his friends desert him. A realist at last, Timon invites all his former parasites to a last banquet. When they appear, they are served dishes of warm water, which he throws in their faces. He drives them from his home. Cursing mankind, Timon exiles himself in a cave near the sea, where he lives on roots. He comes upon a buried treasure. But he dies alone and neglected in his cave.

ANTONY AND CLEOPATRA

(1606–1607) Based on North's translation of Plutarch. This magnificent play contains in it the most masterful portrait of the "eternal feminine" that ever Shakespeare drew, Cleopatra. It luxuriates in color and liquid music, but the vast number of its scenes makes it difficult to produce. The Mark Antony of this play, though in history he was the same man, has nothing to do with the character of the same name in *Julius Caesar*. Here he is a great soul, a man of magnanimity, one of the pillars of the world. When the play opens he is living at Alexandria, lapped in the luxuries of the ever-resourceful Queen. News comes of the death of his wife Fulvia, and of the rebellion of young Pompey, who threatens to avenge his father. Feeling he must go to Rome to assume his part in the management of the world, Antony takes leave of Cleopatra. After mutual recrimination at Rome, Antony and young Octavius agree to bury their differences in the marriage of Octavia, his sister, to Antony. Because of Antony's interest, Pompey comes to terms.

But Antony longs for Cleopatra. In Egypt the news of his marriage so enrages the Queen that she almost murders the messenger. Before long the rivalry between Octavius and Antony is renewed. Octavius takes the first step by resuming the war against Pompey and making a prisoner of Lepidus, the third member of the Triumvirate. Octavia goes to Rome to beseech her brother not to anger her husband. But hearing that Antony has returned to Egypt, Octavius convinces himself and his sister that Antony has abandoned her.

Octavius begins to war against Antony. Accepting Octavius' dare, Antony determines to fight by sea instead of by land where his superiority would be beyond question. Cleopatra heads her fleet to join Antony's at Actium. Suddenly, when the fight is going best, for no apparent reason, Cleopatra hoists her sails and flies. Antony follows her. He has thus lost his equal footing with Octavius. He sends his schoolmaster to negotiate with Octavius, asking permission to live in Egypt. Octavius denies this request but promises Cleopatra the right to retain her crown if she will put Antony to death. Antony, forgetting the politician he is dealing with, challenges him to personal combat. Octavius sends an envoy to wean Cleopatra from Antony by lavish promises; Antony has the envoy whipped. Octavius naturally spurns the offer of a duel as Antony's followers begin to desert him. Even his most trusted friend, Enobarbus, deserts Antony; realizing he is in his decline, Antony does not blame Enobarbus, but sends his former friend's treasure after him. Enobarbus, overwhelmed at his master's generosity, dies of a broken heart.

The battle opens, and at first Antony is victorious on land. But once more Cleopatra's flight turns everything to defeat. Antony is now convinced that she is in league with Octavius, and determines to kill her. The Queen, in terror, takes refuge in her monument and sends word that she has committed suicide because he no longer loves her. This feminine trick is taken for reality by Antony, and, in despair, he begs his faithful follower, Eros, to kill him. Eros prefers suicide to such an act. Antony runs upon his own sword. Too late, Cleopatra sends word that she is alive. Antony is taken to her; they make their peace and he dies in her arms. Octavius hears of Antony's death and fears that Cleopatra may follow her lover's example and thus cheat Octavius of complete triumph. Determined not to serve Octavius' ends, Cleopatra puts on her most queenly robes and applies a deadly asp to her bosom, and dies. Her devoted servants, Charmian and Iras, die with her. Among the many wonderful passages in this play is Enobarbus' rapturous description of Cleopatra:

> Age cannot wither her, nor custom stale
> Her infinite variety. Other women cloy
> The appetites they feed, but she makes hungry
> Where most she satisfies, for vilest things
> Become themselves in her

CORIOLANUS

(1607–1608) Based on North's translation of Plutarch. Shakespeare follows North more closely than usual. Though not as well known to the general public as it deserves to be, this, Shakespeare's last tragedy, is a very noble and somewhat austere masterpiece. Shakespeare is nowhere more superb in his characterizations than in those of the proud, impractical patriot and fearless hero, Coriolanus; the talkative, worldly-wise, and mellowed old Menenius; the aristocratic, Juno-like Volumnia, Coriolanus' mother, a true Roman matron; and the unscrupulous demagogues, Sicinius and Junius, tribunes of the people. Because of a famine in Rome the citizens rebel; Menenius tries to reason with the mob, but Coriolanus spurns it with contempt. Suddenly news comes of a threat from the army of the Volsces under the leadership of Aufidius. At the siege of Corioli, the Romans are losing until Coriolanus (up to this time known as Caius Marcius), infuriated with the cowardice of his troops, follows the fleeing Volsces into their city. His heroic example shames the Romans into taking the city. They crown him with a garland and give him the title of Coriolanus; but he loathes their praise and refuses any of the spoils. On his return to Rome the Senate nominates him to the office of Consul. Unwillingly, he accepts the convention of standing in the forum to ask the votes of the citizens. Miraculously, despite his open contempt for them, he wins the support of the citizens.

Once he is off the scene, however, the tribunes of the people convince them that Coriolanus is a menace to their liberties. The citizens determine that he shall not take office after all. When Coriolanus is confronted with their change of mind, he throws discretion to the winds and insults them. The tribunes take advantage of his rash temper and bait him. Before he is through, they are demanding his death. His friends and his mother fear for his safety, and convince him that he must make amends by being humble before the populace in the Forum. The vicious accusations of the tribunes, however, prove too much for him. As a result of his tactless fury, he is banished. He takes leave of his family and friends, and, his heart filled with a desire for revenge against ungrateful Rome, he goes to Antium to offer his services to Aufidius. Aufidius is only too glad to have Coriolanus' aid, and they march upon Rome, but the former resents Coriolanus' pride and vows to be quits with him when the time comes. At the gates of Rome, Menenius comes to plead with Coriolanus to save the city, but Coriolanus refuses to speak with him. It is his mother who at last softens his heart. In Aufidius' presence, Coriolanus decides to spare Rome, and withdraws his troops. Aufidius now declares Coriolanus a traitor, and hires assassins to put an end to his old rival. Coriolanus is stabbed by them.

PERICLES, PRINCE OF TYRE

(1608–1609) Based upon Lawrence Twine's romance *The Pattern of Painful Adventures,* which was an adaptation of a story in Gower's *Confessio Amantis.* Though there is some good poetry in the play, not much of the drama is by Shakespeare. He seems to have touched up an older play that was none too good to begin with. His hand may be seen in the parts relating to the birth and the recovery of Marina.

10
SHAKESPEARE'S PERIOD OF DRAMATIC ROMANCES

CYMBELINE

(1609–1610) Based upon a story in Boccaccio's *Decameron* with historical material taken from Holinshed's *Chronicles*. This play is transitional between the tragedies and the last comedies. The work opens with the darkness and threat of disaster common to some of the tragedies, but ends in sweetness and peace like the dramatic romances. These dramatic romances are all tragicomedies. And *Cymbeline, The Winter's Tale,* and *The Tempest,* which form the group, have certain traits in common. They all deal with the separation and eventual reunion of families; they show just people unfairly wronged, finally justified, and forgiving their persecutors; the plays contain elements of suspense and surprise, not common to Shakespeare's work before this; and, as might be expected, they show Shakespeare's characterization at its profoundest and mellowest. The character of Imogen in *Cymbeline* is almost an idealization of the perfect wife; but she is too warm, too human to be thought of as an abstraction. The play, too, is filled with inspired poetry throughout. Some critics object to the multiplicity of events in this play and it is true that there are too many to make the play successful on the stage. *Antony and Cleopatra* has more scenes, but the story of that play is not diffuse. In *Cymbeline* something new seems to be happening all the time.

Imogen has married a poor gentleman, Posthumus, without the consent of her father, Cymbeline, king of Britain. He had expected her to wed Cloten, a clownish son of his second wife's former marriage. The King banishes Posthumus. As he parts from Imogen, Posthumus gives her a bracelet as a token, and she gives him a diamond ring. Posthumus goes to Rome as the guest of Philario. There he meets the Italian Iachimo, who sneers at the idea of a virtuous woman. Before he knows it Posthumus is wagering Iachimo ten thousand ducats against Imogen's diamond ring that Imogen is incorruptible. Iachimo, armed with a letter of introduction from Posthumus, goes to Britain to attempt Imogen's chastity. Finding that flattery makes no impression upon her, Iachimo pretends that Posthumus is leading a riotous life in Rome, and suggests she revenge herself by accepting him as her lover. She scorns his story and his protestations. He now pretends that he was only testing her and that he is delighted with her constancy. She is overjoyed to hear that her husband is faithful, and willingly offers to hold a treasure chest for Iachimo in her room for the night. Iachimo hides in the chest, which is carried into Imogen's room, comes out of it when she is asleep, makes notes of the room's decorations and her particularly personal physical traits, steals the bracelet, and creeps back into the chest. In the meantime, Cloten's mother, a crafty, devilish woman, has been experimenting with poisons; her physician, fearing her purposes, gives her a drug that induces a coma, pretending the drug is lethal. The Queen gives the drug to Pisanio, the trusted servant of Posthumus, as though it were a gift of health-giving qualities.

Iachimo, back in Italy, easily convinces Posthumus that Imogen has been unfaithful. In Britain, Cloten continues his objectionable overtures to Imogen; in disgust she assures him that any garment of Posthumus' would be dearer to her than all of Cloten himself.

Lucius, the Roman ambassador, arrives in Britain for the tribute due Augustus Caesar. Spurred on to revolt by his Queen, Cymbeline refuses the tribute. The Romans begin war against the Britains. In the meantime, Posthumus has written to Pisanio ordering him to kill Imogen because she has been faithless; to aid Pisanio he has also written to her, feigning he is in Britain, and asking her to join him at Milford Haven. Pisanio, convinced of her innocence, urges Imogen to adopt the disguise of a boy, and aids her escape from court. He gives her as a parting gift the vial containing the Queen's draught, which he has been told is a restorative. Imogen, lost on the mountains of Wales, finds refuge in a cave. In this cave a nobleman unjustly banished by Cymbeline twenty years before, Belarius, lives with two boys, who do not know themselves to be sons of Cymbeline. (Belarius had taken them with him on his banishment as revenge against the King.) The young men, Arviragus and Guiderius, who are actually Imogen's brothers, feel drawn to her in her disguise as the page Fidele. They plead with Fidele to live with them. Imogen's flight being discovered at court, Pisanio encourages Cloten on a false scent by showing him Posthumus' letter to Imogen. Remembering Imogen's scornful declaration, Cloten dresses himself in Pisanio's clothes, purposing to kill Posthumus and rape Imogen.

Cloten comes upon Belarius. Guidarius, taking a violent dislike to Cloten, fights him, kills him and cuts off his head. Imogen, despairing of her position, takes the Queen's draught. The brothers come upon her, apparently dead, and sorrow over Fidele's body. They carry it to the forest and place it beside the headless corpse of Cloten, strewing fresh flowers on her. Here they sing the exquisite dirge:

> Fear no more the heat o' the sun,
> Nor the furious winter's rages;
> Thou thy worldy task hast done,
> Home art gone, and ta'en thy wages.
> Golden lads and girls all must,
> As chimney-sweepers, come to dust

Imogen recovers from her coma, recognizes Posthumus' clothes on the corpse beside her, and faints. The general Lucius happens to be passing by when she comes to, and employs Fidele as a servant. Learning of the war, the two princes are anxious to join in the action. With the Roman armies Iachimo returns, as does Posthumus disguised as a peasant. Imogen's husband is now so grief-stricken at his rash command for Imogen's death, that he seeks death in battle, though unsuccessfully. He is captured by the Britons. In the meantime, the wicked Queen, who has been raging over Cloten's disappearance, confesses her crimes, and dies. Iachimo, Fidele, and the Roman Lucius are all captured and brought before Cymbeline. Fidele begs the King to demand why Iachimo is wearing a certain diamond ring. Iachimo confesses. Posthumus, overwhelmed by grief, reveals himself, and strikes Fidele for trying to comfort him. Pisanio then tells what he knows, Belarius reveals the identity of the princes, and all are reunited. The King makes his peace with Rome and frees all the prisoners. The play contains the beautiful song that later inspired Schubert to write his well-known music for it:

> Hark, hark! the lark at Heaven's gate sings
> And Phoebus 'gins arise

THE WINTER'S TALE

(1610–1611) Based upon Robert Greene's pastoral romance, *Pandosto*. This is one of Shakespeare's most enchanting plays; he never painted a more exquisite girl than Perdita, a nobler woman than Hermione, a more realistic out-spoken woman of righteousness than Paulina, or a more delightful rogue than the ballad-monger Autolycus. On the other hand, Shakespeare never attempted so daring an indifference to the laws of dramatic structure as in this play, when he allows sixteen years to elapse between the third and fourth acts. All that can be said of his boldness is that he manages it well. There is a wonderful feeling of authentic rusticity in the country scenes; and the last scene, in which a statue comes to life, is one of his most engaging ideas.

Leontes, King of Sicily, and Polixenes, King of Bohemia (which in this play is on a seacoast), have been close friends since childhood. Polixenes has been visiting with his friend and is entreated unsuccessfully by Leontes to remain longer. Leontes asks his wife Hermione to plead for him. She succeeds, and Leontes suddenly becomes curiously jealous. Before long he is convinced that his wife and Polixenes are lovers. He orders Camillo, his trusted counselor, to poison Polixenes. Camillo, certain that the Queen and Polixenes are innocent, warns Polixenes of his danger, and flees with him to Bohemia. This flight is taken by Leontes as proof that his suspicions are justified. He denounces Hermione for adultery, takes away their young son Mamillius, and imprisons her even though she is about to bear another child. Hermione conducts herself with great dignity, though unable to convince her husband of her innocence. A daughter is born to the Queen in prison. Hoping to soften the King's heart, Paulina, the Queen's waiting woman, takes the little princess to him. He declares the child not to be his. Paulina courageously upbraids him. Angered the more, the King orders Paulina's husband to abandon the infant in some deserted place. Hermione is brought to trial, quietly asserts her innocence and the innocence of Polixenes, and leaves her fate to the oracle of Apollo, to which Leontes has already sent ambassadors to learn the truth. The oracle exonerates Hermione, Polixenes, and Camillo, declares Leontes to be a tyrant, and warns him that he shall live without an heir "if that which is lost be not found." Even this heavenly admonition is unprevailing; the trial continues. But the news that little Mamillius has died of grief because of separation from his mother brings the King to his senses. Hermione swoons, is carried out, and reported dead. Now Leontes is full of bitterness at his folly when it seems too late. In the meantime, Paulina's husband has left the baby on the abandoned coast of Bohemia. A shepherd finds the child. Paulina's husband is attacked by a bear, and so the King does not learn the fate of his daughter.

Sixteen years elapse. Florizel, Polixenes' son, has been seen very often at the home of a shepherd because of the shepherd's beautiful daughter, Perdita. Polixenes and the now elderly Camillo play the detective; disguised, they attend a sheep-shearing festival, are taken with Perdita, and listen to the merry-making of the rogue Autolycus. But when the prince is about to become engaged to Perdita, the King makes himself known, threatening everyone present for his son's attempt to marry a low-born girl. Florizel, however, will not give Perdita up, and is determined to elope with her. They find sympathy in old Camillo, who, in offering to accompany them to Sicily, sees an opportunity of returning to his native land again. Perdita's "father," to secure his own position, decides to reveal to the King that Perdita is not really his daughter. En route to the King's palace with Perdita's baby clothes, he meets Autolycus, who is now an ally of the prince, and is taken on the ship with the lovers to Camillo's homeland. The prince and Perdita are welcomed by Leontes. But Polixenes and Camillo soon appear. The two Kings make up their misunderstanding, Camillo is greeted by Leontes, and the old shepherd makes it clear that Perdita is Leontes' lost daughter. Only the loss of Hermione prevents Leontes' giving way to complete joy. Paulina now offers to show them all a life-like statue of the Queen in her home. They go to view it, are amazed at its perfection, and while music is played see it turn into a flesh-and-blood Hermione. The Queen has secretly been housed by Paulina all these years. Thus, all that has been lost is found, and the play ends in general happiness.

THE TEMPEST

(1611–1612) Based on contemporary accounts of ocean voyages for some details of the Bermudas. The plot of this play seems to be Shakespeare's own invention. If so, it was only in one of his earliest (*Love's Labour's Lost*) and in his last comedy that he troubled to invent his own plot. It is almost irresistible to interpret this play as Shakespeare's conscious farewell to the theatre. Through Prospero he seems at last to be speaking to us, though there are many scholars who would sneer at such an idea. But like Prospero he had been banished from his own kingdom (Stratford); like him he had made himself master of no mean magic in his new abode (the London theater), where he was lord of all the spirits there; and like Prospero he was prepared to abandon all the wonders of his magic art and return home. No play of Shakespeare's has such quiet mellow depths as this one. Brief though it is, it is so condensed in expression that it is likely to take longer to read than other of his more lengthy plays. The portrait of the gruff-mannered, tender-hearted, and all-forgiving Prospero is incomparable; Ariel, the delicate spirit who serves Prospero, seems to be woven out of the colors of the atmosphere; but nothing is more amazing than the conception of Caliban, the freckled whelp, barbarous and inhuman as only a savage can be, yet far superior to the scum of civilized life. In the second scene of this play, Shakespeare, perhaps deliberately, breaks one of the most solemn rules of dramatic composition: he has Prospero relate at considerable length all the facts that precede the opening of the play. It is as though he delighted to show that there was nothing impossible to his art.

Prospero and his lovely daughter Miranda inhabit a tropical island, where through the study of magic he has made himself complete master. Twelve years earlier he had been the Duke of Milan. Unknown to him, his brother Antonio had plotted to seize the Dukedom through the help of Alonso, King of Naples. They had hurried Prospero and the infant Miranda into a boat, and set it adrift. Luckily a loyal nobleman, Gonzalo, had provided food, clothes, and Prospero's books of magic. The boat had drifted to the island, where the only inhabitant was Caliban, an ugly, earthy creature, the son of a witch. One other being, the dainty sprite Ariel, was there imprisoned in a tree. Prospero had set Ariel free, and in recompense Ariel had agreed to serve Prospero's wishes for a certain term. Prospero had also tried to civilize Caliban, but all his attempts had been unsuccessful in taming the evil in the monster's nature; Caliban now acted as general porter for the household. His magic informs Prospero that his old enemies are sailing in the neighboring waters. The play opens with a storm at sea, in which the ship is apparently capsized and the passengers compelled to jump overboard for their lives. But with Ariel's help, Prospero has them all safely led to shore, though in different groups. Ferdinand, the courageous and sweet-tempered son of Alonso, follows the invisible Ariel's singing to Prospero's cave. There he and Miranda meet. Miranda, knowing no other man than her father, decides that Ferdinand is the most beautiful creature in the world. The young people fall in love. Prospero, however, will not have their course of love run too smoothly lest Miranda be not sufficiently prized, pretends hostility to Ferdinand, and overpowers the prince with his magic.

Alonso, Antonio, Gonzalo, and Alonso's treacherous brother Sebastian have landed elsewhere on the island, feeling certain that Ferdinand is dead.

While the rest are put to sleep by Ariel's music, Sebastian and Antonio plot Alonso's death. They are about to carry out their scheme when Ariel wakens the others in time. In another part of the island Trinculo, the King's cowardly jester; Stephano, a drunken butler; and Caliban meet. Stephano gives Caliban some of the liquor, and the monster is so entranced with its effects that of his own accord he offers himself as Stephano's slave. Caliban now urges the two drunkards to murder Prospero and seize control of the island. Stephano is only too willing to be king when he learns of Miranda, who is to be his queen. Ariel, overhearing this absurd plot, informs Prospero. In the meantime the love between Miranda and Ferdinand is progressing rapidly, just as Prospero would have it. Prospero employs Ariel to punish Alonso's party with a lavish banquet that vanishes just as the famished men sit down to eat it. They are rebuked for their crimes against Prospero.

Prospero, convinced that Ferdinand will make a satisfactory husband, gives his consent to the lovers, and for their entertainment presents a masque enacted by spirits. Before the masque is quite over, the time has arrived for dealing with Caliban's plot. Ariel is commissioned to hang some vulgar tinseled clothes on a line; the sight of these delays the drunken conspiracy. Then the spirits, in the shape of dogs, drive the three about the island in terror.

Under the spell of Ariel's music, Alonso's party is brought to Prospero's cell. Prospero, now dressed as the Duke of Milan, demands his Dukedom back, and reveals Sebastian's mischievous intentions. Convinced that Alonso is fully repentant, Prospero shows him his son and Miranda playing chess in the cave. We learn that the King's ship is in perfectly good condition with the sailors aboard. The three other conspirators are led in in a sorry state. Caliban sees the light at last, and will strive to be wiser. Prospero gives up his magic, frees Ariel at last, and prepares for his return to Milan.

While everyone speaks the most masterful kind of poetry (except the drunkards), some of the most beautiful lines are allotted to Caliban; in them we are conscious of how his brutish mind is touched by the beauties of nature, as for instance:

> *The isle is full of noises,*
> *Sounds and sweet airs, that give delight and hurt not.*
> *Sometimes a thousand twangling instruments*
> *Will hum about mine ears, and sometimes voices*
> *That, if I then had wak'd after long sleep,*
> *Will make me sleep again; and then in dreaming,*
> *The clouds methought would open and show riches*
> *Ready to drop upon me, that, when I wak'd,*
> *I cried to dream again.*

No passage in Shakespeare has been more often quoted than Prospero's:

> *We are such stuff*
> *As dreams are made on, and our little life*
> *Is rounded with a sleep*

The Tempest also contains two of his most exquisite songs, both sung by Ariel:

> *Come unto these yellow sands,*
> *And then take hands.*
> *Curtsied when you have, and kissed*
> *The wild waves whist,*
> *Foot it featly here and there*

and,

> *Full fathom five thy father lies;*
> *Of his bones are coral made;*
> *Those are pearls that were his eyes:*
> *Nothing of him that doth fade*
> *But doth suffer a sea-change*
> *Into something rich and strange*

COLLABORATIONS

Henry VIII (1612–1613) Always included among Shakespeare's plays. Actually it is a collaboration, probably with Fletcher, a leading dramatist of the day; a few scenes are unmistakably Shakespeare's. Based upon Holinshed's *Chronicles,* this history deals with Henry's break with his first wife, Katherine of Arragon, when he falls in love with Anne Bullen, a maid of honor, and with the machinations and fall of Cardinal Wolsey.

The Two Noble Kinsmen (1613), although not included among Shakespeare's works in popular editions, is now thought also to be partly by him. It is a tragicomedy, written in collaboration with Fletcher, and is based upon Chaucer's *Knight's Tale*. It has genuine poetic excellence, but could not be considered a great play.

IMPORTANCE

Shakespeare has never been equaled as a poet, and it may be questioned whether he has ever been equaled as a dramatist. He must have been a man of the vastest interests. Although not elaborate, his vocabulary is the largest in English and drawn from every department of human experience—not only from transactions of everyday living, but from music, sports, the law, business, farming, popular superstition, and numberless other realms as well. No man has ever been a subtler understander of the workings of the human heart, and no one has had so unflagging an interest in the complicated relationships of men and women. He is perhaps the most perfect example of an objective artist. Though his works reveal nothing of his own character, they show us, timelessly, the world. It is a fact that simple, uneducated people in all lands read him and love him with no less enthusiasm than the most cultivated.

11
OTHER ELIZABETHAN DRAMATISTS

Shakespeare's genius had led the English drama from its infancy to full maturity. The plays written before he began his career are more or less inept; his contemporaries and successors wrote plays some of which would be hard to equal for quality and imagination. Even without his plays, the Elizabethan drama is perhaps the most impressive period in the history of the theater. The outstanding dramatists were Ben Jonson, John Fletcher, Francis Beaumont, Thomas Heywood, Philip Massinger, Thomas Dekker, George Chapman, Thomas Middleton, John Marston, Cyril Tourneur, John Webster, John Ford, and James Shirley.

BEN JONSON (1573–1637)

Ben Jonson, one of the most interesting personalities of his day, was born into poverty, for a while was a bricklayer, managed to study at Cambridge, made an unfortunate marriage, fought with the army in Flanders, and around 1597 took up the profession of playwright in London. Within a few years, the new king, James I, became interested in Jonson's work, and gave him the post of providing entertainment for the Court. Jonson's powerful character impressed itself upon many of the younger men; his abilities and enthusiastic scholarship won him many disciples, among whom he was practically the literary dictator. He was a belligerent advocate of the Latin classics, and scorned the romantic tastes of his time. He first became famous with two comedies, *Every Man In His Humor* (1598) and *Every Man Out of His Humor* (1599). In these plays Jonson introduced the so-called *"comedy of humors,"* that is, comedy revealing not a rounded character, but equipping each person of the drama with one predominant trait (the Braggart, the Spendthrift, the Parasite, and so on). The result is really caricature rather than characterization. Perhaps the chief value of Jonson's comedies is their realism. Jonson persisted in painting contemporary London as he saw it with a satirical eye. He was thus actually following in the traditions of Plautus and Terence, who had done the same for Rome of their day. Besides the two comedies mentioned, Jonson's *Volpone, or the Fox* (1606), *Epicoene, or the Silent Woman* (1609), *The Alchemist* (1610), and *Bartholomew Fair* (1614) are important.

Major Plays

Every Man in His Humor: Presents a jealous man (Kitely), a country simpleton (Stephen), a town simpleton (Matthew), an irate father (Knowell), a wayward son (Edward), a knavish plotter of intrigue (Brainworm), and a braggart-warrior (Captain Bobadil). The main interest revolves about a clandestine marriage, mistaken identity, and the exhibition of the "humor" of each character.

Volpone, or the Fox: One of Jonson's best plays. Its satire is leveled at all kinds of human beings. Its dialogue is lively and ironically conceived, and its tone powerful though bitter. Volpone employs his servant Mosca to circulate the rumour that he is near death. His purpose is to encourage a collection of rascals each to believe that he will be his heir. They outdo each other in bestowing lavish gifts and inheritances upon Volpone, each desiring to prove his affection greatest for the "dying" man. He fleeces the corrupt lawyer Voltore, the miser Corbaccio (who even disinherits his son to impress Volpone), and the dishonorable merchant Corvino (who goes so far as to bring his wife to Volpone's bed). In the end judgment is visited upon Volpone and Mosca.

Epicoene, or the Silent Woman: One of Jonson's cleverest plays. A miser (Morose) has a passionate hatred of noise. For this reason he willingly engages to marry a silent woman, who is actually a boy in disguise. This little trick has been arranged by Morose's nephew, Sir Dauphine. After the nuptials, the boy begins at once to become a noisy chatterbox. Nor is he silenced until Morose agrees to allow his nephew an income and a large inheritance.

The Alchemist: This contains some of Jonson's best portraits and is a brilliantly constructed play. A quack (Subtle) and his wife (Common) conspire with others to force Sir Epicure Mammon into financing the discovery of the philosopher's stone and the elixir of life. Involved in the conspiracy are Captain Face, Drugger, and Dapper. The unexpected return of Lovewit, the master of the house, to town puts an end to the deception.

Bartholomew Fair: This farce is sometimes bawdy but often realistic. Bartholomew Fair is the occasion for the undoing of all who come to it: Cokes (a squire), Wasp (his servant), Busy (a puritan), and Overdo (a Justice of the Peace). There are also vivid portraits of a pickpocket, a prostitute, and other representatives of London low life.

Minor Works

Jonson is also the author of two tragedies, *Sejanus* (1603) and *Catiline* (1611), both Roman plays written on the model of Seneca. They are too pompous to be of interest to us. But the masques and court entertainments that Jonson wrote after 1603 contain some of his best work; there are many of them, the most admired being *The Hue and Cry After Cupid* (1608). The *masque* is a little drama, its story taken from mythology, often employed for allegorical complimentary purposes, and its plot rarely more than an excuse for singing, dancing, music, and scenic effects.

Jonson, a prodigious worker, is also the author of an English grammar, a volume of epigrams, a collection of stray thoughts (which he entitled *Timber*), and two volumes of verse. None of his works is more often referred to than his poem *"To The Memory of My Beloved Master, William Shakespeare"* written for the First Folio edition of Shakespeare's plays. It is full of now-famous phrases:

> *Soul of the age!*
> *The applause delight, the wonder of our stage*
>
> *Thou art a monument without a tomb*
>
> *...thou hadst small Latin and less Greek*
>
> *He was not of an age, but for all time!*
>
> *...though the poet's matter nature be,*
> *His art doth give the fashion*
>
> *For a good poet's made, as well as born*
>
> *Sweet swan of Avon!*

FRANCIS BEAUMONT (1584–1616) AND JOHN FLETCHER (1579–1624)

Francis Beaumont and John Fletcher wrote most of their best works in collaboration. Beaumont died at the age of thirty-two, and Fletcher collaborated with many other writers. Together their output includes some fifty-two plays, and some poems. Beaumont was the greater master of tragic effect, was a better craftsman, and wrote a more direct verse; Fletcher's gifts were largely lyrical and fanciful. Their plays attain a high level of excellence, but compared to Shakespeare's tend toward the melodramatic rather than the tragic. Their best tragedies are *The Maid's Tragedy* (around 1611) and *A King and No King* (1611); *The Knight of the Burning Pestle* (around 1608) is their best comedy; and *Philaster, or Love Lies A-Bleeding* (around 1611) is their best tragicomedy.

The Maid's Tragedy contains some of the most dramatic writing of the age. In reward for his services to the Crown, the King marries Amintor to the most desirable lady of his Court, Evadne. In order to make this advantageous match, Amintor breaks his engagement to the lovely Aspatia. After the ceremony, when they are alone, Evadne discloses to Amintor that she will never sleep with him, that she is the King's mistress, and that the King has arranged the marriage so that her children may have a father. Unable to avenge himself on the King because of the "divine right of kings," Amintor reveals his sorrow to Evadne's brother, Melantius. Melantius forces Evadne to slay the King. Amintor refuses to condone her act, and she commits suicide. Aspatia, who cannot live without Amintor, disguises herself as a youth, and arranges to have herself slain by Amintor's own hand.

The Knight of the Burning Pestle is particularly interesting to us for the lively picture it affords of an Elizabethan audience at the playhouse. It contains some delightful burlesques on military heroism as exemplified in the exploits of Ralph, the Grocer-Knight, whose chivalric device is the pestle. The main plot deals with the success of a lover in winning his girl over parental opposition. There are forty songs strewn throughout the play.

Among the plays that Fletcher wrote alone should be mentioned *The Faithful Shepherdess* (around 1609), a pastoral tragicomedy with some fine poetic writing, and *The Wild Goose Chase* (1621), a very clever romantic comedy. Fletcher also, as has been mentioned, collaborated with Shakespeare on *The Two Noble Kinsmen* and *Henry VIII*.

THOMAS HEYWOOD (c. 1575–1641)

Thomas Heywood was one of the most original of Elizabethan dramatists. He is the author of *A Woman Killed With Kindness* (1603), one of the most moving tragedies of the period, and probably the first real example of "domestic tragedy" in English. (This is a type of drama that was to become extremely popular in the eighteenth century, and culminated in Europe in the dramas of Ibsen.) Heywood's play is written with great sincerity, compassion, and quiet strength. It tells the story of the adultery of Anne Frankford with Wendoll, he husband's best friend, to whom he has been generous in the extreme. Her sin was due less to viciousness than to weakness of will. Her husband, Frankford, is a man of great personal nobility. His revenge is to treat her with every consideration, though separating himself from her. He removes her to another house, where she eventually dies of a broken heart. On her deathbed he forgives her.

PHILIP MASSINGER (1583–1640)

Philip Massinger is the author of some fifteen original plays and of many others in collaboration with fellow dramatists. There is not much poetry in his verse, but he is a master of satire and of a natural directness of language. His best play is *A New Way to Pay Old Debts* (around 1625), a brilliantly contrived satirical comedy. Wellborn, a spendthrift, induces a wealthy widow, Lady Allworth, to create the impression that they are to marry. His purpose is to impress his uncle, Sir Giles Overreach, that Wellborn has a wealthy future. Overreach, who intends to get his hands on the widow's holdings, wipes out his nephew's debts as a kind of investment for himself. Actually Lady Allworth is in love with Lord Lovell, whom she eventually marries. The old rascal is therefore not only deprived of his miserly hopes, but also foiled in his attempts to prevent his daughter Margaret from marrying the man she loves.

THOMAS DEKKER (c. 1572–1632)

Thomas Dekker, one of the most industrious of the Elizabethans, must have had a particularly happy nature. There is an air of light-heartedness and a strong sense of the "common touch" throughout his work. His most important comedies are *The Shoemaker's Holiday* (1600) and *Old Fortunatus* (1599); *The Honest Whore* (1604) is his most striking drama, realistic in its depiction of domestic catastrophe, and was unquestionably influenced by Shakespeare. He is also the author of many prose works of London life, notably *The Gull's Hornbook*, a piece of good-natured satire at the expense of town fops; *The Belman of London* (1608), a lively tract on the lives and manners of the men of London streets; and *The Wonderful Year* (1603), a vivid picture, diversified by humor, of the plague. *The Shoemaker's Holiday* remains his most popular work; it is a lively comedy whose characters are drawn to the life from London tradesmen. The chief plot is the romantic love of Lacey for Rose, the daughter of the Lord Mayor of London. The Earl of Lincoln, Lacey's father, and the Lord Mayor both object. Lacey thereupon disguises himself as a shoemaker from Holland, and enters the employ of Simon Eyre, master of the trade. At length the lovers elope. The mixture of romanticism and realism is very felicitous in this play.

GEORGE CHAPMAN (C. 1559–1634)

George Chapman will always be remembered because of the fact that his translation of Homer inspired Keats's great sonnet "On Looking Into Chapman's Homer." Chapman was the master of a resounding verse, but his style is marred by many inflations and a certain pedantry. The subjects for his plays were usually drawn from French history. His best-known tragedies are *Bussy D'Ambois* (1607) and *The Revenge of Bussy D'Ambois* (1613), the latter quite inferior to the first. He is also the author of a good comedy, *All Fools* (1605), and a tragicomedy, *The Gentleman Usher* (1606). The most frequently mentioned play with which Chapman is associated, however, is a comedy written in collaboration with Marston and Jonson, *Eastward Ho!* (1605). This play offended King James so much because of its satire on the Scots that Chapman and Marston were thrown into prison for a while, where, out of principle, Jonson soon voluntarily joined them.

THOMAS MIDDLETON (1580–1627)

Thomas Middleton was a writer of no considerable poetical ability, whose plays are not profoundly touching, but who was skillful in plotting a play and was a master of spirited dialogue. He was a prolific writer. His best comedies are *A Trick to Catch the Old One* (1608), *The Roaring Girl* (1611), *A Chaste Maid in Cheapside* (1612)—all amusing and realistic—and a tragi-comedy, *The Witch* (c. 1615). His best work, however, is in the field of tragedy, particularly in *Women Beware Women* (c. 1612), and the powerful blood-and-thunder *The Changeling* (1624) written in collaboration with Rowley.

JOHN MARSTON (c. 1575–1634)

John Marston was a writer of a violent cynical turn who collaborated with a number of his contemporaries, and whose coarse but powerful satire *The Metamorphosis of Pygmalion's Image* (1598) was ordered burned. His plays *The History of Antonio and Mellida* (1599), in two parts, and *The Malcontent* (1604) show markedly the influence of Kyd's blood-and-thunder tragedy. *The Malcontent* has often been compared to *Hamlet* because of the central character.

CYRIL TOURNEUR (c. 1584–1626)

Cyril Tourneur is remembered for two remarkable plays—*The Atheist's Tragedy* (before 1607) and *The Revenger's Tragedy* (before 1611), both in the blood-and-thunder school. *The Atheist's Tragedy*, though curiously inept in plot, exhibits a great nobility of style. *The Revenger's Tragedy*, which must have had considerable influence on Webster, is a much superior play, and parts of it are as fine and elevated as anything in English drama. Though an uneven writer, at his best moments Tourneur was an inspired genius, and it is as a poet that he will always be most admired.

JOHN WEBSTER (c. 1580–c. 1625)

John Webster is by common consent considered the greatest Elizabethan dramatist after Shakespeare by reason of two plays—*The White Devil, or Vittoria Corombona* (before 1611), and *The Duchess of Malfi* (before 1613), both tragedies of blood. Webster was without a peer in depicting the dark, richly vibrant atmosphere of the late Italian Renaissance, and its world of lust, crime, and cruel intrigue. He is a great poet, and the startling quality of his imagery flashes like lightning through the horror and gloom of the plays. His plays have a quality all their own, and are the first that would come to mind if one wished to name anything equal to *Macbeth*.

The White Devil, or Vittoria Corombona: The play is based upon a recent piece of Italian history. Webster's heroine was actually murdered in 1585. The story is of the vengeance of the Duke of Florence for the death of his daughter, who was poisoned by her husband. Before he is through, several others involved meet their death, and Vittoria, named The White Devil for her beauty, is stabbed to death. The dialogue is brilliant throughout; and the trial scene is one of the finest pieces of dramatic writing in our literature. There is also a famous dirge: "Call for the robin redbreast and the wren..."

The Duchess of Malfi: Here is Webster's genius at its most breath-taking. The story tells of the marriage of the Duchess to Antonio, her steward, in secret to avoid the animosity of her brothers, the Cardinal and the Duke. They are anxious to keep their sister unmarried because they look forward to being her heirs. They hire Bosola to spy on her. Bosola discovers the truth, and that the Duchess is about to bear a child to Antonio. The Duke and the Cardinal put their sister through dreadful agonies, and murder her children. Bosola, repenting his role, unintentionally kills Antonio and then murders the Cardinal. The Duke, now demented, kills Bosola and is himself killed. The portraits of the cunning, cruel Cardinal, the violent, tortured Duke, and the noble, patient Duchess are masterful.

JOHN FORD (1586–c. 1639)

John Ford reveals in his work the gradual decaying of the Elizabethan spirit, once so fresh and healthy, and by his time tainted by a hectic intensity, a feverish interest in the less common aspects of human experience. His plays are among the best of the Elizabethan period, because of the subtlety with which he understands the psychology of eroticism, the sweetness and directness of his verse, and his ability to create scenes of intense passion. His best plays are *'Tis a Pity She's a Whore* (1633) and *The Broken Heart* (1633), both tragedies, and his history play *Perkin Warbeck* (1634).

'Tis a Pity She's a Whore: A study of incest, it exhibits Ford's ability to take the most difficult kind of subject and manage it superbly without offense. It is a heartbreaking story of a brother and sister who are thrust almost by circumstances into each other's arms. Then, that their child may have a father, the sister is forced to marry after all. But her husband's servant discovers the sin of which she has been guilty. In order to save her from the punishment that has been planned for her, her brother-lover stabs her himself, kills her husband, and comes to his own death. It is a profoundly moving play.

The Broken Heart: The best contrived of Ford's plays, it has many exquisite lines and wonderfully realized characters. The King's daughter is overwhelmed with catastrophe —the death of her father, her lover, and her friend. In the end, although she has been apparently unmoved by these circumstances, she dies of a broken heart.

Perkin Warbeck: A well-written chronicle history dealing with the unwarranted claim of Warbeck to England's throne, his acts to come nearer his desire, his capture and death. This play is considered inferior of its kind only to Shakespeare's histories.

JAMES SHIRLEY (1596–1666)

James Shirley was the last important Elizabethan dramatist. His entire career, of course, falls in the years when the Stuarts were on the throne. And his work shows quite completely the final enervation of the freshness and imagination of the earlier Elizabethan period. His verse is good, his dialogue easy, his humor pleasant, but nevertheless all of the zest of his great predecessors is missing. When we read him, we can understand how the period was drawing to its close. In 1642 a Puritan Parliament closed the last of the theaters. But it is safe to assume that even without Parliamentary edict the theater could not have been kept alive. The great public that had supported the theater under Elizabeth and James had become under Charles more and more Puritan. And Puritans did not go to the theater. Shirley's comedies include *Hyde Park* (1632) and *The Lady of Pleasure* (1635); his tragedies are *The Maid's Revenge* (1626), *Love's Cruelty* (1631), and *The Cardinal* (1641), the last named being perhaps his best. *The Lady of Pleasure* is interesting as somewhat anticipating Sheridan's *The School For Scandal* of the eighteenth century.

12
ELIZABETHAN NONDRAMATIC POETRY, PROSE, AND TRANSLATIONS

ELIZABETHAN NONDRAMATIC POETRY

It is true that many of the great Elizabethan poets wrote for the stage. And because the age loved song as well as drama, the plays are flooded with the most exquisite songs in our literature. But some of the nondramatic poets wrote songs too. A song requires no heavy burden of meaning, and by definition its first quality must be musical. But there is an undercurrent of good health, kindliness, and zest for living that gives dignity to these songs. Even the most mediocre writers could apparently at that time turn out a good song. Queen Elizabeth herself wrote, not badly for a queen. Miscellanies of lyrics were very popular, and in them have been preserved for us many choice ones. It would be impossible to specify any great number of songs amidst so many treasures. But aside from the songs of Sidney and Spenser, some typical songs may be briefly indicated. There are some that are anonymous, such as "Hey Nonny No!" which asserts: "Men are fools that wish to die!" and a song from *Gammer Gurton's Needle*, "Back and side, go bare, go bare," which lauds the pleasures of good ale. Queen Elizabeth sang with only half earnest melancholy in "When I Was Fair and Young" of the many hearts that she had vanquished in earlier days. Edward Dyer (1543–1607) in "My Mind to Me a Kingdom Is," tells how much better it is to live in moderate circumstances with a clear conscience than to be wealthy and without peace of mind:

> *But all the pleasure that I find*
> *Is to maintain a quiet mind.*

In "Apelles' Song," John Lyly tells how the singer's sweetheart has robbed Cupid of all his beauties, including his eyes, at a card game:

> *O love, has she done this to thee?*
> *What shall, alas! become of me?*

George Peele indited to Queen Elizabeth his "Farewell to Arms":

> *Blessed be the hearts that wish my sovereign well,*
> *Cursed be the souls that think her any wrong.*

In "Sweet Are The Thoughts That Savour of Content," Robert Greene maintains that: "The quiet mind is richer than a crown." Christopher Marlowe's "The Passionate Shepherd to His Love," a pastoral lyric, was very popular in its time; in it the shepherd sings of all the delights of the country that he is prepared to offer his sweetheart if she will come and live with him: "And I will make thee beds of roses..." Sir Walter Ralegh, a friend of Marlowe's, answered it in "The Nymph's Reply to the Shepherd," in which the girl declines because all that the shepherd offers must die or wither; she would live with him if joys and youth could last. One of the loveliest of the songs is Thomas Dekker's "Content," in which once more a humble honest life is much preferred to a wealthy burdened one:

> *Art thou poor, yet hast thou golden slumbers?*
> *O sweet content!*
> *Art thou rich, yet is thy mind perplexed?*
> *O punishment!...*
> *Work apace! apace! apace! apace!*
> *Honest labor bears a lovely face.*

No song of the period has achieved such immortality as Ben Jonson's "To Celia," which he adapted from a piece of ancient Greek prose. One has only to quote its opening lines to identify it:

> *Drink to me only with thine eyes,*
> *And I will pledge with mine*

Another song of Jonson's, "Simplex Munditiis" (In Simple Elegance), is also well-known; in it the poet asks for naturalness and simplicity in his sweetheart's dress:

> *Give me a look, give me a face,*
> *That makes simplicity a grace*

In conclusion, it should be remembered that the plays of Shakespeare as well as those of Webster, Beaumont and Fletcher and their fellows are full of wonderful songs.

Thomas Campion (1567–1620)

One song writer deserves special notice. Thomas Campion wrote exclusively in this form, and was perhaps the subtlest songwriter of the age. His career was varied, for he was a practicing physician, a student of law, and a gifted musical composer. He published four books of *Airs* (1601–1617), in which he supplied the music for his own words. Some of his songs are adaptations from the lyric poets of the ancient world, but they all have the stamp of his own composition. Among the best of the songs are "My Sweetest Lesbia," an invitation to make the most out of this life:

> *But soon as once set is our little light,*
> *Then must we sleep one ever-during night;*

"When Thou Must Home," in which the sweetheart is asked to tell in Hades of all the revels and joys that were indulged for her sake, and:

> *When thou hast told these honors done to thee,*
> *Then tell, o tell, how thou didst murder me;*

"When To Her Lute Corinna Sings," in which the poet tells how his sweetheart can sway all his emotions by her singing; and "Cherry Ripe," in which the poet makes an inventory of the garden that is in his sweetheart's face.

Sonnets

Besides songs, Elizabethan lyrical poetry is notable for a number of *sonnet sequences*, a series of sonnets connected in theme or idea. We have already spoken of Shakespeare's sonnet sequence, and shall presently deal with the sonnet sequences of Sidney and Spenser. But there are others worthy of mention. All through the Renaissance the sonnet had a great vogue. In the thirteenth century Dante and his friends in Italy were writing one another sonnets to do the service of letters; and the great sonnets of Petrarch increased the prestige of the form. In England, after the initial experiments of Wyatt and Surrey, Sidney made the sonnet even more popular. After that, many men, even those who were not professional poets, prided themselves in their abililty to turn out a creditable sonnet on occasion. In addition to Sidney's, Shakespeare's, and Spenser's sequences, however, the two most important sonnet sequences were those of Daniel and Drayton.

Samuel Daniel (1562–1619), known as "the well-languaged," was the author of an ambitious historical poem on the War of the Roses written in *ottava rima* (a stanza of eight iambic pentameter lines, rhyming *ababbcc*); *A Defense of Rime* (1603); sundry other poems; and the sonnet sequence *Delia* (1592). *Delia* contains fifty sonnets, addressed to a lady who is thought to have been the Countess of Pembroke. Many of them are excellent. The most famous is the one beginning, "Care-charmer Sleep, son of the sable Night."

Michael Drayton (1563–1631), a writer of very uneven quality, was one of the busiest of Elizabethan poets. His works include an uninspired religious poem, *The Harmony of the Church* (1591); *England's Heroical Epistles* (1597), a series of letters in verse put over the signature of various historical personages; *Poems Lyrical and Pastoral* (1606), which contains one of his most celebrated poems, "The Battle of Agincourt," with its famous opening line:

> *Fair stood the wind for France*

(a breezy song celebrating a victory of noble King Harry); *Poly-Olbion* (1613–1622), his most ambitious work, celebrating the glories of English history; and the sonnet sequence *Idea* (1593). *Idea* contains fifty-one sonnets addressed in all probability to Anne, the daughter of Drayton's patron, Sir

Henry Goodere. The title *Idea* refers to Plato's conception of ideal beauty. The most famous of these sonnets is the deeply human, "Since there's no help, come let us kiss and part."

Sir Philip Sidney (1554–1586)

Sir Philip Sidney was the brightest star in the firmament that revolved about Elizabeth in her early days as Queen. His life was brief but illustrious. He has remained the type of what was best in the Renaissance gentleman. Scholar, diplomat, poet, courtier, soldier, and gentleman, Sidney was admired for his attainments in all of these pursuits. He was widely traveled, went to Germany as ambassador, then to Holland as Governor of Flushing, and lost his life in an engagement in Flanders. Everyone knows the story of how as he lay wounded on the battlefield, he refused a cup of water so that it could be given to a dying common soldier. Universally admired for his high principles as well as his learning, Sidney was a patron of poetry and a poet himself. It was he who gave the great Spenser his first encouragement.

Sidney's most important works are his *Astrophel and Stella*, a sonnet sequence; the *Arcadia*, a pastoral romance; and the noble *Defence of Poesie*.

Astrophel and Stella: (1591) The first important sonnet sequence in England, it may be held accountable for the subsequent popularity of that form. The sonnets were addressed to Penelope Devereux, Lord Essex's daughter, to whom Sidney had for a brief time been engaged before her marriage to Lord Rich. She is his star (Stella) and he is the star-lover (Astrophel). There are 108 sonnets in the series, uneven in quality, but at times brilliant in image, and profoundly touching in their sincerity. Most of them are in the Petrarchan form. The most famous sonnets of the sequence are the first, where the poet, helpless in finding the right words for his love:

> *Biting my truant pen, beating myself for spite*
> *"Fool," said my Muse to me, "look in thy heart, and write."*

the thirty-first, with its memorable opening line, "With how sad steps, O Moon, thou climb'st the sky"; and the thirty-ninth, whose opening line is: "Come, Sleep! O Sleep, the certain knot of peace..."

The Arcadia: (1590) The first important pastoral in English, it is written in alternate prose and verse and was originally composed to entertain Sidney's sister, the Countess of Pembroke. The *Arcadia* contains many episodes, a highly complicated plot, and a considerable artificiality of style. Its chief importance lies not in itself, but in its introducing the pastoral to English literature. Noteworthy is the fact that Shakespeare took the plot of Gloucester and his sons from it for *King Lear*, and that Beaumont and Fletcher adapted another tale from it for their *Philaster*.

Pastoral poetry owes its history to the writings of Theocritus (3rd century B.C.), a Sicilian Greek poet. In Theocritus the characters of the poems are always shepherds, light-hearted peasants who love to sing and dance. It is even thought by some scholars that Theocritus and his disciples were shepherds themselves, and that the flocks and swains they sang of were a reflection of their actual experience. Among the Greeks who followed in the tradition of Theocritus were Moschus (around 150 B.C.) and Bion (around 100 B.C.). One of the most important of Greek pastoral poems is Bion's *Lament for Moschus*. With the Roman poet Virgil (70–19 B.C.), the pastoral developed certain conventions. Temperamentally Virgil was essentially a man of the city; but out of admiration for Theocritus he wrote a series of pastoral poems, the *Eclogues*. Virgil's pastoral poems are exquisite but artificial. Where Theocritus is fresh and of the countryside, Virgil is "literary." The most important change that took place in the pastoral under Virgil's hand was that he pretended that he himself and his friends (politicians, generals, writers) were shepherds. Under the guise of this graceful artifice, he sometimes discussed contemporary events. All this is foreign to the simplicity of Theocritus. With Virgil the pastoral begins its history as one of the most artificial forms of literary expression. During the Italian Renaissance Virgil's pastorals were imitated, writers called themselves and their friends shepherds, and, in the guise of shepherds, discussed current events. This fashion passed into Spain and France, and through Sidney's *Arcadia* into England. In English pastoral poetry we are forever meeting thereafter shepherds and shepherdesses of exquisite delicacy and refinement placed in pseudo-rustic settings.

***Defence of Poesie*:** (1595) This work was written to answer Stephen Gosson's *School of Abuse* (1579). Gosson had written this savage attack on the theater and poets in general as corrupters of English morality. Without permission he had dedicated his treatise to Sidney, so that the latter felt obliged to answer. Although, like Sidney's other work, it was not published until after his death, the *Defence of Poesie* must have been written soon after Gosson's attack. But the *Defence of Poesie* is more than an answer. Nobly he defends poetry from the charge of being inimical to morality. In his sketch of poetry's noble lineage, he praises Chaucer, admits the shortcomings of (early) Elizabethan drama, and anticipates great things in the future for English literature. No work of Sidney's better exhibits his own gentleness and sweetness as well as his austerity of mind.

Edmund Spenser (1552–1599)

Spenser was the greatest nondramatic poet of the Elizabethan age. He was educated at the Merchant Taylors' School, and went from there to Cambridge, where he received his M.A. in 1576. It was at the University that he became the friend of the celebrated pedant, Gabriel Harvey. Probably it was Harvey who introduced Spenser to Sir Philip Sidney, and to Queen Elizabeth's favorite, the Earl of Leicester. For a while he had a position in Leicester's household. *The Shepherd's Calendar* (1579) was written at about this time, and was probably inspired by his friend Sidney. It is a collection of twelve pastorals, one for each month of the year. In a desire to escape the artificiality of the pastoral, Spenser actually undertook to employ country dialect in these poems. He soon began his masterpiece, *The Faerie Queene*, and was admitted to a literary group that included Sidney and Dyer.

In 1580 he was appointed Secretary to the Lord Deputy of Ireland, and Spenser spent most of his remaining years in that country. Lord Grey, in his enthusiasm for subduing Ireland, devastated the length and breadth of that land with fire and sword. It became necessary for Spenser to vindicate his master's methods, and Spenser's *View of the Present State of Ireland*, written around 1596, is one of the most amazing productions ever penned by a sensitive poet, for in it Spenser concludes that Lord Grey's savagery was the only method of subjugating a backward people like the Irish. Spenser himself was very unhappy in Ireland, even though he was promoted to higher positions and given the confiscated castle of Kilcolman. He was visited there in 1589 by Sir Walter Ralegh, who lived nearby, and to whom he read what he had composed of *The Faerie Queene*. Ralegh urged Spenser to accompany him to London, and in London the first three books of *The Faerie Queene* were published in 1590. The poem was immediately praised and earned him a small pension from Elizabeth, to whom the work was dedicated.

Shorter Poems: Returning to Ireland, he wrote a charming pastoral, *Colin Clout's Come Home Again*, a poetic record of his experiences at court, with some satirical touches on the intrigue of Elizabeth's courtiers. In 1594 he married his sweetheart, to whom he had already written the love sonnets that make the sequence *Amoretti*. And to celebrate his marriage to her, he wrote the noble marriage song, "Epithalamion." These two works were published in 1595. The next year he was in London with three more books of *The Faerie Queene*, which were published there. Later in the same year (1596), he wrote the "Prothalamion," an exquisite marriage hymn on the wedding of two daughters of the Earl of Worcester. He returned again to Ireland, bitterly disappointed at his failure to be awarded any desirable posts in England. In 1598 his home was burned by the rebels, and he fled with his family to London. Neglected, ill, and without hope, he died suddenly in an inn in 1599. The Earl of Essex had him buried near Chaucer in The Poet's Corner at Westminster Abbey.

The Shepherd's Calendar is dedicated to Sidney. In addition to compliments paid to Spenser's friends and patrons, and references to contemporary political events, the twelve pastoral poems that form this work are held together by the theme of Colin Clout's unsuccessful love for a girl named Rosalind. Spenser appears as Colin in the poems. They are written in a considerable variety of forms, and exhibit Spenser's wide reading in the classics as well as in the Italian, Spanish, and French writers of the Renaissance.

The Amoretti, as has been said, were Spenser's love poems to his future wife, Elizabeth. There are eighty-nine sonnets in the sequence, rhymed in a way Spenser invented for himself: *ababbcbccdcdee* (a rhyme scheme somewhat similar to the stanza he invented for *The Faerie Queene*). The sonnets are among the most easy-flowing and musical in our language. The most famous are: the first, a dedicatory sonnet, which says of his poems:

> *Leaves, lines, and rymes, seeke her to please alone,*
> *Whom if ye please, I care for other none;*

the thirty-fourth, beginning "Lyke as a ship, that through the Ocean wyde", the seventy-fifth, beginning "One day I wrote her name upon the strand," and the seventy-ninth, beginning "Men call you fayre, and you doe credit it."

The "Epithalamion" is perhaps Spenser's most personal poem, wonderful in melody, and full of noble passion. It contains twenty-three stanzas and an envoy at the end. The final line of each stanza contains the refrain "That all the woods may answer, and your eccho ring."

The "Prothalamion" is equally exquisite. The occasion for its composition was the marriage of Lady Elizabeth Somerset and Lady Katherine Somerset, daughters of the Earl of Worcester, to two noblemen. The music is especially delicate in this poem, in which the two brides are presented picturesquely as two swans. This marriage song also has a lovely refrain at the end of each of its ten stanzas, "Sweet Themmes, runne softly, till I end my song."

The Faerie Queene: *The Faerie Queene* is the first important epic attempted in English by a major poet. Only six books and two cantos of the seventh book, of the twelve books intended, are extant. It is possible that other books of this work went up in the smoke when Spenser's home in Ireland was burned. This poem is many things besides an epic poem, it should be noted; it has allegorical purposes as well. The plan called for a series of knightly exploits, one on each of twelve successive days, and the hero-knight of each exploit was to stand for one of the twelve virtues that Aristotle had proposed as the cardinal ones. These twelve virtues were to exemplify the qualities that should go into making the perfect gentleman.

At the court of Gloriana, Queen of Fairyland, a twelve-day feast is being held. On each day a stranger appears and asks for help against some enemy in the form of a dragon, giant, and so on. To each of these strangers a knight is assigned as help. Spenser made it very clear that he was personifying Queen Elizabeth as Gloriana—the handsomest compliment of the many literary compliments paid to her in her age. King Arthur, who stands for Magnificence (Highmindedness), was to have been the unifying element in the twelve intended books; he appears in each book at a critical moment to give the advice and help that are needed. The allegory in *The Faerie Queene* is on several levels: the twelve ideal virtues for a gentleman are personified in each of the hero-knights; Queen Elizabeth and various of her courtiers are glorified in the representation of Gloriana's court; and the struggle of the English Church to free itself from the "paganism" of Rome is also depicted. In connection with the last matter, it should be remembered that Spenser himself was of Puritan persuasion.

The Faerie Queene proves Spenser to have been the most learned poet of his day; indeed, after Milton, he is the most learned poet in English literature. The work shows an intimate acquaintance with and digestion of many of the world's great classics, among which the most important are Ariosto's *Orlando Furioso*, Tasso's *Jerusalem Delivered*, and Malory's *Morte d'Arthur*, and to a lesser degree, Virgil's *Eclogues*, the *Iliad*, the *Odyssey*, Plato, Aristotle, Dante's *Divine Comedy*, Chaucer, Langland, and others.

For *The Faerie Queene* Spenser invented a stanza, now called the *Spenserian stanza*, which was not only perfect for his purposes but for those of a number of celebrated poets after him. Major works of Thomson, Burns, Byron, Shelley, Keats, and Tennyson, for instance, were later to be written in the Spenserian stanza. (The *Spenserian stanza* consists of nine lines, the first eight in iambic pentameter, the ninth in iambic hexameter, and rhyming *ababbcbcc*.)

Book One: The prologue contains an appeal to the Muse for inspiration as is common in epic poems; Spenser declares that his poem will be a moral one concerning "fierce wars and faithful loves."

Canto I: On the plain the Red Cross Knight is riding confidently beside Una, who is borne by a white ass; she leads a milk-white lamb. In the rear lags a dwarf. Suddenly the atmosphere threatens, the sky darkens, and it begins to rain. They seek shelter in a thickly wooded forest. When the storm has passed over, they cannot find their way out of the woods. Despite Una's warning, the inexperienced knight takes a beaten path, and hands over his spear to the dwarf. The most beaten path often leads to error, just as this one does. They come to the den of Error, guarded by that hideous monster, half-serpent, half-woman. The knight slays her; Error's countless young ones begin to suck up their mother's blood, and burst with it. Una congratulates the knight, and they find their way out of the wood. They encounter an aged religious-looking man, who seems all simplicity and goodness, one Archimago, who takes them to his lowly hut. The weary travelers are soon asleep. Archimago, who is really a scheming hypocrite, summons by magic two sprites from Hell, and dispatches one to Morpheus, god of sleep, for an evil dream to trouble his guests. Morpheus, prodded from his sleep, grants the dream. Meanwhile, Archimago shapes the other sprite into the form of Una, and orders it to lie beside the Red Cross Knight; the dream he places in the knight's thoughts. The knight dreams a carnal dream of Una, awakes, and apparently finds her by his side. He is angered enough to kill her, but the sprite pleads for his pity. He comforts her, and is soon asleep again.

Canto II: In the morning Archimago transforms the dream-sprite into a squire, and places the Una-sprite with the former on the grass in close embrace. He then awakens the knight to view the sight. Barely restraining himself from slaying them both, the knight returns in torment to his bed. At dawn he leaves with the dwarf. A little later the real Una, innocent of the night's events, finds her protector is gone. Dismayed, she sets out in search of him, but her little ass cannot overtake the knight's fine steed. Archimago, still bent on mischief, disguises himself as the knight and follows her. By this time the Red Cross Knight has wandered far; he suddenly encounters a belligerent heathen, Sansfoy (Without Faith), who is accompanied by a beautiful lady in glittering array, Fidessa (as she is called). Sansfoy challenges Red Cross, and a furious battle ensues. Red Cross slays his adversary, pursues the fleeing Fidessa (Faithful), and catches up with her. Pleading for mercy, she tells him she has been a captive to Sansfoy. He believes her, and after a while they pause to rest in the shade of a tree. When he tries to pluck a garland for Fidessa, whose charms have moved him, he sees blood trickling from the tree, and hears a hideous cry. The tree, once a man, begins to speak. The tree's story is of his having once been in love with Fraelissa, and, encountering a knight and lady, of his having conquered the other knight; with two ladies on his hands, he had to choose between the new one, the sorceress Duessa, who reviled Fraelissa's virtue, and Fraelissa; deeming Fraelissa truly false, he changed his allegiance; but one day seeing Duessa bathing, he discovered that she was really a deformed old witch; whereupon she transformed him into a tree. Grieved, the Red Cross Knight patches up the torn bark, still unaware that his Fidessa is actually the false Duessa.

Canto III: Una, still alone, lies down to rest. A fierce lion rushes at her, but seeing her beauty and innocence, is docile, and becomes her protector. They come upon a maid, who runs away in terror at sight of the lion. Una, following her, comes to the cabin where she and her mother dwell. The girl, Abessa, is huddled in a corner; but Una's gentleness wins the confidence of Abessa and her blind mother. Una and the lion remain the night. The girl has a lover, Kirkrapine (Church-robber), a thief, who leaves his loot usually in the cabin. When Kirkrapine arrives, the lion kills him. When Una departs in the morning, realizing that their breadwinner is dead, the pair pursues Una with imprecations, but she is deaf to their curses. Meanwhile Archimago, disguised as Red Cross, overtakes Una. Mistaking his true identity, she is overjoyed. But an angry knight, Sansloy (Without Law), brother of the slain Sansfoy, encounters them, and is bent on revenge. Thinking Archimago the Red Cross Knight, he quickly dismounts Archimago; seeing his white hair and wrinkled face, he recognizes him as the old hypocrite, and leaves him lying on the ground. Sansloy turns to Una, handles her roughly, and is attacked by the lion. But even the king of beasts is no match for the lawless. Sansloy kills the noble animal, and Una is his captive.

Canto IV: The true Red Cross is traveling with the false Duessa. They come upon a glittering castle built on sand, its foundaffons always shifting. A closer view reveals hideousness behind the first effect of beauty. Inside there are all sorts of people peering at each other from the galleries. The place is gaudily bedecked; everyone is waiting for the queen, the fair Lucifera (Pride). Everyone in this place is concerned only with physical appearances, and Red Cross feels ill at ease among these peacocks. Lucifera rises from her throne and calls for her coach, which is drawn by six creatures, the personification of vices; the beasts are mounted by six deadly sins, Lucifera's counsellors. Satan is the coachman. Out to the plain they ride, followed by the people, Duessa, and Red Cross. A new knight, Sansjoy, appears; he is the brother of Sansfoy and Sansloy. Seeing Sansfoy's armor in Red Cross's possession, he charges at the latter. But the queen will not have such uncouth conduct; the fight must be postponed until it can take place in the lists tomorrow. That night there is a great feast, Gluttony being the host. While everyone is asleep, Duessa steals off to Sansjoy, and promises him her love.

Canto V: In the morning, the terms of the battle are arranged; the victor is to win Duessa and Sansfoy's armor. Lucifera arrives, the trumpets sound, and the battle begins. Both contenders are fierce, and presently are covered with blood. At length Red Cross unseats Sansjoy. Rushing to find him, the victor sees his opponent has disappeared; Duessa has hidden him under a dark cloud. Duessa journeys to the witch of night, an aunt of Sansjoy's, who returns with her to earth. Together they bring Sansjoy to Hades, where the doctor Aesculapius heals Sansjoy. Meanwhile, in the palace of Pride, the dwarf discovers the dungeons are full of the corpses of those who fell into Lucifera's clutches. Many famous men lie dead there. The Red Cross Knight flees before Duessa's return.

Canto VI: Una rebuffs the advances of Sansloy; when she removes her veil and he perceives her incomparable beauty, he is more determined than ever to have her. Her anguished cries ring through the forest, and are heard by the aged Sylvanus and his troops of fauns and satyrs. These come running to the rescue, and the frightened Sansloy flees. Una is also terrified of them, but soon is won over by their friendliness. They worship her for her beauty, and she tries to teach them truth and to civilize them. Some time later, the knight Satyrane, whom the wild beasts fear, wanders into this part of the forest. He falls in love with Una, but she does not reciprocate his feelings. They become friends, and Una tells him that she must be on her way to find Red Cross. He says he saw the latter, dead by the hand of a knight who is near at hand. They leave and find Sansloy. He denies he killed Red Cross, but regrets that he did not. Satyrane and he battle. The fight is long but evenly matched; unable to control his lechery, Sansloy makes a lunge towards his former captive, Una, who flees into the forest while the fight proceeds. Archimago, disguised as an old man, is a spectator of the encounter.

Canto VII: Duessa sets out to find the Red Cross Knight; she sees him by the brink of a stream. Cleverly she explains her strange behavior in a way that satisfies him. Unaware that the stream is drugged, the knight drinks of it; his senses are stupified. He is suddenly confronted by the giant Orgoglio swinging an uprooted oak as a weapon. Red Cross is felled before he can don his armor. Promising herself to the giant, Duessa intervenes before he can destroy Red Cross; she suggests that the knight be thrown in a dungeon. They go off to his castle, and he bestows a seven-headed serpent upon her to serve as a steed. The dwarf, who has been watching from afar, gathers his master's armor, and chances upon the fleeing Una. She faints at the sight of her knight's armor but is revived by the dwarf, who relates Red Cross's adventures. In despair they decide to try to find him. En route they meet Prince Arthur, magnificently accoutred, who offers to befriend them. She tells Arthur her story, and he vows to rescue her knight.

Canto VIII: The dwarf leads them to the giant's castle, where Arthur's charmed horn blows down the gate with one blast. The giant, Duessa, and her seven-headed serpent appear. A fierce contest ensues. Arthur's squire succeeds in keeping the dragon at bay until Duessa enchants the youth. Arthur's shield of diamond dazzles Orgoglio and the serpent, both of whom are slain by Arthur. Duessa tries to escape, but the squire corners her. Una thanks Arthur. They now behold a stupid-looking old porter, Ignaro, from whom Arthur takes the keys to begin a search of the castle. He comes upon the corpses of many babes and martyrs. Finally he discovers an iron cell with no keyhole; breaking down the door, he finds an emaciated Red Cross, who is brought back to the grateful Una. The latter now takes care of Duessa, stripping her of her finery to reveal her in all her native ugliness and deformity. Only then is the traitress allowed to go her way.

Canto IX: When Red Cross has somewhat regained his strength, Arthur is ready to leave. To please Una, the King reveals how he was raised by Timon and Merlin without knowledge of his parentage; the Faerie Queene has appeared to him in a dream, and now he is in search of her. The others predict that he and the Faerie Queene will make an ideal couple. The adventurers part with an exchange of gifts. Red Cross and Una travel on. They come upon a pale harried knight with a rope about his neck, Sir Trevisan, who tells his story. He had been traveling with a lovelorn companion when they met hellish Despair, who hypnotized them into deep distress, giving one a rope and the other a knife, and suggesting suicide to them. His friend has taken the advice, and Trevisan is fleeing, afraid that he will commit the same act. He warns Red Cross to keep clear of Despair. Red Cross and Una come upon Despair's cave, where they find the aged creature clothed in rags and thorns guarding his new victim. Despair tries his charms upon the knight, reminding him how sinful a creature man is, and offering him the weapons with which to destroy himself. Red Cross is about to yield to the suggestion when Una seizes the knife from his hands, recalling to him the existence of mercy for those who sin. They leave Despair, who tries to hang himself, but cannot, being chained to time.

Canto X: Una, realizing that her knight must recover his strength, brings him to the House of Holiness, where Humilta, the porter, admits them. Dame Celia welcomes them. Her daughters are: Fidelia (Faith), Speranza (Hope) and Charissa (Charity). The franklin Zeal and the squire Reverence are there, but Charissa is absent in the discharge of her good works. The groom Obedience leads Red Cross off to a much-needed rest. Later, at Una's request, Fidelia teaches Red Cross the limitlessness of faith. Seeing him distressed, Speranza tries to instil him with hope despite his foolish past. Finally, doctor Patience is called in to ease his mental anguish. Penance, Remorse, and Repentance complete the cure. He suffers much, but his soul is cleansed.

Charissa now appears to teach him the ways of charity and love. An ancient matron, Mercy, takes him to a holy hospital, where seven holy men serve. Here the knight's education continues. Then the holy man, Heavenly Contemplation, after fast and prayer, leads him up a steep mountain, once ascended by Moses and Christ. After that he is granted a vision of the New Jerusalem, where dwell the spiritually whole. Dazzled by the city's beauty, Red Cross wishes to remain. But Contemplation informs him that he can return here only after accomplishing his mission, the liberation of Una's parents from the dragon. The holy man also tells the knight he is a descendant of ancient kings, and that he is to become St. George. After much thanks, Una and her knight depart.

Canto XI: Una and Red Cross reach the besieged castle. After a fierce struggle, the dragon fells the knight with his tail, and attempts to fly over him, emitting flames. The dragon makes off in triumph, though wounded in the wing. But the waters of the Well of Life, into which Red Cross has fallen, restore him. During the night all his wounds are healed. In the morning he is ready for a new fight, much to the monster's astonishment. Red Cross smites the dragon heavily and wounds him on the head. The dragon counters with a wound on the knight's shoulder, and overpowers him with his flames and stench. Red Cross has fallen under the Tree of Life, which drips a balm that restores him. The deadly dragon is unable to approach this tree, and withdraws at the second coming of night. Una still keeps watch by her hero. The third day finds the dragon wearied and confused. He opens his jaws to swallow his foe, but the knight is too quick for him and thrusts his sword into the monster's throat. With a crash the dragon goes down to death. Una praises God and her knight.

Canto XII: The watchman on the wall tells Una's parents, the king and queen, the joyful news. Trumpets sound, and the rusted gates are thrown open. The royal pair come forth in humble thanks to their rescuer. There follow dancing, singing, and feasting. The commoners flock around the dragon, not without fear. The knight moves his hosts with the story of his adventures; they bestow Una's hand upon him, and insist he remain with them. Una appears, glitteringly robed, more beautiful than ever, now that all fear is banished. But the Red Cross Knight cannot stay now. He must first serve the Faerie Queene for six years, according to his vow. The celebration is suddenly interrupted by an excited messenger, bearing tidings from Duessa. She claims Red Cross as her betrothed. In explanation Red Cross tells how he was deceived by the false Fidessa; Una adds her pleas to his, and reveals that the messenger is old Archunago himself. The hypocrite is seized and imprisoned; the feast continues. Red Cross is forgiven, and an elaborate marriage ceremony takes place. Red Cross takes leave of his loved wife for the present. Holiness, personified by the Red Cross Knight, and Truth, personified by Una, have thus been united forever, and he is now ready to serve the Faerie Queene fitly. This book of Spenser's poem is supposed also to exhibit the freeing of the English Church from Roman falsehood.

Book Two: This deals with the legend of Sir Guyon, who stands for Temperance. This section opens with an address to Elizabeth, whom Spenser assures that time will unfold the truth of his fable just as it has unfolded a New World in the West. In the mirror of his story, the Queen will behold her face, her realm, and her ancestry.

Canto I: The Red Cross Knight now being wise, Archimago attempts Guyon. Duessa pretends having been ravished by the Red Cross Knight, whom Guyon soon encounters. They part friends. Guyon and the palmer come upon Amavia, whose husband, Mortdant, was undone by the witch Acrasia, whose dominion is the Bower of Bliss. Amavia has stabbed herself. Guyon and the palmer take Ruddymane, her newborn babe, whose hands, stained with the blood of her mother's breast, they cannot wash.

Canto II: Guyon tries to wash the blood off in a stream, which is formed by the tears of a virgin Diana has turned to stone to prevent her being raped by a faun. The virgin's virtues, passing into the water, will allow of no stain. Guyon's horse is stolen. On foot they reach the house of Medina (the Golden Mean), who has two sisters, extreme opposites, Elissa and Perissa, whose lovers are the malcontent Sir Huddibras and Sansloy. The two knights fight alternately with each other and against Guyon. Medina makes the peace. Before continuing on his adventure to overthrow Acrasia, Guyon leaves Ruddymane with Medina.

Canto III: Braggadochio, riding Guyon's horse, puts Trompart in vassalage. Archimago gets Braggadochio to vow vengeance on Guyon and the Red Cross Knight for having killed Sir Mortdant and his lady. Archimago magically disappears to procure Arthur's sword; petrified, Braggadochio and Trompart hide in the forest. They are come upon by the handsome Diana-like huntress Belphoebe. Braggadochio's lust is aroused, but he is afraid to pursue her.

Canto IV: Guyon comes upon Furor dragging Phedon along the ground. On the palmer's advice he trusses up Occasion, Furor's mother; Furor flies. Phedon tells of his having been betrayed; he killed his betrothed and his friend, and was in pursuit of his lady's maid, who had revealed the treachery, when Furor caught him. Atin (Strife), running by, berates Guyon for having fought with a woman.

Canto V: Pyrochles sets upon Guyon, but is too hot-headed to overcome the cool knight. Guyon spares him, and on learning his motive, sets Occasion and Furor free. The mother provokes her son to attack Pyrochles, and the palmer counsels Guyon to allow Pyrochles to taste his own folly. In the meantime Atin has run to Pyrochles's brother, Cymochles, who is luxuriating in the Bower of Bliss.

Canto VI: Cymochles, in haste to find vengeance, comes to Idle Lake, where the wanton Phaedria (Immodest Mirth) is dallying in a little boat. She refuses Atin passage, and ferries Cymochles to her island, where she charms him to sleep. She merrily returns for Guyon, and leaves the palmer ashore. The knights battle; she parts them, and sends Guyon on his way. In the meantime Pyrochles has plunged into the lake to ease his furious burning. Archimago succors him.

Canto VII: Guyon comes upon Mammon, who pretends to godhead, and takes Guyon to his treasury adjoining Hades, where the knight glimpses Pain, Revenge, Treason, Hate, and Sorrow. Care guards the house of Riches. An ugly fiend stalks Guyon, ready to pounce on him should he be tempted. Guyon is offered the very fountain of worldly goods and even Mammon's daughter; then he is taken into the Garden of Proserpine, where the golden apples are. In the river Cocytus he sees Tantalus and Pilate. Finally the Money God takes him back to earth where, because of lack of food and sleep, he faints.

Canto VIII: The palmer finds Guyon; the angel guarding the hero commits him to the palmer's care. Pyrochles, Cymochles and Archimago (who has stolen Arthur's sword) come by, and are about to finish off the knight when Arthur rides up. He speaks temperately; they attack him; with Guyon's sword he kills Cymochles and then Pyrochles, who has refused to give Arthur allegiance. Arthur cuts Guyon's thanks short, for he has done nothing but his duty. Archimago and Atin run away.

Canto IX: The two knights reach Alma's House of Temperance, whose castle is being besieged. She escorts them on a tour of the premises. Prince Arthur speaks with Prays-Desire, and Guyon with Steadfastness. They are then taken to the three men who have all knowledge of the future, past, and present.

Canto X: Arthur reads *Briton Moniments*, which goes back into prelegendary time and then begins the chronicle of British kings with Brute, whose seven-hundred-year line includes Guendolene, the first woman ruler, Lear, and ends with Ferrex and Porrex. In Roman days Joseph of Arimathy brought the Holy Grail. The next great woman ruler was Bonduca. The story stops with Uther. The Prince rhapsodizes on his country. Guyon reads the *Antiquitee of Faery Lond*. The first Elf was created by Prometheus; he mated with a Fay in the garden of Adonis. They are the first ancestors of Eliza. Alma at last calls the two knights to dine.

Canto XI: Guyon and the palmer leave by boat. The enemies of Temperance besiege the castle. Seven of the troops attack the gates; the other five each attack one of the bulwarks (the Five Senses). Arthur prances out on Spumador and engages the captain Maleger, who rides a swift tiger and is attended by two hags, Impotence and Impatience. When Arthur is overthrown by the hags, his squire beats them off. Since Maleger is the son of Earth, who continually revives him, Arthur finally kills him by throwing him into a lake; the hags kill themselves.

Canto XII: Guyon's boat passes by the Gulf of Greediness and the Rock of Vile Reproach, past the Wandering Isles where Phaedria dallies, past the Whirlpool of Decay, past hideous sea beasts whom the palmer's staff disperses, past the mermaids from whose temptation the palmer restrains Guyon, and finally reaches the Island. The palmer's staff tames the wild beasts. Near the Bower of Bliss, Guyon almost succumbs to two naked ladies. In the Bower, the palmer and Guyon throw a net over Acrasia and her lover, who are gathering the rose of love while yet there is time. Her lover, Verdant, is set loose and given sage counsel. They destroy the Bower. The palmer's staff changes the beasts, Acrasia's former lovers, back to men, but they prefer beasthood.

Book Three: The legend of Britomart, who stands for Chastity, is told. The poet avers that the greatest example of chastity is not in Faery but in his Sovereign's breast.

Canto I: Arthur and Guyon sojourn at Alma's castle, then go abroad for adventure, sending Acrasia under heavy guard to the Faerie Queene. They come on Britomart, who unseats the charging Guyon. The palmer and the Prince make concord, and they all travel on together. Rushing out of a forest comes fair Florimell, pursued by a rapacious forester. Arthur and Guyon pursue Florimell; Arthur's squire chases the forester. Britomart comes upon six knights attacking the Red Cross Knight, who will not love the Errant Damozel. She subdues them, and they become her liegemen. They all enter Castle Joyous, ruled by the Lady of Delight. On an arras is the story of Venus and Adonis; squires and damozels swim in sensual delights. The lady of the castle, Malecasta, lusts for Britomart, and at night steals into her bed. Threatened mortally by Britomart, Malecasta shrieks. Britomart and the Red Cross Knight rout the castle, and proceed together.

Canto II: The knight persuades Britomart to tell her story. She disparaged the love she is seeking, Arthegall, only to listen to praise of him. She once beheld him in a magic mirror that Merlin devised for her father, King Ryence. Her nurse, Glauce, tried to purge her of her love by magic charms, to no avail.

Canto III: To cure her of her grief, Glauce took her to Merlin, who told the girl that the will of Eternal Providence was unfolding, that from Britomart and Arthegall would spring a great race of rulers. Arthegall is to take the crown from Constantius and fight against the Saxons. Merlin continued the history down to the reign of Eliza. Glauce advised that since Uther was now warring against the pagans in Brittany, for their safety Britomart should follow the example of the martial virgin Angela. From her father's chapel they took Angela's armor, a virtuous spear and shield; Glauce disguised herself as a squire.

Canto IV: Britomart and the Knight having parted ways, she rests sorrowfully by a seacoast and prays to Neptune for relief. Marinell, guardian of the Rich Strond, arrogantly challenges Britomart, knowing only a woman can undo him. He receives a deadly wound. His mother, daughter of Nereus, takes him to her bower at the bottom of the sea, and sends for Tryphon, physician to the sea gods. Guyon and the Prince meanwhile each follow a different road. The Prince sees Florimell, but night overtakes him.

Canto V: The Prince finds a dwarf in the forest who is also looking for Florimell, whom he loves unrequitedly. They go on together. Meanwhile Arthur's squire comes upon the savage forester and his two brothers; he kills them but is badly wounded himself. Belphoebe finds and nurses him. He falls desperately in love with her, and though recovering from his wounds begins to waste away. Belphoebe cannot give him her love honorably, and he would rather die than entreat dishonorably for it.

Canto VI: Chrysogone, impregnated by the sun, conceived the twins Belphoebe and Amoretta in the forest. The nymphs took the children: Phoebe raised Belphoebe in the woods and Venus in the garden of Adonis. Psyche trained Amoretta along with her own daughter, Pleasure.

Canto VII: Florimell's white palfrey gives out. On foot she reaches a little cottage; the witch there would worship her; the witch's son makes advances. Florimell escapes on the revived palfrey. To solace her son, the witch makes a false Florimell when a hyena-fiend returns bloody from gorging himself on the palfrey and bringing Florimell's belt. Florimell, however, has escaped in a fishing boat. Satyrane comes on the feasting hyena, recognizes belt and palfrey, and though he cannot kill the charmed beast, binds it. A giantess, Argante, twin of Ollyphant, gallops towards him, a knight athwart her saddle. Stopped by Satyrane, she unseats him, but because her pursuer came so close, she throws off the Squire of Dames, whom she wanted for her lust. The pursuer is the chaste virgin Palladine. The Squire tells his story. He has brought the names of his three hundred conquests to his love, Columbell, at the end of the year; she had demanded he serve ladies. Angered, she then commanded that he bring her the names of three hundred who had resisted him. In three years there have been only three: a prostitute, a nun, and a country girl. Satyrane finds the beast has broken its bonds.

Canto VIII: The witch makes a false Florimell for her son, but Braggadochio takes her from the churl and yields her in turn to a knight. Meanwhile the old fisherman tries to rape the true Florimell in the boat; Proteus rescues her, but when she will not yield to him, places her in a dungeon. Satyrane meets Paridell, who is searching for Florimell.

Canto IX: The Squire of Dames tells Satyrane and Paridell why the castle offers no hospitality: old, miserly, jealous Malbecco guards his young Hellenore, whom he wishes no one to see. While they are taking shelter under a shed, Britomart comes. They storm the gates. At dinner Paridell traces his ancestry to Troy, and tells Britomart of Aeneas and the Trojan Brutus.

Canto X: Paridell complains of the hurt he has received in the fight with Britomart, and stays behind. He runs off with Hellenore, who has stolen a large sum from Malbecco. The latter, disguised as a pilgrim, follows them. Braggadochio and Trompart join him because of his wealth. Meanwhile Paridell, having had his fill, travels on alone, and Hellenore joins a band of satyrs. Malbecco cannot persuade his wife to leave them, though he is ready to forgive her. On also finding his buried treasure stolen by Trompart, he runs mad, and finally is transformed into Gelosy.

Canto XI: Britomart, in pursuing the beastly giant Ollyphant, finds Sir Scudamour, who tells of Amoret's being captured by Busirane. They go to the castle. Britomart gallops through the gates of flame, but Scudamour cannot.

She finds various love affairs depicted on the tapestries: Jove's, Apollo's, Neptune's. There are also a statue in gold of love, and many warlike spoils. She waits for whatever is to happen.

Canto XII: A shrill trumpet sounds, heralding a storm. The iron door flies open. Britomart looks on a masque of Cupid. Ease, Fancy, Desire, Doubt, Danger, Fear, Hope, Dissemblance, Grief, and Fury come in. Then a naked lady, her heart in a silver basin, enters, flanked by Despite and Cruelty. The God himself is next. After come Repentance, Shame, Strife, Loss of Time, Disloyalty, Sorrow, and Death with Infamy. Britomart waits until the next night, and when the door opens, rushes through. She finds a magician and Amoret. She forces the evil man to cure the girl. On their way out she notes the richly furnished rooms have vanished; the flaming gates are gone. But Scudamour and Britomart think the worst has happened, and leave. In this tale Amoret stands for Female Devotion and Busirane for Illicit Love.

Book Four: The legend of Cambell and Triamond, who stand for Friendship, it is a continuation of Book Three in the sense that Book Three concerns love between the sexes, and Book Four concerns friendship (or love without regard to sex).

Canto I: Amoret is a little fearful of Britomart; but at the castle where one must win a leman or stay outside, Britomart reveals her sex. Going on the next day, they encounter fickle Blandamour and false Paridell travelling with Duessa and Ate, the goddess of mischief. The knights attack and are overthrown. Paridell later falls to Scudamour, whom they convince of Britomart's lust for Amoret.

Canto II: Glauce cannot calm Scudamour. They all meet Sir Ferraugh, from whom Blandamour wins the false Florimell. Ate stirs up strife. Coming to the scene, the Squire of Dames stops the fight by telling of the tourney to take place for Florimell's girdle. Blandamour and Paridell, ceasing, make accord; they will stand against all others. They overtake Cambell and Triamond with their wives and sisters, Canacee and Cambina. Cambell has announced that anyone who could overthrow him can claim Canacee; he has a magic ring that staunches all wounds. Triamond's mother, Agape (Love), a fairy, made the Fates promise that when her eldest son, Priamond, should die, his spirit would go into Diamond, and Diamond's into Triamond.

Canto III: The brothers take up the challenge. Cambell defeats the elder two. With the youngest, who has three lives, the battle hangs in doubtful balance, when Cambina appears in a chariot drawn by lions; her magic arts despoil them of arms. They drink her Nepenthe and become fast friends. There is a double wedding.

Canto IV: Satyrane's tournament for the love of Florimell is the scene. The heroes of three days' contest are Satyrane, Cambell, and Triamond. Arthegall, disguised as the Salvage Knight, defeats all on the third day, until he is overthrown by Britomart.

Canto V: The ladies are paraded for the beauty's prize, the girdle of Venus. The golden belt is awarded to the counterfeit Florimell, but will fit only Amoret. Britomart does not desire Florimell; the Salvage Knight is gone; Satyrane suggests that Florimell choose to avoid strife, and she goes to Braggadochio. Britomart and Amoret go on, to seek Scudamour, who spends a miserable night in the workshop of Care, a blacksmith.

Canto VI: Scudamour finds Arthegall, who is nursing grievance against Britomart; they join forces. She comes. Her enchanted ebony spear unseats Scudamour, and then Arthegall. The latter attacks with his sword, which her armor deflects to her horse. Without her spear she is being worsted, when her helmet comes off; her beauty brings him to his knees. Scudamour, too, worships her. Glauce persuades the knights to raise their visors. Britomart recognizes Arthegall. He woos, she yields. But he must leave her to go on a hard adventure for three months. Britomart and Scudamour go to the forest, where she has lost Amoret.

Canto VII: Lust carries Amoret to his cave. Aemylia is there, and an old woman who substitutes for her in satisfying Lust's appetite. Amoret escapes but he overtakes her. Arthur's squire engages him, and Belphoebe kills him. Belphoebe goes for Aemylia, and on her return finds Arthur's squire kissing Amoret; haughtily she banishes him from her presence. He lives penitently in a cabin, wasting away. Even Prince Arthur, passing, does not recognize him.

Canto VIII: A turtle dove who lost her mate lives with the squire, who ties a jewel of Belphoebe's around her neck. The dove lures Belphoebe to the squire. She receives him back again in favor. Arthur meets Aemylia and Amoret and cures them with a precious liquor. They stay at Scalaunder's cottage, who continually slanders them. The next day Arthur rescues the squire from a pagan giant, Corflambo (Amorous Passion). The dwarf leads them back to the castle. The squire marries the giant's daughter Poeana, who reforms.

Canto IX: Arthur joins Aemylia with her squire of low degree, his own squire and Poeana, and travels on with Amoret. They come to where Britomart and Scudamour have found Blandamour and Paridell fighting with two other knights for the false Florimell, whom they took from Braggadochio. The Prince puts an end to the quarrel.

Canto X: Scudamour tells how he won the Shield of Love and Amoret, defeating twenty knights. In the castle, past Doubt, Delay and Danger, he proceeded to a second paradise where lovers and friends walked. Concord let him into the Temple of Venus, and the Goddess smiled upon his claiming Amoret.

Canto XI: Marinell's wound having been cured by Tryphon, his mother Cymodoce takes him to the wedding of Thames and Medway. There is a feast for all the gods of streams, rivers, and seas.

Canto XII: Being half mortal, Marinell cannot eat the immortal food. Walking abroad, he hears the complaint of Florimell. He is deeply moved but has no power to offer redress. In his mother's bower he wastes away. But Tryphon and Apollo tell her there is nothing physically wrong with him. She guesses at his grief but thinks he loves a nymph. When she learns that it is Florimell he loves, she chafes him, but finally decides that he will certainly die unless he wins his love. She appeals to Neptune, who commands Proteus to set the girl free, and seeing her, she admires Florimell's beauty. Marinell begins to recover and Florimell modestly hides her joy.

Book Five: The legend of Sir Arthegall, who stands for Justice, illustrates the fact that justice may be for a while turned aside, but never permanently. Commenting that he is living in a stone age, Spenser begins by assuring us that he is writing of the Golden Age.

Canto I: Arthegall, raised by the goddess of Justice, Astraea, sets out to rescue Eirene (Peace) from Grantorto (Spain), equipped by Justice with the iron man Talus (Power) as a groom. They come upon a squire and a headless lady undone by Sanglier; Sanglier has the mistress of the squire. Arthegall understands that she belongs to the latter since he was willing to give her up rather than have her die. Talus enforces the judgment.

Canto II: Dony, Florimell's dwarf, tells of the coming marriage at the Castle of the Strond. The pagan Pollente allows no one to pass over the bridge without payment; his daughter Munera (Bribery) keeps the treasury, and buys up all the country round. Arthegall kills the father; Talus, the daughter; the castle is razed. They next come upon a giant who is descanting on justice, wanting to restore all things to equality in his scales. Arthegall refutes him, and Talus tumbles him down a cliff into the sea. The listeners rebel, but Talus quells them.

Canto III: Marinell and Florimell are wedded. Marinell does himself and his lady great honor in the tourney. Braggadochio brings out the false Florimell and exhibits Arthegall's shield. Arthegall exposes him, and puts the golden belt on the true Florimell. Sir Guyon claims his horse, and Talus throws Braggadochio out.

Canto IV: Arthegall comes upon two brothers and two maidens arguing over an island, the sea having shifted most of one island on to another; they are also disputing the possession of a rich coffer that the sea washed onto the smaller isle. Amidas is given the island and Placidas the coffer. Later on Arthegall sees a troop of women holding Sir Terpin captive; Talus rescues him. Terpin tells of Radigund the Amazon, who forces many knights to do women's work. Arthegall and Radigund agree to a tourney.

Canto V: At the fight, Arthegall, about to deliver the fatal blow, sees her face and will not strike again. She takes him captive and hangs Terpin; Talus escapes. The author reflects that women, until Heaven decrees otherwise, should obey men. Radigund falls in love with Arthegall, and sends her maid Clarinda to win him over; the maid herself is smitten by love for him, and promises him his freedom in exchange for his favors. He seems not unwilling.

Canto VI: But Arthegall remains loyal to Britomart, whom Talus tells of his captivity. Britomart has a jealous mood, but finally masters her grief and sets out to rescue him. She lodges at the house of Dolon (Deceiver), in a tricky bed that begins to descend. Talus routs those who come to her door. Safe, Britomart meets Dolon's sons on a bridge and kills them.

Canto VII: Britomart stays in the temple of Isis, where she has a vision of herself adorned with jewels; the crocodile at the foot of Isis devours flames, then couples with Isis, who gives birth to a lion. The priests foretell her glorious future by this dream. She reaches the land of the Amazons, kills Radigund, and frees Arthegall and the other subdued knight. Arthegall continues on his adventures.

Canto VIII: He sees a maid being chased by two knights, who in turn are pursued by Arthur. Each hero kills one of the pagans, and then they begin to fight each other. The maiden stops them; they become friends. Samient (an emissary of Mercilla, exponent of mercy) takes them to the castle of the Souldan and his wife Adicia (Injustice). Arthur kills the terrible-charioted Souldan, while Arthegall subdues Adicia and the castle.

Canto IX: Next they rid the world of Malengin (Guile) with the help of Talus. They reach Mercilla's castle; two of her people are Awe and Order. She is to judge a trial, Duessa being the accused. Zele is the prosecutor; the witnesses are Kingdom's Care and Religion. Duessa has aspired to the crown. Mercilla (a personification of Queen Elizabeth) with tears passes judgment. Arthur then goes to rescue Belgae (The Netherlands).

Canto X: Arthur kills Geryoneo (Spanish Rule in The Netherlands), who has three bodies, and then the monster guarding the tyrant's idol (the monster being the Inquisition, the idol the Roman faith). In the meantime Arthegall meets the good Sir Sergis.

Canto XI: The old knight tells him that Irena (Ireland) will soon be killed by Grantorto unless a champion rescues her in ten days. Arthegall reproaches himself for his delays, and they sail to the Salvage Islands. But before setting sail they rescue Burbon (Henry of Navarre), who unchivalrously had thrown his shield away, from the attacks of a rabble; the shield had been given him by Red Cross. They also rescue Flourdelis from the peasants, but she will have none of Burbon until Arthegall upbraids her.

Canto XII: Talus clears the way for the landing party the day before the crucial one. With his sword Chrysaor he decapitates Grantorto. Then he gives true justice to the land; but before he can reform it thoroughly he is called back to Faery Court. Two hags, Envy and Detraction, annoy him on the road back. They set the Blatant Beast (Infamy) to bark and bray. Arthegall pays no attention to them, nor does he allow Talus to chastise them.

Book Six: The legend of Sir Calidore, who stands for Courtesy. The author begins by confessing that he is cheered on his long journey to Faery by the beauty of the road, and that for his pattern of Book Six he turns to his sovereign, Queen Elizabeth.

Canto I: Calidore meets Arthegall and tells him he is pursuing the Blatant Beast, a dog with one hundred heads. He overthrows Maleffort, the seneschal of Briana, who collects the beards of knights and the hair of ladies for her lover, Crudor. Calidore overthrows Crudor but spares his life. Crudor and Briana marry.

Cantos II–III: Calidore sees Tristram, who though untutored in arms kills a knight maltreating a lady. Calidore makes Tristram his squire. He returns the lost Aladine and Priscilla to their respective castles, and then comes on a loving couple, Calepine and Serena. The latter is seized by the Blatant Beast; Calidore pursues the monster. Calepine catches up with his lady; he and Serena are refused help by Turpine in crossing a stream, and are not granted by him a night's lodging.

Canto IV: Turpine attacks the weak Calepine, who is saved by a gentle savage. The savage nurses the lovers back to health. Calepine wanders in the woods, rescues a baby from a bear, but loses his own way. The baby has been given to the barren Mathilde, wife to Sir Bruin.

Canto V: Arthur and Timias encounter Serena and the gentle savage. They all go to a hermitage. Timias, who has been wounded by the Blatant Beast, and Serena remain there. Arthur and the savage go on.

Canto VI: The hermit heals Timias and Serena. Arthur defeats Turpine, and spares his life on condition that he never use arms again.

Canto VII: Turpine tricks two knights into attacking Arthur, who kills one and forces the other to bring Turpine to him. He hangs Turpine by the heels. In the meantime Timias and Serena meet Mirabella attended by Disdain and Scorn; Cupid has condemned her to save as many lovers as she has destroyed. Disdain knocks down Timias; Serena runs away.

Canto VIII: Prince Arthur rescues Timias, but Mirabella tells him not to kill Disdain, who is a needful adjunct to her penance. Serena, meantime, is captured by savages and stripped to be offered as a sacrifice. Calepine rescues her.

Canto IX: Calidore is still chasing the Blatant Beast over the face of the earth. He rests with some shepherds, and thus falls in love with Pastorella. He stays as the guest of her fosterfather Meliboe. (This passage is a tribute to Sir Philip Sidney. Pastorella is the latter's wife; Meliboe her father, Sir Francis Walsingham. The whole episode is suggested by the fame of Sidney's *Arcadia*.) The rustic Coridon is jealous.

Canto X: Calidore comes upon the Graces dancing to the melody of Colin Clout (Spenser himself). Colin and Calidore (Sir Philip Sidney) discourse. On his return Calidore kills a tiger that is attacking Pastorella. Coridon, coward that he is, runs away. One day while Calidore is away, brigands despoil the houses and flocks of the shepherds, and take many of the people to sell as slaves.

Canto XI: The captain of the brigands falls in love with Pastorella, and therefore will not have her sold. The thieves begin to quarrel; many are killed. Coridon escapes, finds Calidore, and tells him of all that has happened. Calidore comes to the rescue and frees Pastorella.

Canto XII: Calidore leaves his love at Castle Belgard. Sir Bellamour and Claribell turn out to be the true parents of Pastorella. Calidore finds the Blatant Beast, overtakes him, puts him in chains. Later the Blatant Beast breaks free.

In addition to these six books of *The Faerie Queene* we possess two cantos and two stanzas of an uncompleted Book, known to us as the "Cantos of Mutabilitie." The first, called Canto VI, tells how Mutability, daughter of Earth and Titan, challenges the sovereignty of Jove. Canto VII shows Nature, judging the contention, giving the award to Jove. In the two stanzas remaining, Spenser prays for the sight of God.

IMPORTANCE

Spenser has been called the poet's poet because of his superb technical skill. No one has ever written with greater fluency, ease, or sweeter music. The air of effortlessness that emanates from his lines everywhere may, of course, be entirely deceptive; for all we know, that apparent artlessness may have been achieved only by the most arduous kind of labor combining words for their maximum musical sweetness. Spenser has exerted a great influence on later poets—he was, for instance, Milton's favorite poet. His poetry would seem to lack none of the qualities belonging to the greatest excepting only two: power and unity. While Spenser is always equal to the music of sweetness, or even grotesqueness, when a passage calls for powerful music, his verse is sometimes too sweet. *The Faerie Queene* also suffers from a great diffuseness, and a consequent tendency to confuse the line of the story. Nevertheless, *The Faerie Queene* is likely always to be an inspiration to other poets; and some of the *Amoretti*, the "Prothalamion" and the "Epithalamion" are among the most exquisite pieces of English lyrical poetry.

Spenser had something of the antiquarian spirit, and was very fond of archaic language and words which in his own time were already obsolete. This affection for the antique was doubtless nourished by his love of Chaucer, whom he openly acknowledged to be his master, and on occasion Spenser will employ a Chaucerian expression, even though many of his contemporaries might have had some difficulty in understanding it. It is from these considerations that Ben Jonson said of him rather gruffly that he "writ no language." But one need not take Jonson's expression of annoyance too literally, for Jonson himself was perhaps too much addicted to the language of the London streets in his plays; at any rate, his vocabulary in them requires more footnoting than Spenser's works today.

ELIZABETHAN PROSE

There was not to be any tradition for English prose until the late seventeenth century. Until that time poetry was ever the chief medium for literary expression. But there are several pieces of Elizabethan prose worthy of mention for either historical reasons or reasons of intrinsic merit.

John Lyly (1554–1606)

John Lyly, who has been noted above as a dramatist and songwriter, was responsible for the creation of a highly affected prose style that had considerable vogue with the Elizabethans and became the favorite idiom at court. This prose first appeared in Lyly's *Euphues, or The Anatomy of Wit* (1578) and the sequel, *Euphues and His England* (1580). The work is a cross between a novel (a form that had not yet been invented) and a tract. The plot is merely an excuse for a series of dissertations on love, friendship, education, morals, and so on, and there is very little characterization. The style of *Euphues* is far more important than its content. Lyly, in his desire to evolve an elegant style for English prose, invented a style that to us is largely ridiculous. His sentences are full of carefully balanced clauses, antitheses, alliteration, plays upon words, and references to Pliny's highly unnatural *Natural History*. This style has come to be known as *Euphuism*. Shakespeare burlesques this style in the mouth of Falstaff (*Henry IV Part 1*, Act II, Scene 4). The following sentences from *Euphues and His England*, part of a compliment to Queen Elizabeth, are typical of the Euphuistic style:

> This is that Caesar, that first bound the crocodile to the palm tree, bridling those that sought to rein her. This is that good pelican, that to feed her people spareth not to rend her own person.

Sir Walter Ralegh (1552–1618)

Sir Walter Ralegh was one of the finest examples of the breadth of experience to which Elizabethan humanism invited. He was equally famous as explorer, soldier, sailor, statesman, poet, and historian, and he had also mastered more than a smattering of music and chemistry. Once very close to the Queen, he won her enmity by falling in love with and marrying one of her ladies-in-waiting. Thrice he attempted to colonize Virginia, and he also explored the Orinoco River. Marlowe and Spenser boasted of his friendship. When James I came to the throne, one of his earliest acts was to sentence Ralegh to the Tower on the charge of complicity against the King's life. He remained in the Tower for thirteen years, and was released in 1616 in order to undertake a voyage in search of gold in the New World. The expedition failed, and Ralegh was rearrested and condemned to die. His great courage facing death has become almost legendary. When asked to alter the position of his head on the block, he answered: "What matter how the head lies, so the heart be right."

Many of Ralegh's poems were printed in miscellanies and as complimentary verses in the volumes of other men. His most famous poems are his answer to Marlowe's "Passionate Shepherd" (mentioned above) and his sonnet on the *Faerie Queene*. His prose works include *A Report of the Truth of the Fight About the Isle of Azores* (1591), from which Tennyson took the material for his ballad "The Revenge"; his account of *The Discovery of Guiana* (1596); and his *History of the World* (1614), written in prison. Only one volume of the *History* was completed. The conclusion is justly celebrated:

> O eloquent, just, and mighty Death! whom none could advise, thou hast persuaded; what none hath dared, thou hast done; . . . thou hast drawn together all the far-stretched greatness, all the pride, cruelty, and ambition of man, and covered it all over with these two narrow words, hic jacet (here lies)!

Robert Greene (c. 1560–1592)
Among the pamphleteers and professional writers, already mentioned for their verse, were a number who wrote some lively prose. Robert Greene was the author of a racy piece of autobiography, *A Groatsworth of Wit Bought With a Million of Repentance* (1592), an attack on Shakespeare, and two romances, *Pandosto* (1588), the source of Shakespeare's *Winter's Tale*, and *Menaphon* (1589)—both quite Euphuistic.

Thomas Nashe (1567–1601)
Nashe is best remembered for the only work of the period that may lay just claim to being the first English novel, *The Unfortunate Traveller, or the Life of Jack Wilton* (1594), a lively journalistic tale of adventure. Thomas Dekker (c. 1572–1632) wrote an ironic picture of London lowlife in *The Gull's Hornbook* (1609).

Richard Hooker (c. 1554–1600)
Mention should also be made of a remarkable piece of Elizabethan prose by Richard Hooker, minister and Hebrew scholar. His *The Laws of Ecclesiastical Polity* (1593), defending the English Church against incipient Puritanism, is a splendid and often inspired example of the Ciceronean style imported into English.

ELIZABETHAN TRANSLATIONS

It is not surprising that with the excitement of the Renaissance at its height in the Elizabethan Age, and the language itself at its freshest and most stimulating, Elizabethan scholars and men of letters should have been tempted to introduce the treasures of ancient and modern literature into their own language. Some of these translations are among the best that have ever been made in our language. The most important are Thomas Nicoll's Thucydides (1550); Holland's Livy (1600) and Suetonius (1616); Golding's Caesar (1565); Newton's Seneca (1581), Sir Thomas North's Plutarch (1579); Chapman's Homer (1598–1614); Jonson's *Art of Poetry* by Horace; Florio's Montaigne (1603); Harrington's Ariosto; and Fairfax's *Jerusalem Delivered* of Tasso (1600). In addition, Painter's *Palace of Pleasure* (1556–1557) and Fenton's *Certain Tragical Discourses* (1567) are collections of a number of classic and Renaissance tales. Fairfax's translation of Tasso is still considered the best. Florio's Montaigne is still admired and was the means of introducing the essay form into English. Chapman's Homer not only was to inspire Keats, but is thought to have more of the Homeric sweep than any translation since made. North's Plutarch was a favorite source book for Shakespeare, and the great dramatist did not disdain to incorporate whole passages almost verbatim into his works.

The great Bible of 1611 is, in a way, a culmination of Elizabethan translating, and will be discussed later.

REVIEW QUESTIONS

THE RENAISSANCE, THE REFORMATION, AND THE ELIZABETHANS

Multiple Choice

1. _____ The Renaissance came to England
   a. at about the same time it came to continental Europe
   b. earlier than it came to continental Europe
   c. later than it came to continental Europe
   d. in 1457

2. _____ A powerful influence on the Renaissance was
   a. medieval Latin works
   b. classical Latin and Greek works
   c. native English writings
   d. literature from the Orient

3. _____ In 1534 Henry VIII declared himself to be
   a. a loyal subject of the Pope
   b. a follower of Martin Luther
   c. head of the English Church
   d. an atheist

4. _____ Sir Thomas Wyatt is remembered primarily for
   a. his novels
   b. his sonnets
   c. his translations
   d. his romances

5. _____ Blank verse is
   a. unrhymed iambic pentameter
   b. rhymed iambic pentameter
   c. unrhymed iambic tetrameter
   d. rhymed iambic tetrameter

6. _____ Which of the following are considered revenge tragedies?
   a. *Macbeth, Dr. Faustus*
   b. *The Spanish Tragedy, Hamlet*
   c. *Volpone, The Revenger's Tragedy*
   d. *Gorboduc, A Woman Killed With Kindness*

7. _____ Christopher Marlowe, the greatest dramatist before Shakespeare, wrote
   a. *The Spanish Tragedy*
   b. *Dr. Faustus*
   c. *Coriolanus*
   d. *Edward I*

8. _____ In which of these plays are women wrongly accused of infidelity?
   a. *Much Ado About Nothing, Othello*
   b. *King Lear, Hamlet*
   c. *A Winter's Tale, The Tempest*
   d. *Measure for Measure, The Taming of the Shrew*

9. _____ Among Shakespeare's earliest plays were
   a. experiments in romantic comedy
   b. the great tragedies
   c. the Henry IV history plays
   d. several pastoral romances

10. _____ The dramas of Webster, Tourneur, and Ford generally
    a. deal with the concerns of the growing middle class
    b. present a more optimistic view of human nature than Shakespeare did
    c. deal with violence and extremes of passion
    d. can be classified as tragicomedies

True or False

11. _____ The sonnets were published with Shakespeare's consent.

12. _____ *Romeo and Juliet* is the first romantic tragedy of the English stage.

13. _____ In developing his plots and choosing names and attributes for his characters, Shakespeare seldom relied on previously existing story materials.

14. _____ Claudius, Laertes, and Gertrude appear as central characters in *Othello.*

15. _____ Cordelia dies by hanging at the end of *King Lear.*

16. _____ Social satire is the major element in Shakespeare's comedies.

17. _____ Ben Jonson collaborated with Shakespeare on several tragedies.

18. _____ Chapman is remembered primarily for his translation of Homeric epics.

19. _____ Sidney was unique among Elizabethan poets in that he devoted himself almost exclusively to the writing of poetry throughout most of his life.

20. _____ Spenser wrote *The Faerie Queene* in part as a tribute to Queen Elizabeth.

Fill-in

21. The *Amoretti* was a sequence of _____ written by Spenser to his future wife.

22. Each of the hero-knights in *The Faerie Queene* exemplifies an ideal

    _____ .

23. The nine-line Spenserian stanza used in *The Faerie Queene* follows the rhyme pattern _____ .

24. An important prose stylist, John Lyly is most famous for his work,
    _____ .

25. Mary Stuart's religion was _____ .

26. In *Henry IV, Part I,* Prince Hal's character is contrasted with that of
    _____ , a man of similar age.

27. The story of Katherina and her terrifying temper is told in
    _____ .

28. Cordelia's sisters were Goneril and _____ .

29. The comedy of humours was introduced to the English stage by
    _____ .

30. Thomas Campion is remembered primarily as a writer of
    _____ .

Matching

31. _____ Sidney	a.	Translation of Homer
32. _____ Jonson	b.	Translation of the Bible
33. _____ Tournear	c.	*The Revenger's Tragedy*
34. _____ Webster	d.	*Utopia*
35. _____ Chapman	e.	*Tamburlaine*
36. _____ Marlowe	f.	Theological reformer
37. _____ Beaumont and Fletcher	g.	*The Duchess of Malfi*
38. _____ Calvin	h.	*Volpone*
39. _____ More	i.	*Arcadia*
40. _____ Covedale	j.	*The Maid's Tragedy*

Answers

1.	c	16.	t	30.	songs
2.	b	17.	f	31.	i
3.	c	18.	t	32.	h
4.	b	19.	f	33.	c
5.	a	20.	t	34.	g
6.	b	21.	sonnets	35.	a
7.	b	22.	virtues	36.	e
8.	a	23.	ababbcbcc	37.	j
9.	a	24.	*Euphues*	38.	f
10.	c	25.	Catholicism	39.	d
11.	f	26.	Hotspur	40.	b
12.	t	27.	*Taming of the*		
13.	f		*Shrew*		
14.	f	28.	Regan		
15.	t	29.	Jonson		

Part 4

THE SEVENTEENTH CENTURY

WORKS AT A GLANCE*

Francis Bacon

1597–1625	*Essays*	1620	*Novum Organum*
1605	*The Advancement of Learning*	1627	*The New Atlantis*

Thomas Carew

1640   *Poems*

Richard Lovelace

1649   *Lucasta*

Robert Herrick

1648   *Hesperides*
        Noble Numbers

John Donne

1633   *Go and Catch a Falling Star*
        A Valediction Forbidding Mourning

George Herbert

1633   *The Temple*

Henry Vaughan

1650, 1655	*Silex Scintillans* published in two parts	1678	*Thalia Rediviva*

Richard Crashaw

1648	*Steps to the Temple*	1653	*Carmen Deo Nostro*

Andrew Cowley

1633	*Poetical Blossoms*	1638	*Love's Riddle*

---

*Dates refer to dates of publication unless otherwise noted.
**Denotes date of composition.

Andrew Marvell

1681	*The Garden*

Izaak Walton

1653	*The Compleat Angler*

Sir Thomas Browne

1642**	*Religio Medici*	1646	*Vulgar Errors*

Robert Burton

1606**	*Philosophaster*	1621	*Anatomy of Melancholy*

Thomas Fuller

1662	*The History of the Worthies of England*

John Bunyan

1666	*Grace Abounding to the Chief of Sinners*	1682	*The Holy War*
1678	*Pilgrim's Progress (Part One)*	1684	*Pilgrim's Progress (Part Two)*

Joseph Hall

1608	*The Characters of Virtues and Vices*

Sir Thomas Overbury

1614	*A Wife*

Anonymous

1628	*Microcosmogrophie*

John Milton

1631–1632**	*L'Allegro*	1665**	*Paradise Lost*
	Il Penseroso	1671	*Paradise Regained*
1637	"Lycidas"		*Samson Agonistes*

---

*Dates refer to dates of publication unless otherwise noted.
**Denotes date of composition.

John Dryden

1666**	*Annus Mirabilis*	1687	*A Song for St. Cecilia's Day*
1683**	*Religio Laici*	1697	*Alexander's Feast*

John Evelyn

1818	*Memoirs*

Samuel Pepys

1690	*Memoirs Relating to the State of the Royal Navy*

Samuel Butler

1663, 1664, 1668	*Hubridas* published in three parts

William Congreve

1700	*The Way of the World*

*Dates refer to dates of publication unless otherwise noted.
**Denotes date of composition.

13
HISTORY, PHILOSOPHY, AND RELIGION

THE STUARTS

The seventeenth was one of the most crucial of centuries in the history of western European thought. It saw the development and growth of three of the most important factors that have made for the modern spirit: puritanism, rationalism, and the scientific spirit. Puritanism had far-reaching consequences in the world of political theory as well as in the world of morals; its offspring in the seventeenth century was the democratic ideal. Rationalism completed the break with the Middle Ages and broke the yoke of authority; among its many results was the turning of thought towards new fields of psychological investigation. The scientific spirit, to a large degree a byproduct of rationalism, evoked a new interest in the study of human experience and the gathering of experimental data.

In the more limited field of English literature, the century was equally remarkable. It began with the plays of Shakespeare and his great contemporaries and successors, the philosophic ventures of Francis Bacon, and the great Bible of 1611. Following these come the incomparable poetry of John Milton, our greatest nondramatic poet and the splendid prose of Burton, Browne, Walton, and Taylor. As the century proceeded to its close, there are the poetry and prose of Dryden, and Restoration Comedy.

The political history of the century is also of cardinal importance. In 1603 James I succeeded Elizabeth to the throne. The first of the Stuarts, he had little of his predecessor's talent for holding the kingdom together. He was a bigot, and ill-fitted to exemplify "the divine right of kings," which he revived from the Middle Ages. He was determined to make the English Church subservient to his will, and persecuted Puritans and Catholics with ferocity. It was because of his policies that the first American colonists preferred the unknown terrors of the New World to their familiar homes in England. He was extravagant and wasteful, and to raise money sold peerages and monopolies in trade to the highest bidder. The English public soon grew to resent his despotism, and the Puritan philosophy gained by leaps and bounds its hold on Englishmen. The Puritan's believed their destiny to be exclusively in the hands of God; as Stuart unreasonableness increased, average Englishmen began to think that even a king, if he stand between a man and God, must be removed. This is how the concept of a democracy first became effective in Western Europe.

Charles I, James' son, succeeded to the throne in 1625. He proved a thoroughly unreliable and treacherous monarch. Before long he found himself faced with the opposition of a large section of the people. In 1629 Charles, in anger, dissolved Parliament, and ruled without it for eleven years. With the aid of the Earl of Strafford and Archbishop Laud, he attempted to establish an absolute system of control. But it was too late for that. The lines were already drawn between the Cavaliers (his adherents) and the Roundheads (the Puritans). In 1639 Charles found himself involved in a war with the Scottish Presbyterians and was forced to reconvene Parliament; when it refused to grant his demands for money, he dismissed it again. A new Parliament met in 1640, the so-called Long Parliament, and decided to espouse the Scottish cause. The break came in 1641, and Civil War ensued. In 1649, a Parliament entirely Puritan in membership beheaded Charles. For the next few years Puritan extremists tried valiantly to establish a government something like a democracy. In 1653 Cromwell established a rigid Protectorate in the hope that a firm hand might succeed in forming a free state. For the first time, for instance, religious toleration was extended to all except those who followed "popery and prelacy." Jews were readmitted into England after having been banished for centuries.

When Cromwell died in 1658, his weak son proved unequal to the task of guiding the helm of government, and anarchy ensued. The Puritan sects, which had greatly multiplied in number, were at each other's throats. Sick of dissension, the public seized the occasion of General Monk's march on London to recall the son of Charles I to the throne, as Charles II. For twenty-eight years thereafter the English people tried vainly to live happily under the Stuarts again. But in 1688 Charles II's brother, James II, had to flee the country, and England was done with the Stuarts and absolute monarchy forever. The Puritan Revolution had not been in vain.

FRANCIS BACON (1561–1626)

Francis Bacon, although he might be treated as an Elizabethan, is actually the herald of the new century. To him more than to any other may be credited the leading impetus for the development of the scientific spirit in the new century. Though not a scientist himself, except in an amateur way, he was not only a great popularizer of the scientific method and a leading underminer of tradition, but a profound theoretician on the ways and means of developing science. It cannot be proved that he invented the inductive method of reasoning, which has been so indispensible to scientific research, but he certainly was the man to give the inductive method of reasoning its first important exposition to the public.

The disparity between the nobility of Bacon's mind and the wretchedness of his personal character is amazing. In his own time, few seem to have trusted him—and with good reason. He was an opportunist, a treacherous friend, and almost deficient in any human warmth. But his devotion to knowledge is one of the most awe-inspiring facts of history. If the knowledge be limited to knowledge of a strictly scientific nature, it must be admitted that Bacon did not boast when he said: "I have taken all knowledge to be my province."

He was the son of the Lord Keeper of the Great Seal to Elizabeth, and studied at Cambridge and at Gray's Inn. He left no stone unturned to advance himself at court, but the Queen refused to do anything for him. In hopes of gaining support, he became a kind of adviser to Essex, the last favorite of Elizabeth. Still unsuccessful in his ambition, when Essex headed a rebellion against the Queen, Bacon stepped forward to accuse his benefactor, and even undertook the role of prosecutor against Essex. That Bacon could have expected Elizabeth's gratitude for this shows how little he understood human nature. Elizabeth died soon after Essex, and James I proved more friendly. Bacon became a member of Parliament, later Attorney General, and in 1618 Lord Chancellor. His elevation included the titles of Baron Verulam and Viscount St. Albans. Two years later he was found guilty of accepting bribes, and forfeited his offices. He lived in retirement until his death in 1626, after he caught cold as a result of an experiment with the use of snow for preserving animal food.

His place is more properly in philosophy than in literature. He planned a huge work that would be a complete survey of existing knowledge and an index of the road to future knowledge. The first part of this work was written in Latin and translated into English as *The Advancement of Learning* (1605). This was an attempt to examine the methods of acquiring knowledge, and to advance the claims of logic and reason in its pursuit. The second part, the epochal *Novum Organum* (1620), describes the inductive method of reasoning. (The inductive method of reasoning is the process of collecting a mass of individual facts before arriving at a general truth.) In this work he also identifies the obstacles that lie in the path of scientific research: the power of tradition, the personal limitations of the investigator, the confusion inherent in the use of language, and the public fear of new ideas.

After his death his picture of a scientific utopia, *The New Atlantis* (1627), was published. There we read his picture of a university for scientific research, the "House of Solomon," fully equipped with laboratories. It was upon this model that the Royal Society was soon to be founded.

Bacon's place in literature, strictly speaking, is secured by his *Essays*, which he himself considered to be only trifles. They are his collection of "dispersed meditations" on life and human behavior. They are hardly more striking for the powerful succinctness of their style than for the observations they contain. In matters of the intellect, Bacon's mind is revealed to us in them in all its profundity; in matters human, Bacon's indifference to human emotion is sometimes repellantly materialistic.

These *Essays* were undoubtedly inspired by Montaigne's. Bacon published originally ten essays in 1597. By 1625 he had fifty-eight to publish. The name "essay" is borrowed from Montaigne, but nothing could be more dissimilar than the essays written by these two men. Montaigne is intimate, warm, genial, and profoundly humane; Bacon is cold, objective, utterly unemotional. Montaigne's manner is leisurely and follows freely the law of association of ideas; Bacon's is pointed, sententious, and steadily logical. In Montaigne's essays we are everywhere aware of the author's personality (such essays we call *informal* or *familiar*); in Bacon's we are confined to the object under discussion, and the tone is impersonal (such essays we call *formal*). Bacon's diction is direct and clear, and more modern than that of any other prose writer of the time. But the style does not flow. There are gaps in thought between sentences, which the reader must fill in, and which a modern prose writer would not allow. The best essays are "Of Truth," "Of Studies," "Of Adversity," "Of Great Place," "Of Innovations," and "Of Seeming Wise." Among Bacon's famous observations are:

> Certainly virtue is like precious odors, most fragrant when they are incensed or crushed: for prosperity doth best discover vice, but adversity doth best discover virtue. (From "Of Adversity")

> Some books are to be tasted, others to be swallowed, and some few to be chewed and digested. (From "Of Studies")

> He that hath wife and children hath given hostages to fortune. (From "Of Marriage and Single Life")

THE BIBLE OF 1611

The *King James Bible*, so-called because it was dedicated to James I, is also known as the *Authorized Version*. It is more than a translation, it is a great English book. No other European country witnessed so many attempts at translation of the Bible as England. The Bible of 1611 is in a way only a culmination of English translations of the Bible. Even in Anglo-Saxon days many attempts were made at partial translations in the popular tongue—among others those by Aldhem, Bede, Alfred, Aldred, Alfric, and the anonymous authors of the *Vespasian Psalter*, the *Rushwell Gospels* and the tenth century West Saxon translation. In 1384, followers of the reformer John Wyclif made a complete translation, the so-called *Wyclif Bible*, and a revision followed in 1396. The New Testament and the Pentateuch were translated by Tindale (1525–1535). Miles Coverdale made the first complete English Bible to be printed (1535), using Luther's version and the Vulgate as basic texts for his translation. A new edition of the *Coverdale*, including revisions made after consultation with the original Hebrew and Greek, was issued in 1539, and is known as *The Great Bible*. In Switzerland, the most popular of all English Bibles, *The Geneva Bible*, was printed in 1560. In 1568 a revision of the *Great Bible* was published and is now known as the *Bishop's Bible*. At Rheims a literal translation of the New Testament was printed in 1582.

For the monumental Bible of 1611, at the instance of King James, some fifty scholars from Oxford, Cambridge, and Westminster were engaged. The resulting translation is actually the product of the labors of all these men. They referred to Hebrew, Syriac, Greek, Latin, and modern language versions, and—what is more important—based their translation wherever possible on the work of their English predecessors. They everywhere preferred to use the homely, racy diction of the common people. The result of this tireless search for perfect expression is that the beauty of their prose has been surpassed by nothing else in English literature. The echoes of its cadences and diction are to be found throughout English literature thereafter. The *King James Bible* has been the fundamental book in the education of the Protestant English-speaking world.

14
CAVALIER AND METAPHYSICAL POETRY

CAVALIER POETS

With the major exception of the works of Milton, most of the literature of the seventeenth century was written by men of the King's party. As a general rule, the Puritans did not approve of secular poetry, and in that too Milton is a conspicuous exception. The typical Cavalier poet wrote gay, very clever, superficial verses,—amorous lines to various sweethearts or else verses in which the poet makes himself out to be a devil of a gay dog. The leading Cavalier poets of this school were George Wither, Thomas Carew, Sir John Suckling, Richard Lovelace, Edmund Waller—and in a class by himself, Robert Herrick.

George Wither (1588–1667)

George Wither was the author of elegies, satires, and pastorals. Unlike the other poets in this group, he became sympathetic to the Puritan cause, and was a captain in the Puritan Army. His great bulk of Puritan writings have now been forgotten, and he is remembered only for his early light verse, for the rediscovery of which we are indebted to Charles Lamb. His two most famous songs are: "Shall I, Wasting in Despair," in which the poet fortifies himself against female charms, and concludes:

> For if she be not for me,
> What care I for whom she be?

and "I Loved a Lass," in which the poet complains lightly about a lovely girl who has deserted him, and concludes that all women are false, frail, and untrue.

Thomas Carew (1595–1640)

Thomas Carew for a while considered the law as a profession, but his cleverness and tact won him a place of esteem as a poet in aristocratic circles. His verse is a perfect example of the best in Cavalier taste, and was published as *Poems* in 1640. Among his best songs are "Ingrateful Beauty Threatened," "Persuasions To Joy," "Would You Know What's Soft," and "The Unfading Beauty." Like other poets in this school, he reminds the girls that time plays tricks with beauty and youth, and that they had better take their joy now.

Sir John Suckling (1609–1642)

Sir John Suckling was one of Charles' courtiers and a notorious gambler. He sided with the King and, for his part in attempting to rescue Strafford from the Tower, was forced to flee to France, where, it is thought, he took his life. His poems exhibit the gay, devil-may-care tone of Cavalier life. The most famous of them are "A Doubt of Martyrdom"; "The Constant Lover," in which he expresses surprise at his having loved one woman "three whole days together"; and "Why So Pale and Wan, Fond Lover?" which concludes:

> *If of herself she will not love,*
> *Nothing can make her.*
> *The devil take her!*

Richard Lovelace (1618–1657)

Richard Lovelace was celebrated in his circle for his personal beauty as well as for his undying devotion to the King's cause. In 1648 he was imprisoned by the Puritans and there wrote his famous "To Althea." He was released next year and published his poems in a volume called *Lucasta*. His verse exhibits the more serious side of Cavalier life, its courage and elegance, and reminds us that any cause may evoke the best in a man if he believes in it whole-heartedly. Lovelace will always be remembered for "To Lucasta, Going to The Wars," a farewell to his sweetheart before going into battle, with its celebrated concluding lines:

> *I could not love thee, Dear, so much,*
> *Loved I not honor more*

and "To Althea, From Prison," in which he sings of the liberty he still can feel though in prison:

> *Stone walls do not a prison make,*
> *Nor iron bars a cage.*

Edmund Waller (1606–1687)

Edmund Waller came from a Royalist family, but first sided with the Puritans. He was banished from England for a while, but came back to write in praise of Cromwell. However, when Charles II was restored to the throne, like most of his contemporaries, he rejoiced in seeing a king again at the helm. He was very popular during the Restoration, and in the eighteenth century he was one of the most admired of English poets. There is perhaps a greater mixture of dignity and sweetness in his work than in that of any of the poets thus far mentioned in this period. His two best known lyrics are "Go, Lovely Rose," a message sent with the flower to remind his sweetheart that all lovely things must die in time; and "On A Girdle," a most graceful poem on his sweetheart's belt, concluding:

> *Give me but what this ribband bound,*
> *Take all the rest the sun goes round.*

Robert Herrick (1591–1674)

Robert Herrick was certainly the most gifted and enchanting poet of the group. There is an important difference in his work in that, unlike his fellow Cavaliers, his lines are fresh with the authentic feeling of the country, and have a sweetness and a guilelessness of tone. This fact may be owing to the peculiar circumstances of his life. Herrick was a graduate of Cambridge and spent a good many years in London in the company of poets and wits, "the sons of Ben [Jonson]." Without any apparent profound calling, he accepted the vicarship of Dean Prior in Devonshire in 1629. Here he lived, feeling exiled from London, yet learning to make most of the simple country life about him. The Puritan victory cost him his living, and he was back in London in 1648, in which year he published the works by which he is remembered: *Hesperides,* his human poems, and *Noble Numbers,* his divine poems. After the Restoration he was restored to the Vicarship at Dean Prior.

There is little of the exaggerated sophistication of the Cavaliers in Herrick. In his sweetness and freshness, he is a son of the Elizabethans, although he lacks their romancing and conceits. He is perhaps nearer than any other English poet to the tone of the Greek and Latin lyric poets. Within the radius of his parish he found any number of wonderful trifles to write about. "The Argument of His Book" tells fittingly the nature of his subject matter:

> *I sing of brooks, of blossoms, birds, and bowers,*
> *Of April, May, of June, and July flowers . . .*
> *I write of youth, of love, and have access*
> *By these, to sing of cleanly wantonness;*
> *I sing of dews, of rains, and, piece by piece,*
> *Of balm, of oil, of spice, and ambergris;*
> *I sing of time's trans-shifting; and I write*
> *How roses first came red, and lilies white; . . .*
> *I write of Hell; I sing and ever shall,*
> *Of Heaven, and hope to have it after all.*

He writes of the coming of May and how the young folk troop through the woods to greet it in "Corinna's Going A-Maying," which says (his favorite theme):

> *Come, let us go, while we are in our prime,*
> *And take the harmless folly of the time!*

The opening lines of "To the Virgins, To Make Much of Time," containing the same idea, are quite famous:

> *Gather ye rosebuds while ye may,*
> *Old Time is still a-flying.*

In "To Daffodils" he sees the same lesson in the short life of the flower. Herrick was also a studious observer of the fleeting moments of beauty. A woman walks across the room and he notes (in "Upon Julia's Clothes"):

how sweetly flows
The liquefaction of her clothes.

Among his religious poems are "A Thanksgiving To God For His House," in which he gives thanks with touching sincerity for the simple food and drink on which he lives; and "His Litany To The Holy Spirit," one of his few deeply religious poems, written in one of his rare moods of depression, in which every stanza concludes with the refrain "Sweet Spirit, comfort me!"

THE METAPHYSICAL POETS

During the Cavalier period there was a group of remarkable poets whose work formed what is now called "The Metaphysical School"—a name given to them in the eighteenth century by Samuel Johnson. The father of the school was John Donne, born in Elizabethan times, and his most important successors were Herbert, Vaughan, Crashaw, and Traherne; to this group may be added the name of Abraham Cowley, a poet less gifted than the others. Most of the Metaphysical poets were at their best when writing religious poetry. Indeed, their contribution in this field remains unsurpassed for intensity and mystical vision.

Johnson fixed the label upon the group to describe certain qualities which these poets all have in common. Their poetry exhibits a strenuous exercise of intelligence in their desire to combine dissimilar images, or to discover kinship in things apparently unlike. Their normal vehicle for reconciling contradictions is the poetic conceit.

John Donne (1572–1631)

John Donne, the originator of the school, has been rediscovered and greatly admired in our time. Because he was born a Catholic, he could not take a degree at Oxford or Cambridge, at both of which universities he studied. He tried studying law at Lincoln's Inn, and found it not to his liking. He then turned to writing poetry. He served under Essex at Cadiz in 1596 and at the Azores in 1597. When he returned to London, he entered the service of Sir Thomas Egerton, fell in love with Egerton's niece, and married her without her family's consent. Dismissed, he spent the next years in great poverty. On the advice of his friends he took orders in the English Church and was ordained in 1615. His sermons soon made him famous, and in 1621 he was made Dean of St. Paul's.

Very few of Donne's verses were published in his lifetime, and he regretted the publication of even these. But his poems had a wide circulation in manuscript. Two years after his death, they were published and were received with enthusiasm. His work is something of a revolt against the sweetness of the Elizabethans. He deliberately avoids charm and delicacy, but writes instead with passion and intensity of his own intellectual and emotional experiences. There is a feverish intellectuality about his verses, and almost no music in them. The younger poets were delighted with them, and began to imitate them, sometimes to their own undoing.

Some of his poems are in the amorous Cavalier tradition; such is his celebrated song "Go and Catch a Falling Star," which avers that nowhere lives a woman true and fair. In something of the same tradition is the poem "Love's Deity," beginning:

> *I long to talk with some old lover's ghost*
> *Who died before the god of love was born.*

In a somewhat different strain, one more like his religious poems, is "A Valediction Forbidding Mourning." It is for his religious poetry, however, that Donne is most admired. Among the best of these are the masterful sonnet "Death," with the inspired couplet:

> *One short sleep past, we wake eternally,*
> *And Death shall be no more; Death, thou shalt die!*

and the powerful "A Hymn To God The Father," spun out of amazing puns on the poet's own name: "When Thou hast done, Thou hast not done . . ."

George Herbert (1593–1633)

George Herbert has expressed the beauty of holiness more perfectly than any English poet. When he was at Cambridge he was already writing religious verse. He entered the Church of England and became Rector at Bemerton, near Salisbury. He was very much interested in his work, and it is with justice that Izaak Walton, his first biographer, called him "holy Mr. Herbert." Sometimes he was troubled with a desire to participate in worldly affairs, but expressing the conflict in poetry brought him peace. When he was dying, he gave the manuscript of his poems, none of which had yet been published, to a friend, with the request that they were to be published only if they could be of any help to "any dejected poor soul"; otherwise they were to be burned. The volume, called *The Temple*, came out in 1633, and made disciples of Crashaw and Vaughan. It had a large sale. Although he was a follower of Donne, there is a sweetness and saintliness peculiar to Herbert's poetry. In common with other writers of this school, there are often startling images in his poems. "Virtue" compares the virtuous soul to seasoned timber, which:

> *. . . though the whole world turn to coal,*
> *Then chiefly lives.*

"The Pulley" tells how God gave Man every blessing but restfulness because:

> *If goodness lead him not, yet weariness*
> *May toss him to My breast.*

"The Collar" finds the poet apparently tired of a virtuous, self-denying life, and yearning for the world's pleasures:

> But as I raved, and grew more fierce and wild
> At every word,
> Methought I heard one calling, Child!
> And I replied, My Lord.

Henry Vaughan (1621–1695)

Henry Vaughan, a disciple of Herbert's, has little in common with his master. His inspiration was not the English Church, but his perception of God in Nature—in this respect resembling Traherne, Blake, and Wordsworth later. He was a Welshman who attended Oxford, studied law in London, and during the Civil War returned to Wales to study medicine. For the rest of his life he lived the unexciting existence of a country doctor. The two parts of his *Silex Scintillans* appeared in 1650 and 1655; in 1678 he published *Thalia Rediviva*. His talent was very uneven, and he was not always happy imitating Herbert's complicated verse forms. Yet when he achieves ecstasy, it is quite beyond anything Herbert could attain. His two best-known poems are "The Retreat," which says we are closest to God when we are children, and that as we live in the world we forget our heavenly home, and expresses the poet's desire to return there:

> But I by backward steps would move;
> And when this dust falls to the urn,
> In that state I came, return.

and "The World," with its wonderful opening lines:

> I saw Eternity the other night,
> Like a great ring of pure and endless light,
> All calm, as it was bright.

Richard Crashaw (c. 1613–1649)

Richard Crashaw was a minister's son, took his degree at Cambridge, and fled to the Continent during the Civil War. There he became converted to Catholicism, went to Rome, and in 1647 entered the household of Cardinal Pallotto. The title of his first volume *Steps to the Temple* (1648) indicates his discipleship to Herbert. A new volume, *Carmen Deo Nostro*, appeared in 1652. Crashaw is the most daring of the metaphysical poets in his imagery, and his verse alternates between sublimity and uncertainty. His best known poems are "The Tear," "On The Blessed Virgin's Bashfulness," and "Upon the Body of Our Blessed Lord."

Thomas Traherne (1637–1674)

Thomas Traherne published no poetry during his lifetime. His very name was forgotten until a manuscript of his poems was discovered and published in 1903. Another manuscript was discovered in the British Museum and published in 1910. Traherne is often verbose and prosy, but at some moments he achieves wonderful rapture. He is at his best when dealing, like Wordsworth later, with the simple things in nature and childhood. One of his best poems is "Shadows in the Water."

Abraham Cowley (1618–1667)

Abraham Cowley was a prodigy who, like many others, failed to justify the great promise of his childhood. He was only fifteen when his volume of *Poetical Blossoms* (1633) appeared. Five years later he issued a pastoral comedy, *Love's Riddle* (1638). He was busy writing at Cambridge but was expelled from there as a Royalist. He went to Oxford and is thought there to have acted as a secret agent for the Royalists. He went to France, returned after the Restoration to England, and ended his life on a small estate given to him by the Duke of Buckingham.

Although vastly admired in his own time, his reputation has steadily declined. He is one of the most extreme of the metaphysical poets, and Johnson later particularly condemned him for indulging in "the unexpected and surprising." Today he is admired much more for his essays than for his poetry. His best known poems are "The Wish," in which he states his preference for life in the country; and "The Thief," an address to his sweetheart, who steals his thoughts from God.

Andrew Marvell (1621–1678)

Andrew Marvell is in something of a class by himself, and is a kind of forerunner of the classicism that was to come later in the century. Marvell was a man of such scholarly attainments that he won the praise and friendship of Milton. After Milton became blind, he was appointed the great poet's assistant in affairs of state, (1657), and two years later he was elected to Parliament. He continued to be reelected there until his death. He took his political duties so seriously, however, that he neglected his considerable poetic gifts. It is rather remarkable that despite his being a partisan of Cromwell, he was able to win the respect of Charles II. He is the author of a number of satires, written mostly during the Restoration, and of some fresh and virile lyrical poems. Of the latter his most celebrated are "On A Drop Of Dew," and "The Garden," with its beautiful lines:

> *Annihilating all that's made*
> *To a green thought in a green shade*

THE SCHOOL OF SPENSER

There were a number of poets in this period, none of any considerable importance, who wrote in the Spenserian tradition. Giles Fletcher

(c. 1584–1623) is best remembered for an elegy on Elizabeth, "A Canto Upon the Death of Eliza" (1603), and "Christ's Victory" (1610), a versification of Satan's temptation of Christ—both in modified Spenserian stanza. His elder brother, Phineas Fletcher (1582–1650), is the author of "The Locusts" (1637), an allegory attacking the Jesuits, "The Purple Island" (1633), an allegorical poem on the human body, and *Piscatory Eclogs* (1633)—all imitative of the music of Spenser. William Browne (1591–1643) was the author of *Britannia's Pastorals* (1613 and 1616), an imitation of Sidney's *Arcadia*, which impressed Milton and Keats later; *Shepherd's Pipe* (1614), pastorals in imitation of *The Shepherd's Calendar*, and an epitaph "Upon The Countess Dowager of Pembroke," whose six lines constitute his best known poem, concluding:

> *Death, ere thou hast slain another*
> *Fair and learned and good as she,*
> *Time shall throw a dart at thee.*

15
PROSE AND CHARACTER WRITERS

SEVENTEENTH CENTURY PROSE

The prose writers of the seventeenth century before Dryden are, in the opinion of some critics, the greatest masters of prose in our language. There was not yet an English prose style, and the work of these men is as highly individualized in style as if they were poets. Some of the best of them were not consciously writing "literature," but the fascination of their personalities as revealed in their prose has won them a high place in critical regard. Of these worthies, the best are Izaak Walton, Sir Thomas Browne, Robert Burton, Thomas Fuller, Jeremy Taylor, John Bunyan—and the Character Writers, Joseph Hall, Sir Thomas Overbury, and John Earle.

Izaak Walton (1593–1683)
Izaak Walton is one of the best-loved of English writers. Somehow or other he managed to keep clear of the fierce contention of his times, although he was a Royalist in sympathies. For a while he was a dealer in ironware at London. He began to write in his late forties. His first work was a short *Life Of Donne* (1640), in whose parish he had worshipped. He added a *Life of Sir Henry Wotton* (1651), a *Life of Hooker* (1665), and a *Life of Herbert* (1670), all of which were collected in 1670 to form one of the first important books of biography in our literature. Delightful as these anecdotal biographies are, Walton is best known to the general public for a book on his favorite hobby, a book dear to the hearts of all fishermen, *The Compleat Angler* (1653). With Walton fishing was more than a hobby, it was almost a holy and most Christian exercise. The work is written in a style of almost effortless charm and clarity. It is full of invaluable information on the art of angling, but is delightfully interspersed with anecdotes, verses, and interesting characters. A famous passage in it is the one in which Walton encounters a milkmaid who sings Marlowe's "Passionate Shepherd" and her mother who sings Ralegh's answer. If all fishermen are like Walton, we can agree that they are, as he asserts, all "honest, civil, quiet men."

Sir Thomas Browne (1605–1682)
Sir Thomas Browne is considered by many to be the best prose stylist in English, although Browne himself probably never thought of himself as a

man of letters. He was a man of superb learning; after receiving an education at Oxford, he studied medicine on the Continent at Montpelier, Padua, and Leyden. On his return to England, he lived a few years in London, and then settled down in 1687 as a provincial doctor in the little town of Norwich. Although sympathetic to the Crown, he was too busy with his studies and his profession to participate in the Civil War. Charles II knighted him in 1671.

Naturally Browne was vastly interested in the new science. He kept up a large correspondence with the Royal Society and other scientific bodies. But in spite of all he knew—and he owned one of the largest scientific libraries in England—his knowledge only increased his wonder at the mysteriousness of God's creation. His scientific research deepened his innate mysticism. As a scientist he issued the *Pseudodoxia Epidemica, or Vulgar Errors* (1646), his most elaborate work, in which he undertook to disprove the existence of such monsters as the phoenix and the unicorn, discussed the location of the human heart, and warned against submitting the intelligence to the dicta of authority. On the other hand, he warns against "obstinate incredulity," and everywhere exhibits his own mystical turn of thought.

The two books, however, by which Browne earns his place in English literature were written one at the beginning and the other towards the close of his career as a writer. The *Religio Medici* (1642)—the Religion of a Physician—was his first book; *Hydriotaphia, or Urn-Burial* (1658) was his last. It is in these that we meet most perfectly the exaltation of Browne's spirit and mind. The *Religio Medici*, which became one of Charles Lamb's favorite books, is an exposition of its author's belief: for himself he prefers the Church of England, but has no prejudice against anyone worshipping God in any other place. For him the mysteries of religion were no impediment to faith. "Methinks," he says, "there be not impossibilities enough." He has little taste for religious controversy and is convinced that most men are fundamentally good. Above all, he assures us that his religion brings him only joy: "I fear God, yet am not afraid of him."

Hydriotaphia was written on the occasion of some burial urns having been discovered in Norfolk. Browne's book is a meditation on methods of disposing of the dead, man's faith in immortality, and the impermanence of worldly things. The work is like a magnificent poem in prose, full of dazzling imagery clothed in rich, darkly colored Latinized diction. The sombre majestic music Browne evokes is wonderfully suited to the peculiar cast of his temperament.

Robert Burton (1577–1640)

Robert Burton was one of the most amazing writers England produced. He was a widely read man, particularly in the most obscure and little-known books. Educated at Oxford, he became vicar of St. Thomas Church in his university town.

Only passing mention need be made of the Latin comedy he wrote in 1606 under the influence of Ben Jonson, *Philosophaster*, a satirical comedy on the charlatans of learning. But his massive *The Anatomy of Melancholy* (1621), which is an analysis of the causes, species, symptoms, and cure of melancholy, has been one of the most influential books in English literature. He continued to add new material in succeeding editions. Sam Johnson confessed that it was the only book that could make him rise two hours earlier than he had intended, to read it. Charles Lamb was an untiring reader of its voluminous contents; and his style and very habit of thinking were influenced by Burton. Among the great writers who also felt this influence have been the dramatist Ford, the poets Milton and Keats, and the novelist Thackeray. As for Laurence Sterne, his novel *Tristram Shandy* is full of passages which are hardly more than plagiarisms from *The Anatomy of Melancholy*.

In addition to the subject announced in the title, the interest in this book has been even greater in the wealth of quotations Burton makes from the writings of Latin, Greek, and French authors, and the Bible. The book is indeed an inexhaustible treasure-house of learning, fancy, wit, noble ideals, sentiment, charm, and deep irony. It is the only book of its kind in literature.

Thomas Fuller (1608–1661)

Thomas Fuller was a celebrated clergyman and antiquarian, who eventually became chaplain to Charles II. Naturally, he too was a Royalist, though a man of mild temper, very learned and witty. He was a master of the pun. His style is quiet and quaint with sudden thrusts of humor and brilliant manipulations of the language. His works include *The History of the Holy War* (1639), on the Crusades; *The Holy and Profane State* (1642), a collection of little essays on social conduct, and including some very pleasant descriptions of good and evil human types; and *The History of the Worthies of England* (1662), a compendium of information on all sorts of things including contemporary manners, descriptions, and reflections on various trades, and a series of short biographies—one of them on Sir Walter Ralegh.

Jeremy Taylor (1613–1667)

Jeremy Taylor was at Cambridge during the same time as Milton. The two men eventually became prominent on opposing sides during the Civil War. While Milton was preparing himself to aid the Puritans, Taylor joined the Royalist forces, and was later taken prisoner. After the War he spent most of his remaining life in Ireland, and was one of the men who signed the request for Charles II's return. After the restoration of Charles, he was elevated to a bishopric in the English Church. Most of Taylor's work is theological. In his own time that fact in no way limited his audience. Sermons were popular reading in the seventeenth and eighteenth centuries, and Taylor's style is magnificent.

In all of his works one is aware of a mild, cultivated, and beautiful character. His *Liberty of Prophesying* (1647) was the first work on religious tolerance to be written by a clergyman of the Church of England. Of all his many works the two that are still read are *The Rule and Exercises of Holy Living*

(1650) and *The Rule and Exercises of Holy Dying* (1651)—both classic Anglican views of ideal religious conduct. If he seems extraordinarily preoccupied
with the subject of death, one must remember that it was a favorite topic in
his century. But it is as a stylist that people of taste read Taylor, no matter
what his subject. He has been called "the Shakespeare of English prose."
There are almost as many critics who call him the greatest of English prose
stylists as claim the same position for Sir Thomas Browne. Nothing could be
further from Browne's sombre complicated music than Taylor's simplicity and
naturalness. As Coleridge said of his work: it is "a miraculous combination of
erudition, broad, deep . . . and of genuine imagination." It is chiefly for the
splendor of his imagery that Taylor has few peers in English prose.

John Bunyan (1628–1688)

John Bunyan was the only great Puritan prose writer of his era. His biography is interesting. He was born the son of a tinker in a little village. While
still a boy he served in the Puritan Army. Reading in the gloomiest of the
Puritan theologians plunged him into a time of mental torture during which
he was convinced that he was doomed to everlasting damnation. Almost at
the point of madness because of this conviction, he was saved just in time by
a Baptist minister, Mr. Gifford, who was able to win him to mental peace.
Bunyan himself began to preach now in tiny villages. His reputation grew,
crowds came to hear him, and he was arrested under a new Restoration law
prohibiting such meetings. While in prison for twelve years, he was allowed
to read and write. It may be that this confinement was the luckiest thing that
happened to him. For now, unable to address an audience in person, he was
forced to channel his energies into writing. In prison he wrote an amazing
autobiography, *Grace Abounding To the Chief of Sinners* (1666), a vivid
account of the period of his life when he lived in spiritual anguish. Bunyan
was released in 1672, and became pastor of a small church. Three years later
he was again thrown into prison for six months. This time he began the composition of his masterpiece, *Pilgrim's Progress* (Part One, 1678; Part Two,
1684). No book, with the exception of the Bible of 1611, was to be so widely
read in English homes for the next three centuries. It has been translated into
more than a hundred languages. In Bunyan's own lifetime 100,000 copies
were sold.

Pilgrim's Progress is a simple allegory in which the hero Christian flees the
City of Destruction to find the City of God, Zion. His journey is past the
Slough of Despond, the Valley of Humiliation, the Valley of the Shadow of
Death, Vanity Fair, the Delectable Mountains, and the River of Death until he
reaches the Holy City. On his way he meets Faithful, Ignorance, Sincere, Mr.
Money-love, Little-Faith, Lord Hate-Good, Talkative, Mr. Fearing, and Mr.
Greatheart—characters drawn with great vividness and so true to life that the
simplest country folk of England came to know them as intimates of their
homes. Part two tells how Christian's wife, Christiana, and their sons—
Matthew, Samuel, Joseph and James—set out with their neighbor, Mercy, for

the same destination, and how Mr. Greatheart helps bring them there. The allegory of *Pilgrim's Progress* is, of course, perfectly transparent. But it has been the excitement of the simple story itself that has won the book its high place in the hearts of the English-speaking world.

Among Bunyan's many other works there are three that have been widely read: *The Life and Death of Mr. Badman* (1680), in which a rogue makes his pilgrimage to damnation; *The Holy War* (1682), his longest work, which is a picture of the Fall and Saving of Mankind; and *The Heavenly Footman* (1698), a description of the man that is destined to go to Heaven.

CHARACTER WRITERS

The character was a literary type that flourished in the seventeenth century, and was to play an important role in the development of both the essay and the novel. The character is a brief, objective account of the qualities of a type person, place or thing. The best characters are those that describe types through action rather than through comment. These experiments in depicting human character remain an important part of the essay as it was to be written later, and also prepared the way for mole extensive depiction in the novel. The three most important character writers (in addition to those characters interspersed in the writings of Fuller, as discussed above) are Joseph Hall, Sir Thomas Overbury, and John Earle.

Joseph Hall (1574–1656)

Joseph Hall made a collection of English characters, the first on record, called *The Characters of Virtues and Vices* (1608). More than his successors, he follows the writings of Theophrastus (died 287 B.C.), the father of the character. Theophrastus had defined his purpose as the depiction of "the manners of each several kind of men, both good and bad, and . . . the behavior proper to them." Hall, who was a bishop in the Church of England, wrote characters on The Happy Man, The Hypocrite, The Superstitious, The Covetous, and so on.

Sir Thomas Overbury (1581–1613)

Sir Thomas Overbury was a poet as well as a character writer. In *A Wife* (1614) he describes in verse the qualities to be desired in a wife. But his important work is the collection of *Characters* (1614) in prose that were published as an appendix to the poem. (It is known that some of these characters were written by his friends.) These characters move further away from Theophrastus's models. Overbury describes the character as "a picture (real or personal) quaintly drawn in various colors, all of them heightened by one shadowing." His subjects include a Country Gentleman, a Melancholy Man, a Tinker, an Inns of Court Man, a Fair and Happy Milk Maid, an Improvident

Young Gallant, a Devilish Usurer, a Dunce, and so on. These prove to exhibit a much wider range than Hall's characters.

John Earle (c. 1601–1665)

The finest examples of characters were written by John Earle. He was born in Yorkshire and took his M.A. at Oxford. It was while he was an undergraduate at the University that he composed his book of characters. It circulated in manuscript for a number of years before being published anonymously as *Microcosmographie* (1628). The book went through many editions, although its author seems never to have been tempted to repeat his success. He led a varied life, was chaplain to Charles II during the latter's exile, and made Dean of Westminster during the Restoration. The *Microcosmographie* is the profoundest of the character books as well as the most powerfully written. Earle was a fairly subtle psychologist, unlike his predecessors, and makes us familiar with the causes of the actions of his types. His subjects include a Child, a Downright Scholar, a Mere Young Gentleman of the University, a Vulgar-Spirited Man, a Pretender to Learning, an Affected Man, and so on.

Other character books worthy of mention are John Stephens' *Satirical Essays, Characters and Others* (1615) and Owen Feltham's *Resolves* (c. 1620).

16
JOHN MILTON

IMPORTANCE

Milton is our greatest poet after Shakespeare. But no two poets have less in common. Understanding Shakespeare is above all a profound experience in broadening one's humanity; understanding Milton is a profound experience in deepening one's aesthetic perceptions and widening one's intellectual horizon. Everybody is a potential audience of Shakespeare; only the intellectually cultivated will love Milton. His learning and erudition are greater than those of any other poet on record. And as a literary artist he has exerted the widest of all influences over later poets. You may read his influence in the work of Dryden, Pope, Cowper, Collins, Gray, Wordsworth, Coleridge, Shelley, Keats, Tennyson, and Browning.

Milton was fortunate in his parents. His father, a scrivener by profession, was well known as a composer of music. His mother was a woman noted for her deeds of charity. Their home was cultivated, well-to-do, and firmly Puritan. They lived on Bread Street, Cheapside, London, and Milton was born there on December 9, 1608. His father decided early on that Milton was to have a literary career, and Milton himself tells us: "From twelve years of age I hardly ever left my studies or went to bed before midnight." After studying at St. Paul's School, Milton entered Christ College, Cambridge in 1625. At Cambridge he decided that he was to be a great poet, a poet who would write such poetry as posterity "should not willingly let die." To that end he felt he must lead a life of austerity and integrity. For not participating in the riots of his schoolmates, he was affectionately dubbed "the lady of Christ's."

EARLY WORKS

In 1632 he took his M.A. and went to live at his father's new house in the village of Horton, a few miles from London. His literary output up to this time is not very impressive. He had written some Latin verses and a handful of English poems. There are many good lines in his "On the Morning of Christ's Nativity,"

(1629); the poem "On Shakespeare" (1630) is better intended than executed; the sonnet "To a Nightingale" (1631) has a certain charm. But Milton himself in his sonnet "On His Being Arrived to the Age of Twenty-three" (1631) realized full well that he had accomplished very little of which he could be proud. Milton's father, however, had faith in his son and allowed him to continue his studies at Horton from 1632 to 1638. During these years he made himself master of everything worth knowing in the literature of Rome, Greece, Italy, France, Spain, and England; the Bible, the Talmud, and the writings of the early Christian Fathers were perfectly familiar to him. Toward the close of his stay at Horton, Milton's genius began to produce its first important fruits: "L'Allegro," (1631–2) and "Il Penseroso" (1631–2), *Comus* (1634), and "Lycidas" (1637). These great English poems constitute what is known as Milton's first period.

"L'Allegro" and "Il Penseroso"

"L'Allegro" and "Il Penseroso" are companion pieces. The titles are taken from musicology, and mean respectively "the joyful man" and "the thoughtful man." Considered together they are like a musical composition in two movements, the first gay, the second pensive. They are approximately of the same length and each opens with a ten line introduction banishing the mood hostile to the spirit of the piece. They are both written in the same meter, which for the bulk of each poem is iambic tetrameter rhyming in couplets. Together they record twenty-four hours in the experience of the poet. The Joyful Man and the Thoughtful Man are the same individual, and the poems exhibit two aspects of his temperament. "L'Allegro" opens at dawn and ends at dark; "Il Penseroso" opens there and closes with the new dawn.

"L'Allegro," after banishing the spirit of "loathed melancholy," welcomes the Goddess of Mirth, Euphrosyne. With her are also invited Jest, Jollity, Sport, Laughter, and Liberty. The poet, as the lark begins his morning song, commences a tour of the day: the cock strutting before the barnyard door; the sounds of hounds and horn on the hill; the sun rising; the ploughman busy over the soil; the milk maid, the mower, and the shepherd, at their tasks; the flocks on the sunlit meadows; the flowers and brooks; the village cottages; the hayloft; country dances. Then, as daylight fails: the "nutbrown ale"; folk tales at the fireside; the reading of books of romance and the comedies of Shakespeare and Jonson. The poem concludes with a desire to be lapped "in soft Lydian airs":

> *In notes with many a winding bout*
> *Of linked sweetness long drawn out*
> *With wanton heed and giddy cunning,*
> *The melting voice through mazes running,*
> *Untwisting all the chains that tie*
> *The hidden soul of harmony.*

"Il Penseroso," after banishing "deluding joys," welcomes the Goddess Melancholy. With her are also invited Peace, Quiet, Fast, Leisure, Contemplation. The poet, as the nightingale sings

> *In her sweetest, saddest plight*
> *Smoothing the rugged brow of night . . .*
> *Sweet bird, that shun'st the noise of folly,*
> *Most musical, most melancholy!*

begins a tour of the night: the woods; the wandering moon shedding its light through *"Heaven's wide, pathless way,"* and on the lawns; the far-off curfew; at home again

> *Where glowing embers through the room*
> *Teach light to counterfeit a gloom;*

the bellman's song; the watcher in the tower of the mysteries of astronomy. Then, the world of books again: the tragedies of the great Greeks, the *Iliad*, the writings of Chaucer, and Spenser's *Faerie Queene*

> *Of forests, and enchantments drear*
> *Where more is meant than meets the ear . . .*

As Dawn approaches, the poet escapes the morning light by seeking heavy woods and some quiet brook, or else the cathedral where the organ plays and the full-voiced choir sings so as to dissolve him into ecstasy

> *And bring all Heaven before mine eyes.*

Comus

Comus is a masque written, as masques often were, for a particular occasion: an entertainment of the family of the Countess of Derby. Henry Lawes, the distinguished composer, to whom Milton later indited a sonnet, wrote the music to Milton's words. Although Milton was familiar with Jonson's masques, his earnestness of moral purpose differs widely from the tradition of court masques. The story presents an allegory on the ideal of chastity that was so dear to Milton. A girl and her two brothers lose their way in a forest, and she becomes separated from them. Comus, the son of Bacchus and Circe, finds the girl, and conducts her to his dwelling where many creatures whom his enchantments have overcome are sunk in bestiality. Comus tries to work his sorcery on the girl, but she is strong against his powerful appeals to sensuality. A guardian spirit leads her two brothers to her rescue. The leading idea in the poem is that the virtuous mind is safe from the attacks of evil:

> *Love virtue, she alone is free;*
> *She can teach ye how to climb*
> *Higher than the sphery chime;*
> *Or if Virtue feeble were,*
> *Heaven itself would stoop to her.*

Among the many beauties of *Comus* are two wonderful songs:

> *Sabrina fair,*
> *Listen where thou art sitting*
> *Under the glassy, cool translucent wave . . .*

and

> *Sweet echo, sweetest nymph that liv'st unseen*
> *Within thy airy shell*
> *By slow Meander's margent green.*

Comus was presented on September 29th, 1634 in honor of the Earl of Bridgewater.

"Lycidas"

"Lycidas" has been called by many critics the greatest achievement of English lyrical poetry. It is an elegy written upon the death of a fellow alumnus of Milton's, Edward King, who was drowned in the Irish Sea in 1637. A group of King's former school mates at Cambridge issued a commemorative volume titled *Obsequies to the Memory of Mr. Edward King* (1638). It was in this limited publication that "Lycidas" first appeared. Heretofore, of his great poems only *Comus* had been published, and that anonymously.

"Lycidas" is not an expression of personal grief (personal grief was to be eloquent in Milton's next important poem, the Latin "Epitaphium Damonis"), but rather a record of the thoughts that King's death evoked in the poet. King had written verses himself and had prepared himself for the Church. These two facts of the dead man's career form the basis for what Milton had to say. Outwardly the poem is written in the tradition of pastoral poetry, and more particularly in the tradition of the pastoral elegy as exhibited in the ancient Greek "Lament for Bion" by Moschus. The poet is spoken of as a shepherd. But Milton introduces the innovation of identifying the Christian idea of shepherd (pastor) as meaning *priest*. In a wonderful fusion of pagan and Chistian tradition, Milton makes his elegy the occasion for a scathing attack on the corruptions of the clergy in his time, with parenthetical thrusts of scorn at his trivial contemporaries, the Cavalier poets. The lament for King concludes with a burst of glorious poetry:

> *Weep no more, woeful shepherds, weep no more,*
> *For Lycidas, your sorrow, is not dead,*
> *Sunk though he be beneath the watery floor;*
> *So sinks the day-star in the ocean bed,*
> *And yet anon repairs his drooping head,*
> *And tricks his beams, and with new-spangled ore*
> *Flames in the forehead of the morning sky.*

The poem concludes with a hint that the poet hereafter will sing in another strain.

POLITICAL WORK

In April, 1638, Milton left Horton for a tour of the continent. He visited Paris, Nice, Genoa, Leghorn, and Pisa. At Florence, the great center of cultural activity in Italy, he made many friendships among prominent Italian writers. He went on to Siena, Rome, and Naples. He was about to proceed to the East when he learned of civil discords brewing in England, and felt it was his duty to come home. When he arrived in England he discovered that his best friend, Charles Diodati, had died. In memory of their friendship Milton wrote his greatest Latin poem, the "Epitaphium Damonis," which may be considered the last poem in his first period. The first period of Milton's career may be summarized as exhibiting him as a son of the Elizabethans, interested primarily in love of beauty and learning, with the Puritan side of his nature present but not emphatic.

The second period of Milton's career (1641–1654) finds him so much the Puritan that he writes very little poetry. On his return from the continent he settled in London and began to tutor. In 1641 begins a long period of pamphleteering in the service of democracy and Puritanism. He had already decided that he must write a great poem. But he felt that his duty to his country required his laying aside his own creative ambitions and placing his talents at the service of those who were fighting for liberty. His first piece of argumentative prose was *Of Reformation* (1641), an attack on the political corruption of the clergy in the English Church, and a plea for democracy in the structure of the Church. In the same year he wrote *Of Prelatical Episcopacy*, an argument to prove the superiority of the Presbyterian system of Church government; and *Animadversions*, an attack on Bishop Hall (the character writer), a powerful prelate of the English Church. *The Reason of Church Government* (1642) is Milton's longest ecclesiastical tract, and urges the separation of church and state. The last of the anti-episcopal pamphlets, published the same year, was *An Apology*, an answer to personal attacks on him made by the opposition.

In 1643, Milton went into the country on a commission for his father, met Mary Powell, daughter of a Cavalier family, and married her. After a month with her he left her presumably to make her farewells to her friends. Once he was in London, however, she refused to rejoin him. The sudden failure of his marriage turned Milton's thoughts to the subject of divorce. In 1643, 1644 and 1645 he issued four tracts on divorce: *The Doctrine and Discipline of Divorce*, *The Judgment of Martin Bucer*, *Tetrachordon*, and *Colasterion*. It is Milton's view in these pamphlets that all that should be necessary to disrupt a marriage tie is the willingness of both parties to separate. He believed incompatibility to be a better argument for divorce than adultery. Naturally, Milton was bitterly attacked for these revolutionary opinions. It is interesting that in spite of his stand, when his wife pleaded with him to be taken back in 1645, he was willing to have her return. She bore him three daughters and died in 1652.

Milton's defense of divorce began a series that continued his defense of personal liberty, as he had already defended religious liberty. His next important tract was *Of Education* (1644), in which he urges the supplementing of books with personal contact and practical experience. The same year saw the publication of his most important treatise, *Areopagitica*, a noble defense of the freedom of the press. Parliament had passed a law requiring all books to be licensed by a censor. The Presbyterians, now in control, were attempting to bring all of England to their way of thinking. Milton was indignant that a Puritan party should revive Charles I's licensing act. The *Areopagitica* was addressed to Parliament in the hope of convincing it to repeal the act. It is a magnificent example of the classic oration. (The title is derived from a speech addressed by Isocrates to the Athenian court of the Areopagus.) Milton argues that only enemies of truth have ever tried to crush a free press, and that it is impossible to make men good by external restraints. Most of all he is concerned by the danger to the pursuit of truth. He has complete faith in the ability of people who can read to find their own salvation. The *Areopagitica* has remained a source of inspiration to all who have fought for freedom of speech and of the press, and Milton's arguments were to be repeated in France in the era preceding the French Revolution.

The struggle between the King and Parliament now came to a head. Charles was tried, and, in February 1649, beheaded. Milton's next tract begins his series on political liberty. In *Of the Tenure of Kings and Magistrates* (1649) he attempted to quiet the public's reaction of fear to the beheading of Charles. His argument was that a people may end whenever they see fit the rule of their monarch. The new Commonwealth recognized the importance of Milton's service in this pamphlet, and appointed him Latin Secretary in March 1649. Among his many duties was to defend his country against the many attacks that the monarchies of Europe were aiming at it in print. His energies were now completely absorbed in this work. *Eikonoklastes* (1649) was an answer to a monarchist attempt to paint Charles as a martyred saint. This kind of work and the mass of state correspondence that it was his duty to answer resulted in Milton's losing the sight of one eye in 1650. A very dangerous book against the Commonwealth now appeared, but Milton was threatened with the loss of the sight of his other eye if he did not cease his labors. Fully aware of the risk he was taking, he answered in *The Defense of the English People* (1651). In 1652 he was a blind man.

Blindness, terrible to all its victims, must have been tragic beyond description to a poet who loved books more than anyone we know of, and who was, moreover, an expert musician on the organ. Yet no where in Milton do we read of regret for having sacrificed his eyesight. When another enemy of the Republic, learning of Milton's blindness, attacked him in particular, and cited Milton's affliction as God's punishment for his part in the execution of

Charles, Milton dictated his spirited *Second Defense of the English People* (1654), which contains a noble defense of his conduct. The *Second Defense of the English People* is in one respect Milton's most interesting prose work, for it contains a long and very informative autobiographical section.

Milton continued his defense of the republic despite his blindness. His later treatises are *Pro Se Defensio*, (1655), *A Treatise of Civil Power* (1659), *Considerations* (1659), and, in 1660, when Charles Stuart was preparing to return to assume his father's throne, Milton's warning against the restoration of the Stuarts, *The Ready and Easy Way to Establish a Free Commonwealth*. His prose works also include a *History of Britain* (1646–1660), *Of Christian Doctrine* (1655–1660), *Of True Religion* (1672), a Latin grammar, a Latin dictionary, and a book on Russia.

In the meantime, because of his blindness, he had retired from active service in the Council. He married Katherine Woodcock in November of 1656, but she died in February 1658 with the daughter to whom she had given birth. It was on her that he wrote his most touching sonnet.

LATE WORK

It is ironical that it was his blindness that gave him the freedom again to take up his vocation of poet. His third, and last period, may be said to begin in 1655 with his great sonnets, and includes his major works: *Paradise Lost*, *Paradise Regained*, and *Samson Agonistes*. But these great works were not written in peace. At the Restoration Milton was forced to remain in hiding for some time because of his services to the Commonwealth. He was even arrested for a while, but was released on the payment of a heavy fine. His declining years were embittered by the neglect and dislike of his three daughters. Needing someone to take care of him, in 1663 he married Elizabeth Minshull, who was thirty years his junior. His will left his estate to her because of his disagreements with his daughters.

Paradise Lost
Paradise Lost (1665) is the great poem that Milton for many years knew he was to write. During the years of political activity, he had been seeking about for a subject, and for a time toyed with the idea of writing on the Arthurian legend. But eventually he chose a far greater subject—the Fall of Adam and Eve from God's grace, and through them, the fall of the human race. The poem is, of course, entirely the work of a blind man. It was composed as Milton lay abed nights, and dictated during the day to his secretary. When it was issued to the public, its sale was small; nevertheless, it has exerted a greater influence on the history of English poetry than any other single poem ever written. It was Milton's own testament of faith in the Puritan philosophy, and was sent into the world in days when the public was mocking everything Milton had fought for.

No other poem contains such treasures of learning. To the outlines of the story the Bible, the Talmud, and the Church Fathers contributed. The structure and tragic tone of the poem are indebted to Homer and Virgil. But everywhere one will find transfigured for Milton's own purposes a world of literary tradition: Greek mythology, the Scriptures, Ovid, Ariosto, Tasso, Spenser, and many Renaissance writers in Italian, Latin, French, and English. The reference in Milton to the lore of learning is not decoration; it is the very tissue of his thinking. The endless richness of allusion deepens his ideas at every turn.

No story of such vastness was ever told by a poet before as in this epic. The immensities of the physical universe are the background for the events. We are now in Hell, now in Heaven, now in the vast depths of Chaos, now in the ten concentric spheres which, (in the Ptolemaic system of astronomy), encircle the Earth, now in the Garden of Eden. The following is a summary of each of the twelve books of *Paradise Lost*.

Book 1: States the subject (Man's first disobedience and the loss therefore of Paradise) and the purpose of the poem (to "justify the ways of God to men"). The story begins in the middle, showing Satan and his cohorts, the fallen angels, lying on a burning lake of Hell where they have been hurled after their defeat in the Battle of Heaven. Satan awakens his overwhelmed legions, and addresses Beelzebub, one of his chief captains. Satan speaks to his troops, comforts them with the possibility of their regaining Heaven, and bids them form a council to decide upon the next course of action. The fallen angels proceed to build a palace for Satan, Pandemonium, and in it the leaders of the fallen angels sit in council. The opening lines of this book are memorable:

> *Of Man's first disobedience, and the fruit*
> *Of that forbidden tree, whose mortal taste*
> *Brought death into the world, and all our woe,*
> *With loss of Eden, till one greater Man*
> *Restore us, and regain the blissful seat,*
> *Sing, heavenly Muse.*

There are many glorious and tragic passages in this book. The lines describing Satan's fall from Heaven are magnificent:

> *Him the Almighty Power*
> *Hurled headlong flaming from the ethereal sky,*
> *With hideous ruin and combustion, down*
> *To bottomless perdition; there to dwell*
> *In adamantine chains and penal fire,*
> *Who durst defy the Omnipotent to arms.*

Satan's words to Beelzebub are full of tragic grandeur:

> *What though the field be lost?*
> *All is not lost; the unconquerable will,*
> *And study of revenge, immortal hate,*
> *And courage never to submit or yield,*
> *And what is else not to be overcome?*

Book 2: Opens with the Council in Hell. Should they attempt another battle in Heaven? Some of the fallen angels are for the plan, some against it. Satan proposes a third plan—to find out whether it be true, as tradition has it, that another world and another kind of creature inhabiting that world, have been recently created. The fallen angels prefer to work their revenge against God through His new creation, Man. But no one except Satan is willing to undertake the perilous voyage through Chaos. He is applauded for his courage. The council ends, and Satan sets forth on his journey. He comes first to Hell Gates, which he finds shut. Sitting there to guard them are Sin, who turns out to be an offspring of Satan himself, and Sin's son, Death. They open the gates for him, and he proceeds on his painful journey through Chaos. In this book the dark magnificence of the poetry is continued. The meeting of Satan with Sin and Death is a triumph in evoking a sense of horror and revulsion.

Book 3: In Heaven. God, on His throne, seeing Satan making for the newly created Universe, shows him to His Son, and predicts Satan's success in deceiving mankind. God explains that Man has been created with a free will, and the ability to withstand the tempter. But Man will fall. The Son of God offers himself as a ransom for mankind; and God accepts that sacrifice, and ordains His Son's eventual incarnation. All the angels in Heaven, singing to harps, celebrate the glory of God and His Son. Meanwhile, Satan alights on the outside shell of the universe. He makes his way towards the Gate of Heaven, which is reached from this shell by ascending stairs. Satan, on his way down to the Earth, manages to pass through the spheres down to the orb of the Sun. There he finds Uriel, the angel in charge. Changing himself into the shape of a lesser angel, Satan converses with Uriel and pretends that he has come to see the new creation and Man. Uriel directs him to Man's habitation. Satan reaches the Earth, and alights on Mt. Niphates. The opening of this book is one of the most radiant passages in poetry:

> *Hail holy light, offspring of Heaven's first-born . . .*
> *Bright effluence of bright essence increate*

Milton goes on to speak of what blindness means to him:

> *thee I revisit safe,*
> *And feel thy sovereign vital Lamp; but thou*
> *Revisit'st not these eyes, that roll in vain*
> *To find thy piercing ray, and find no dawn; . . .*
> *. . . Thus with the year*
> *Seasons return, but not to me returns*

> *Day, or the sweet approach of even or morn,*
> *Or sight of vernal bloom, or summer's rose,*
> *Or flocks or herds, or human face divine;*
> *But cloud instead, and ever-during dark*
> *Surrounds me, from the cheerful ways of men*
> *Cut off . . .*
> *So much the rather thou celestial light,*
> *Shine inward, and the mind through all her powers*
> *Irradiate, there plant eyes, all mist from thence*
> *Purge and disperse, that I may see and tell*
> *Of things invisible to mortal sight.*

Book 4: Brings Satan in view of Eden. He experiences fear, envy, and despair at the sight of God's creation. At length, confirming himself in his evil purposes, he journeys on to this earthly Paradise. The Garden of Eden and Adam and Eve are described. Satan marvels at the beauty he sees. He overhears a conversation between Adam and Eve and learns that they have been forbidden under the penalty of death to eat of the fruit of the Tree of Knowledge of Good and Evil. He leaves them a while. In the meantime, Uriel descends to the Gate of Paradise, which is in charge of the angel Gabriel, and warns Gabriel that an evil spirit had slipped by him in the guise of a good angel. Gabriel promises to find the evil one before morning. Night comes on, Adam and Eve worship God in their bower, and go to their rest. Gabriel summons his watch to guard Paradise. Satan is found at the ear of Eve, tempting her in a dream. He is brought before Gabriel, tries to resist, but at a sign from Heaven flies out of Eden. The passages describing Eden, in this book, are among the greatest descriptive passages in English poetry.

Book 5: Eve tells Adam of her troublesome dream, and he comforts her. They come forth to their day's labor, the tending of the plants in the Garden, and sing a hymn to God. In order to give Man all the knowledge he needs to resist Satan, God sends Raphael down to warn him. Raphael comes to Eden, is greeted by Adam, and is entertained with their choicest fruits. Raphael delivers his message, warning Adam of his enemy, and, at Adam's request, enlarges on Satan's history. We are thus brought to the actual beginning of the story of the epic, with Raphael's account of how Satan was first moved by envy to gather a third of the angels in Heaven under his leadership, and incited them to rebel against God.

Book 6: Raphael's narrative continues. Michael and Gabriel were sent forth to battle against Satan and his followers. The first fight is described. Satan and his cohorts were forced to retire. Satan called a council, invented devilish instruments of destruction, and in the second day's fight caused confusion among Michael's ranks. But the loyal angels pulled up mountains and with them overwhelmed Satan's forces. On the third day God sent His Son to crush the rebellion. Driving into the midst of the enemy, the Son pursued them to the wall of Heaven, which opened; and Satan's troops fell down into the vast abyss of Chaos. They fell for nine days into Hell, which had been prepared for them.

Book 7: At Adam's request, Raphael relates how the new universe was created because God had desired to fill up the lost ranks of the angels with a new creature, Man. God sent His Son to create in six days the miracles of the universe. The process is related by Raphael.

Book 8: The archangel's comments on the motions of the heavenly bodies. To satisfy his guest's curiosity, Adam relates his own story. He tells what he remembers of his own creation, his first experiences in Eden, his interview with God, the creation of Eve, and of his first meeting and nuptials with her. After another warning against Satan, Raphael departs.

Book 9: Contains the climax of the story, and is the longest book in the epic. Satan returns at night to Eden in the shape of a mist. He finds a serpent sleeping and enters into it. Morning comes, and Adam and Eve go forth again to their labors. Eve argues that they will accomplish more if they work separately. Adam, against his better judgment, agrees to this plan. The serpent finds Eve alone. He extolls her with elaborate flattery over all other creatures. Eve is astonished to hear the serpent speak and asks how he came by such understanding. The serpent replies that the fruit of a certain tree in the Garden has given him speech and reason. Eve asks to be brought to the tree. The serpent brings Eve to the forbidden Tree of the Knowledge of Good and Evil. The serpent, now emboldened, induces her with much flattery to eat of the forbidden fruit. She yields and is pleased with its taste. She comes to Adam with the fruit and relates her reasons for eating it. Adam, overwhelmed with dismay at her sin, is unable to face the prospect of losing her, and knowing that he too must be lost, also eats of the fruit. The first reaction is a kind of drunken excitement. They both exult in their trespass. Suddenly aware of their nakedness, they seek covering for it. After their lascivious pleasure passes, they are appalled at what awaits them, and fall to accusing each other.

Book 10: Man's sin is known in Heaven. God sends his Son to Eden to pass sentence on the transgressors. But He takes pity on them and clothes them. Sin and Death, waiting at the Gates of Hell, are aware of Satan's victory over Man, and decide to follow Satan up to Man's universe. To make the way easier from Hell, they pave a broad highway over Chaos. They meet Satan and congratulate him. He returns to Pandemonium, where he relates his success. When his audience would applaud, the fallen angels are all turned into serpents who can only hiss. God in Heaven commands his angels to make certain alterations in the elements. In Eden Adam now rejects Eve's attempts to comfort him. At length, however, she succeeds in appeasing him. She remembers a promise made to her that her seed should be revenged on the serpent, and she urges Adam to seek peace of offended God.

Book 11: The Son of God presents the prayers of Adam and Eve to God. God accepts His Son's intercession, but declares that they can no longer live in Eden. Michael is sent down with a band of cherubim to dispossess them. Michael is also commanded to give Adam a view of the future of his race. Adam sees Michael approaching, and goes to meet him. The angel announces that they must leave Eden. Eve weeps bitterly; Adam pleads but submits. The angel now leads Adam up to a high hill and sets before him in vision a series of events in the history of his offspring, up to the Flood.

Book 12: Michael's vision continues. Events after the Flood, through Abraham, and the incarnation, death, and resurrection of the Saviour, are shown to Adam. Adam, satisfied at the eventual redemption of his race, descends the hill with Michael. Eve, in the meantime, in her sleep, has had dreams which have composed her mind to submission. Michael takes Adam and Eve, each by the hand, and leads them out of Eden. When they look back they see a fiery sword and ranks of cherubim guarding the entrance to Eden. The concluding lines of the poem are as triumphantly beautiful as anything in the poem:

> In either hand the hastening Angel caught
> Our lingering parents, and to the Eastern Gate
> Led them direct, and down the cliff as fast
> To the subjected plain; then disappeared.
> They looking back, all the Eastern side beheld
> Of Paradise, so late their happy seat,
> Waved over by that flaming brand, the Gate
> With dreadful faces thronged and fiery arms.
> Some natural tears they dropped, but wiped them soon;
> The world was all before them, where to choose
> Their place of rest, and Providence their guide.
> They, hand in hand, with wandering steps and slow,
> Through Eden took their solitary way.

Style: *Paradise Lost*, as an art epic, follows certain epic conventions. These conventions are based upon Homer's usage, and Virgil's deliberate imitation of Homer. These epic conventions include:

1—the statement of the subject in the opening lines
2—an appeal to the Muse for inspiration
3—beginning the story in the middle of the action (in Horace's phrase: to begin *in medias res*)
4—the enumeration of the host of warriors

5—long dramatic dialogue
6—extended descriptive passages
7—elaborate similes ("the epic simile")

Paradise Lost is written in blank verse of such power and grandeur as have won for it the description of "Milton's organ tone."

IMPORTANCE

In the early books of *Paradise Lost* Satan emerges as the most heroic figure, proud, tragic, unwilling to submit to defeat. But that is because Milton was too great an artist not to do full justice to his villain. The hero of his tragedy is Adam, who at first may seem less magnificent than Satan. But as Satan's character becomes more and more debased through his evil plans and actions, Adam's, somewhat because of his human frailty, rises higher in comparison. At the end, because Adam faces his guilt, he emerges in truly heroic proportions. The relations between Adam and Eve, especially before the Fall, are described with charm and with many touching details. Indeed, *Paradise Lost* contains an almost endless variety of poetry: the tragic, the luxuriantly descriptive, the tender, the intellectual, the exalted.

It has sometimes been said that the only parts of this poem that are a failure are those that take place in Heaven. The observation is certainly untrue for the many seraphic outbursts in song of the angels. But it must be admitted that by definition it is impossible to represent Deity with any human qualities, and it is not surprising, therefore, that the passages in which God speaks are too severe and cold in comparison with the rest of the poem. But those passages, after all, are few in number. *Paradise Lost* is the greatest single accomplishment in English non-dramatic poetry.

Paradise Regained

Paradise Regained (1665–7), a short epic that is a sequel to *Paradise Lost*, was published in 1671 together with *Samson Agonistes*. It relates how man's lost Paradise was regained through the victory of Christ over Satan, the victory foretold of Eve's seed over the serpent. The theme here is of Christ's obedience to God, as tried through all temptations. The poem deals with the period in Christ's life immediately following his baptism by John and preceding his ministry in the world. Milton had mentioned the *Book of Job* in the Bible as a model for the short epic. *Paradise Regained* follows the *Book of Job* in having passages chiefly of dialogue with short connecting narrative sections. Here again Milton's learning and memory are astounding. But the blank verse is austere and pared to the naked essentials of the meaning. The four books deal with Satan's temptation of Christ in the order recounted in *Luke*, Chapter 4.

Book 1: Jesus, after baptism at Jordan, is led by the Holy Spirit into the wilderness. For forty days he has had nothing to eat. Satan approaches him in his hunger and bids him, if he is indeed the Son of God, to convert a stone into bread. Jesus overcomes this first temptation of distrust by observing that man does not live by bread alone. It is not his purpose to change the natural order of things.

Books 2 and 3: Satan takes Jesus up to a high mountain and shows him all the kingdoms of the world. Satan promises to give all the power over them to Jesus, if Jesus will worship him.

Book 4: This second temptation of earthly glory is resolved when Jesus disdainfully says, "*Get thee behind me Satan*"; it is God alone whom Jesus worships. Satan now brings Jesus to Jerusalem and sets him on a pinnacle of the Temple, remarking that if Jesus be indeed the Son of God he can test it by casting himself down, assured that God will not allow him to be hurt. But Jesus repels this last temptation, unwilling as he is to tempt God, and perfect in his faith. Satan recognizes Jesus's invincibility, and disappears, while Jesus stands safely on the pinnacle. A band of angels ease Jesus from his station and bear him to the valley where all manner of food and drink are set before him.

Paradise Regained, because it is less dramatic and more severe, has been less read than *Paradise Lost*, but it was Wordsworth's favorite. It has a quieter, but a no less powerful, tone. And Milton's summary of the civilizations of the world and the learning of Greece are among the most notable examples of his erudition applied to the purposes of great poetry.

Samson Agonistes

Samson Agonistes (1668–70) was published with *Paradise Regained* in 1671. It is the culminating work of Milton's career, and exhibits his style at its greatest elevation of austerity. Not a word could be spared, there is no decoration, and the poetry has the massiveness of bronze. For his last work Milton employed the form of Greek tragedy, especially as practiced by the greatest of Greek dramatists, Sophocles. In fact the very situation of the play and certain of its events remind one of Sophocles' *Oedipus at Colonus*.

Like all Greek tragedies, there is in this work a basic conception of five acts. The first act terminates at line 325 and contains Samson's soliloquy and discourse to the Chorus. The second act ends at line 710 and contains the Manoa episode. The third act ends at line 1060 and contains the Delilah episode. The fourth act terminates at line 1440 and contains the episodes of Harapha and the Officer. The fifth act deals with Manoa's reappearance and the announcement of the catastrophe.

The story is concerned with the last day in the life of the great Hebrew hero Samson. We find him blind and captive, working for the Philistines in their city of Gaza. It is a festival day, and he is released for the day from his heavy labors. He comes forth into the open air and bemoans his condition. He receives a visit of certain friends of his people (constituting the Chorus) who comfort him as well as they can. Then his old father, Manoa, comes to see him and announces his intention of trying to win Samson's freedom by paying a ransom. It is a matter of anguish to both father and son that the Philistines on this day are celebrating in thanksgiving for their deliverance from Samson. After Manoa departs to sue to the Philistian lords for his son's liberty, Delilah, Samson's wife, a daughter of the Philistines, comes to see her husband. Delilah attempts to win Samson's forgiveness for her act of treachery in delivering him to the hands of his enemies. Her excuse is that out of love for Samson she wanted to keep him with her in her own country. He rejects her deceptive wiles, and in a fit of wrath she reveals herself for the traitress that she really is. Next comes Harapha, the athlete, a bully who insults Samson now that he is blind and apparently without strength. A public officer arrives to summon Samson to appear before the lords at their feast in an exhibition of his strength. He at first refuses. But suddenly, inwardly persuaded that God desires him to go, he consents to accompany the officer on the latter's reappearance. To the Chorus Manoa returns with great hope that he can procure his son's deliverance. In the midst of his account, a messenger comes to relate how Samson has sacrificed his life for God, in pulling down the roof on the heads of the Philistian assembly. He and all present lost their lives. But in his death he has regained God's favor. The material for the play Milton found in the Book of *Judges*, Chapters 3–16.

It is impossible to escape the conviction that Milton to a certain extent was writing about himself in *Samson Agonistes*. Like Samson, he was living blind and alone among his enemies (the period of the Restoration); like Samson, he had taken to wife a daughter of the enemy (his first wife, of Cavalier family); like Samson, he placed his trust in God to justify his beliefs. The play thus becomes one more assertion of Milton's unquenchable spirit of integrity. But there is a very special pathos that readers of the play will feel. For in Samson's mouth Milton at last speaks to us of the horrors of blindness.

Sonnets

Milton wrote a total of nineteen English sonnets and five in Italian over the course of thirty years in his adult life. The first of these, "To the Nightingale," is a delicate, yet yearning love poem. One of the last is a rapt vision of his recently deceased wife. Through these sonnets, Milton, like Sidney before him, traced the details of his emotional and poetic development. Unlike the Shakespearean sonnet in form, the Miltonic sonnet follows the Italian form of an octave (the first eight lines, usually rhymed *abba abba*) and a sestet (typically rhymed *cde cde*). In the octave a dilemma or complexity of some kind is revealed; in the sestet that tension is dissipated, though not always by a clear solution.

The most important of the sonnets are three written in 1655, when he had been blind for three years: "On His Blindness," "To Cyriack Skinner," and

"On The Late Massacre in Piedmont"; and the sonnet written in 1658, "On His Deceased Wife."

The sonnet "On His Blindness," asks the question "Does God expect Milton to continue his labors in God's cause even though he is blind?" The answer is that Milton must have patience, and then he will know what is expected of him:

> *They also serve who only stand and wait.*

"To Cyriack Skinner" is also on the subject of Milton's blindness. The poet declares proudly that he has no doubt in the justice of the cause for which he sacrificed his eyesight:

> *My noble task,*
> *Of which all Europe talks from side to side*

"On The Late Massacre in Piedmont" contains the most resounding music of any of Milton's sonnets. In April, 1655, the Duke of Savoy, in an excess of religious enthusiasm massacred the Protestants living in the mountains of Piedmont. As England's great Protestant poet, Milton, in this sonnet, nobly exclaims:

> *Avenge, O Lord, thy slaughtered saints, whose bones*
> *Lie scattered on the Alpine Mountains cold*

"On His Deceased Wife" is Milton's most touching sonnet. Milton was already blind when in 1656 he married Katherine Woodcock. Milton, who had loved her, had never seen her. When she died in 1658, he wrote this poignant sonnet. In his dreams he imagines his wife coming to him dressed all in white:

> *Her face was veiled; yet to my fancied sight*
> *Love, sweetness, goodness, in her person shined*
> *So clear as in no face with more delight.*
> *But, Oh! as to embrace me she inclined,*
> *I waked, she fled, and day brought back my night.*

Milton's other sonnets include one to Henry Lawes, the musician, one to Cromwell, and another one to Cyriack Skinner.

17
THE RESTORATION

HISTORICAL BACKGROUND

When Charles II was restored to the throne of England after the collapse of the Commonwealth, Englishmen began a period of twenty-eight years of submission to the absolutism of the Stuarts. During these years English liberty was quiescent rather than dead. For the moment the nobility seemed to triumph. The people looked to the crown to establish moderation and order after the hysteria of Puritan disputation. Charles reestablished the Anglican Church. The expulsion of about one-fifth of the English clergy from their parishes as nonconformists formed the basis for political division in the country, and this division is the origin of the Whig and Tory parties, the liberal and conservative parties respectively.

Charles II led a carefree and reckless life. The exile of his court in France had improved the wit and manners of his courtiers. Now they set themselves up as patrons of the arts. A tone of cynicism in discourse became fashionable with them. Charles changed his mistresses frequently, created new titles for his illegitimate sons, and devoted himself to the pastimes of drinking and gambling. Virtue, honor and gratitude were mocked at as too "lower class" to be worthy of respect. But all this frivolity of the King and his Court was something of a mask for the fact that Charles was carefully recapturing all the power he could for the Crown, and building himself a standing army. Opposition to his plans was led by Shaftesbury, whose purpose was to have Charles's illegitimate son, the Duke of Monmouth, named as successor to the throne. The plot collapsed, and when Charles died soon thereafter (1685), his hated brother James, crowned as James II, succeeded to the throne. For the first time since Mary Tudor, England had a monarch who openly avowed membership in the Roman Catholic Church. The nonconformists in the Whig party raised a revolt against him, which was put down with bloody cruelty. James began a policy of public terror, and turned to France for aid. He replaced many high officials who refused to accept the Roman Catholic faith, and attempted to override the decrees of Parliament. Such behavior lost him the support of even the Tories. James even went to the extremes of ousting some of the teachers at Oxford in a desire to convert a Protestant seminary into one of his own faith. When both houses of Parliament opposed him, he dismissed the House of Commons.

In June, 1688, both Whigs and Tories united in an invitation to James's son-in-law, William of Orange, to intervene in behalf of English liberty.

James suddenly found himself deserted by every sector of his people. On November 5, 1688, William landed with an army on English soil amidst the enthusiastic support of Englishmen. Commoners and nobles alike flocked to his standard. The King's army, in chaos over desertions, gave way. William entered London triumphantly and James fled to France. Parliament met and voted that James "has abdicated the government." A Parliamentary committee drew up a Declaration of Rights, affirming the liberty of Englishmen, denying the king any privilege to supersede law, insuring free worship to all Protestants and binding the new monarchs (William and Mary) to maintain the Protestant religion and obey the laws of the land. This is the famous bloodless, or so-called Glorious Revolution of 1688. The next year the Declaration of Rights became the Bill of Rights, and the theories of divine or hereditary right to the throne were ended. Since then every English monarch rules by permission of Parliament.

THE AGE OF DRYDEN

Background

This period is often known as the Age of Dryden because Dryden was the most imposing literary figure of the time; and the period is generally considered as concluding with his death in 1700. As might have been expected from the history of the period, we find that literature of the Restoration was aristocratic in tone, and was addressed particularly to the Court. The drama was one of the most favored of literary forms, but the audience was limited to the nobility, and was not large enough to support more than one of the two theaters in London at a time. The prevailing tone of drama and literature in general was elegant, cynical, and witty. In such an atmosphere, great works of imagination can find no nourishment, and it is not surprising that satire becomes the most typical form of literature. The exile of the court in France had taught the Royalist audience to admire classic form and ease as exhibited in French literature of the period; English writers of the Restoration emphasized these qualities.

John Dryden (1631–1700)

Dryden was not only the greatest literary man of his age, but also to a great extent the man who determined the literary characteristics of his age. Curiously, he was a mirror of the times too. In him we find all that was admirable in the Restoration, and much that was not. He held undisputed sway over the field of literature, and his practice in poetry and prose exerted the dominant influence on the course of English literature for another century.

He was born in Northamptonshire into a Puritan family of Republican convictions. He studied at Westminster and at Trinity College, Cambridge, where he took his B.A. in 1654. An early poem, "Upon the Death of Lord Hastings"

(1650) is an elegy marred by the worst excesses of the metaphysical school. A stiff elegy on Cromwell, "A Poem Upon the Death of His Late Highness, Cromwell, Lord Protector of England" (1659), is full of praise for the great Puritan. However, when Charles II was restored to the throne, Dryden enthusiastically welcomed him in a panegyric, "Astraea Redux" (1660), and followed it the next year with "To His Sacred Majesty, A Panegyric on His Coronation" (1661). Charles made Dryden Poet Laureate and Historiographer Royal. With this shift in Dryden's political views came a change in his religious stand. In 1683 he wrote a poem, *Religio Laici*, to defend the Anglican Church against Presbyterians and Catholics. But by 1687, like many of the courtiers, he had been converted to Roman Catholicism, the religion of James II, and so wrote *The Hind and the Panther*, an allegorical poem in defense of the Catholic Church against the Anglican. It would be too easy to interpret Dryden's changes in politics and religion as opportunistic. These changes were true not only of him when they occurred but of vast numbers of his fellow countrymen as well. They merely show how much Dryden was a man of his times.

In the coffeehouses and taverns of London, frequented by men of letters, Dryden was acknowledged dictator in matters literary. The keynote of the period of the Restoration is a desire for moderation and conformity in the social scene after the Puritan chaos. In literature, conformity and reasonableness became the dominant traits too. Dryden approached his art with much forethought, and developed a style in prose and poetry to achieve the maximum of clarity, pointedness, and energy. He was a man of extensive learning and even larger gifts than his actual creations would show. He had command over pathos as well as wit. There is an incredible variety in his work. He wrote tragedies, comedies, operas, narrative verse, satires, songs, odes, epistles, translations, prologues, epilogues, and critical essays. These were to be the leading literary types for over a century.

Dryden devoted some twenty years of his career to the drama, though his plays do not show him at his best. It was financial necessity which moved him to turn out these plays rather than to write his great ambition, an English epic. His comedies include *The Wild Gallant* (1662–1663), *Sir Martin Mar-all* (1667), *Marriage à la Mode* (1672), *The Spanish Friar* (1679), and his best (for which the great English composer Purcell wrote music), *Amphitryon* (1690). The first two mentioned are adaptations from Molière, whose great comedies set the ideal for Restoration Comedy. Dryden's tragedies include *The Indian Emperor* (1665), the two parts of *The Conquest of Granada* (1669–1670), *Aurengzebe* (1675), *Don Sebastian* (1689), and his finest (based on Shakespeare's *Antony and Cleopatra*), *All For Love, Or The World Well Lost* (1677). This is but a portion of his actual dramatic output; among other dramatic works of Dryden should be mentioned the opera libretto that he made on Milton's *Paradise Lost*, which he called *The State of Innocence*, and an adaptation (which was no improvement) of Shakespeare's *The Tempest* (in collaboration with the dramatist D'Avenant).

To us the critical prefaces Dryden wrote for his plays are far more important than the dramas accompanying them. Dryden's prefaces form a highly important series of critical essays, the first imposing body of literary criticism in English. In addition they are responsible for establishing the traditional style for English prose. It is because of them that Dryden has been called "the father of English prose." Before him the great prose writers forged each for himself the style best suited to his temperament. But with Dryden begins the conception of what a sound, clear, and solid sentence in English should be. On the critical side, we find Dryden discussing every kind of literary question in these prefaces: the Aristotelian conception of tragedy, the unities, dramatic technique, poetical justice, estimates of various writers, the criteria for translations, the rules for writing epics, and the history and nature of satire.

One of Dryden's early prose pieces was issued by itself: *Essay of Dramatic Poesy*, which is considered to be the first important piece of modern English literary criticism. It is cast in the form of a dialogue, and demonstrates the clarity and variety of Dryden's prose as well as anything he ever wrote. Throughout, his sanity and good judgment are in evidence. The subject was an old favorite of the Renaissance writers: the relative superiority of the Ancients and the Moderns. The persons of the Dialogue are Crites (Sir Robert Howard, Dryden's brother-in-law), Eugenius (Lord Buckhurst), Lisideius (Sir Charles Sedley), and Neander (Dryden himself). As Dryden looked back on the history of English literature for something resembling a literary tradition, he could point out only Ben Jonson as a man who had respected classic order and clarity. The Elizabethan taste for wild imagination Dryden shows to be inferior to the elegance and orderliness of the French in their drama. Dryden is sure, however, that contemporary English drama can go higher than the French. He vindicates the use of rhyme in drama. But despite his taste for the classics and the French, Dryden makes special allowance for Shakespeare despite the latter's unclassical practice. He admires Jonson more, but Shakespeare he loves.

In writing his critical prose, Dryden was trying to clarify his own ideas on the way poetry should be written. The great age of Elizabethan poetry had passed; and in France the French critics had been busy laying the foundations for a lucid style in French poetry with many notable results. Dryden desired to find a method that might bring England to such a golden age as France was experiencing in his own time. England was ready for rules and standards. Dryden therefore decided upon the heroic couplet as best suited for the writing of clear intelligible verse. In an heroic couplet he himself says:

> *And this unpolished rugged verse I chose*
> *As fittest for discourse, and nearest prose.*

(The *heroic couplet* consists of two lines of iambic pentameter rhyming and containing a complete unit of thought.)

IMPORTANCE

Dryden was not interested in the wonderful imagination and delicate music of his Elizabethan predecessors. What he wished to achieve in an era that was crying for stability was precision, energy, and lucidity. For those ends, the heroic couplet is admirably suited. The prestige of Dryden's name made the heroic couplet the form in which the vast bulk of English verse was to be cast for a century.

Dryden's chief poems are *Annus Mirabilis* (1666), on the Dutch War, the plague, and the great fire of London, all of which occurred in that "wonderful year"; *Absolom and Achitophel* (1681), a satire that is also an allegory on the frustrated attempt of the Whigs to place the Duke of Monmouth as Charles II's successor to the throne; *MacFlecknoe* (1682), a savage satire on Thomas Shadwell, who had attacked Dryden for his lampoon on the Whigs, and in which other literary rivals come in for a lashing; *Religio Laici* (1683), "the faith of a layman" supporting the Church of England against her enemies among the Deists, Catholics, and nonconformists; *The Hind and the Panther* (1687), a defense of the Roman Catholic Church against the Church of England, and in which the Catholic Church figures allegorically as a milk-white hind, and the English Church as a panther; a translation of Virgil (1697); translations and adaptations of Theocritus, Lucretius, Horace, Ovid, Juvenal, Persius, Boccaccio, and Chaucer; and two remarkable lyrics, "A Song for St. Cecilia's Day" (1687) and "Alexander's Feast" (1697). Both these last named odes were written in praise of St. Cecilia, patron saint of music and thought to be the inventor of the organ. The "Song for St. Cecilia's Day" opens with the celebrated lines:

> *From harmony, from heavenly harmony*
> *This universal frame began*

and proceeds to describe in sound the effects of various musical instruments: the trumpet, the drum, the flute, the violin, and the organ. "Alexander's Feast" (subtitled "The Power of Music") is a more elaborate ode. The scene is at a royal feast celebrating victory over Persia by Alexander the Great. Lovely Thais sits by Alexander's side ("None but the brave deserves the fair!" says Dryden), as the musician Timotheus sings to his lyre. First he sings of Alexander's reputed descent from Jove, and the audience cries: "a present deity." Next Timotheus sings the praises of wine and the joy of battle. As Alexander begins to fight his battles over again, the musician changes the mood, and sings of the King of Persia, who now is "fallen from his high estate." Having evoked pity in Alexander's bosom, Timotheus now sings of love:

> 'Twas but a kindred sound to move,
> For pity melts the mind to love.

Alexander sinks on Thais's breast. Now Timotheus strikes the lyre in a loud strain to remind Alexander of the Grecian dead that must be revenged. The King rushes out to battle. Thus a musician could master a world conqueror to his will. But at last, Dryden concludes, Cecilia came and accomplished more than old Timotheus when she invented the organ:

> He raised a mortal to the skies;
> She drew an angel down.

These two odes indicate that Dryden had vast lyrical resources as a poet, which in his heroic couplet satires he preferred to leave untapped.

John Evelyn (1620–1706)

We owe a great deal of what we know about the Restoration to the personal memoirs of several diarists. John Evelyn, an erudite writer of various treatises, kept a comprehensive diary and collection of letters covering the years 1640 to 1706. Evelyn's *Memoirs* were published in 1818. He maintains an objective flow of observation, and provides some excellent portraits of his contemporaries and the world of fashion.

Samuel Pepys (1633–1703)

But it is to Samuel Pepys that we are most indebted for a lively picture of London from January 1st, 1660 to May 31st, 1669. Pepys, though born the son of a tailor, progressed from post to post until at the time of James II he was virtually Minister of the Navy. He managed to acquire a considerable fortune for himself and at the same time to introduce important economies into the British Navy. In 1679 he served in the House of Commons. He was elected president of the Royal Society in 1684. But James II's flight into France terminated Pepys's political career. He spent the rest of his life in retirement, devoting himself to correspondence and his large library. In 1690 he published his *Memoirs Relating to the State of the Royal Navy*. On his death in 1703, his books were bequeathed to his college, Magdalen College, Cambridge. More than a century later the Reverend John Smith discovered, among the volumes in Pepys's bequest, six bound volumes of an original shorthand closely written. He worked over them until they were deciphered, and in 1825 gave the world a new Samuel Pepys.

The *Diary* was of course never intended for publication, and for that reason it gives us a complete insight into the private life of the author as well as an amazingly complete picture of a decade in Restoration London. When Pepys ended his diary he wrote:

> And thus ends all that I doubt I shall ever be able to do with
> my own eyes in the keeping of my Journal . . . Having done now
> so long as to undo my eyes almost every time I take a pen in my

hand . . . And therefore resolve from this time forward to have it kept by my people in long hand, and must therefore be contented to set down no more than is fit for them and all the world to know.

It is the secrecy with which the diary was kept that gives it its value. He felt free to tell his Journal everything: the small talk at tavern, court, and church; his own eccentricities; his troubles with his French wife; his tastes in the theatre, books, food, music, and dress; his lapses from virtue; and the daily traffic of London life. He was a man of most mediocre tastes, and that is perhaps the secret of the place he has won in literature. The complete honesty of his record has given us a portrait of the average man in undress. He didn't like *Romeo and Juliet;* he delighted to see others trapped in the miserable condition of matrimony; he experienced bad headaches after too much drinking the night before; he thought the *Midsummer Night's Dream* the most insipid play he had ever seen; he dreaded taking his ill-natured sister under his roof; he gave an unintentional blow to his wife in the midst of sleep; he rejoiced to see his wife dressed in the newest fashion at church; at a friend's he met a most beautiful fat woman; he noted with envy Charles's facility at changing beautiful mistresses; he was in the middle of the confusion during the Great Fire; he saw the horrors of the Great Plague—all these and more are recorded blandly, trivial events receiving no less attention than historic happenings. No other book gives one such a sense of living in a period.

MINOR RESTORATION POETS

Samuel Butler (1612–1680)

Among the lesser poets of Dryden's age few achieved the success of Samuel Butler. His *Hudibras*, published in three parts (1663, 1664, 1678), though never finished, was enormously popular, and went through many editions, largely because it supplied a public demand. *Hudibras* is a coarse and outrageously bigoted satire at the expense of the Puritans. Taking the plan for his book from *Don Quixote*, and the name of his hero from *The Faerie Queene*, and copying some of his wit from the French of Scarron, Butler pilloried the Roundheads, who were now safely out of favor. It was exactly what the public desired in the first aftermath of the collapse of the Commonwealth. The hypocritical Puritan Hudibras, in the company of his squire Ralpho, wanders through the ten thousand lines of the poem in a series of complicated experiences; his purpose is to see to it that the strict laws of a Puritan Parliament, intended to put an end to all pleasure among the people, are being enforced. Among his more famous adventures are his exploits with a bear-baiter (Crowdero), an astrologer (Sidrophel), and other buffoons. The verse of *Hudibras* is largely doggerel, written in iambic tetrameter couplets; many of the rhymes are deliberately absurd, and the real merit of the book is to be found in the somersaults of language in which Butler indulges. Of course, his poem was too much of the day to have much more than historical interest now.

John Oldham (1653–1683)

Among other satirists should be mentioned John Oldham, himself the subject of a noble commemorative ode by Dryden. His *Satyrs Upon the Jesuits* (1681), is a violent attack on the order.

Court Poets

Several court poets are worthy of mention. The Earl of Rochester, John Wilmot, (1647–1680), managed to crowd into his brief life enough viciousness to make his name a synonym for libertinism. His verse, although sometimes outrageously obscene, is on occasion admirable for powerful irony and intellectual straightforwardness. His "Satire Against Mankind" reveals his talents at their best; and his "Epitaph on Charles II" is celebrated:

> *Here lies our sovereign Lord the King,*
> *Whose word no man relies on,*
> *Who never said a foolish thing*
> *Nor ever did a wise one.*

The Earl of Dorset, Charles Sackville, Lord Buckhurst (1638–1706) was the courtier to whom Dryden dedicated his *Essay of Dramatic Poesy.* He is the author of some biting satires, but is now remembered for a number of very graceful light verses. Among the best known are the songs, "Phyllis for Shame! Let Us Improve"; "Corydon Beneath the Willow"; "To All You Ladies Now at Land"; and "Dorinda's Sparkling Wit and Eyes."

The Duke of Buckingham, John Sheffield, Earl of Mulgrave (1648–1721) was of all these men the least interested in being a rake. His verses are written with considerable ease. Among his best known are "The Relapse," "The Reconcilement," and "Inconstancy Excused."

The Earl of Roscommon, Wentworth Dillon (1633–1685), was a celebrated Irish critic, one of the earliest to recognize the importance of *Paradise Lost.* His translation into blank verse of Horace's *Art of Poetry* (1680) provided the public with what was for a long time its favorite translation of that important critical work. His verse, *Essay on Translated Verse* (1684), is important historically for urging the use of a refined and rarefied vocabulary in poetry; his suggestions in this direction were destined to develop into a classical theory of "poetic diction."

LATE RESTORATION PROSE WRITERS

As has been said, the Age of Dryden, largely through Dryden's own influence, witnessed the first evolution of a tradition for English prose. The rational, as opposed to the imaginative, approach to life, characteristic of the age, was congenial to the development of prose. We find, therefore, a number of interesting critics, historians, philosophers, and religious writers in this period, as well as the first significant women writers in our literature.

Critics

Thomas Rymer (1641–1713) was one of the best-known critics, though today he is more notorious than famous for his shortsighted condemnation of Shakespeare and the Elizabethan dramatists. A smaller man than Dryden, he was therefore far more inflexible in applying the measurements of what he thought was Aristotelian dogma to the plays of the Elizabethan masters. His *Short View of Tragedy* (1693) is full of narrow-minded applying of rules to the works of genius.

Historians

To the formation of a regular prose style for English, the historical writers of the period made valuable contributions. Sir William Temple (1628–1699) was the master of a lucid style, and is best remembered for his part in the controversy on the relative merits of the ancients and moderns; his *On Ancient and Modern Learning* was the cause for launching his young friend, Swift, into a literary career.

The Marquis of Halifax, George Savile (1633–1695) wrote with epigrammatic pointedness; his best works are *A Lady's Gift, or Advice to a Daughter* (1688), written for his own daughter with much charm; *The Character of Charles II* (published in 1750), a brilliant portrait of the monarch; and *The Character of a Trimmer* (1688), a self-portrait of a man who prefers the middle-of-the-road in politics.

The Earl of Clarendon, Edward Hyde (1609–1674), is remembered for the portraits of contemporaries in his *History of the Rebellion and Civil Wars in England* (1702–1704).

Philosophers

The philosopher of the Restoration was Thomas Hobbes (1588–1679), the master of one of the most flawless and direct styles ever penned. He was not at home in Puritan England; but his heretical religious views made him equally unwelcome in the Stuart entourage during its exile in France. Hobbes nonetheless believed that an absolute monarchy was the form of government best suited to the needs of men. At basis, according to Hobbes, man is evil, and his natural state is one of war. Hobbes's great contribution to philosophy is his insistence on making natural science the foundation of human knowledge. As a materialist, Hobbes's thinking led him to become a pioneer in the unknown science of psychology, and in basing ethics on naturalism. *The Leviathan* (1651) contains the fullest statement of his philosophy and is written in clear powerful prose.

John Locke (1632–1704) exerted even a wider influence in the next and the subsequent generation. It was Locke who dethroned the Platonic concept that at birth the human mind is equipped with certain fundamental ideas (innate ideas). He taught that in infancy the human mind is a blank (*tabula rasa*) on which experience is to write. All our knowledge and our material for reasoning comes, he argued, from experience alone. This line of thought has earned Locke the title of the "father of empiricism." His writings exerted a vast influence over the philosophers Hume and Berkeley, and the French philosophers Rousseau and Voltaire. His fundamental book is *Essay Concerning Human Understanding* (1690), the first important attempt to trace the foundations of thought.

Locke was also a herald of eighteenth-century religious toleration, and the democratic ideas therewith associated. His *Letters on Toleration* (1689, 1690, 1692) not only urges the toleration of all religious sects, but also rejects the idea of absolute monarchy as being against all reason.

Three other works of Locke are worthy of mention. His *Two Treatises of Government* (1690), is an argument for democratic government as the natural one. His *Some Thoughts Concerning Education* (1693) stresses the importance of experience in learning. *The Reasonableness of Christianity* (1695) argues that natural religion must be founded on reason.

Religious Writers

Religious writings and sermons had a considerable vogue in the seventeenth and eighteenth centuries. The most popular of these during the Restoration, besides Bunyan and Jeremy Taylor, were John Tillotson (1630–1694), Archbishop of Canterbury, whose sermons are admirable for their clarity of style; Robert South (1634–1716), the author of some vigorous though bigoted sermons; and Thomas Sprat (1635–1713), Bishop of Rochester, who is best remembered for his *History of the Royal Society*, a work overflowing with patriotic enthusiasm.

Women Writers

One of Charles Lamb's favorite books was *The Life of William Cavendish, Duke of Newcastle* (1667), written by the Duchess of Newcastle, Margaret Cavendish (1624–1674)—although Pepys, her contemporary, thought the author insane and conceited, and her hero-husband a fool to have allowed her to write it. Lamb felt that there could be no casket magnificent enough to contain this jewel of a book. Margaret Cavendish was a writer of plays, essays, philosophy and poetry, in the last of which she is at her best.

Lucy Hutchinson (1620–1675) was also the author of a biography of her husband, *The Memoirs of the Life of Colonel Hutchinson*, a graceful account of the Civil War from the Puritan point of view.

The first woman to be a professional writer; that is, to earn her living by her pen, was Aphra Behn (1640–1689). Her life was filled with varied experiences. As a child she lived in Guiana. After coming to England she was married to a London merchant. Charles II, after her husband's death, employed her for a couple of years as a spy in the Netherlands. Some time later she was in debtor's prison in London. It was upon her release that she began to be the first female hack writer. Her pen name was usually Astraea. She is the author of many novels, plays and poems, nearly all astoundingly indecent. But she had a light touch, and was sometimes even charming. Of her many works the only one that need be noted is her novel *Oroonoko, or the Royal Slave* (1688), remarkable not only for being one of the earliest of English novels, but, as well, for being the first of them to be strongly partisan for the Negroes and bitterly critical of the slave trade. This work achieves realism, largely as a result of her childhood recollections.

18
RESTORATION DRAMA

CHANGES IN THE THEATER

The theaters had been closed in 1642 by order of a Puritan Parliament. During the ensuing years, despite Puritan authority, there were occasional theatrical performances. But so far as the general public went, it would be fair to say that the period of the Commonwealth was a period without drama. The Restoration brought with it the opening of theaters again.

Sir William D'Avenant, an enthusiast in matters theatrical, formed a connecting link with the glorious Elizabethan age; indeed, he did nothing to discourage the rumor that he was an illegitimate son of Shakespeare; what is important, D'Avenant had written plays before the closing of the theaters in 1642, and now was active in enterprises of the theater under Charles II. William Beeston opened a theater; D'Avenant, his friend, collected a company together; and Killigrew founded a company of his own. Charles II, who loved the theater, decreed that there must not be more than two companies in London. At first these were D'Avenant's and Killigrew's. But in 1682 the two companies became one.

The audience was no longer the butcher, the baker, and the candlestick maker of Shakespeare's day. Most Londoners, still Puritan at heart, kept away from the theater. The playhouse became the resort of the world of fashion and the aristocracy.

The Restoration theater shows important changes in the physical aspects of dramatic representation. The playhouse becomes oblong in shape, is roofed in, and employs lighting and scenery on the stage. Women, instead of boys, enact the feminine roles for the first time. But the quality of the plays themselves is no less remarkably different from Elizabethan practice. To please an audience of sophisticates, two types of plays came to be favorites with the dramatists: the *heroic tragedy* and the *comedy of manners*. The *heroic tragedy* appealed to the court's interest in men of rank; the *comedy of manners* reflected the loose morals and witty talk of aristocratic private life.

HEROIC TRAGEDY

The *heroic tragedy* centers around a hero of enormous prowess and extravagantly noble ideals; the heroine is a combination of perfect beauty and unalloyed faithfulness; the conflict is between love and honor; the background is war; and the verse is cast in inflated rhetoric and rhymes in couplets. It is not surprising that no really distinguished tragedy was written in this style. These plays, inspired by the plays of Corneille in France, were written best by Dryden. Indeed, it was Dryden's *Indian Queen* (1664) that set the fashion. Among other plays of this school may be mentioned Nathaniel Lee's *The Tragedy of Nero* (1675) and *The Rival Queens* (1677)—the latter written in blank verse. Sir Charles Sedley's *Antony and Cleopatra* (1667); and Dryden's *The Indian Emperor* (1665), *Tyrannic Love* (1669), *The Conquest of Granada* (1669–1670) and *Aurengzebe* (1675). John Sheffield, Duke of Buckingham, ridiculed the whole school of heroic tragedy in his witty burlesque, *The Rehearsal* (1671).

Thomas Otway (1652–1685)

The only great tragedies of the period are written in another manner. Dryden's best, *All For Love* (1677), as we have already said, is an imitation of Shakespeare's blank verse tragedy. The best of the Restoration writers of tragedy, Thomas Otway, produced the two finest tragedies of the period without following the fashion. Otway's *The Orphan* (1680) is a domestic tragedy, somewhat influenced by Shakespeare's *Cymbeline*; its language is simple and direct, its pathos genuine, and its psychology valid. His *Venice Preserved* (1682) is so much in the Elizabethan manner that it has been called the last of the Elizabethan plays; its sombre blank verse is well adapted to a typical Elizabethan plot, somewhat suggesting *Othello* and *Julius Caesar*.

COMEDY OF MANNERS

It was in the field of comedy that Restoration drama achieved distinction. Whereas classical precedent since the Renaissance had made for pomposity in tragedy, classic tradition in comedy (because of the example of Plautus and Terence) had made for realism. Moreover, the Restoration desire to work within the limits of common sense and logic tempered by wit, provided an atmosphere in which comedy could thrive. The newly perfected lucid prose style naturally suggested itself as superior to poetry for the purposes of comedy. Thus, while Restoration tragedy tends to be boring for its inflated qualities, Restoration comedy tends to be amusing for its ease and cleverness. The leading writers of comedy in the period were Etherege, Wycherley, Congreve, Vanbrugh, and Farquhar.

Sir George Etherege (c. 1633–c. 1688)

Sir George Etherege was first heard of when his first play *The Comical Revenge, or Love In A Tub* appeared in 1664. Everything else concerning his birth, private life, and death is uncertain. (Scholars are still arguing as to whether he was born in Bermuda or England.) This play is the first *comedy of manners* of the period. Written in prose, with occasional rhymed couplets, its tone is one of broad farce. Etherege knew his Molière, and the best touches in him are indebted to the French master. Like Molière, Etherege deals with individuals rather than types. His second comedy is *She Would If She Could* (1668), which Pepys, who was no judge, thought a silly play. His last comedy is *The Man of Mode, or Sir Fopling Flutter* (1676), the best-contrived of his plays, and it contains his clearest portraits and satire. Sir Fopling Flutter, prince of fops, is right out of Molière. The story of *The Man of Mode* deals with the complicated love life of Dorimant, the fop, and his two mistresses, Mrs. Loveit and Belinda. He deserts them in order to sue for the hand of a wealthy lady of fashion. Dorimant succeeds in procuring the consent of the heiress's mother by making love to her too.

In all of Etherege's comedies the central character is a delightful woman, and the prevailing atmosphere is one of gaiety, licentiousness, and frivolity. These characteristics remain true of most Restoration comedies.

William Wycherley (c. 1640–1716)

William Wycherley was in France while the court was exiled. He studied for a while at Oxford, went to sea for a time, and secretly married when he was around forty the furiously jealous Countess of Drogheda. Upon her death, unable to discharge his debts, he was imprisoned for a number of years. A few days before his death he married again. As a writer, Wycherley is the most vigorous of the Restoration comic dramatists; his dramatic construction is particularly admirable. His worst flaw is that in an age given to excessive coarseness, he is outstandingly coarse. His first three plays, *Love in a Wood, or St. James' Park* (1671), *The Gentleman Dancing Master* (1672), and *The Country Wife* (1675) are written in imitation of Etherege. The first of these is the most indecent and most loosely put together; the second is better written and the most engaging of the three. *The Country Wife* is the bitterest, and is based upon a play of Terence; its farce is bold, bawdy, but very witty, and its action swift. In these three plays the characters are all gallants, fops, and fools, and the plot is always one of amorous intrigue.

The plot of *The Country Wife* centers about the girl described in the title, one Mrs. Margery Pinchwife, who, although her husband keeps an unrelaxed guard over her, is not proof against the temptations of illicit love. Mr. Pinchwife believes Mr. Horner, a bachelor, to have only a platonic interest in women. Actually Horner is a philanderer. He succeeds in having an affair with Margery. When that is over he becomes interested in Lady Fidget, and Pinchwife consoles himself with the thought that he is only one of many cuckolded London husbands.

Wycherley's last play, *The Plain Dealer* (1676), is his best. It is a brilliant adaptation, with many original additions, of Molière's masterpiece, *The Misanthrope*. This play shows a departure from Wycherley's earlier vulgarity; it is a powerful and biting social satire, lashing out at the very vices that

Wycherley once had found so very amusing. It provides one of the liveliest pictures we have of Restoration manners. The plot concerns the loss of faith in almost everyone by a ship's captain, Manly. He trusts only his sweetheart, Olivia, in whose care he leaves his money, and his friend, Vernish. Fidelia is a girl who is secretly in love with him. When he goes off to sea, Fidelia dresses like a man and follows him. On his return, Manly discovers that Olivia has been married to a man at first not named, and that she is evasive about returning his money. Her husband turns out to be Vernish. A fight ensues, and the disguised Fidelia is wounded while attempting to save Manly. When Manly learns of Fidelia's loyalty and identity, he returns her love and marries her.

William Congreve (1670–1729)

William Congreve is the greatest of Restoration writers of comedy. Voltaire says of him that he raised the art of comedy "to a greater height than any English writer before or since." He was born near Leeds, the son of an army officer, and educated in Ireland at Kilkenny's School, and later at Trinity College, Dublin. He went to London, entered the Inner Temple, and was for a number of years in government service. In the meantime he had produced his first literary work, an immature novel of intrigue, *Incognita* (1691). Two years later he won acclaim with his first comedy, written under Wycherley's influence, *The Old Bachelor* (1693). This play shows that Congreve already had a more superb wit than any of his Restoration predecessors. *The Double Dealer* (1694), which is a great advance in subtlety of irony, made little impression upon the public, though Dryden was highly pleased with it. The next year found him very popular again with his best constructed play (by reason of its deftness called by many his masterpiece), *Love for Love* (1695). Here he is very close to Molière in spirit and is wonderfully delicate in satirizing contemporary manners. The plot of *Love for Love* centers around Valentine, a very elegant young man, besieged by creditors, and out of favor with his father. The latter, Sir Sampson, offers to pay Valentine's debts if he will sign over his inheritance to his brother. Pressed by his creditors, Valentine agrees. But reflection causes him to regret his rashness, and he invents the idea of pretending to be insane. As an insane man he could not be responsible for his signature on a document. He is aided by the girl he loves, Angelica. She feigns to encourage the attentions of Sir Sampson, manages to have the old man propose to her, and thus procures possession of the valuable document. Because she has never clearly agreed to marry him, Valentine believes that she intends marrying his father, and never imagines that her actions are in his own behalf. In anger he declares himself ready to give up his inheritance. She is finally forced to admit her love for Valentine, and, explaining her successful ruse, she tears up the document. The other characters include Benjamin Legend, Valentine's brother, a lively portrait of a British tar; Prue, a lass fresh from the country; and typical Londoners of the aristocracy.

The Mourning Bride (1697) is Congreve's only tragedy. It is written in blank verse that is effectively pathetic. But the plot is too improbable to be interesting. The first line of the play, however, has become famous:

Music hath charms to soothe the savage breast

His last play, *The Way of the World* (1700), is probably his best, and is one of the most important of English comedies. Certainly here Congreve seems to have found his perfect expression. It is true that it contains less action than *Love for Love*, but the characterization is Congreve's most brilliant. The chief figures were probably inspired by Beatrice and Benedick of Shakespeare's *Much Ado About Nothing*. But Millamant is a thoroughly Restoration version of Beatrice. She is enchantingly the lady of fashion, the mistress of dazzling repartee, and is deliciously feminine in her perverse delight in keeping her lover guessing. Only Beatrice can vie with her for the honor of being the most brilliant girl in English comedy.

Paradoxically, *The Way of the World* was not successful when produced. Its failure is probably the reason why Congreve never wrote anything of consequence for the remaining twenty-nine years of his life. The hostility of the public to this marvelous comedy was somewhat owing to a controversy then raging among audiences, playwrights, and actors. The agitation began with the publication of a pamphlet, *A Short View of the Profaneness and Immorality of the English Stage* (1698), written by the nonconformist clergyman Jeremy Collier (1650–1726). This tract, full of absurd argument, nevertheless was basically sound in its attack on the corrupt morals of Restoration drama. Even Dryden, who came in for particular abuse, was forced to admit in his characteristic manly way, that the charges were just. Congreve, however, was infuriated at Collier's invective. Unhappily for the dramatist, the public was not of Congreve's mind. *The Way of The World*, despite the admiration it has since evoked, appeared before a public that at the moment was out of patience with the loose morality exhibited in the story. It mattered not that this play is on that score the least objectionable of all Restoration comedies. The tide was turning against Restoration frivolity.

The hero of *The Way of the World* is Mirabell. He is in love with Millamant, "a fine lady." But Lady Wishfort, her aunt, is furious with Mirabell for having once falsely pretended to be in love with her. In revenge she plans to deprive Millamant of her inheritance. Mirabell, who would like to have the fortune as well as the girl, enlists the aid of a former mistress of his. Their plot is successful, and Lady Wishfort finally agrees to the marriage in order to save her own face. The play abounds in incomparable wit, and is an elegant reflection of the manners of the aristocracy of the time.

Sir John Vanbrugh (1664–1726)

Sir John Vanbrugh was a celebrated architect as well as a dramatist. Among his famous architectural accomplishments were the building of Blenheim Castle for the Duke of Marlborough, and the construction of the

Haymarket Theatre (1705), which he himself managed. He is the author of a number of fables, several translations from Molière, and two excellent comedies, *The Relapse, or Virtue in Danger* (1697) and *The Provoked Wife* (1697). Vanbrugh's gift is especially in lively dialogue and an unbroken gaiety of tone.

The Relapse was written as a kind of protest against the false sentiment of Colly Cibber's play *Love's Last Shift.* In Vanbrugh's play, Loveless (who in Cibber's play had been reformed from extreme libertinism to virtuousness) is living in the country with his wife Amanda, who had reformed him. But they are obliged to go to London. There Loveless meets an unscrupulous but attractive widow, Berinthia, who arouses his dormant weakness. A former lover of hers, Worthy, is attracted to Amanda. In order to further his own chances for seducing Amanda, Worthy persuades Berinthia to encourage Loveless. Loveless falls from grace, but Amanda, though resentful, remains chaste. Vanbrugh's point is that overnight reformations, such as Loveless experienced in Cibber's play, cannot last long.

The Provoked Wife sustains Vanbrugh's title as a "lesser Congreve." If he has less elegance and sparkle than Congreve, his sense of fun never deserts him, and his characters are less artificial. In this, his best play, Sir John Brute mistreats his wife outrageously. Although she is pursued by the attentions of Constant, Lady Brute remains faithful. Her niece, Belinda, evokes the love of Constant's friend, Heartfree. The two ladies agree to meet Constant and Heartfree one night, but they are discovered in an apparently suspicious rendezvous by the jealous Lady Fanciful. Lady Fanciful tries to stir up Sir John's fury, and for a while succeeds. In the end, all is explained happily.

George Farquhar (1678–1707)

George Farquhar was born in Ireland and studied at Trinity College, Dublin. He was for a while an actor in Dublin, then came to London, where he became an officer in the army. He is the author of a number of highly indecent comedies, an adaptation of Molière's *Would-be Gentleman,* and two good comedies: *The Recruiting Officer* (1706) and *The Beaux Stratagem* (1707).

The Recruiting Officer is a fresh satire, the product of his own experience in the service during the War of the Spanish Succession. The locale of the story is a country town where recruiting for the army is going on. Captain Plume is anxious to fill up the ranks, and makes love to the ladies so that the ladies will induce their admirers to enlist. Sylvia, the delightful heroine, is the Sheriff's daughter and is in love with Plume. She leaves home disguised as a man and manages to get arrested for misconduct. When she is brought before her father, the Sheriff, he delivers her to Captain Plume as a recruit.

The Beaux Stratagem is considered Farquhar's masterpiece; it is somewhat more artificial than *The Recruiting Officer* but is more brilliantly constructed both in plot and dialogue. It marks also an important step in incorporating some sentiment in the midst of Restoration scintillation of wit, and so is generally accounted to be the last important Restoration comedy of manners. It is said that the dramatist wrote the play in six weeks to divert himself from the pain of an illness that proved fatal; if this story is true the buoyancy of the wit is all the more remarkable. The plot deals with two gentlemen in reduced circumstances, Archer and Aimwell, who decide to masquerade as master and servant in an effort to recoup their fortunes. The other characters include Lady Bountiful, a philanthropist known all over the countryside (her name has passed into colloquial usage); an innkeeper, Boniface; Scrub, a servant to Lady Bountiful's son, and the receiver of young ladies' confidences; Dorinda, Lady Bountiful's daughter; and Mrs. Sullen, Lady Bountiful's daughter-in-law. After complications, the two beaux (Archer and Aimwell) are back in fortune's favor when Archer marries Dorinda and Aimwell Mrs. Sullen.

Among other Restoration comedies of manners may be mentioned Otway's adaptation from Molière, *The Cheats of Scapin* (1677); Sedley's adaptation from Molière, *The Mulberry Garden* (1668), and *Bellamira, or The Mistress* (1687); and Aphra Behn's *The Rover, or The Banished Cavaliers* (1677), her adaptation from Molière, *Sir Patient Fancy* (1678), and *The Lucky Chance, or An Alderman's Bargain* (1686).

REVIEW QUESTIONS

THE SEVENTEENTH CENTURY

Multiple Choice

1. _____ The seventeenth century witnessed the influence of all of the following social and intellectual forces except
   a. Puritanism
   b. Rationalism
   c. Transcendentalism
   d. the scientific spirit

2. _____ Dryden wrote *All for Love* as an attempt to make Shakespeare's *Antony and Cleopatra*
   a. fit the moral standards of the Puritans
   b. conform to Greek and Roman literary models
   c. more historically accurate
   d. easier to perform

3. _____ The King James Bible of 1611 is also known as
   a. the Coverdale Bible
   b. the *Vulgate*
   c. the *Vespasian Psalter*
   d. the *Authorized Version*

4. _____ Members of the Cavalier School of poetry included all of the following EXCEPT
   a. Milton
   b. Wither
   c. Carew
   d. Suckling

5. _____ Metaphysical poets are so called for their tendency to
   a. discover kinship in apparently unlike things
   b. concentrate on heavenly rather than earthly topics
   c. use magical terms and incantations in their poetry
   d. end poems with a spiritual message

6. _____ Milton wrote "Lycidas" as
   a. the expression of deep personal grief over the loss of a dear friend
   b. a submission to a commemorative volume for Edward King
   c. a poem in the epic tradition
   d. a companion piece for *Paradise Lost*

7. _____ *Comus* is a
   a. pastoral elegy
   b. masque
   c. sonnet
   d. ode

8. _____ By the mid-1650s, Milton suffered from complete
   a. paralysis
   b. deafness
   c. blindness
   d. insanity

9. _____ *Paradise Lost* is a poetic narration of
   a. the birth, death, and resurrection of Jesus
   b. the events relating to the Garden of Eden and the banishment of Satan
   c. the *Book of Revelations*
   d. the prophecies of Jeremiah

10. _____ *Paradise Regained* tells the story of
    a. Christ's baptism, temptation, and triumph
    b. Samson's struggle against the Philistines
    c. the driving out of Romans from England
    d. the reign of Elizabeth

True or False

11. _____ In his sonnets, Milton used the same rhyme scheme as that used by Shakespeare.

12. _____ The Restoration (1660–1688) followed the collapse of the Commonwealth.

13. _____ In Dryden's day, the usual location for literary debate was the coffeehouse.

14. _____ *An Essay of Dramatic Poesy* concerns itself with the question of whether ancient poetry surpasses modern poetry in excellence.

15. _____ Samuel Pepys wrote a closely detailed diary of Parisian life.

16. _____ Heroic tragedy, by using middle-class characters as protagonists, reflects the easing of class distinctions during the Restoration.

17. _____ Social behavior rather than human nature is the target of satire in Restoration comedy.

18. _____ Mirabell and Millamant appear as central characters in *The Way of the World*.

19. _____ In *Hudibras*, Samuel Butler satirizes the Puritans.

20. _____ *The Leviathan* is a sea-story along the lines of *Moby Dick*.

Fill-in

21. The two major political philosophers of the seventeenth century were _____ and _____ .

22. The fencing of formerly common lands by English nobility for their own use was called the _____ .

23. A prose allegory that belongs to the tradition going back to the medieval *Everyman* is _____ .

24. Aphra Behn's *Oroonoko* argued powerfully against the _____ .
25. The Restoration drama that closely resembles the earlier "blood and thunder" tragedies is _____ .
26. Truth, Studies, Adversity, and Innovation are all topics dealt with in Bacon's _____ .
27. The poet who also served as Dean of St. Paul's was _____ .
28. Clever analogies as exemplified in "The Pulley" and "The Collar" are the hallmark of the poet, _____ .
29. Izaak Walton, although ostensibly writing about the sport of fishing, included many other topics and reflections in his book, _____ .
30. Sir Thomas Browne remains known primarily for his skill as a _____ .

Matching

31. _____ Milton
32. _____ Donne
33. _____ Hobbes
34. _____ Locke
35. _____ Dryden
36. _____ Wycherley
37. _____ Overbury
38. _____ Etherege
39. _____ Burton
40. _____ Herrick

a. "Upon Julia's Clothes"
b. *The Leviathan*
c. Characters
d. *Essay On Human Understanding*
e. "A Valediction Forbidding Mourning"
f. *All for Love*
g. *The Man of Mode*
h. "L'Allegro"
i. *The Country Wife*
j. *Anatomy of Melancholy*

Answers

1. c	16. f	27. John Donne
2. b	17. t	28. George Herbert
3. d	18. t	29. *The Compleat Angler*
4. a	19. t	30. prose stylist
5. a	20. f	31. h
6. b	21. John Locke,	32. e
7. b	Thomas Hobbes	33. b
8. c	22. Enclosure	34. d
9. b	Movement	35. f
10. a	23. Bunyon's *Pilgrim's*	36. i
11. f	*Progress*	37. c
12. t	24. slave trade	38. g
13. t	25. Otway's *Venice*	39. j
14. t	*Preserved*	40. a
15. f	26. *Essays*	

Part **5**

THE EIGHTEENTH CENTURY

WORKS AT A GLANCE*

Daniel Defoe

1701	*The True-Born Englishman*	1720	*Captain Singleton*
1702	*The Shortest Way with the Dissenters*	1722	*Moll Flanders*
			A Journal of the Plague Year
1719	*Robinson Crusoe*	1724	*Roxana*

Alexander Pope

1709	*Pastorals*	1732–1734	*Essay on Man*
1711	*Essay on Criticism*	1731–1735	*Moral Essays*
1712	*The Rape of the Lock*	1733–1739	*Imitations of Horace*
1717	*Eloïsa to Abelard*	1735	*Epistle to*
1715–1720	*Iliad*		*Dr. Arbuthnot*
1725–1726	*Odyssey*		
1728, 1729, 1743	*The Dunciad* published in three parts		

John Gay

1714	*The Sheperd's Week*	1728	*The Beggar's Opera*
1715	*The What D'Ye Call It?*	1729	*Polly*
1716	*Trivia*		
1727, 1738	*Fables* published in two parts		

Jonathan Swift

1704	*The Battle of the Books*	1720	*A Proposal for the Universal Use of Irish Manufacture*
	A Tale of a Tub		
1708**	*Abolishing of Christianity*	1724	*The Drapier's Letters*
		1726	*Gulliver's Travels*
1710	*Meditation Upon a Broomstick*	1727	*A Short View of the State of Ireland*
1710–1713**	*The Journal to Stella*	1729	*A Modest Proposal*

*Dates refer to dates of publication unless otherwise noted.
**Denotes date of composition.

Joseph Addison

1704	*The Campaign*	1711	*The Spectator* (with Steele)
1709	*The Tatler* (with Steele)	1713	*Cato*

Richard Steele

1701	*The Christian Hero*	1709	*The Tatler* (with Addison)
	The Funeral	1711	*The Spectator* (with Addison)
1703	*The Lying Lover*	1722	*The Conscious Lovers*
1705	*The Tender Husband*		

Samuel Johnson

1738	*London*	1758-1760	*The Idler*
1744	*The Life of Savage*	1759	*Rasselas*
1749	*The Vanity of Human Wishes*	1775	*Journey to the Western Islands of Scotland*
1750-1752	*The Rambler*	1779, 1781	*Lives of the English Poets*
1755	*Dictionary of the English Language*		

James Boswell

1768	*Account of Corsica*	1791	*The Life of Samuel Johnson*
1785	*Journal of a Tour to the Hebrides*		

Oliver Goldsmith

1759	*An Enquiry into the Present State of Polite Learning in Europe*	1764	*The Traveler*
		1766	*The Vicar of Wakefield*
		1778	"The Deserted Village"
1762	*The Citizen of the World*	1773	*She Stoops to Conquer*

Edmund Burke

1756	*The Sublime and the Beautiful*	1790	*Reflections on the Revolution in France*
	Vindication of Natural Society	1796	*Letters on a Regicide Peace*
1774	*On American Taxation*		*Letter to a Noble Lord*
1775	*On Conciliation with America*		

Richard Brinsley Sheridan

1776	*The Duenna*	1777	*The School for Scandal*
	The Rivals	1779	*The Critic*

*Dates refer to dates of publication unless otherwise noted.
**Denotes date of composition.

Philip Stanhope, Earl of Chesterfield

1774	*Letters*

Edward Gibbon

1776, 1781, 1788	*History of the Decline and Fall of the Roman Empire*

Thomas Paine

1791–1792	*The Rights of Man*

William Godwin

1793	*An Enquiry Concerning the Principles of Political Justice*	1794	*Caleb Williams*

Samuel Richardson

1741–1742	*Pamela*	1754	*Sir Charles Grandison*
1747–1748	*Clarissa Harlowe*		

Henry Fielding

1742	*Joseph Andrews*	1749	*Tom Jones*
1743	*Jonathan Wild*	1751	*Amelia*

Tobias Smollett

1748	*Roderick Random*	1771	*Humphrey Clinker*
1751	*Peregrine Pickle*		

Laurence Sterne

1759–1767	*Tristam Shandy*

Henry Mackenzie

1771	*The Man of Feeling*	1773	*The Man of the World*

Frances Burney

1778	*Evelina*	1796	*Camilla*
1782	*Cecilia*		

---

*Dates refer to dates of publication unless otherwise noted.
**Denotes date of composition.

Horace Walpole

| 1764 | *The Castle of Otranto* | 1788 | *The Mysterious Mother* |

Anne Radcliffe

| 1794 | *The Mysteries of Udolpho* | 1797 | *The Italian* |

---

*Dates refer to dates of publication unless otherwise noted.
**Denotes date of composition.

19
THE RISE OF THE MIDDLE CLASS

GEORGIAN ERA

The Glorious Revolution of 1688 established the political authority of the English middle class over the crown. The eighteenth century saw the gradual and eventually complete ascendancy of the middle class in the life of the nation, coincidentally with the development of commerce and industry.

The literature of the eighteenth century has a calmness of tone that might indicate that the political life of the century was more peaceful than it actually was. Queen Anne, who was on the throne from 1702 to 1714, although the elegant literature of her day is known somewhat deceptively to us as the literature of the Age of Queen Anne, was a woman completely lacking in taste and judgment. Under her, England became involved in numerous intrigues on the continent. The War of the Spanish Succession (Queen Anne's War) found England and France as foes in international conflict. The military genius of the Earl of Marlborough, who won a decisive victory at Blenheim, became the excuse for another furious war in England itself between the Whigs and the Tories. The Peace of Utrecht (1714) marked the beginning of a new role for England in the affairs of Europe when the principle of "the balance of power," established at Utrecht, consigned England to be the special guardian of this principle. England thus began to be brought into closer contact than ever with the culture of western Europe, and the philosophy and literature of England began to exert great influence on the continent. London became for western Europe a new Athens inspiring the poets and philosophers of France and Germany.

This era also witnessed the union of Scotland with England into the nation of Great Britain, in 1707. Queen Anne's line ended with her, and the House of Hanover, whose claims were supported by the Whigs, came to the throne. George I (1714–1727) and George II (1727–1760) made little effort to understand the country, and were more or less strangers even to its language. During their reigns the Whig Party was able to rule England for a period of thirty years without a rival, and did all it could to further the interests of the middle class. The mid-century found the nation in new wars, most important of which were the campaigns of Clive in India (1756–1760) and the Seven Years' War (1756–1763).

When George III came to the throne in 1760, Britain had unrivaled prestige in Europe, and empires in America and India. But the third George was not inclined to allow the country to be run by his ministers. He was the last king to attempt recapturing the royal power. His failure was almost complete. He succeeded only in discrediting himself with his own people, in forcing the American colonies to revolt for their independence, and in bringing England near the brink of ruin. His obstinacy was equalled only by the smallness of his mind and meanness of his abilities. The Tory Party, long out of power, was ready to do his bidding. The consequence of the union of Tory and king towards the end of the century was the growth of very radical thought in England, under the influence of the French *philosophes*. When the Bastille fell in 1789, English sentiment was largely in enthusiastic support of the French Revolution. Indeed, when the French National Assembly declared war on England in 1793, many English liberals hoped for a French victory. Of course, the later excesses of the French Revolution soon alienated English sympathy almost completely.

The steady growth of industry during the century was of course accelerated by important mechanical inventions, such as the spinning jenny, the flying shuttle, the water frame, and the steam engine. The middle class, as its wealth increased, began to have the leisure to absorb the intellectual accomplishments of the preceding century. In science these had been formidable. To list but a few of the advances of science made since the second half of the seventeenth century: the telescope's development by the invention of Newton's reflector; the thermometer; the barometer; the pendulum clock; Newton's law of gravitation; the development of analytical geometry and calculus; the beginnings of entomology.

The admiration for classical ease, symmetry, balance, and common sense which had been fostered by the age of Dryden continued during the entire eighteenth century. But the culture of the new century differed in one important aspect from that of the Restoration. Dryden and his contemporaries had addressed their works to the aristocracy. The eighteenth century found the men of the middle class taking a new interest in the arts. The Court was no longer the center of patronage for the arts; instead the well-to-do tradesmen of London began to form the audience for creative effort. As this public increased, writers began more and more to cease depending on noble patrons for their livelihood, and turned to the average citizen for their support. Good taste and elegance began to characterize the lives and interests of the wealthier members of the middle class, as was reflected in their gracious new homes and furnishings.

In most other respects the characteristic writers of the eighteenth century continued the traditions established by Dryden. Above all they were interested in achieving perfect form, which they felt to be found best exemplified in the literature of ancient Greece and Rome. For this reason the century has been called Neoclassic. As in the Restoration, writers of this century tended to distrust the imagination and to prefer to write within the limits of logic and common sense. The century has therefore also been called the Age of Reason. It is customary to separate the literature of the century into two subdivisions: the first part, during which time the leading writers were Addison, Steele, Swift, and Pope, known as the Age of Queen Anne, or the Augustan Age, or the Age of Pope; the second part, during which time the leading writers were Samuel Johnson, Goldsmith, Boswell, and Burke, known as the Age of Johnson.

INDUSTRIAL REVOLUTION

The term "Industrial Revolution" is assigned rather arbitrarily to the latter half of the eighteenth century. In fact, elements of revolutionary change in production, transportation, and communication began earlier than 1760 and certainly have continued unabated throughout the nineteenth and twentieth centuries. But to writers, historians, and other social observers in the latter half of the eighteenth century, the changes taking place in the creation of factories, the invention of the steam engine, and other developments qualified as a bona fide revolution on the same scale as the French Revolution.

The impact of the Industrial Revolution was noted in several spheres. Men, women, and eventually children were taken from home occupations to become laborers in centralized (and often dismal) mines, factories, and warehouses. Many of these workers were driven out of agricultural occupations by the Enclosure Movement, a series of legislative acts beginning in 1709 that allowed major landowners to fence their entire deeded properties, including open-field lands traditionally farmed by villagers. The intention of the Enclosure Movement was to make English agricultural production more efficient. It resulted, however, in massive social dislocation.

The textile industry underwent a dramatic change from the "putting-out" system (in which a supplier provided raw materials to workers who performed artisan production activities in their homes) to factories employing power gins (Eli Whitney, 1793) and looms (Edmund Cartwright, 1785). To work in these factories, whole populations of villagers left their age-old family homes for rented and often squalid rooms in burgeoning cities.

Powering such industrial centers were new dynamos made possible by the invention of the steam engine (James Watt, 1763). Prior to Watt's invention, textile and other factories had to be located near major rivers for waterpower. The steam engine made it possible to drive mills wherever wood or coal could be made available to stoke the engine.

Steam transportation enabled industrial centers to forge links with supply regions and urban markets for their finished goods. The first iron bridge was built in England in 1779. The creation of a network of canals followed shortly thereafter so that heavy industrial materials and products could be shipped inexpensively.

For all their influence in making improved products more widely available, these industrial developments also carried a terrible price in human suffering. Factory work conditions were frequently abysmal, with workers spending long hours at repetitive tasks in poorly lighted, unventilated workhouses. Cities grew with plan or provision; Manchester, for example, had a population of more than 50,000 before a police force was organized. Living conditions in the cities for those already-poor victims of the Enclosure Movement were harsh, unsanitary, and dangerous. In 1798 Thomas Malthus in his *Essay on the Principle of Population* provided the intellectual grist for English lawmakers to view poor living conditions and haphazard food supplies as necessary, even inevitable, factors restraining overpopulation. The British economist David Ricardo bolstered Malthus's argument by asserting that wages would always adjust downward to the bare level of subsistence. If a worker demanded more, another poorer, more desperate applicant would be ready to take his or her place.

DANIEL DEFOE (1660–1731)

Background

Daniel Defoe, who was born Daniel Foe, is a transitional figure between the Restoration and the eighteenth century. He was forty years old when Dryden died, but most of his works were written after 1700. He was the son of a London butcher, a staunch Presbyterian, and spent some years at his father's trade. Defoe did not begin to write until after he was thirty. His career was, in fact, too varied to be followed now with any ease; and it is even more difficult to understand. He seems to have had the ideal temperament for a journalist, and once he discovered that his gifts lay that way, he did not cease until he had produced more than two hundred and fifty works. Besides these there are some one hundred and fifty other works of which it is highly likely that he is also the author. One would imagine that so much writing would make enough to fill a lifetime. But Defoe was very busy as a secret political agent as well. Despite his apparent adherence to the Puritan belief, and his serving time in jail for it, we find him sometimes in the pay of the Whigs, sometimes in the pay of the Tories, and sometimes in the pay of both—as a spy. He seems to have had no interest in his writing beyond the profit he could make out of it. Naturally the quantity of his productions implies a haste in composition that would have made artistic considerations impossible. Without any taste for form or elegance himself, he was inevitably considered by the best writers of his time to be an unimportant and illiterate scribbler.

In 1701 he wrote a rugged poem, *The True-Born Englishman*, an attack on English notions of superiority to all foreigners. The next year his *Shortest Way With the Dissenters* (1702), one of his best works, satirized the intolerance of the Church of England. In it Defoe, with elaborate irony, suggested the severest persecution of Nonconformists as the only way to save the Established Church. The Tories, at first, took him literally, and were pleased. When they realized that they had been deceived by his tone, they had the work burned publicly, and its author first placed in a pillory, and then fined and imprisoned for having too much sense of humor.

On his release, with nothing else to turn to, he entered the employ of the Whigs as pamphleteer and spy. Soon he began to write, almost entirely by himself, a periodical, *The Review* (1704–1713), a highly important paper in the history of English periodicals. A department in it, which he entitled "Advice from the Scandalous Club," a weekly account of contemporary "Nonsense, Impertinence, Vice and Debauchery," inspired Steele with the idea for his *Tatler*, and is thought to be the beginning of the periodical essay. While he was thus busy writing about all kinds of subjects, and selling political secrets to opposing parties, he had not yet discovered his real talent.

Indeed, he was nearly sixty years of age before it developed that his greatest ability was for fiction. A Scottish sailor, Alexander Selkirk, had just published an account of his experiences on an island off Chile where he had lived for five years after being shipwrecked there. Defoe decided that he would like to write something similar. In 1719 Defoe published a book that has made his name famous all over the world, *The Life and Strange Surprising Adventures of Robinson Crusoe*. It immediately had enormous success, and was the beginning of a series of racy journalistic narratives by its author. The best of these are *The Life, Adventures, and Piracies of the Famous Captain Singleton* (1720), a story about the raids of a pirate on the African coast; *The Fortunes and Misfortunes of the Famous Moll Flanders* (1722), a romance about a prostitute-pickpocket who is eventually sent to the penal colony in Virginia, where she in the end reforms; *Roxana, or the Fortunate Mistress* (1724), a romance on the life of a courtesan among the upper classes. The reason for the great success of these romances with the public is somewhat the result of Defoe's lack of artistry: they all have an air of fact and unadorned realism. Also, their being written as "autobiographies" and the very plainness of their style gave them something of the sham air of truthfulness that the "confessions" (written by professional ghostwriters) of criminals in our own day have. They also had the added attraction of being concerned with the adventures of malefactors. Defoe managed to keep an air of piousness in these romances by having his criminal reform on the last page. Defoe had no interest, of course, in serving the purposes of English literature. Although he seems to have lacked artistic conscience as much as any other kind, he nevertheless prepared the way for the novel in these romances. All that is missing in his romances to make a novel is a unified plot to tie the loose incidents together. His portraits are admirable, his style is racy, if inelegant, and he certainly increased the audience for books among the public. Also, his very indifference to style did much to overcome the false elegance with which some of his contemporaries wrote, and helped to fix the tone of prose that ordinary Englishmen use in daily intercourse.

Moll Flanders

Our heroine's mother is sent to a penal colony when Moll is still an infant. Taken up by a band of gypsies, the child is abandoned by them at Colchester, where the Essex parish officers become her guardians. Moll is well liked in the little town. At the age of fourteen she is taken into the home of a kind gentlewoman to be the companion to her two daughters. Educated with the two girls, she is a credit to her rearing, and at seventeen is a beautiful young woman. Her benefactress' elder son becomes enamored of her, promises marriage, and makes her his mistress without the knowledge of the family. He is generous with gifts, and Moll is deeply in love with him. Robin, the younger son, now falls in love with her, and much to his family's displeasure wishes to marry her. She becomes ill when her lover urges her to accept the opportunity, but he prevails upon her, and she agrees to marry Robin. They wed, and she makes him a good wife. When he dies five years later, she is left with a little money; their two children are cared for by her husband's parents. Moll goes to London, becomes attracted to a draper, marries him, and allows him to spend all her money. In two years he is arrested for his debts. Escaping, he promises never to trouble her again. She sells what she can of the remaining goods, and is left with a pittance. She assumes the name of Mrs. Flanders. Taking lodgings in that part of London frequented by sailors, she meets a sea captain who sues for her love, thinking her a widow. She marries him and goes off with him to his plantation in Virginia. Her happiness there is doomed; her mother-in-law turns out to be her own mother; she is wedded to her half-brother! After eight years, she leaves her spouse, and returns to England, where she settles at Bath, a town noted for its loose living. She gives herself to a gentleman, who treats her handsomely; for six years they live together and she bears him three children. After a seizure of illness her lover repents of his adultery (all this time he has had a wife who is mentally deranged). He makes Moll a parting gift and relieves her of the responsibility of their offspring. Alone again in London, Moll flirts with a bank clerk who thinks her wealthy; he offers to guard her money, divorce his wife, and marry her, but Moll joins a friend in Lancashire. There she weds an Irishman she believes to be very rich; they both soon discover that each has been lying. Though fond of each other, they separate—he to pursue his profession of highwayman. She meets by appointment her bank clerk, now free, and they marry at the inn. The next day she sees her highwayman-ex-husband in the courtyard, and saves him from prison. Moll and her new husband live contentedly for five years. The loss of his money kills her spouse. Now forty-eight, Moll has two children to support. Impoverished, she yields to temptation and steals a bundle from an apothecary's shop. Soon she is stealing whatever she can get her hands on, and keeps at it for twelve years. Moll goes to live with an old friend, a female pawnbroker connected with thieves. From her she learns the arts of picking pockets and shoplifting. She becomes so expert that after a time Moll is at the top of her profession. Though rich enough to retire, she has become so enamored of her work that she continues for the love of it. During this period she has an affair with another gentleman. At last caught stealing some silk, she is sent to Newgate, where she meets her highwayman again. She is to be hanged. But her sentence and his are both commuted to banishment. The two decide to reform and leave for America. They start life afresh together, and settle in Maryland, where they prosper. The death of her mother and ex-husband-brother frees her of their shame. When she is seventy the now-wealthy pair return repentant to England.

A Journal of the Plague Year

His best work, *A Journal of the Plague Year* (1722), is highly typical of its author. The book pretends that it is a factual record maintained by a citizen who was in London all during the terrible plague of the year 1665. That year, of course, Defoe was only five years of age. But no adult eyewitness could have written a more painstakingly accurate-sounding account of actual events, public and private. All the imposing statistics were Defoe's own inventions, and certainly not one of his "facts" can be trusted. But the book was issued and accepted solemnly as an honest historical account. As a child Defoe must have heard many stories about that terrible year, and therefore his picture in general must be true enough. But his ability to create the feeling of fact and actual occurrence in this *Journal* is of the same kind that makes his romances seem so real.

20
THE NEOCLASSICAL
(AUGUSTAN) AGE

NEOCLASSICISM

The writers of the days of Queen Anne were conscious of the superiority of their efforts. During the days of the Emperor Augustus, Rome had had her greatest period of literature; Pope's contemporaries therefore modestly referred to themselves as forming a new "Augustan Age." The coffeehouse played an important role in the dissemination of literary tastes in those times. By Dryden's time the coffeehouse had already assumed importance in the life of London; it was there that the younger men went to hear Dryden preside as a monarch over the literary world. By Pope's time there were a great many of these meeting places popular in London: Will's, White's, Button's, Child's, Lloyd's, The Grecian, and St. James's, among others. It was for the patrons of these that Addison and Steele especially published their periodicals. Indeed, Addison expressly says that his purpose was to bring learning out of the schools into the coffeehouses.

The conformity overcasting the literature of this period makes it fairly easy to summarize some of its general characteristics. The respect for cities, which began in the Renaissance, reached its height at this time as a result of the new importance of industry. Augustan writers considered it catastrophic to be forced to live in the country away from the intellectual excitement of London. Mountain scenery and the sight of meadow or brook were only a bore to them. When they tolerated nature at all, it was only when it was tamed as in the gardens of Versailles. In the literature of the eighteenth century we look in vain for enthusiasm or inspiration, as we come to know these qualities in nineteenth century poetry. Pope and his contemporaries had little interest in the concerns of individuals; they were far more interested in the general laws of conduct for urban society as a whole. With their proudly rationalistic view of the world, they tended to be chiefly interested in satire as a form of expression, for in satire one attacks those individuals or institutions that do not conform to the common sense of society. Wit was at a premium; good manners were required in writing as in con- duct; and the world in which they lived and the concerns of contemporary life were their chief interest. They were classicists only in the sense that they imitated the literary *forms* of the ancients. Their subject matter was always the life of their own times.

ALEXANDER POPE (1688–1744)

Pope is beyond question the greatest of early eighteenth century English poets. He was born into a Roman Catholic family that operated a profitable business as linen drapers. Because of his religion the great schools and universities were closed to him, as was also any important public office. His education was therefore necessarily private. These limitations left him all the more free to bury himself in books and to exercise his thirst for poetic composition. He lived under the most grievous physical handicap. A serious illness as a child left him an invalid for the rest of his life. He never grew taller than four and a half feet and was humpbacked, and only rarely was free from some ailment. It is not surprising that he developed into an oversensitive, proud, and irritable man.

When he was still a boy, he had already read widely in the poetry of the modern and ancient world. By the age of fifteen he had written an epic poem, which he decided to destroy. His first volume was his *Pastorals* (1709), four poems on the seasons, inspired by Virgil and quite stilted; the music of his verses, however, so plainly indicated his genius that he was soon well-known to the public. Two years later he published his *Essay on Criticism* (1711), modelled on Horace's *Art of Poetry* and on the Frenchman Boileau's treatise on poetry (which was itself also derived from Horace). The *Essay on Criticism* was a remarkable accomplishment for a boy of twenty-three.

Essay on Criticism

Naturally the *Essay on Criticism* is not very profound or original. Pope makes no such claims. He is satisfied to follow the lead of Aristotle, Horace, and Boileau in formulating the principles of neoclassical art. Nature (by which he meant *human nature* in its universal aspects) and reason he believes to be the best guides to poetic inspiration. It is the business of art to reflect what is sane and commonsense in life. The rules that the ancients evolved for literary composition are derived from nature, and are only "nature methodized." The classics have faithfully reflected what is natural, and that is why they are the best guide for writers. The rules of the ancients are therefore only a means, not an end. But the rules cannot make a good poet, because a poet must have genius, just as a critic must have taste.

The poem is called an essay because of its informal tone. In it we can already see the qualities that make Pope without a rival in his peculiar gifts: wit, polish, and charming melody of verse. In it too we can find the weaknesses that he never overcame at any time: an inability to organize his intellectual concepts into a consistent philosophy, and an almost total lack of human warmth.

Part I: It is as great a crime to be an inferior critic as to be a wretched author; poor criticism is indeed more dangerous to the public, for it augments bad taste among readers. True taste among critics is as rare as true genius among authors; a good critic, like a good author, must be born with his gift. Nature gives most of us some judgment, but a faulty education impairs it. Too many fools turn critic out of a spiteful impulse to deride others. A good critic must begin by knowing his own powers and limitations, and never go beyond his depth. A man should confine himself to his own province for

One science only will one genius fit;
So vast is art, so narrow human wit.

Follow Nature, whose standards are unchanging, and frame your judgment according to her rules. The rules of the ancients were "discovered," not invented; they merely show "Nature methodized." Among the Greeks the critic "fanned the poet's fire," and taught the world what among the poets' works must be admired. Later, criticism ceased being the "Muse's handmaid," and tended to turn against the poets. Some critics began to prey on the great authors' ideas; others, unable to create for themselves, presumed to lay down dull laws to teach others how to write; the whole ambition of such men was to display their own feeble learning. To be a good critic: study the ancients; give your days and nights to Homer; compare his works with Virgil's (since the Roman poet found that Homer and Nature were "the same"). But it must be remembered that some beauties are beyond the analysis of rules; we should remember that if Homer does seem to nod on occasion, it is more likely that it is "we that dream." A modern, however, is wisest to hold close to the rules.

Part II: There are ten causes of a warped critical judgment. The first is pride; too many have but a desire to swell their own importance when they approach letters. The second fault is imperfect learning; sheer ignorance is safer than a mere smattering of learning. The third mistake is the practice of judging masterpieces by the qualities or defects of the parts, instead of viewing each work as a whole; it is the business of the critic to "regard the writer's end." Some critics pay all their attention to clever plays upon words; yet one can have

One glaring chaos and a wild heap of wit;

others are indifferent to an author's thought, and dwell only on his language, which is "but the dress of thought"; most critics judge a poet by the quality of his verse—such are not interested in mending their minds, like folk who go to church only to hear the music. The fourth error of the critic comes from his being either too hard or too easy to please. Avoid extremes; don't cavil at each trifling fault and don't lose your judgment because of one lucky phrase. The fifth fault lies in being too partial either to ancients or moderns; equally foolish is to admire only foreign writers or only our own. The sixth fault is to indulge prejudice or merely follow the mode of the moment. The seventh flaw is a love of being original. The eighth proceeds from an inability to stick to one judgment for twenty-four hours. The ninth is the unjust "party spirit," which praises only those with the right alliances. The tenth, worst of all, is envy. Good nature is one of the best attributes possible to a critic; a critic should be the first to discern merit. Let abuse be confined to those who earn it.

Part III: The best equipment for a critic is a combination of candor, modesty, good breeding, sincerity. The great critics of the past were Aristotle, Horace, Dionysius, Petronius, Quintilian, Longinus, Erasmus, Vida, and Boileau.

The Rape of the Lock

In 1712 Pope issued what many believe to be his masterpiece, *The Rape of the Lock*. Two years later he enlarged the original two cantos into five. In this final form, *The Rape of the Lock* stands as the most brilliant of English poetical satires. All of Pope's best qualities are in evidence throughout the poem. The heroic couplet has never been managed with greater elegance, pointedness, sweetness of music, or wit. It is also the finest example in English of the mock-heroic epic (a burlesque on the epic form). The poem was written at the suggestion of Pope's friend John Caryll. The very triviality of the occasion it celebrates makes Pope's infallible artistry all the more delightful. Lord Petre had stolen a lock of hair from the head of Miss Arabella Fermor, with the result that their respective families had broken off all friendly relations. The ostensible purpose of Pope's poem was to reconcile the two families. That the poet should have succeeded seems astonishing enough to a modern reader. But the Age of Queen Anne placed such a premium on wit that Miss Fermor, instead of being indignant at the satirical picture drawn of her, exhibited Pope's poem with pride to her friends.

The Rape of the Lock gives us one of the most brilliant pictures we have of the foibles and artifices of the aristocracy in Pope's day.

Canto 1: Belinda wakes up one midday, recollecting a dream she has just had, in which a guardian sylph, Ariel by name, has informed her that she is surrounded by thousands of delicate spirits guarding her honor and beauty, and warning her that something dreadful is fated to happen to her this day. But as Belinda reads the love letters waiting for her, she forgets the warning and goes to her toilet table to enhance her beauty with cosmetics.

Canto 2: That same morning the Baron, who admires her, coveting the possession of two of Belinda's lovely locks, has offered a prayer to Heaven, sacrificing in fire:

> *. . . twelve vast French romances, neatly gilt . . .*
> *. . . three garters, half a pair of gloves;*
> *And all the trophies of his former loves.*

The scene is now on board a pleasure launch going up the Thames to Hampton Court. Everyone is gay except the sylph Ariel. He summons the other sylphs, in a passage that proves Pope a master of the melody of verse:

> *The lucid squadrons round the sails repair . . .*
> *Some to the sun their insect-wings unfold,*
> *Waft on the breeze, or sink in clouds of gold;*
> *Transparent forms, too fine for mortal sight,*
> *Their fluid bodies half dissolved in light,*
> *Loose to the wind their airy garments flew,*
> *Thin glittering textures of the filmy dew,*
> *Dipped in the richest tincture of the skies,*
> *Where light disports in ever-mingling dyes,*
> *While every beam new transient colors flings,*
> *Colors that change whene'er they wave their wings.*

and warns them that they must be very attentive to Belinda this day because catastrophe threatens her. He doesn't know what the event will be: Will she lose her chastity? Will she break a valuable porcelain? Will she "stain her honor or her new brocade"? "Or lose her heart or necklace at a ball"? Or, worst of all, is her lapdog Shock to die? Each sylph hastens to defend some part of Belinda's person.

Canto 3: The gay party arrives at Hampton Court:

> *Here thou, great Anna! whom three realms obey,*
> *Dost sometimes counsel take—and sometimes tea*

A game of cards is started, and a bloody battle (of cards) ensues:

> *The Knave of Diamonds tries his wily arts,*
> *And wins (oh shameful chance!) the Queen of Hearts.*

Coffee is then served. As Belinda bends over her cup, the Baron takes a pair of shears, spreads them to enclose the lock, and joins them again. Just as he is about to cut:

> *A wretched sylph too fondly interposed;*
> *Fate urged the shears, and cut the sylph in twain*
> *(But airy substance soon unites again)*

and the lock is cut from Belinda's head "forever and forever." Shrieks go up to Heaven, louder than when husbands or lapdogs die.

Canto 4: Umbriel, a gloomy sylph, hastens down to the Cave of Spleen, and brings from there a bag of chagrin, and hastily returns to Hampton. He breaks the bag over Belinda's head, and Belinda's fury breaks forth. She curses the day that brought her to Hampton Court. She bitterly bemoans the loss of her beautiful lock, and cries to the Baron:

> *O hadst thou, cruel! been content to seize*
> *Hairs less in sight, or any hairs but these!*

Canto 5: The Baron is entreated to return the lock but he refuses to do so. A fight ensues, and in the scuffle, the lock is lost. Where could it have gone? Some think that it went to limbo. But the Muse saw it rise upward and become suddenly transformed as part of a constellation in the heavens. This new star will be sacred to lovers, and in its course almanac-makers will read the destiny of nations. Surely such an end must console Belinda for the lost lock.

The Rape of the Lock, as a mock-heroic poem, introduces much of the machinery of the epic: the announcement of the subject, the appeal to the muse, beginning in the middle of the story, a mythology (the sylphs), a battle scene (game of cards), a descent into Hades (the Cave of Spleen), and long epic speeches. The poem is a triumph of wit and satire.

Pope commemorated the happy life he had had for a few years in the country, in his next work, *Windsor Forest* (1713). It contains descriptive passages interpolated with political and historical ideas. Pope's praise in it of the Peace of Utrecht delighted the Tories but angered the Whig Addison and the latter's friends. The poem also won Pope the friendship of Swift. Thus Pope, at the age of twenty-five, was recognized in literary circles already as the greatest living poet.

Translations of Homer

In order to provide an income for himself, Pope announced in 1718 his intention of translating Homer. Subscriptions came pouring in in advance. The six volumes of the Iliad, which appeared between 1715 and 1720, brought him the handsome royalties of £5,000; the *Odyssey* (1725–1726) brought him some £4,000 more. This was the first time in English history that a writer had made a fortune by his pen. Pope made sound investments, and was able to live thereafter in security. He bought the lease of an estate on the Thames, near London, at Twickenham, which was converted into a miniature Versailles. Twickenham has been immortalized by the friends who visited Pope there.

The ten years spent in translating Homer (the *Odyssey* was a collaboration of Pope, Broome, and Fenton) resulted in a translation that belonged far more to Pope's own age than to ancient Greece. Pope's brilliant heroic couplet has little in common with the simple majesty of Homer; somehow or other Pope manages also to envelop the heroes of the Trojan War with the artificial manners and polish of the eighteenth century. This translation, moreover, because it was so widely read, was destined to have a blighting effect on later eighteenth century poetry: the abstract terms, the epithets, the chill formality of diction, which Pope employed in an effort to capture the dignity of the Greek (which he did not know very well), became the model for a "poetic diction" by Pope's imitators. It was against this theory of poetic diction that the *Lyrical Ballads* of Wordsworth and Coleridge in 1798 rebelled. Pope's *Homer* has one virtue, however, exceeding all other translations of the same works: It is certainly the raciest ever made.

In 1717 Pope published *Eloïsa To Abelard*, the sweetest of his poems. Though concerned with a pair of the most famous lovers in history, the poem is rhetorical rather than passionate. In 1725 Pope issued his edition of Shakespeare, which, except for a few interesting ideas, does little credit to his scholarship.

With the publication of his *Homer*, Pope had now achieved brilliant success in various types of poetry. He thereafter focussed his attention on the two kinds of poetry in which he has never been equalled: the satiric and the didactic. *The Dunciad* (1728, 1729, 1743), is almost a sequel to Dryden's *MacFlecknoe*, as an attack on literary charlatanism. When first issued, it was intended as an attack chiefly against a rival editor of Shakespeare, Lewis Theobald, who made many important contributions to Shakespearean scholarship, and had quite justifiably objected to Pope's edition. But in the final revision of *The Dunciad* Pope substituted the Poet Laureate, Colley Cibber, as Monarch of Dullness. Other less prominent people come in for savage criticism too. Like Dryden, Pope pillories people who would no longer be remembered if he had not attacked them. But one should note that these now insignificant writers were thought very important in their day. It is a tribute to Pope's discernment that he understood their worthlessness.

Essay on Man

The *Essay on Man* (1732–1734) is Pope's adventure into philosophy. The poem is almost as remarkable for its lack of consistency as for its literary perfection. It was translated into many other languages and admired all over Europe. Originally published anonymously, the *Essay* won immediate acclaim. It had been written at the suggestion of Pope's friend Bolingbroke, a nobleman-philosopher, man of letters, and politician. Bolingbroke was a free thinker, and Pope never gave up his acceptance of the Roman Catholic Church. The *Essay on Man* thus fluctuates between all shades of opinion from orthodoxy to deism. The four epistles that compose the poem discuss man's relation to the universe, to himself, to society, and to his ultimate happiness. One would search in vain for a philosophic system in this work. There is, of course, the basic eighteenth-century optimism, propounded by Leibnitz, throughout the poem, that "Whatever is, is right." Actually it was Locke who had first propounded the basis for this optimism with the concept of "the chain of being." According to this theory there is a gradual scale of the species in this world, "from plant to man," so that "the little transitions and deviations from one species to another are almost insensible." And so, from man to God there is a like chain of being. Pope says that many may ask questions about the ordering of the universe on the basis of the little he can observe; but could man, like God, see all things in the universe, he would understand that everything exists as part of a perfect harmony of the whole. The fly exists for the spider, and the spider exists for the fly. Thus man, too, is suited to his place in the scheme of things. Man is wisest when he studies himself rather than God. Vice and virtue are mixed in man's nature; but that very mixture is part, too, of the eternal plan of things. The *Essay on Man* is essentially a brilliant collection of epigrams on popular philosophic ideas of the time.

Epistle I: Let us take a view of "this scene of man." Labyrinth though the creation seems to be, it is "not without a plan." In looking over the whole let us

> *Laugh where we must, be candid where we can,*
> *But vindicate the ways of God to man.*

(The last remark is an adaptation of *And justify the ways of God to men*—with a difference!) We can reason only about our own world, not at all about "the worlds unnumbered" in the universe. Man ought not complain that he is "formed so weak"; rather should he ask "Why formed no weaker?" Man indeed is not imperfect; he is a being perfectly adapted to his place in the general scheme of things, and is in exact harmony with the larger order of creation, had he but the wit to understand as much. That thing which to man may seem wrong, must in relation to the larger order be right, for man sees but a part of the whole. No more than the "dull ox" can understand why at various times he has been a victim or a god (as in Egypt), so man cannot understand the meaning of the vicissitudes of his destiny. Indeed, man's very felicity depends as much on his ignorance of future events as on his hopes for a future state. God sees with "equal eye"

> *A hero perish, or a sparrow fall.*

Trust God and hope, though He does not reveal His plans for the soul in the world to come. The poor Indian is content to trust to his god in his hopes for "some happier island." Man builds for himself much misery and error in aiming at more knowledge than this, and in yearning to achieve greater perfection. Thus man foolishly puts himself in God's place, and vainly strives to judge of the fitness or unfitness of things, of what he deems justice or injustice—indeed calls God unjust if he finds himself unhappy. It is not for man to question God's dispensations. It is absurd that man should think of himself as the final cause of creation, or that he should expect the moral order to contain what may seem to him greater perfection but may actually be against Nature's plan. Man in his complaints is wholly inconsistent: he stipulates for the perfections of angels and at the same time enjoys the bodily qualifications of animals. If man were more sensitively constituted than he is, he would only be miserable. The "bliss of man"

> *Is not to act or think beyond mankind.*

Man has not a microscopic eye because "man is not a fly." If his sense of hearing were acuter, the sounds of Nature would but stun him. Throughout the created world there exists a universal order in which the faculties are graded from species to species; every creature is subordinated to some other creature, and all are subordinated to man. Man's reason gives the powers of all created things to him. There exists a

> *Vast chain of being! which from God began,*
> *Natures ethereal, human, angel, man,*
> *Beast, bird, fish, insect, what no eye can see,*
> *No glass can reach.*

In this great plan, were

> *one step broken, the great scale's destroyed,*

and the whole system must fall. Any desire to interfere with the grand scheme is therefore pure madness. Consequently, we owe to Providence absolute submission both as to our present and future state.

Epistle II: The business of man is to study himself, not to pry into God's purposes. Let scientific speculation increase, but with all modesty. In man two principles operate: Self-love and Reason. Of these Self-love is the stronger, but both tend to the same end: the avoidance of pain and the discovery of pleasure. The passions are "modes" of Self-love. Each man has a Ruling Passion, towards which all his faculties tend:

> *Nature its mother, Habit is its nurse;*
> *Wit, spirit, faculties, but make it worse.*

Even Reason is at its service; at its best Reason cannot conquer this natural predisposition, but can only modify it. But the Ruling Passion serves to direct men to different pursuits. Moreover, our best qualities issue from it:

> *Thus Nature gives us (let it check our pride)*
> *The Virtue nearest to our Vice allied:*
> *Reason the bias turns to good from ill.*

Vice, though odious, can too easily become a habit through self-justification. All men have some virtue and some vice, few in either extreme. In all cases, the ends of Providence are answered—in our imperfections no less than our virtues. Everyone ought to be happy with his place in the scheme of things, the master as the servant.

> *The learned is happy Nature to explore,*
> *The fool is happy that he knows no more;*
> *The rich is happy in the plenty given,*
> *The poor contents him with the care of Heaven.*

Every stage of life has its own contentment: the baby a rattle, the young man finery, the old man beads and prayerbooks.

Epistle III: The whole universe forms one system; nothing is made wholly for itself; nothing is made wholly for another

> *All served, all serving: nothing stands alone.*

Reason and Instinct both operate for the good of each individual, in the animal world as among human beings. Instinct prompts the mother to take care of its young until they are able to take care of themselves; Instinct perpetuates the species. Reason begins where Instinct ends, making life more benevolent and ever nobler. The state of Nature was "the reign of God." Then there was neither pride nor arts, and men and beasts lived in harmony. But later man became a murderer of his own species as well as of the brutes. Thus, as men began to vie with one another, the arts developed. Man built cities, nations were born. Wars began, and out of common interest men placed kings to rule over them. Fear, the origin of superstition, became also the parent of tyranny. When man saw that monarchs were only men, man began to worship God. Self-love became the incentive to the seizure of power but also the cause of self-restraint and the birth of law. Mankind now owns many kinds of government and religion:

> *In Faith and Hope the world will disagree,*
> *But all mankind's concern is Charity.*

So, Self-love taught man to be a social animal.

Epistle IV: Happiness is the desire of all men and is attainable by all. God intends all men to be happy, and therefore happiness must be social, for the welfare of the individual depends upon the welfare of the general. Man must submit, thus, to general, not particular, laws. Since the peace and welfare of society depend on material inequalities, it is not in material wealth that men should seek happiness. Providence maintains the balance of happiness through the passions of Hope and Fear. Health, Peace, and Competence are the true sources of felicity. But Health depends on Temperance. The good man is therefore more likely to be happy than the bad man. Nor are we wise to deem that because the good experience tragedy, that they are ill repaid; we forget that "partial ill" may be "universal good." God cannot alter his great plans for individuals. Riches, honors, rank, fame, and genius cannot make the unvirtuous happy. Virtue alone constitutes happiness, whose object is universal and whose prospects are eternal. The perfection of virtue and happiness depends on harmony with universal order.

Continuing his philosophic speculations, Pope published his *Moral Essays* (1731–1735), four epistles on contemporary manners, riches, and the use of wealth; and his *Imitations of Horace* (1733–1739), a series of satires on contemporary life. These final philosophical works show Pope in the perfection of his style. *The Epistle To Dr. Arbuthnot* (1735) was intended as a prologue to the *Imitations of Horace*, and is one of his most perfect poems. It is especially interesting to us because it is largely autobiographical.

IMPORTANCE

No poet in English has bequeathed more of his lines than Pope to the common vocabulary of the English-speaking world, excepting only Shakespeare. The reason that so many of Pope's phrases have passed into common usage is that he had an incomparable gift for pointed and succinct expression.

The following are only a handful of some of the better known lines:

A little learning is a dangerous thing;
Drink deep, or taste not the Pierian spring
(From *Essay on Criticism*)

True wit is Nature to advantage dressed,
What oft was thought, but ne'er so well expressed.
(From *Essay on Criticism*)

To err is human, to forgive divine
(From *Essay on Criticism*)

For fools rush in where angels fear to tread
(From *Essay on Criticism*)

And beauty draws us with a single hair
(From *The Rape of the Lock*)

At every word a reputation dies
(From *The Rape of the Lock*)

Hope springs eternal in the human breast:
Man never is, but always to be, blessed.
(From *Essay on Man*)

Lo, the poor Indian!
(From *Essay on Man*)

Whatever is, is right.
(From *Essay on Man*)

The proper study of mankind is man
(From *Essay on Man*)

> *Vice is a monster of so frightful mien,*
> *As to be hated needs but to be seen;*
> *Yet seen too oft, familiar with her face,*
> *We first endure, then pity, then embrace*
> (From *Essay on Man*)
>
> *Who shall decide when doctors disagree?*
> (From *Moral Essays*)

JOHN GAY (1685–1732)

John Gay, poet and playwright, has the unusual distinction of being perhaps the only literary figure in Pope's age who never quarreled with any of his literary confrères. He was born of humble Devonshire stock, and in London served as an apprentice for a while to a silk merchant. Later he was secretary to the Duchess of Monmouth and to the Earl of Clarendon. These were followed by other sinecures. Gay was universally liked, and was a good friend to Pope, Swift, and Arbuthnot. On his death he was buried in Westminster Abbey.

After publishing several unimportant volumes, Gay issued *The Shepherd's Week* (1714), a set of six pastorals, the best of their kind in the period, and remarkable in that age for their endeavor to be faithful to the spirit of country life. Gay's best known poetical work, however, is his *Trivia*, or *The Art of Walking the Streets* (1716), the finest poem in English on London life. It contains three books devoted to many realistic details of contemporary London, its sights, its scenes, its characters, its shady persons. His *Fables* (Part 1-1727; Part 2-1738) are among the best fables in English. Each poem tells very wittily a neat story with a moral at the end. The *Fables* were written to please a six-year-old boy who later became the Duke of Cumberland.

Gay, however, is best known to us as the author of a perennially revived opera, *The Beggar's Opera* (1728), which from its first presentation has been a favorite of the public. It was a satire on Italian opera, and Gay proved by his use of native popular tunes and folk songs that the English language is perfectly well suited to the purpose of opera. He thus started a tradition that was to achieve its greatest flourishing in the operettas of Gilbert and Sullivan a century and a half later. *The Beggar's Opera* is also a satire on Sir Robert Walpole and the party in power. The characters of the plot are thieves and criminals. Macheath, a leader of a gang of highwaymen, is handsome, a lover of the ladies, and much loved by them. He has married Polly Peachum secretly; she is the daughter of Peachum, an unscrupulous fence and stool pigeon. Peachum decides to betray Macheath to the law. In jail, Macheath wins the affections of Lucy Lockit, the jailor's daughter. Lucy helps Macheath to escape. But he is recaptured and brought to trial. He is condemned to death, but is reprieved. At this juncture he openly acknowledges that Polly, who has been faithful to him despite her parents' advice, is his wife.

Gay wrote a sequel to *The Beggar's Opera, Polly* (1729), in the same spirit. He also is the author of a satire on contemporary tragedy: *The What D'Ye Call It?* (1715).

MINOR POETS

Matthew Prior (1664–1721), a friend of Gay and Swift, called himself "only a poet by accident." He is best known for his graceful light verse. He is an expert in *vers de société* (clever, occasional verse). One of his lines has become famous: "*The end must justify the means.*" Bernard Mandeville (1670–1733), a Dutch physician living in London, was the author of a work of no great quality though of a certain historical importance, *The Fable of the Bees, or Private Vices, Public Benefits* (1705–1714). This poem undertook to defend the luxury and extravagance of the wealthy on the grounds that the money expended to satisfy pride and lust was responsible for providing the livelihood of the community. If men lived with the abstinence and moderation advocated by philosophy and religion, Mandeville argued, society would rapidly lapse into a state of economic chaos. The book was discussed everywhere, and denounced by the clergy. It did much to influence some aspects of the thought of Adam Smith, the economist, and Voltaire.

JONATHAN SWIFT (1667–1745)

Background

Outside of the poetry of Pope, the eighteenth century, until its closing years, was more remarkable for its prose than for its verse. Among English prose stylists none exceeds Jonathan Swift as a master of a perfectly clear, exact, and firm prose. It is a prose exactly opposite in its virtues to that of Sir Thomas Browne, and on the artistic side is the best expression of the Age of Reason. Swift himself had little to say about matters artistic. His writing was based upon purely rational criteria. But despite the firm outline and lucidity of his style, one is aware that the author was a man of violent passions.

Everything concerning Swift's career is a paradox. He despised office seekers and men whose principles were for sale; no man of his times was more eager in the search for personal advancement. Everyone has admired him for his wit; his private life was an unrelieved tragedy. He was fond of practical jokes; it is said of him that he laughed only twice in his life. He was merciless in his satire; no man suffered more in reaction to the miseries of others. He loathed having to spend so many years in Ireland, which he compared to a rat hole; he is still honored in Ireland for employing his pen in behalf of the Irish against their English oppressors.

He was descended from the same great-grandfather as Dryden. Swift's parents were English, and had settled in Dublin. There he was born after the death of his father, into abject poverty. It was only through the help of an uncle that he received any education at all. At Killkenny Grammar School he came to know Congreve. Later he studied at Trinity College in his native city. When he had taken his degree, he was given a position as private secretary in Surrey by a distant relative, Sir William Temple, politician and man of letters. In this post he remained from 1688 to 1699. Temple was aware of the genius of his protégé, but Swift found his employment too servile for his happiness. During these years Swift wrote a considerable amount of verse; but Dryden, on examining it, said (with justice): "Cousin Swift, you will never be a poet."

Early Works

His position left him plenty of leisure for reading and literary composition. Before 1699 he had written his two earliest major works, *The Battle of the Books* and *The Tale of a Tub*, both published in 1704. *The Battle of the Books* was written in defense of Temple, who was in the midst of a revival of the old argument on the comparative merits of the Ancients and the Moderns. Swift's work is written in the form of a prose mock-epic. He has the books in a Library take up the quarrel; such Ancients as Homer, Virgil, Plato, and Aristotle come to grips with such Moderns as Milton, Hobbes, and Descartes. Neither side is granted victory, but Swift's sympathies are plainly with the Ancients because of their fidelity to Nature.

The Tale of a Tub is a satire on the divisions of the Christian religion, and shows Swift's genius already in full maturity. Here, as is usual with him, the satire is managed by an extraordinarily simple device. A father dies and leaves bequests to his three sons, Peter (St. Peter), Martin (Luther), and Jack (John Calvin), who stand for the Roman Catholic Church and the Protestant Churches. The father has left each son a good coat, which each proceeds to alter in his own way, even though the father's will expressly prohibits any alteration of the coat. The brothers begin to squabble among themselves in justification of their own perversion of their father's intention. Through this simple story, Swift was able to satirize many matters of theological controversy. The book gave Carlyle, in the next century, the idea for his masterpiece *Sartor Resartus*.

While he was in Temple's employ, Swift formed the deepest attachment he had in his life, for Esther Johnson, a protégée of Temple's, whom it was his duty to tutor. She has been immortalized as Swift's "Stella," but everything connected with their relationship is still a mystery. While it is thought that they may have been married at some time or other, even this is not certain. Swift persuaded her to live with a friend near him, but they are said never to have met alone. After his death, among his papers was found a lock of her hair, identified as "only a woman's hair."

During these years Swift was ordained in the Church of England. When Temple died in 1699, Swift accepted the living of Laracor, a small parish near Dublin. From there he made frequent trips to London in search of a better position. In the metropolis he became well known to the clients of the coffee houses as an agreeable companion. Addison was soon calling him "the greatest genius of the age"—which was probably the truth. His position with Temple won him the friendship of the Whigs, and for them he wrote a number of pamphlets, none of which need be listed here. In 1708 he wrote a fanciful satire against the Deists, entitled, *An Argument To Prove That the Abolishing of Christianity in England May, As Things Now Stand, Be Attended With Some Inconveniences*; in it we find Swift's characteristic irony, and his skill in demolishing a point of view by advancing absurd arguments in its behalf. The same year saw the publication of the gayest of his work, *The Partridge Predictions* (1708). John Partridge was a quack dispenser of pills and patent medicines, who edited a yearly almanac; he had achieved something of a reputation as a prophet of coming events. In February, 1708, there was issued what Swift pretended to be a rival almanac by one Isaac Bickerstaff, in which the death of Partridge was prophesied to occur on March 29th. On March 30th there appeared another pamphlet with a full description of the last hours and death of Partridge. Poor Partridge tried to prove that he was still alive, but Mr. Bickerstaff answered that Partridge's death had been incontestably proved, and that the matter was ended. Indeed, Swift had killed Partridge, while aiming a heavy blow at the "science" of astrology. In 1710 Swift wrote another delightful piece in the same mood. As secretary to Lord Berkeley, it had been his duty to read, at Lady Berkeley's request, Boyle's dull *Meditations*. One day, Swift substituted a gay parody of it, his *Meditation Upon a Broomstick* (1710).

The Whigs had promised much to Swift, but had done little for him. As a firm believer in the Church of England, he was fundamentally not of their conviction. Seeing himself unrewarded in his hopes for advancement, he allied himself, in 1710, with the Tories, a party with which he had closer sympathies. For the next three years he devoted himself almost exclusively to their cause. The Tories were now in power, and made good use of Swift's phenomenal abilities. It is now history that Swift kept them in office. Of this period, when he was the most important man in England, he kept an account in a series of letters which he sent at intervals to Stella in Ireland. These were published eventually as *The Journal To Stella* (1710–1713). The *Journal* shows us Swift most intimately, and we realize what his other work little proves, that he was a man of tenderness and warmth, capable of the most delightful playfulness and sweetness.

His giving up his allegiance to the Whigs cost him the friendship of Addison. Pope, Gay, Prior, and their friends who formed the Scriblerus Club, remained devoted friends. Queen Anne, who had no liking for Swift, in 1713 granted him a post that he did not especially want, the Deanship of St. Patrick's in Dublin. She died the next year, the Tories went out of power for more than forty years, and Swift was forced to remain in exile in Ireland for the rest of his life.

Later Works

Swift's retirement in Ireland was a source of unending bitterness to him. Nevertheless his conscience was tortured by the spectacle of the dreadful misery in which the Irish suffered at the hands of the English. In *A Proposal for the Universal Use of Irish Manufacture* (1720), he urged the Irish to boycott English clothing and furniture. In *The Drapier's Letters* (1724), famous in the history of Ireland, he actually succeeded in sponsoring something of a national boycott, with the result that the Whigs in power were forced to come to terms on their proposal of debasing Irish money. He continued his championing of the Irish in *A Short View of the State of Ireland* (1727) (in which he proves how impoverished the country is) and in *A Modest Proposal for Preventing the Children of Poor People in Ireland From Being a Burden to Their Parents or Country, And For Making Them Beneficial to the Public* (1729). *A Modest Proposal* is one of Swift's most savage and perfectly written satires. The inability of the Irish to find relief or assistance in the midst of starvation, enraged Swift. Here we find his bitter irony at its best. As is common with him, he attacks an evil by pretending to advocate something even more preposterous and dreadful. The tone is cold and calm, and the prose cuts like steel. In it Swift declares that a young healthy child, if it is well nursed until it is a year old, will make "a most delicious, nourishing, and wholesome food, whether stewed, roasted, baked or boiled; . . . it will equally serve in a fricassee or ragout." He argues that if children will be raised in Ireland for the purposes of food supply, both the poor and the rich will be better off—the latter for food, the former for a small income, and that the plan will also reduce the number of Catholics in Ireland. In addition, this new source of income will provide an incentive for poor people to marry, since they have no other means of an assured livelihood. The work is a masterpiece of bitterness and irony.

Gulliver's Travels

While occupied in behalf of the Irish people, Swift wrote and published his masterpiece, *Gulliver's Travels*, or *Travels Into Several Remote Nations of the World by Lemuel Gulliver*, as it was first entitled. This is one of the greatest satires in the world. Ostensibly the satire could have been taken as a burlesque of travel books, which for a long time were commonly filled with incredible adventures. Actually *Gulliver's Travels* contains as bitter a denunciation of mankind as has ever been penned.

Book One: Book One relates the adventures in Lilliput.

Chap. I: The shipwrecked Gulliver awakens in a strange land to find himself bound by slender bands and surrounded by hundreds of diminutive inhabitants of the Empire of Lilliput.

Chap. II: The Emperor, taller by almost the breath of a nail than the rest of his court, treats the navigator with great hospitality, although he removes Gulliver's scimitar and pistols to a safe place.

Chap. III: The diversions of the country are shown the stranger-giant. Candidates for important posts and high favor at court are wont to procure their offices according to their skill in rope dancing. Needless to say, the chief ministers are able to jump higher on the slender white thread than anyone else. Royal favor is shown to those who have the greatest skill in jumping over or creeping under a stick held parallel to the ground; that favor is indicated by the conferring of blue, red, and green silken threads. Gulliver is anxious to be set free; the council of Lilliput confers and decides on certain conditions under which the "Man-Mountain" may obtain his liberty. One of these is that he must be the country's ally against the isle of Blefescu, ancient enemy to Lilliput.

Chap. IV: The reason for the feud is explained to Gulliver by the Principal Secretary. Lilliput labors under two evils: a violent faction at home and the threat of Blefescu. The two Lilliputian parties are distinguished by the height of the heels on their shoes. High heels are most friendly to the ancient constitution, but His Majesty now allows only low heels in the administration. The cause of the war between Lilliput and Blefescu is ancient: the old way for breaking eggs was to use the larger end; however, the present Majesty's grandfather once cut his finger in the operation; the next monarch proclaimed that all subjects must thenceforth break their eggs at the smaller end; six rebellions against the decree ensued, and Big-Endian exiles fled to Blefescu, where their resentment was encouraged; Big-Endians are denied civil employment in Lilliput, and their books are burned; in Blefescu, the Big-Endians charge the Small-Endians with causing a schism in the traditional religion.

Chap. V: Gulliver, at liberty, prevents an invasion, captures fifty of the enemy's ships, and is therefore honored by His Majesty. The Emperor is so excited about the victory that he wishes to become the sole monarch of the world by forcing everyone to become a Small-Endian. Gulliver, the liberal Englishman, dissuades the Emperor from this attempt. Though his advice is heeded, he is thereafter marked for destruction. The ambassadors from Blefescu arrive and concur in a peace. Gulliver does them several good offices, thereby further incurring the resentment of His Majesty, who lends an ear to the wicked counsels of Flimnap and Bolgolam. In this way Gulliver learns about court proceedings.

Chap. VI: The natives of Lilliput are about six inches high. They write aslant from one corner of the paper to the other, "like ladies in England." All crimes against the state are punished severely, but if the defendant is found innocent, his accuser is immediately put to death. Fraud is regarded as a greater crime than theft; ingratitude is a capital crime. Lilliput is remarkable by the extent to which it follows the principle of rewards and punishments; elsewhere only penalties seem to be enforced. Good morals in Lilliput are more highly esteemed than abilities in the awarding of employment. A child is under no obligation to his parents, and is educated by the state according to his rank; laborers, however, keep their offspring at home.

Chap. VII: Gulliver is secretly informed of an intrigue against his life contrived by Flimnap (the High Treasurer) and Bolgolam (the High Admiral). These two have maintained that Gulliver by all his actions tends to aid the enemy. Gulliver hears that they had wanted him put to death ignominiously, but that his friend Redresal has pleaded for him and urged that Man-Mountain's eyes be put out instead. His Majesty is inclined towards this leniency, but, hearing economic arguments on the depletion of the Treasury, agrees to a compromise; Gulliver is to be starved by degrees and also to have his eyes put out. The former plan is kept secret, the latter entered on the books. It is a custom in Lilliput after an execution has been decreed that the Emperor should make a speech expressing his tenderness and lenity; the more he commends his own goodness, the severer the punishment visited on the victim; the most innocent naturally are most harshly treated of all. No courtier by temperament, Gulliver is perplexed about the declared mercifulness of his sentence. He escapes to Blefescu, though living to regret the rash act; had he known the true nature of courts and kings, and the punishment allotted to criminals, he might have preferred the gentleness of Lilliputian ways.

Chap. VIII: Gulliver finds a boat; the ruler of Blefescu is glad enough to be rid of him; our navigator prepares to leave. He refuses the offer of service in His Majesty's employment, for he is resolved nevermore to trust princes or ministers.

The satire of Book One is aimed at the littleness of human beings. It is also more particularly concerned with English public affairs. The diplomatic relations of Lilliput and Blefescu mimic those of England and France. The High-heels are the Tories; the Low-heels the Whigs. But the domestic convulsions of Lilliput form a picture of human failings everywhere.

Book Two: Book Two shows us Brobdingnag, a land of giants, where Swift makes the same points in reverse.

Chap. I: Two years later, Gulliver embarks again for distant lands. During a great storm, he and his men are cast adrift upon a large island. The men flee to the boat, pursued by a large creature; Gulliver takes refuge in a field where the corn is forty feet high. Soon he is discovered by a huge man dressed like a laborer, who takes the diminutive Gulliver to his master. Gulliver is brought to the farmer's house, where he is amazed at the spectacle of these monstrous giants with blemishes on their skin; he reflects on the fair skin of English ladies, "who appear so beautiful only because they are of our size."

Chap. II: Gulliver is cared for by the farmer's daughter, Glumdalclitch, who is nine years old and only forty feet tall. The farmer, foreseeing profits, decides to exhibit Gulliver as an oddity.

Chap. III: By royal command Gulliver is carried to the Court. The Queen purchases him from the farmer; Glumdalclitch is retained as nurse to the little monster. Gulliver tells of his background, but the King's three philosophers are sceptical. The monarch, wiser than they, is almost persuaded to belief. Every Wednesday, the Sabbath of the Brobdingnagians, Gulliver dines in His Majesty's apartments. After he talks of his beloved England in glowing terms, the King observes that human grandeur is indeed contemptible when it can "be mimicked by such diminutive insects" as his guest. The latter is first incensed, then realizes how ridiculous he must seem to these superior people. Gulliver has many narrow escapes from the malice of the Queen's dwarf, a scurvy fellow; he is also tortured by the flies, which to him are as big as larks.

Chap. IV: Brobdingnag is six thousand miles long, and about four thousand miles wide, being a peninsula terminated on the northeast by impassable mountains. Gulliver views the metropolis. He sees a group of beggars, filthy and odious to his keen vision; he notes, as though magnified, the lice crawling about their clothes.

Chap. V: He has many dangerous experiences in the Queen's garden. One day a monkey as big as an elephant makes so bold as to carry him up to the roof and there try to feed him with the victuals stored in his chaps, much to the amusement of the whole court. He becomes ill, and the King questions him on his reactions to the accident. Gulliver replies hotly that had he had his weapon, he would have killed the monkey. The King laughs loudly at this response.

Chap. VI: In order to dispel the King's contempt for his native land, Gulliver tells him of England: of the illustrious House of Lords; of the saintly, erudite Bishops; of the House of Commons, formed of the representatives of the people, culled for their great abilities and love of country; of the Court of Justice and its interpretations of the law. The King asks questions: has the humor of a prince, a court-lady bribed, the whim of a Prime Minister, or party politics ever been responsible for the creation of new Lords? How much knowledge of the laws do the Lords possess that they should make important decisions on the properties of men? Do they ever take bribes? Are Bishops ever in slavish subjection to the whims of the nobility? Could a stranger with a full purse influence voters in the elections to the House of Commons? Do lawyers have the right to plead cases they know have no merit or right? Do party—or religious—alliances bear any weight in the scale of justice? Gulliver, having been almost ruined by a long lawsuit, is well qualified to answer. His Majesty is astounded to learn the history of the extensive wars and the use of mercenary armies in Gulliver's world. The account he hears leads the monarch to the opinion that the last century has been only a mass of "conspiracies, rebellions, murders, massacres, revolutions, banishments, the very worst effects that avarice, faction, hypocrisy, perfidiousness, cruelty, rage, madness, hatred, envy, lust, malice, or ambition could produce." In England what might have been tolerable has been vitiated by corruption; ignorance, idleness, and vice seem to be the chief qualifications for a legislator, and the majority of Englishmen must be "the most pernicious race of odious little vermin that nature ever suffered to crawl upon the surface of the earth."

Chap. VII: Gulliver begs the reader to forgive the King for such views, since His Majesty's standards must be narrower than the European. To illustrate, Gulliver tells how he begged His Majesty to make use of the invention of cannon, and how the King was horror-struck at such a devilish machine, and refused. The King's ignorance must be excused on the grounds that his people have not reduced politics to a science, as in Europe. The King indeed professes to despise all mystery in government. But these people are all defective in cleverness: their mathematics is applied only to what is useful; their laws never exceed twenty-two words; and it is a capital offense to write a commentary on the laws.

Chap. VIII: Gulliver leaves Brobdingnag in a strange way. Left alone one day in the third year of his visit, his box is picked up by an eagle, who then engaging in a fight with other birds, drops Gulliver into the sea. He is rescued by a ship, is glad to be among men of his own stature, and returns home.

Book Three: This book is devoted to an attack on abstract philosophers and pedants.

Chap. I: The author again sets sail for the East Indies, is captured by pirates, and set adrift in a little canoe. He lands and suddenly sees a vast opaque body moving towards him. It is the flying island of Laputa, with a flat, smooth, shining bottom, several gradations of galleries and stairs exhibiting many people. Gulliver is drawn up to the island by pulleys.

Chap. II: He meets a singular group of people. Their heads all incline to the left or right, and one eye is turned inward, the other eye being fixed on the zenith. Their garments are adorned with figures of suns, moons, and musical instruments. Each person is attended by a servant, who bears a blown bladder filled with pebbles which he uses to flap the mouth and ears of his master. These people are so rapt in speculation that they cannot speak or heed the discourse of others without being aroused by some external stimulus. Extreme danger awaits all who walk abroad without their flappers, since there are steep inclines and precipices everywhere. Only the minds of the vulgar are more disengaged. Gulliver waits one hour for the King to solve a problem before he is noticed; he is then treated to a meal of mutton cut into an equilateral triangle, ducks trussed up like fiddles, and other morsels geometrically arranged. The next day a tailor measures him for some new clothes by taking his altitude with a quadrant, describing the dimensions of his body with a rule and compass, and making elaborate calculations. The results are very ill-tailored because of a mistake in computation. The houses are all ill-built, with no visible right angles; these people despise practical geometry. The whole of their lives depends on mathematics; they are adroit on paper, but very clumsy in deed. The most important issue in their lives is the perpetual changes of the celestial bodies; they fear certain portents—such as the earth's being swallowed by the sun or being brushed by a comet's tail; a man rising from bed in the morning first asks fearfully about the sun's health, how it looked at sun up, and what hopes there are for avoiding a comet. The women like strangers, and indulge in every sort of intimacy before their husbands, who are too much immersed in speculation to notice. The women long to leave the island, and are always flitting off to the metropolis on the continent below.

Chap. III: The Floating Island is circular; its bottom is adamant. In the center of the island is the astronomer's cave, deep in the earth, where is found the loadstone upon which the fate of the island depends; this magnet is sustained by an axle which the weakest of hands could turn; by means of the loadstone the island rises or falls according to its attracting or repelling the King's domains below. Should a rebellion arise below, the King can hover over the town and deprive it of rain or sunshine, or pelt the inhabitants from above with stones.

Chap. IV: Gulliver, heartily weary of these people, goes to the metropolis of Lagado, where he is entertained by the great lord Munodi; the houses are wretched, the lands wasted, the people wild. The next day he visits the Lord's beautiful country house, classic in design. Munodi is melancholy because his compatriots despise him for managing his life no better; he must tear down his buildings and rebuild them according to the new mode; forty years ago certain people went to Laputa, acquired a smattering of mathematics, and were ready to change all things; they formed an Academy of Projectors for new experiments; but no project has ever been finished, so that the whole country is in a ruined state.

Chap. V: Gulliver meets the Projectors. One professor endeavors to extract sunbeams out of cucumbers; another ancient one is trying to reduce human excrement to its original state as food; another, emulating the bee and the spider, is trying to devise a method of building houses by beginning at the top. A new machinery-saving method for ploughing is to bury dates and acorns in parallel lines and have six hundred hogs driven into the field; the hogs will root up the earth and manure it at the same time; the method is brilliant, but expensive and troublesome, and has yielded no crops as yet. A great medico cures the colic with a huge pair of bellows; drawing in the wind, he can make the guts as lank as a dried bladder. Next Gulliver sees the speculative philosophers. One professor has proved that anyone can write a book on any subject without knowledge or genius; he has invented a machine which scrambles words, with the twist of a crank, and the lines that emerge are written down; already he has collected volumes of broken sentences that should in toto provide the world with a complete body of information on the arts and sciences. Another brilliant scheme is to abolish all words by utilizing the things for which words are only symbols; all a man needs for conversation is a knapsack full of the things he wishes to discuss; women, naturally, have no sympathy with this theory.

Chap. VI: The political Projectors make Gulliver very sad because of their visionary ideas. They wish monarchs to select officers by the criteria of wisdom, virtue, and the peoples' interest. Some ideas are pleasant, however. One professor wishes each senator, after having argued his position, to vote directly contrary to it for the good of the public.

Chap. VII: Gulliver leaves Lagado, and goes to the Island of the Sorcerers. He calls up the spirits of the dead. Homer and Aristotle appear at the head of their commentators, not recognizing any of the latter.

Chap. VIII: The commentators, out of shame for their past misrepresentations, have been in hiding. Three kings assure Gulliver that it is an error to prefer a person of merit, for virtue is a great clog in public affairs.

Chap. IX: Gulliver sails to Luggnagg, and learns of their Struldbrugs (the Immortals). He is enchanted at the thought of these happy beings perpetually storing up rich experience. But he learns that his conception presupposes perpetual youth and health. Actually the Struldbrugs are most unfortunate; at eighty they have all the follies of old men in addition to many more that come from the prospect of never dying. They can never rest; they remember only dimly their past; they lose their teeth; they cannot converse or read because the language is forever changing; they cannot even understand one another. Everyone shuns them.

Chap. X: Gulliver sails to Japan, and finally reaches England.

Book Four: This last book contains Swift's most vehement denunciation of the human species.

Chap. I: Setting sail as captain of the *Adventure*, Gulliver is threatened by mutiny of the crew, and is at last set ashore in a strange land. In a field he notices several animals, the most repulsive he has ever beheld. They are bearded like goats; their heads and breasts are covered with thick hair; and the rest of their bodies are bare and of a brown-buff color. These beasts attack him but are suddenly driven off by the appearance of a horse, who walks softly in the field, looking at Gulliver with amazement. Soon other horses join the first, and Gulliver observes that they converse like human beings discussing matters of weight. He recognizes that they are employing the word *Yahoo* as applying to himself. He distinguishes another word, *Houyhnhnm*. He follows the horses where they lead him.

Chap. II: Gulliver reaches a rambling dwelling, and after seeking a human form in vain, realizes that the horse is his host. Gulliver is placed side by side with one of the detestable creatures he first met in the field, and sees to his horror that he is its counterpart, except for the fact that the other's face is flatter and broader, the lips larger, and the body coarser and hairier. The horses, comparing the two, say *Yahoo* several times. An old steed, drawn in a vehicle by four Yahoos, comes to view the stranger along with many other horse-guests. Gulliver pleases the latter by his ability to pick up their language.

Chap. III: Gulliver finds that *Houyhnhnm* means "horse," and etymologically signifies "the perfection of nature." Gulliver tells his horse-master of his own antecedents, but the horse does not believe him. Lying is altogether foreign to the culture of the Houyhnhnms, but the Master cannot conceive of a vessel that can sail the seas. The Master is mystified at the invention of clothes, when Gulliver disrobes; why should Gulliver's race conceal what nature has provided? The horse concludes that Gulliver is a somewhat differing type of the perfect Yahoo. Gulliver announces that in his country the Yahoos are the masters and the Houyhnhnms the brutes.

Chap. IV: The Master is greatly disturbed. Here speech is for the purpose of being understood, and he cannot comprehend lying and is unfamiliar with doubt. If anyone says "the thing which was not," the whole end of speech is defeated. He is indignant to hear of a Yahoo riding a Houyhnhnm. Yahoos are physically too incapable to rule. Gulliver's account of the crew's mutiny, and of human desire for power and money, proves shocking to his Master.

Chap. V: Gulliver discourses to his Master on the state of England. He tells of great wars caused by the ambition of kings or by a mere difference in opinion. His master hears of this with horror and declares that the shame exceeds the dangers since Yahoos cannot bite each other very well and cannot easily kill. To clear up such ignorance Gulliver relates the art of war, describing cannons, bullets, powder, the dying, sinking ships. He proudly paints the valor of his countrymen when they blew up a hundred enemies at once and could behold "the dead bodies come down in pieces from the clouds." His Master's detestation of Yahoos increases with this account. In this country the Yahoos are not blamed for their odious qualities, but when a reasonable creature descends to such enormities, the Master wonders whether the corruption of reason is not more dreadful than brutality. Gulliver goes on to describe the Law; in his world a society of young men is encouraged to prove that black is white and white black, according to who pays them; these are the lawyers; judges are chosen from these men, who all their lives have been biased against truth and justice. The Master is further grieved to hear these things.

Chap. VI: Gulliver describes the use of money; the poor man furnishes by his labors the luxury of the rich; England produces more food than it needs, but sends food away to buy the follies and vices which feed luxury. Thus vast numbers of people must seek food by "begging, robbing, stealing, cheating, pimping, forswearing, flattering." When Gulliver tries to explain the medical profession, the Master cannot understand the meaning of sickness. Gulliver enlarges on the bad eating habits of his countrymen; doctors are skilled in predicting death,—in that they are abler than in aiding recovery. A representative of Gulliver's world is a minister of state; such a man's promise is a curse; he procures office by knowing how to get rid of a wife, daughter, or sister, or by betraying his predecessor. Gulliver's Master being of the opinion that he must be of noble birth because of his cleanliness and color,

Gulliver informs him that he is of humble origin; nobility breeds idleness and disease, dullness, ignorance, and sensuality.

Chap. VII: Gulliver informs the reader that his clarity concerning the human race was owing to his greater enlightenment while living among the horses; truth became so important to him that he wished never to return to his own world again. The Master tells Gulliver of the Yahoos, how they fight over food even when there is an excess of it; how they delight in a shining stone, which, when they find, they hide; how they are given to rapine and stealth; how their greed foments disease.

Chap. VIII: Protected by a strong sorrel nag, Gulliver observes the Yahoos. They are the most unteachable of animals, cunning, malicious, cowardly, with no desire to be governed by reason as are the Houyhnhnms. The latter accept the principles Socrates announced, and look on benevolence and friendship as the two principal virtues. They marry with an eye to perpetuating strength and comeliness. Each family produces a child of each sex; after that they exchange children to equalize matters.

Chap. IX: At the General Assembly of the Houyhnhnms the question is debated as to whether the Yahoos ought to be exterminated from the face of the earth. Asses would be more easily trained and much preferable to live with. Gulliver's Master, having learned from his guest of the castrating of horses, suggests the measure be applied to the Yahoos. We learn more of Houyhnhnm culture; their poetry is excellent; they use their limbs with great dexterity for every practical purpose; they die only of old age, and without regret; they own no word to describe the concept of evil; anything unpleasant is indicated by suffixing *Yahoo*.

Chap. X: Gulliver has lived in this land with great happiness; here there were no doctors, no lawyers to ruin him, no politicians, no wits, no bores, no pedants, no scoundrels, no nobles. When dining with the Houyhnhnms he preferred to listen and learn; their talk was only of virtue, friendship, benevolence, reason, and poetry. Thinking of his own world, Gulliver understands his own kind for what they are: Yahoos in shape and temper, using reason only to multiply vice. Seeing his own reflection in a lake, he draws back in horror, and begins to imitate the voice and gestures of the Houyhnhnms. But in the midst of his happiness, Gulliver is exhorted to leave. The General Assembly has taken offence at this Master for treating a Yahoo like one of themselves. Gulliver swoons, and on reviving cries that death were preferable to the horrifying prospect of passing the rest of his days in a world ruled by Yahoos. He builds a canoe, and in two months takes leave of his Master. He feels honored that when he prostrates himself before his Master to kiss the Houyhnhnm's foot, that worthy animal raises his hoof gently to Gulliver's mouth.

Chap. XI: Gulliver sails to a small island where he is attacked by the natives. He sees a ship approaching, is carried off by the sailors against his will, would jump overboard to escape returning to a Yahoo life. Home, his disgust with his family is unconquerable, and he buys two horses with which to converse.

Chap. XII: The purpose of this work is to instruct, not amuse. The author asks all English Yahoos to keep forever out of his sight.

This last book of *Gulliver's Travels* contains so savage a picture of humanity that some critics declare it to be the product of a diseased mind. But such a judgment fails to take into account Swift's own conviction that a life of reason could lift the Yahoo in human beings to a higher level of living. The fourth book is merely an expression of Swift's anger at the cruelty and stupidity of human beings towards each other. Swift himself said, to explain his position: "I hate and detest that animal called man, although I heartily love John, Peter, Thomas, and so forth."

Stella died in 1728, and without her Swift lapsed into deeper and deeper gloom. Towards the end he was the victim of a terrible mental disease; he was tortured by dreadful pain, and for long periods could not even speak. When he died in 1745, he was buried according to his wishes beside Stella in St. Patrick's.

JOSEPH ADDISON (1672–1719) AND RICHARD STEELE (1672–1729)

Addison and Steele formed the most celebrated of literary partnerships. They were born within a few weeks of each other, Addison in a Wiltshire village, Steele in Dublin. In London at Charterhouse, and later at Oxford, they were schoolmates, and all their lives close friends. Temperamentally they were opposites: Addison was the typical scholar, modest and formal; Steele was warm, impulsive, and irresponsible. Nevertheless they had much in common in the way of tastes. Although they did their best work together, each also wrote independently of the other.

Addison was a fellow at Magdalen College, Oxford, after taking his M.A. there in 1689. His studies and his Latin verses won much repute for him. His attainments were of the kind to make him valuable in the politics of those days, and an offer from the Whigs enabled him to travel abroad for four years. In 1704 he was asked to write a poem celebrating the Battle of Blenheim; in answer to this request he wrote *The Campaign*, an elegant but cold poem in heroic couplets. As a reward he was given the post of Undersecretary of State (1706). He entered Parliament in 1708, and kept his seat there until his death. In 1708 he was also made Secretary to Lord Halifax, the next year Secretary to Lord Lieutenant of Ireland, and in 1716 he was made Commissioner for Trade and Colonies. He now married the Countess Dowager of Warwick, and in consequence obtained the post of Secretary of State. When he died in 1719 he was buried in Westminster Abbey. Besides his collaboration with Steele, Addison's work has little importance for us now. *Cato* (1713), a stiff classical tragedy in blank verse written according to the Aristotelian rules, was enormously successful only because both Whigs and Tories saw in it a glorification of their own party's devotion to the cause of liberty.

Steele led a very different kind of life. He left Oxford without taking his degree, and enlisted under an assumed name in the Army. For this act he was disinherited. But his ability was considerable and he was eventually promoted to the rank of Captain. He became known to the patrons of the coffee houses as a wit, and a member of the fashionable set Steele was very much the victim of his own easygoing nature. He found it hard to resist temptation, but was forever earnestly promising himself to reform. In one of the latter moods he composed *The Christian Hero* (1701) to prove that only Christianity could save a man from the temptations that London offered for folly and vice. Then, in order to make up to his fellow soldiers for this outburst of religious fervor, he wrote his first play, *The Funeral or Grief à la Mode* (1701), a satire on undertakers and lawyers.

Steele became one of the most influential writers for the stage, and did as much to kill the spirit of humor and amusement in eighteenth-century comedy as anyone. He is largely responsible for the vogue of sentimentality in comedy, a vogue that has continued into the twentieth century. His next plays set the style. *The Lying Lover* (1703), his first sentimental play, is suffused with piety, and shows up the folly of excessive drinking (one of Steele's own vices) and dueling. *The Tender Husband* (1705), based on Molière (although the comic spirit of the great Frenchman is certainly perverted in it), continues the sentimental tradition. *The Conscious Lovers* (1722), an adaptation of Terence, is in some ways the most characteristic of the "weeping comedies," as sentimental comedy has been called. The plot deals with the love of young Bevil for the orphan Indiana. He is, however, supposed to marry the wealthy Lucinda Sealand. There are many complications until the end, when Indiana turns out to be the long lost daughter of Mr. Sealand by a former marriage, and all ends happily. The trouble with these sentimental comedies is that they are debased by a desire to show that crime and evil are but the product of thoughtlessness; wicked people repent at the last minute and become good—the kind of conversion that never occurs in life. From a literary point of view, they did drama the great disservice of banishing fun from comedy.

In 1706 Steele was appointed gentleman-in-waiting to Queen Anne's husband. In 1707 he was appointed editor of the government newspaper, *The London Gazette*. In the same year he married Mary Scurlock, known to us in his letters as "Dear Prue." Despite his success, Steele was always financially insolvent because of his extravagance. This personal weakness was responsible for his starting the first important English literary periodical, *The Tatler* in 1709. *The Tatler* was followed by *The Spectator* in 1711. These were the most significant years in the lives of both Addison and Steele. After *The Spectator* was discontinued, Steele continued to try other ventures in the field of the periodical, *The Guardian* (1713), *The Englishman* (1714), *Town Talk* (1715), *The Plebeian* (1718), *The Theatre* (1720), and others; but he never succeeded in reproducing the brilliance of *The Tatler* or *The Spectator*. He was elected to Parliament in 1713, lost his seat, but was re-elected. In 1715 George I knighted him for having been a champion of the Hanover dynasty. He was appointed Patentee of Drury Lane Theatre in the same year. But Steele never managed to live within his income. His debts proved too much for him and in 1724 he was forced to retire to a property in Wales.

Before *The Tatler* there had been a certain number of newspapers and newssheets. But Steele's only important predecessor was Defoe's *Review*, particularly in that periodical's department known as *The Scandalous Club*, "a weekly history of nonsense, impertinence, vice and debauchery." It was *The Scandalous Club* that gave Steele his idea. He issued the first number of *The Tatler* on April 12, 1709. It sold first for a penny and later for twopence, and appeared three times a week. Steele borrowed the *nom de plume* of Isaac Bickerstaff, which Swift had invented for his *Partridge Predictions*. The material was to be dated from the various coffee houses, according to the nature of the town gossip connected with each meetingplace. Articles on pleasure and entertainment came under the heading of White's Chocolate House; poetry under Will's Coffee House; learning under The Grecian, and so on.

Addison was in Ireland when the first numbers of *The Tatler* appeared. He was sure that he recognized his friend's hand, and, much to the delight of Steele, began to send him contributions. But the whole tone of *The Tatler* is largely owing to Steele's writings, for he wrote himself 188 out of the 271 papers in the series, while Addison wrote only 42. Steele's policy was to make truth, honor, and virtue attractive. But aside from that commendable objective he succeeded in recording with wonderful vividness the life of the middle-class readers who were his public. He has immortalized their gossip, their taste, their fashions, scandals, and learning. It is probably through Addison's influence that items of news began to be excluded, and that each issue of *The Tatler* tended more and more to become a single essay.

The Tatler made its last appearance on January 2, 1711, to the great disappointment of the coffee houses. Two months later the first number of *The Spectator* appeared, on March 1, 1711. The new periodical was published six times a week and ran until December 6, 1712. Its plan was more carefully thought out than *The Tatler's*, and Addison was the leading contributor. There are 555 essays in *The Spectator;* of these Addison wrote 274, Steele 236, a few were written by both of them; their friends wrote the rest. To give unity to the papers, the editors invented the Spectator Club, whose leading members were Sir Roger de Coverley (a country gentleman), Sir Andrew Freeport (a well-to-do merchant), Will Honeycomb (a man of fashion), and Captain Sentry (one of the military). Other characters, in charge of matters pertaining to learning, were the Templar, the Clergyman, and Mr. Spectator himself. Addison announced that his purpose was to make virtue pleasant through the use of wit, and to bring philosophy out of the schools into homes and coffee houses. In other words, his task was to popularize the learning and good manners that had been practiced at Court during the Restoration, but cleansed of their Restoration indecency. The success of *The Spectator* was spectacular. The public display of goodness soon became as fashionable as vice had been in the preceding era. The prestige of many follies began to dwindle once *The Spectator* aimed its amiable wit against them. Dueling, for instance, was proved by this periodical to be absurd, and its decline began with the laughter of *The Spectator*. More important, middle-class Londoners began to be conscious of literature and literary values. The readers of *The Spectator* were instructed while being entertained. There is no end to the variety of subjects covered in these papers: the sights of London, Italian opera, audiences in a theater, eccentrics, ladies' fashions, suggestions for those in love, the difference between true and false learning, the pleasures of the imagination, anecdotes, literary criticism, religious discussions, and so on. Among the papers on literary criticism is a very important series in which Addison examined *Paradise Lost*, a criticism of Milton that is still among the best ever written.

The Spectator ended on December 6, 1712. It was revived on June 18, 1714 to be issued three times a week until December 20th of the same year. In the meantime Addison had contributed to Steele's *Guardian* (1713). Addison himself edited *The Freeholder* (1715–1716) for 55 issues. But the success of *The Spectator* was never repeated.

The Tatler and *The Spectator* were reprinted in book form for an even larger public. These essays were translated into many languages. In England they had many imitators, notably Johnson's periodical-essays, and Goldsmith's.

In this partnership certain differences can be noted. Steele is warmer, more spontaneous, more colloquial and more slipshod, but more a man of the world. Addison is less interested in sentiment but has a more profound mind, more dignity, more subtlety, and more grace. As a stylist Addison is certainly the superior. His essays are models for classicism at its most polished, elegant, and witty.

Among the most celebrated essays in *The Tatler* are "On Duelling," "The Trumpet Club," "The Character of the Upholsterer," "Ned Softly The Poet," and "Character of Sir Timothy Tittle." Among the best of *The Spectator* are: "The Uses of the Spectator," "Westminster Abbey," "The Vision of Mirza," "Dissection of a Beau's Head," "Dissection of a Coquette's Heart," and "The Fine Lady's Journal."

21
THE AGE OF SAMUEL JOHNSON

CLASSICAL ABSTRACTION

For the rest of the eighteenth century most poets tried to imitate the elegance and grace of Pope. Without his genius, they succeeded chiefly in being pompous rather than elegant. It is true that artifice is to be found in Pope, but his wit somehow managed to impart a gaiety lacking in his imitators. The chief enemy of eighteenth-century poetry as it was written is the theory of "poetic diction." Pope himself preferred "ethereal plane" to *sky*, "main" to *sea* in the interests of elegance. This tendency becomes worse as the century proceeds. We find Gray writing "the orb of day" for the sun, and "golden flood" for sunlight. Besides this inflated diction, eighteenth-century poets preferred vague and general diction to the specific. Thomson speaks of "winter's rough domain," and "the cheerless empire of the sky," and so on. The extreme of this inclination to generalize is found in the practice of using abstractions in their poems. Gray has such phrases as "Conquest's crimson wing," "Thirst and Famine scowl," "the shrine of Luxury and Pride," and so on. These abstractions are highly unpoetic because they convey no image. It is strange to us that Johnson's contemporaries were under the illusion that the practice of using these abstractions made for sublimity. It is not surprising therefore that there is little to record of quality in the poetry of Johnson's day. The self-consciously classical poets of the time are little better than versifiers. The only poets of literary importance were those who were writing in reaction to the classical tradition, and exhibiting certain traits that were leading toward the revolt known as the Romantic movement, a movement that came to a focus a generation after Johnson. These pre-Romantic poets—Thomson, Gray, Collins, Cowper, Chatterton, and MacPherson—will be considered in the next volume in connection with the beginnings of the Romantic movement. Among the Classicists there was only one poem of real quality, Goldsmith's "The Deserted Village," and even that is remarkable for its more or less unconscious Romantic symptoms.

The bulk of literature in the Age of Samuel Johnson, therefore, is in prose. The leading writers in this second half of the Classic period are Johnson, Boswell, Goldsmith, Burke, and Sheridan. These men were all friends, and Johnson was their acknowledged leader as arbiter of classical taste.

PHILOSOPHICAL BACKGROUND

Throughout the eighteenth century and well into the nineteenth century, the most influential philosopher in England was John Locke. His *Essay Concerning Human Understanding* (1690) formed the basis of British empiricism—the view, in general, that only particular, concrete things actually exist, with all other ideas an abstraction from these primal realities. Locke rejected the idea that we are born with innate ideas. The mind, in his famous phrase, is a *tabula rasa*—a blank slate—ready to receive only what sensory experiences write upon it.

This broad philosophical position influenced every aspect of British life, from education to art to politics. In all these areas, the emphasis was placed on what *was* (as empirically defined) rather than what *might be* (via the imagination or visionary). Pope, Swift, Dr. Johnson, and other writers of the century placed emphasis on the central importance of guiding principles, not innovative leaps. Children were schooled to become, as quickly as possible, small versions of adults. Moral and economic systems (in the hands of such men as Thomas Malthus and David Ricardo) focused on what seemed undeniable, not what was theoretically possible.

At the same time (and perhaps as a response to the rigidity of Lockean empiricism), a powerful wave of nostalgia and sentiment is observable in British life during the eighteenth century and beyond. The progress made possible by the Industrial Revolution was weighed by the average citizen against the losses brought about by change. Due to the Enclosure Movement and the factory system, hundreds of thousands of villagers left or lost their places of birth, their accustomed family life, and in many cases their health as well.

The philosophical notions surrounding the French Revolution, with its emphasis on democracy and punishment of oppressors, were a constant source of terror to the English upper class. A comparable social revolution did not occur in England for at least three reasons. First, middle-class and upper-class English industrialists and others could be assimilated into the halls of power such as Parliament in a way not possible in pre-Revolution France; revolutionary fervor was partially defused, therefore, among those with access to social influence and power. Second, the religious fervor of the century (including the rise of Methodism and other evangelistic denominations) emphasized the virtues of patience and long-suffering in this "vale of tears" while awaiting translation to eternal life. Third, the average British citizen, no matter how poor, viewed continental political ideas and enthusiasms with suspicion and disdain. The excesses of the French Revolution (as recounted especially by Edmund Burke) convinced most English men and women that they did not want a similar blood-letting on British soil.

SAMUEL JOHNSON (1709–1784)

During Johnson's lifetime the factory system grew by leaps and bounds. Along with this industrial development came changes in the social scene, and with them changes in literary concepts. Against the beginnings of this revolt to Romanticism, Samuel Johnson stood as a bulwark of the neoclassical ideal. He was completely unmoved by the changes going on about him or the revolutionary ideas being advanced in France—except to detest them. He was a rigid conservative in all the departments of his thinking.

He was born the son of a poor bookseller in Lichfield. He was educated at the Lichfield Grammar School and at Pembroke College, Oxford. At the University he suffered much because of his extreme poverty and ill health. Already he was victimized by the depression that afflicted the rest of his years. Despite his modest way of living, he accumulated many debts, and was compelled to leave Oxford without taking a degree. A few years later he was married to a widow, Elizabeth Porter, many years his senior, whom he dearly loved, and whose death later was the deepest sorrow of his life. Johnson and his wife attempted to run a school, but failed. He came to London in 1737 with his pupil, David Garrick, who became the greatest actor of his day. In London Johnson began a long period of extreme poverty and privation, not rendered easier by his perpetual ill health and melancholy. He was forced to try his hand at anything for even the most trifling sums. At this time most of the little he earned came from the hack work he did for the *Gentleman's Magazine*. He was given notes, and from these it was his duty to invent what pretended to be literal records of the debates in Parliament.

His first significant work is a poem, *London* (1738), an imitation in heroic couplets of Juvenal's *Third Satire*. This poem won the notice and admiration of Pope. Johnson's only other celebrated poem is *The Vanity of Human Wishes* (1749), an imitation of Juvenal's *Tenth Satire*. *London* is a picture of the vices and follies of the city, its pursuit of fashion, and its indifference to poverty. *The Vanity of Human Wishes* is a reflection on the futility of optimism in human endeavors. Both poems exhibit Johnson's strong love of Latinity in expression, his pessimism, and his virile temperament. They are the product of a strong-minded man. In 1749 Johnson's tragedy, *Irene*, with part of which he had first come to London, was produced through the influence of Garrick; it had moderate success, more than it deserved. In the meantime Johnson had also written a critical biography, *The Life of Savage* (1744), on a minor poet who had been his friend. This was the first of a series of such critical studies in which he did some of his best work. *The Life of Savage* gives us some very real pictures of the poverty-ridden Bohemia in which Johnson was compelled to live during these years of complete obscurity.

Although still unknown, in 1747 he issued his plan for a dictionary of the English language that he proposed writing. On the advice of the publisher he addressed the plan to Lord Chesterfield, a nobleman who was proud of his own literary position. Johnson's purpose in undertaking one of the most taxing performances in the history of scholarship was to compile a definitive work that would fix the pronunciation of the language, and help maintain it in its purity. His next eight years were spent chiefly on this project, with almost no aid. The *Dictionary of the English Language* (1755) was almost entirely the product of his own labors. This epical book has provided the basis for all dictionaries since. No dictionary has exercised the authority on our language that Johnson's has. The usage as well as the spelling was fixed forever by Johnson in the case of many words. Only in one respect has his dictionary been subject to justifiable criticism. Occasionally Johnson would permit his sense of humor to intrude on his definitions, as when he defined *patriotism* as "the last refuge of a scoundrel," or *oats* as "a grain which in England is generally given to horses, but in Scotland supports the people."

The financial aid and recognition that Johnson had been led to expect of Chesterfield were nowhere in evidence during all the years in which Johnson was carrying out his enormous task. Johnson was therefore enraged to find Chesterfield writing two papers in *The World* in praise of *The Dictionary* on its publication. Johnson answered at once with a public *Letter to Lord Chesterfield,* which has been called the Declaration of Independence of authors. In it he disclaims any obligation to Chesterfield or any one else for his labors, and asks "Is not a patron, my lord, one who looks with unconcern on a man struggling for life in the water, and, when he has reached ground, encumbers him with help?"

The Dictionary fixed Johnson's reputation as the leading literary figure of his time. While he had been engaged in its compilation, Johnson also wrote periodical essays twice a week in *The Rambler* (1750–1752). Though following Addison's lead in the choice of his subjects, Johnson's style is entirely dissimilar from Addison's. Probably as a result of his researches for the *Dictionary,* Johnson's prose at this time is weighted down with Latinisms. Some years later, when we find him writing another series of essays, *The Idler* (1758–1760), he seems to have discarded the heavy lumber of his vocabulary, and writes with much more lightness and grace. But there is always a note of sadness in Johnson's essays, which has nothing in common with the gaiety of Addison. Johnson was always convinced that the unhappiness in any man's life is in far greater proportion than the joy.

But if it is true that Johnson's essays are not very light or graceful, *The Rambler* and *The Idler* prove him to be a more serious moralist than his predecessors, and a far more thoughtful literary critic. Johnson's sharpness of intellect, lively curiosity on all subjects, and powerful personality are enough to lend his essays interest and importance. The papers reminiscent of his experiences in London's literary Bohemia (Grub Street), and his strong satire at the expense of pretenders to learning (exemplified in his character of Dick Minim, the critic) are the best.

In 1759 Johnson's mother became very ill. She died shortly thereafter. During this period Johnson wrote very rapidly his most widely read piece of prose, *Rasselas*, to pay for the expenses incurred by his mother. Its purpose was to teach the futility of searching for happiness. It is said the composition took no more than ten days. Perhaps this speed accounts for the fact that *Rasselas* is the simplest of Johnson's prose pieces. Rasselas, Prince of Absyssinia, and his sister escape from their Happy Valley together with the philosopher Imlac. After traveling around to observe people in all conditions of life, Rasselas becomes disenchanted with the idea that happiness can be found, and he decides to return to Happy Valley to lead a life of reflection. It is interesting to remark in passing that within a few weeks the French philosopher Voltaire also produced a work on the same idea, *Candide*. But nothing could be more dissimilar than the Frenchman's piercing wit and the Englishman's calm sobriety.

Although Johnson was now celebrated, he was still poor. He was relieved at last of his financial worries in 1762 when he accepted a pension from the government on the condition that there be no duties attached to it. The next year proved very important for us, for in 1763 he met James Boswell, who was to be his biographer. In 1764 Johnson and the great painter, Sir Joshua Reynolds, formed the Club, which was later to be called the Literary Club. Its members included Goldsmith, Burke, Garrick, Adam Smith, Boswell, Bishop Percy, the historian Gibbon, the dramatist Sheridan, and a number of other prominent dramatists and scholars. Of these men Johnson was the acknowledged leader. It is through Boswell that we know that few men had a more ceaseless flow of brilliant conversation than Samuel Johnson; when we read Boswell's biography of Johnson, we can understand why Johnson was the chief talker at the Club, and why the rest preferred usually to be an audience.

Johnson was one of the kindest of men. For years his home provided room and food to a number of needy people. Johnson had announced an edition of Shakespeare, and at last, in 1765, his edition came out. The Preface to his Shakespeare provides one of the finest pieces of criticism ever written of the great poet-dramatist's work. After 1770 he began to be more active in writing. From 1770–1775 he wrote a series of Tory pamphlets, although his private opinion was that he "would not give half a guinea to live under one form of government than another." In 1773 he went with Boswell for a tour of Scotland; two years later he recorded his observations and experiences in his *Journey to the Western Islands of Scotland* (1775).

His last work was the most important of his critical writings. From 1779 to 1781 he wrote a series of biographical-critical essays, originally intended as prefaces to a collected edition of the English poets. But as he became absorbed in them, they became more elaborate, and contained his most mature critical judgments. They were issued under the title of *Lives of the*

Most Eminent English Poets With Critical Observations on Their Works. His *Lives* of Addison, Dryden, and Pope are among his best—naturally, since he was so much in sympathy with their classical literary philosophy. The *Lives* also show his staunch dislike of the rising sentiment of Romanticism. He disliked Gray's *The Bard*, and there seems little reason now to disagree with Johnson. He charged against Collins that he was too much interested in fairies, giants, and monsters. Johnson's most notorious disapproval was of Milton's "Lycidas." Johnson hated all pastoral poetry for its artificiality, and unfortunately lacked the imagination and the ear to understand how much "Lycidas" transcends the conventions of the pastoral. It is too often forgotten that if Johnson disliked "Lycidas," he said of *Paradise Lost* that its design entitles it to first place "among the productions of the human mind." If he attacked Gray's *The Bard*, it is also true that he gave the highest praise to the same poet's *Elegy*.

In 1775 the University of Oxford bestowed on Johnson the honorary degree of Doctor of Laws. When he died in 1784, he was buried in Westminster Abbey. Garrick's remains lie next to his.

IMPORTANCE

It is largely because of his personality that Johnson remains for us the great man of his age. He was the last of England's literary dictators. He believed in what he had to say, and there is great authority in all his utterances. His mind was vigorous, his style at its best forthright and manly. He never failed to uphold the value of sound thinking and common sense in life and literature, and the sturdy clear-eyed quality of his judgments has made him one of the most valuable of English critics. And his style was highly expressive of his own fascinating personality, solid, learned, intelligent, and tinged with melancholy.

JAMES BOSWELL (1740–1795)

It is only fairly recently that Boswell has been understood as the charming gifted man he was. In the nineteenth century critics like Macaulay succeeded in making Boswell out to be a kind of sycophant who hung upon Johnson's coat tails, and permitted himself to be treated with contempt. According to them he became the greatest of biographers only by accident. Macaulay says: "If he had not been a great fool he would never have been a great writer." The witticism is too smug even on the face of it. But within our century, at the residence of one of Boswell's descendants, a now-famous box was discovered containing a vast assortment of Boswell's letters and journals. From these documents a new Boswell has emerged. It would even be possible to say now that Boswell, the heir of a noble house and a literary man himself, might have seemed to his contemporaries to be condescending in knowing Johnson—were it not that Boswell's veneration for Johnson is plain on every page of his great book. It is true that Boswell was well aware that there were materials for a great book in his friend Johnson, and came to feel himself consecrated to the writing of it. Johnson well knew Boswell's intentions, and approved of them. Boswell's devotion to his friend was equal in sincerity to his devotion to the biography he intended to write.

James Boswell was the son of a prominent Scottish judge of ancient family and considerable property. At Edinburgh University young Boswell became acquainted with the great philosopher David Hume. En route to Holland to continue his studies in law, he stopped for a while in London (1763) with the express purpose of becoming Johnson's friend; he was already the great man's profound admirer. On May 16th a lucky accident brought them face to face at last. After a few meetings they were friends, and thereafter a deep affection existed between the two, despite the disparity of their years. To the end of his days Johnson considered Boswell's fidelity "as a greater part of the comforts" that were left him.

Boswell in 1763 proceeded to the continent, and added to his friends four of the most prominent men of his times: Voltaire, Rousseau, John Wilkes, and the Corsican patriot, General Paoli. His close intimacy with Paoli made Boswell become very much interested in the affairs of Corsica. In 1768 he published his *Account of Corsica, The Journal of a Tour to That Island: And Memoirs of Pascal Paoli*. Here Boswell already demonstrates his peculiar gift. He had been able to extract from Paoli a thousand interesting details out of which he made a life-like portrait.

In the meantime he had been admitted to the Scottish bar and had published *Dorando, a Spanish Tale*, and *The Essence of the Douglas Case*. In 1760 he again gave evidence of his interest in the Corsican fight for liberty by supervising the *British Essays in Favor of the Brave Corsicans*. In 1773 he was elected member of Johnson's Club, and so began his friendship with Reynolds and the scholar Malone. During these years he had an active legal practice that required his constant return to Scotland; had he been able to, it was in London that he would have lived. Naturally he was in London as often as he could manage it. From 1777 to 1783 he contributed an essay a month under the name of "The Hypochondriack" to the *London Magazine*.

The year after Johnson's death Boswell published his own *Journal of a Tour to the Hebrides with Samuel Johnson LL.D.* The book was a great success and proved that the public would be more than receptive to Boswell's projected biography. Boswell began to assemble his materials, and to collect what he could from Johnson's other friends. In 1791 his masterpiece, *The Life of Samuel Johnson, LL.D.* appeared. It is the consensus of opinion that this is the greatest biography ever written. Johnson owes his assured immortality more to Boswell's book than to his own work.

Boswell makes good his claim that his biography exhibits Johnson "more completely than any person, ancient or modern." Because of this book few men are known better to readers of English literature than Samuel Johnson. Boswell was a born biographer, but he could not have chosen a more fascinating subject. Johnson had a genius for conversation, and no one in that circle of great men in which he moved could draw him out more completely than Boswell. The very style of Johnson's talk never fails to be consistent—a prose of a very different order from Boswell's own comments. More than this, we can hear the very tone of Johnson's voice, and even, as one critic has it, "the sound of his silences."

Boswell brought to his great task the best talents it could possibly require. He loved Johnson so much that his highest ambition was to present his hero just as he lived and talked. This he perfectly does. Boswell had the patience and the memory to record Johnson's conversation in the notes he regularly made. He had the imagination to give us Johnson's talk in settings so realistic that we always feel we ourselves are present. We feel that we are living day by day at Johnson's side. Nor do we object when Boswell thrusts himself or his own opinions in. For then, although the writing always becomes suddenly pompous and elaborate, Boswell himself is so quaint and lively a character, that we come to like him as much as his hero—for his very failings and egotisms.

EIGHTEENTH CENTURY DRAMA

Developments in the drama during the eighteenth century can be divided into the periods from 1700 to 1750 and from 1750 to the end of the century. During the first period, comedy underwent a moral shift toward less bawdy and, at times, even moralistic and sentimentalized material, when compared to earlier plays. Political commentary (usually through satire or farce) in the first half of the century was pronounced—so much so that Parliament passed in 1737 the Licensing Act, forcing playwrights to have their works approved by deputies of the Lord Chamberlain before these dramas could appear on stage.

The most influential playwright during the period 1700 to 1750 was Colley Cibber (1671–1757), a writer now remembered primarily as a target of Pope's virulent criticism. In such plays as *Love's Last Shift* (1696) and *The Careless Husband* (1704), Cibber uses a plot device typical of his more than twenty plays—the foppish, erring male brought to sudden reformation in the last act. Cibber's handling of such material is never subtle; his plays are driven by plot developments that produce snickers more than laughter and sighs more than tears.

A different personality entirely was Richard Steele (see Chapter 20). Especially his early plays seem to propagandize for middle-class respectability.

Among these are *The Funeral; or Grief à-la-Mode* (1701), *The Lying Lover* (1703), and *The Tender Husband* (1705). Though filled with somewhat dubious intrigues, these plays do address domestic problems, with respectably moral recommendations for their resolution.

The fourteen comedies, two tragedies, and three farces of Susanna Centlivre (c. 1667–1723) had great success in the first two decades of the eighteenth century. The works generally focus, whether for humor or grief, on love relations. Misunderstandings, deceptions, and pretensions between men and women are all anatomized with verve and passion if not great psychological depth. Best known of Centlivre's works are *The Gamester* (1705), *The Busie Body* (1709), and *A Bold Stroke for a Wife* (1718).

Although famous primarily as a novelist, Henry Fielding (1707–1754) played a key role in the midcentury developments of eighteenth century drama. *The Temple Beau* (1730) and *The Modern Husband* (1732) demonstrate Fielding's skill in satirizing or openly condemning London high life and the morally vacuous elite. But Fielding's special contributions to the drama came in the realm of farce rather than comedy or tragedy. John Gay's *The Beggar's Opera* (1728) led the way in this dramatic form with unparalleled stage success. Heroic materials drawn from Italian opera were sent up for ridicule, as, for example, in Gay's *Achilles* (1733), where a Greek hero appears on stage wearing women's clothes over his armor.

These absurd, giddy treatments of formerly serious matters and materials suited both Gay's and Fielding's temperaments and politics well. At heart, both men were using the absurd and irrational to reveal the equally insane elements they located in their society for satire. Among Fielding's most successful farces were *The Mock Doctor* (1732), *The Tumble-down Dick* (1736), and *Welsh Opera* (1731), a work burlesquing the royal family.

Tragedies were less often staged in the first half of the eighteenth century. Among the tragic writers were Nicholas Rowe (*The Ambitious Stepmother*, 1700), Joseph Addison (*Cato*, 1713), and George Lillo (*The London Merchant*, 1731).

Drama in the second half of the eighteenth century underwent a shift toward the primary importance of the star actor, often to the point of eclipsing both play and playwright. David Garrick and Sarah Siddons were immensely famous in the period for their emotive portrayals of tragic heroes and heroines. Shakespearean and other Elizabethan and Renaissance plays returned in revival (and in pieces, according to the star's preferences). Original drama of the period tended to focus either on native English materials (such as Henry Brook's *The Earl of Essex*, 1750, and Hall Hartson's *Countess of Salisbury*, 1767) or on domestic problems and situations (as in Edward Moore's *Gamester*, 1753, and Richard Cumberland's *The Mysterious Husband*, 1783). Other dramatists prominent during the period were Samuel Foote, Arthur Murphy, and George Colman the Elder.

Rising above all playwrights in the period, however, were Oliver Goldsmith and Richard Sheridan. Goldsmith's *She Stoops to Conquer* (1773) was (and remains) a great stage success. It blends farce elements with more sophisticated comedic treatment to produce dramatic entertainment neither antisentimental nor melodramatic. Following Goldsmith's death a year after the staging of *She Stoops to Conquer*, Sheridan carried on his tradition of ingenious plotting in *The Duenna* (1775), a comic opera that surpassed all records at the time for stage runs. His two great comedies, *The Rivals* and *School for Scandal*, followed in the next two years.

Goldsmith's and Sheridan's healthy rebuttal on behalf of sophisticated farce and satire, however, did not stem the tide of sentimentalized, melodramatic plays forming the bulk of dramatic productions throughout the century. George Colman the Younger, Thomas Holcraft, Thomas Morton, and Elizabeth Inchbald collectively wrote dozens of plays that were, in their reliance on stock emotions and unexamined motivations, not dissimilar from the run-of-the-mill television dramas of our own day.

OLIVER GOLDSMITH (1730–1744)

Goldsmith was the most versatile literary man of his time. He was the author of the best essays, one of the best novels, one of the finest comedies, and one of the greatest poems of his generation. Johnson's epitaph on him is indeed fitting: "He touched nothing that he did not adorn." Nevertheless, to his friends, the most gifted member of the Club seemed only to be an awkward, irresponsible, almost incoherent Irishman.

Goldsmith became a writer only when all other likely means of earning a living seemed to fail him. He was born in Ireland, the son of an impoverished Irish clergyman, whom he has immortalized in "The Deserted Village":

> *A man he was to all the country dear,*
> *And passing rich with forty pounds a year;*
> *Remote from towns he ran his godly race,*
> *Nor e'er had changed, nor wish'd to change his place;*
> *Unskillful he to fawn, or seek for power,*
> *By doctrines fashion'd to the varying hour;*
> *Far other aims his heart had learn'd to prize,*
> *More bent to raise the wretched than to rise.*
> *His house was known to all the vagrant train,*
> *He chid their wanderings, but relieved their pain;*
> *The long remember'd beggar was his guest,*
> *Whose beard descending swept his aged breast;*
> *The ruin'd spendthrift, now no longer proud,*
> *Claim'd kindred there, and had his claims allow'd;*
> *The broken soldier, kindly bade to stay,*
> *Sat by his fire, and talk'd the night away;*

Wept o'er his wounds, or, tales of sorrow done,
Shoulder'd his crutch, and show'd how fields were won.
Pleased with his guests, the good man learn'd to glow.
And quite forgot their vices in their woe;
Careless their merits or their faults to scan,
His pity gave ere charity began.

In the little village of Lissoy, where he spent his boyhood he was already considered "little better than a fool" because of his ugly face and clumsy ways, though he was universally liked for his gentleness and good humor. He was a poor student, but nonetheless was sent to Trinity College, Dublin, at the insistence of an uncle. He remained there for five years, miserably poor, and earning when he could a few extra coins by writing popular penny ballads. He paid very little attention to his studies, and was graduated near the bottom of his class. For a while he went back to Lissoy, and by twenty-one seemed a confirmed ne'er-do-well. He was persuaded to try the Church, but his application was rejected. After various abortive attempts at a profession, he was sent by his uncle with fifty pounds to go to London to study law. But he got no further than Dublin, where he gambled away the entire sum, and was forced once more to return to Lissoy. His uncle gave him another chance, and this time he set out for Edinburgh to become a doctor. After a year and a half at Edinburgh, he decided to go to Paris. But, leaving for the Continent, he went instead to Leyden, and began a tour of Europe on one guinea. These youthful indiscretions later provided material for his novel *The Vicar of Wakefield*. From it we gather that Goldsmith made his way through Europe by singing and playing on a flute. He visited Belgium, Switzerland, Italy, and France. In February 1756, he landed penniless at Dover. Making his way somehow or other to London, he found employment in a chemist shop. Although he had no degree, he soon had set himself up as a physician among the poor. Next he was employed by the printer Richardson. After that he was teaching in a school. It was then that a bookseller decided that Goldsmith had literary ability and persuaded him to try his hand at hack writing. It was a series of articles he wrote for the *Monthly Review* that revealed to Goldsmith his true vocation.

But in a short time he had quarreled with his employer and was living in a garret in Fleet Street, where he settled down to hack writing. He was almost thirty before he really applied himself to study. His first ambitious work was *An Enquiry into the Present State of Polite Learning in Europe* (1759), a summary of contemporary European literature; his abysmal ignorance of the subject is hardly greater than the charm and freshness of his style and personality as revealed in it. During the same year he wrote a series of periodical essays for *The Bee*, which he edited, and which did not last very long. As an essayist he proved himself to be the only worthy successor of Addison in the century.

His reputation was now increasing, he moved to better quarters, and by 1761 had become a close friend of Johnson's. The two men, totally opposite in nature, became warm friends. Goldsmith always remained carefree and simple, reckless and extravagant, despite the poverty he had known. And the sombre Johnson was often annoyed at what he considered to be Goldsmith's scatterbrained ignorance. He said of him: "He goes on without knowing how he is to get off." Goldsmith, however, was so simple that he alone of all that illustrious company failed to be terrified by Johnson, and when he was supposed to have been beaten in an argument, failed to realize that it was over. Nevertheless Johnson was devoted to Goldsmith, and Boswell is not able to conceal his jealousy of Johnson's partiality for this "course and vulgar" man. But everyone, even Boswell, liked Goldsmith.

In 1760 and 1761 Goldsmith issued his most important series of essays, the *Chinese Letters* which appeared in the *Public Ledger*. These were collected in two volumes in 1762 as *The Citizen of the World: Or, Letters From a Chinese Philosopher Residing in London, To His Friends in the East*. In some of them Goldsmith borrowed quite glibly from the essays of Montesquieu (*The Persian Letters*), but always managed to be entirely his charming self in them. Between the essays of Addison and those that Charles Lamb was to write in the nineteenth century, *The Citizen of the World* is the choicest collection in English. He has an easy, kind, and warm grace, all his own. Some of his portraits have never been surpassed for their keen observation and kind fun. His prose is almost colloquial in its unstudied ease. Among his best pieces are "The Bookseller," "The Character of an Important Trifler," and "The London Shopkeeper."

The Vicar of Wakefield

One morning Johnson received an urgent message from Goldsmith. came to him, and found that Goldsmith's landlady had arrested him for unpaid rent. Johnson put the cork back on the bottle out of which Goldsmith had been drinking, talked to him, found that he had a novel ready for the press, took it away to a bookseller, and sold it for sixty pounds. Thus *The Vicar of Wakefield* found its way into print in 1766. It was the best-loved novel of the century. The sweet humanity of Dr. Primrose, his simple kindness and hopeless impracticality have made him dear to all. By virtue of his ability to draw from his own Bohemian existence, Goldsmith was able to make this outstanding contribution to our literature.

Dr. Primrose, the gentle vicar, is married to Deborah, who has borne him six children. Olivia is remarkable for her gaiety, Sophia for her modesty— both girls are beauties. His four sons are a credit to him. Being comfortably situated, the good vicar dispenses his salary among the needy. His son George, an Oxonian, is to wed Miss Arabella Wilmot, daughter of their neighbors. But just before the nuptials are to take place, Dr. Primrose and Wilmot argue over the question of second marriages—a purely abstract question in George's case, although Wilmot has married three times. At this juncture, the news arrives that the vicar's fortune has been lost; his broker had run off with it. The marriage is called off. George goes to London to make his way, and Dr. Primrose becomes a curate in a distant village. En route to their new home, the family falls in with Mr. Burchell, who saves Sophia when her horse throws her into a stream. Their new dwelling is on the estate of Squire Thornhill, a wealthy ladykiller. Dropping in for a visit one day, the Squire is enchanted with Olivia. She and Mrs. Primrose's cuisine make him a frequent visitor. Because of his superior position, he is made to feel more welcome than Mr. Burchell, who is also often there to see Sophia. The vicar is worried about Burchell's indifference to improving his fortune. The Squire brings two fine ladies of the town to visit; soon the girls are occupied, despite parental objections, with emulating the fashion in clothes. Mrs. Primrose is willing to have her daughters accompany the women to town as their companions, though Burchell hotly protests. Suddenly, however, the ladies withdraw their offer because of a slanderous letter, which it turns out Burchell has written. Unashamed, he is ordered from the Primrose house. Squire Thornhill comes more often than ever, but matrimony seems not to be his object. Olivia, on her father's urging, considers accepting the hand of Mr. Williams, a young farmer, who is smitten with her. One night Dick Primrose reports seeing Olivia going off with two men in a carriage. Though the Squire seems the instigator, the evidence points to Burchell. The vicar follows in pursuit, falls ill, and three weeks later finds his daughter abandoned at an inn. It was the Squire who tricked her with the false promise of marriage, and Burchell who tried to prevent the catastrophe. The next night, arriving home, the vicar finds his house in flames. No one is hurt, but their home is gone. They are forced to move into a little shack. In the meantime news arrives that the Squire has been paying court to Miss Wilmot. The Squire's final insult is to appear and offer to find a husband for the betrayed Olivia. Primrose orders him out. In anger, the Squire demands his rent, which the vicar cannot pay. He is jailed, and in prison hears that Olivia is dead and that Sophia has been abducted. To make matters worse, George, returned from London, goes to Thornhill Castle to avenge his sister's dishonor, and in the scuffle injures a servant. He is arrested for attempted murder. Dr. Primrose, completely shattered in health and hopes, writes to Sir William Thornhill, the good uncle of the Squire, to tell him of the young man's knavery. When he feels near death from his sufferings, the vicar is suddenly greeted by Sophia and Burchell, who has rescued her. Burchell turns out to be none other than Sir William Thornhill himself. The Squire is confronted with the two knaves he has hired to carry off Sophia. We also learn that the marriage of Olivia and the Squire has been, unknown to the latter, authentic; Olivia is not dead, after all; "Burchell" bestows a fortune on Olivia and allows her husband "a bare competence;" Sophia marries her rescuer, and George, Miss Wilmot. Next day, the vicar hears that his stolen fortune has been recovered.

Poetry

In the meantime a poem of Goldsmith's, *The Traveler, or A Prospect of Society* (1764) had appeared, and was being widely discussed. It was neo-classical in its heroic couplets and diction, but it had a new music. Instead of the hard brilliance of Pope's school, this survey of society which undertook to show that "every state has a particular principle of happiness," had an ease and freshness and tenderness unknown to classicism. It was followed in 1770 by Goldsmith's best poem, "The Deserted Village." It too is written in heroic couplets that aim to be didactic. But luckily Goldsmith did not have it in him to be a neoclassicist in polished verse. A very unclassical warm humanity and the very real pictures of rural life and country folk, have made it one of the important precursors of the Romantic Movement. "The Deserted Village" is a contradiction: on the surface it seems to be a neoclassical satire on the Industrial Revolution. Intrinsically it is a Romantic poem on the sights and simple personalities of the country.

Comedy

In still one more field Goldsmith was to achieve a great triumph. His first comedy, *The Good-Natured Man*, was not entirely successful. It attempted to banish the sentimentality then epidemic in English comedy. Since the very early years of the century there had been no comedies on the stage worthy of production. His second comedy, *She Stoops to Conquer, or the Mistakes of a Night* (1773) is one of the best in the language. In it he restored the sprightliness and wit of Restoration drama without Restoration licentiousness. There is a pervading atmosphere of good health, merriment, and high spirits, which make this play the one bright moment in the history of English drama between the comedies of Congreve and Farquhar and those of Sheridan to follow. The hero, Marlow, is extremely bashful. A match has been proposed between Miss Hardcastle and Marlow, by Marlow's father, Sir Charles. Marlow goes with a friend to visit the Hardcastles. But the two young men lose their way at night, and are directed by Tony Lumpkin, Mrs. Hardcastle's son by previous marriage, to the Hardcastles' home as though it were a public inn; this is the kind of practical joke that Lumpkin is always playing. Marlow, taking Hardcastle for the landlord of the inn, makes free to order what he wants, falls in love with what he believes to be the landlord's daughter. With a servant none of his terrible bashfulness is in evidence. But the idea of meeting Miss Hardcastle is terrifying to him. When Sir Charles arrives, Marlow learns that he has won the heart of Miss Hardcastle, and that the home is no inn. Hardcastle understands at last why his young guest seemed so rude.

EDMUND BURKE (1729–1797)

Burke is the greatest master in English of political eloquence. He was a man of keen intellect, and Johnson, although he was violently of the opposite party, was boundless in his admiration for this member of the Club. Though Burke devoted all his abilities to politics, it was his destiny to be on the losing side in most of his public arguments; ironically, in many instances his position has been justified by history. Goldsmith felt that it was a great pity that Burke, who was "born for the Universe, narrowed his mind, and to Party gave up what was meant for Mankind."

Burke was born in Dublin and educated there at Trinity College; he entered the Middle Temple, in London, in 1750. His *Philosophic Enquiry Into the Origin of Our Ideas of the Sublime and the Beautiful* (1756) won him great respect. The same year he published a satire, *Vindication of Natural Society* (1756), in which he attacks the followers of Rousseau for desiring a society without the restraining influence of legal processes. He became a member of Johnson's Club in 1764. Two years later began his long career in Parliament.

From the very beginning he warmly espoused the cause of the American colonists. In 1774 he delivered his celebrated speech *On American Taxation*, in which he urged the government to do away with the tax on tea in America. The next year his even better known address *On Conciliation With America* (1775) argued that the colonists as free Englishmen were entitled to be treated as such. Had Burke's advice been followed, England might never have had to fight the American Revolution. Burke's interest in the rights of colonials was further demonstrated in his long attack on Warren Hastings' mismanagement and shortsighted policy in India (1788–1794). Burke was a Protestant but he fought for the rights of the Irish as well as for the emancipation of Catholics. He was also one of the first men in English politics to interest himself in the abolition of the slave trade.

Throughout all these contests Burke argued for political liberty on strongly conservative principles. The cornerstone of his thinking was that all English people had won the constitutional right of political freedom and representation in English Parliament. When the French Revolution began, therefore, the English radicals were a little shortsighted in expecting Burke to defend it. Indeed, his was one of the first voices to be raised against it. When Burke's *Reflections on the Revolution in France* (1790) was published, even the Tories were friendly to the Revolutionaries. The Revolution had as yet manifested no violence. The King and Queen of France seemed in no danger, and it appeared that the French were only trying to establish a constitutional monarchy such as the English themselves had. In November, 1789, at a meeting to commemorate the English Revolution of 1688, a Nonconformist minister, Dr. Price, made a speech saluting the French Revolution, and declaring it to be a new era of freedom in Europe. Burke's *Reflections* was written as an answer to Price. Burke was alarmed at what he thought a danger to the fundamental principles by which society can exist. Price had declared that the people possessed the right to choose their own rulers and to dismiss them at their pleasure. Such ideas seemed to Burke to invite revolution in England. The ideas of Voltaire and Rousseau he considered anarchical. In England, he argued, the people and their monarchs had signed a contract in 1688, and since then Englishmen have been bound to be faithful to their agreement. They owned no right to choose another monarch or to dismiss one that they had accepted.

When the *Reflections* came out, Burke's party, the Whigs, thought him a traitor. He was forced to break with them, even though he had been a leader. Abuse was hurled at him from every quarter. But he was not the turncoat that they tried to make him out to be. He had never been a friend of abstract principles, had always reasoned from precedent, and appealed to a love of order in society. He was now convinced that the new theories of the French would bring anarchy and atheism into Europe. In a few years the King and Queen of France were executed, the Reign of Terror began, and many liberals in England became hostile to the French Revolution. It was then that Burke seemed to have been a prophet whom none had heeded.

Burke followed up his attack with *Letters on a Regicide Peace* (1796–1797). In the meantime (1794) he had retired from Parliament in order to make way for his son. But later in the same year Burke was grief-stricken by his son's death. The Crown, recognizing Burke's services, granted Burke a pension. Against this grant the Duke of Bedford, a friend of the Revolution, argued hotly. Burke's last work, *A Letter to a Noble Lord* (1796), his most splendid piece of writing, was an answer to the Duke and a defense of Burke's own career.

Burke has been called one of our finest prose stylists. He has rarely been excelled in the dignity of his style or the richness of his vocabulary.

RICHARD BRINSLEY SHERIDAN (1751–1816)

The finest dramatist of the end of the eighteenth century was born in Dublin in a family that had had many writers. Sheridan's father had been an actor-manager in Dublin theaters for years. When young Sheridan was nine he was taken to England and later sent to Harrow. He studied law in London, but his legal career was ended by his elopement with a famous beauty, Elizabeth Linley, because of whom he fought two duels. Playwriting actually occupied only a small part of his life, from 1773, the year he married, until 1780, when he entered Parliament. In these few years he proved himself to be the most gifted dramatist since the Elizabethans; yet he never went back to writing plays. In Parliament he was greatly admired for his oratory, and his speeches against Warren Hastings are among the best pieces of oratory in our language. He fought by the side of Burke and Fox for the rights of the American Colonists, and remained a friend of the French Revolution. Despite his manifold gifts, he had no talent for finance. In the end he was forced to give up a seat in Parliament because of his debts, and in 1813 was in debtors' prison. When he was on his death bed, there was a Sheriff waiting in the room. His country, however, atoned by giving him a splendid funeral and by burying him in Westminster Abbey.

The only fine contribution to eighteenth-century comedy before Sheridan is Goldsmith's *She Stoops To Conquer.* The sentimentality of the plays that held the boards had debased public taste. But the four comedies of Sheridan are the last bright flourishing of the English comic genius for another century. *The Duenna* (1776), *The Rivals* (1776), *The School For Scandal* (1777), and *The Critic* (1779) revived the Restoration wit and interest in the social behavior of men and women. They are among the finest examples of the English comedy of manners. *The Duenna* is a delightful comic opera that was highly successful. *The Critic* is a satire on sentimental comedy and literary criticism of the time; the leading characters are a plagiarist-versifier (Sir Fretful Plagiary), two critics (Dangle and Sneer), and a shameless practitioner of the science of puffing (Puff); an idiotic tragedy by Puff, *The Spanish Armada*, is introduced to add to the fun. But it is *The Rivals* and *The School For Scandal* that still hold the interest of the English theater-going public.

The Rivals deals with the love of Captain Absolute, son of Sir Anthony, for Lydia Languish, the niece of Mrs. Malaprop. Lydia is a sentimental girl who prefers a lieutenant without any income to the son of a baronet. Therefore, Absolute presents himself as Ensign Beverley, and awakens Lydia's interest. But Mrs. Malaprop is against the match. Sir Anthony arrives in town to promote the match between his son and Lydia, and to this proposal Mrs. Malaprop is very friendly. A rival suitor for Lydia's hand is a numbskull, Bob Acres, who is pushed into challenging Beverley to a duel. Acres asks Absolute to deliver the challenge to Beverley. Another suitor challenges Absolute. Absolute, thus involved in two duels, lacks the courage to reveal to Lydia that her beloved Beverley is Captain Absolute. Acres discovers Absolute's identity, however, and hastens to give up all claim to Lydia. When Lydia finds out who Beverley is, she quarrels with her lover for depriving her of a romantic elopement, but then forgives him. The character of Mrs. Malaprop has become part of English tradition. Her name has become synonymous with all those who use complicated language without understanding it.

The School For Scandal is the favorite of Sheridan's comedies, and one of the most perennially popular in our literature. The screen scene in Act 4 is perhaps the most celebrated single scene in our drama. The play has two distinct themes: The story of the Teazles and the story of the "Scandal School." Lady Teazle belongs in the tradition of Congreve's Millamant, one of the most enchanting women in English comedy. Sheridan was to some extent influenced in this play by Molière's *The Misanthrope*. Charles Surface is a good-natured spendthrift who is in love with Maria, the ward of Sir Peter Teazle. Joseph Surface, a smooth hypocrite, Charles' brother, is paying court to Maria because she is an heiress. At the same time Joseph is annoying Lady Teazle, Sir Peter's young wife, with his attentions. The scandal-mongers, Mrs. Candour, Lady Smearwell, and Sir Benjamin Backbite are always on hand to pick up any gossip. The uncle of Charles and Joseph, Sir Oliver Surface, returns without warning from India, and makes up his mind to find out what his nephews are like. His researches reveal that Charles is fundamentally good, despite his reckless ways. Joseph Surface attempts to seduce Lady

Teazle, but is interrupted by the arrival of Sir Teazle. To save her reputation Lady Teazle hides behind a screen. When Charles comes in Sir Peter also goes in hiding. The talk between the two brothers proves to Sir Peter that his jealousy of Charles has no basis. At this point the screen falls over and Lady Teazle is revealed. Sir Oliver, pretending to be a needy relative, is refused help by Joseph with the excuse that Joseph's uncle is too stingy with him. Joseph is thus completely exposed as a hypocrite and scoundrel, Sir Peter and Lady Teazle make up their quarrel, and Charles and Maria are to be married.

MINOR WRITERS

A number of historians, philosophers, and social activists achieved a modicum of fame in their day and substantial influence upon the course of English and American literature and history thereafter.

Philip Stanhope, Earl of Chesterfield (1694–1773)

Chesterfield was an orator, statesman and a brilliant conversationalist. He had many important political posts on the Continent and in Ireland. Deafness caused his retiring from public life in 1755. His *Letters* are among the best in an age that produced very superior letter writers. Of these the most celebrated were those written to his illegitimate son to instruct him in his education, public demeanor, and his desire to get on in the world. They were published in 1774. Chesterfield's philosophy is completely worldly and practical. He has no interest in ethics and his maxims are aimed only at the success of the young man. The *Letters* are distinguished by considerable polish.

Edward Gibbon (1737–1794)

Gibbon was the most important of eighteenth-century historians. He served for a while in the military and sat for six years in Parliament. His most significant work is *The History of the Decline and Fall of the Roman Empire* (1776; 1781; 1788), a masterful study beginning with the Emperor Trajan in the first century of the Christian era and proceeding through the Fall of Constantinople in 1453. Gibbon's *History* is one of the great monuments of English prose. It is written by a rationalist who sought to prove with his vast erudition that the Fall of the Roman Empire was due to the barbaric triumph of religion. Naturally, Gibbon's work has always been frowned upon by the orthodox.

Thomas Paine (1737–1809)

Paine belongs more properly to American history than to English literature. He played a prominent role in his day in the affairs of his native England and of France. After following various humble trades in England, he came to America in 1774, and became intimately connected with the struggle of the Colonists against England. He joined the Revolutionary Army, even though he was a Quaker, and his papers, *The Crisis*, were of inestimable aid to Washington's forces. When the war was over, Paine returned to England as a great Republican and won the friendship of Burke, whom he very much admired. He also became an associate of the radical writers in London, notably Godwin and William Blake. When Burke published his *Reflections*, Paine, who was shocked at what he considered his former friend's retreat from liberalism, wrote his celebrated *Rights of Man* (1791–1792) as an answer. In simple phrases he supported the principles of the French Revolution. His book became so popular that he was indicted for high treason and forced to flee for France. He never returned to England.

William Godwin (1756–1836)

For a decade Godwin had the reputation of being the leading philosopher in England, quite out of proportion to his merits. He became involved with a number of people of such importance that he is likely always to be remembered for their sake alone. He made a profound impression on younger men like Wordsworth, Coleridge, Hazlitt and Lamb; he married the most remarkable English woman of her age, Mary Wollstonecraft, the great champion of women's rights; their daughter Mary later married the poet Shelley. Godwin was for a while a Nonconformist clergyman, but his reading of the French philosophers caused him to lose his faith, and he became an atheist. In 1793 he published *An Enquiry Concerning the Principles of Political Justice*, the first book to propound philosophical anarchism. The book caused a great stir. Godwin taught the doctrine that the human race was destined to become perfect, in each era becoming more perfect, and that in the millennium it would even conquer death. He believed man by nature to be philanthropic, and that the exercise of reason would completely conquer man's animal and emotional nature, and make government unnecessary. He was an enemy of marriage and family ties as hostile to the exercise of pure reason. Until the campaigns of Napoleon alienated the English radicals, Godwin seemed like the prophet of a new order to the younger generation. Before the century had ended, his reputation was on a decline. He is the author of several novels, of which one is very good: *Things As They Are, or the Adventures of Caleb Williams* (1794), the first detective novel in English, and the first novel to study the psychology of crime. It is well-written and excellently planned. It also is a propaganda novel, for it is above all an indictment of England's penal system and of the injustice that wealth can extend over poverty.

22
THE GROWTH OF THE NOVEL

FORERUNNERS OF THE NOVEL

The novel became in the nineteenth century the most popular of literary forms. Before the eighteenth century there is little to record in its history. Among the ancients, the *Satyricon* of Petronius is a kind of forerunner of realistic narrative writing; Longus' *Daphnis and Chloe*, Heliodorus' *Aethiopica*, and Apuleius's *Golden Ass* were important examples of the romantic story of adventure. During the Renaissance many Italian writers made collections of tales; of these the most famous, of course, is Boccaccio's *Decameron*. In England a number of Elizabethan writers wrote prose romances—Sidney in his *Arcadia*, Greene in his *Pandosto*. But the nearest resemblance to a novel in that age was Nashe's *The Unfortunate Traveller*. None of these, however, is properly speaking a novel. Before the novel could emerge as a type, a prose style for English had to be evolved. Modern prose does not begin until the time of Dryden, and it was Defoe, a man of Dryden's generation, who made the first important contributions toward the development of a novel in his tales of adventure and pseudoautobiographies. Defoe's *Robinson Crusoe* and *Moll Flanders* are actually collections of loosely connected episodes, much in the style of the *picaresque romances* of Spain, which narrate the adventures of a rogue (*Picaro*). But Defoe's characterization is excellent, and his air of realism admirable. What his stories lack in order to be classified as novels is a unified plot. The character writers of the seventeenth century and the essayists of Pope's generation also made notable contributions to the development of the novel in the series of portraits which they presented.

SAMUEL RICHARDSON (1689–1761)

The first English novel was more or less of an accident. A middle-aged printer, Samuel Richardson, who had lived mostly in the company of spinsters, planned a book of model letters for people in humble walks of life. In order to give some unity to the letters, he hit upon the idea of connecting them with a story. His *Pamela, or Virtue Rewarded* (1741–1742) was his first book, and the first English novel. To his astonishment it took the London public by storm. The epistolary form of novel-writing remained thereafter one of the most popular. The plot of Pamela is very simple. Pamela is a maid servant in the service of Mr. B. She is a very good girl. Mr. B. is attracted by her charms, and with dishonorable intentions is in constant pursuit of her in the hopes of winning her favor. She manages to resist him despite his ingenuity in arranging difficult situations. But her resistance becomes increasingly difficult as she finds that she has come to love him. Mr. B. at last becomes convinced that her virtue is unassailable, and consequently proposes marriage to her. She accepts this reward of her virtue, and he turns out to be an ideal husband. The book seems interminable and tedious to modern readers, but in its own day its heavy sentimentality insured it success. To be fair to Richardson, one must admit that he was something of a psychologist in dealing with his heroine, and depicted her struggles with herself with far more insight than many of his successors showed in their works.

Richardson's next novel, *Clarissa Harlowe*, appeared in eight volumes in 1747–1748, also in the form of letters. This time the correspondence is carried on by various people. The plot is more complicated than that of *Pamela* and far more dramatic. Clarissa cannot agree to marry the man her family has chosen for her to marry. She appeals for help to her lover, Lovelace, a roué, and he runs off with her. He tries to seduce her. She tries to escape from him. But he uses drugs on her, and under their influence she yields to him. Eventually she dies from a broken heart, crushed by shame. Lovelace repents, but is slain in a duel by one of Clarissa's relatives. The book had an enormous vogue, chiefly because of the sentimentality. Like *Pamela*, however, *Clarissa Harlowe* reveals Richardson's unusual knowledge of female psychology. The novel made a powerful impression upon the French, and Rousseau's novel *La Nouvelle Héloise* was written in imitation of it.

Richardson's last novel, *The History of Sir Charles Grandison* (1754), is quite inferior to its predecessors. This portrait of a sentimental hero is dull. Richardson knew very little about the emotional processes of men.

HENRY FIELDING (1707–1754)

The career of Henry Fielding as a novelist began after this young aristocrat had starved in London's literary Bohemia, written some twenty farces and comedies, and had thoroughly enjoyed being a gadfly to the party in power. It was largely against Fielding that the Licensing Act of 1737 was passed, and effectively put an end to his career as a playwright. After that Fielding tried the law. But when *Pamela* was published Fielding apparently roared with mirth at Richardson's sentimentalities. There was not a grain of sentimentality in Fielding's own sturdy, rational mind. In his witty fancy, he hit upon the idea of creating a brother to Pamela Andrews, whom he named Joseph, and who was to be the main character in a novel showing how this virtuous youth defended his chastity against the attacks of a lecherous female. Fielding, however, was a born novelist, and actually gave up the more limited idea of making a burlesque, and bestowed upon the world instead an excellent comic novel.

The History of Joseph Andrews

In *The History of Joseph Andrews* (1742), Fielding forgets *Pamela* by the ninth chapter. The central figure becomes a man who is unforgettable, Parson Adams, a simple, learned and brave figure—the first great portrait in the English novel. The story is largely a record of Parson Adams' many experiences. Lady Booby (the female counterpart of *Pamela's* Mr. B.) chases Joseph all over the premises. In the end he marries a humble girl, Fanny. We also meet Pamela's husband, Lord Booby.

Sir Thomas Booby is the uncle of the Mr. B. who eventually married Pamela. Joseph, Pamela's brother, is a servant of Sir Thomas. On the death of his employer, Joseph is retained by Lady Booby, who despite her years finds herself captivated by Joseph's beauty. The young man is innocence itself, like his sister; but even he begins to understand that Lady Booby is out to seduce him. His virtue will not succumb. Chagrined, Lady Booby discharges him despite the pleas of her maid, Slipslop, who is also attracted to the youth. But Joseph is constant to his affection for Fanny, and leaves London to visit her. The first night of his journey his money is stolen by some brutal robbers, who leave him badly beaten up. His cries are heard by passing travelers, who take him into their coach to an inn, where the hostess tends to him. There he comes upon his old teacher, Parson Adams, who pays Joseph's debt to the inn, and agrees to accompany Joseph on his travels. Slipslop, en route to Lady Booby's country house, overtakes them and invites Adams into the coach; thus, Joseph is able to ride the parson's horse. At the next inn, when Joseph is insulted by the innkeeper, Adams takes up the challenge; in the ensuing fracas Slipslop and the hostess join too—the latter throwing a pail of hog's blood over the unlucky parson. When they leave, Adams forgets his horse; Joseph is now in the coach; Adams, on foot, makes better time. The parson comes to the rescue of a young woman being attached by a scoundrel; when some hunters arrive, the rogue accuses the woman and Adams of being robbers. The two are arrested, the parson discovering his friend to be Joseph's Fanny, about to visit Joseph in London. Before the judge, Adams is able to procure their release, and they join Joseph and Slipslop at the tavern where the latter are lodged. Slipslop is outraged to note Joseph's rapture at seeing Fanny, and drives off in the coach. Fanny, Joseph, and Adams are completely stranded, so the parson attempts to borrow money from the local clergyman, to no avail. But the three are enabled to leave the tavern when a poor peddler pays their bill. At the next inn the proprietor is kinder. Later on their travels the gracious Wilsons invite them to stop at their house. Mr. and Mrs. Wilson, originally cousins, would be perfectly happy living in the retired countryside with their two children were it not for their sorrow over their lost third child, stolen by gypsies. The three travel on. Soon the luckless souls find themselves pursued by hunters' dogs as though they were the prey. Adams and Joseph battle the hounds. The hunting squire is furious when he arrives, until he is smitten by Fanny's beauty. He invites all three to dinner, where poor Adams becomes the object of some vulgar jokes. Annoyed, they leave the house for an inn, where, during the night, the squire's servants abduct Fanny. She is happily saved by an old friend, Pounce, who encounters the kidnapping party. They arrive at length at what turns out to be the locale of Lady Booby's country house. Joseph and Fanny go to the parsonage, awaiting the day of their union. Lady Booby arrives and does what she can to prevent the marriage, and manages to have the pair arrested. But Joseph's sister Pamela comes too with her spouse, Squire Booby, who easily procures the release of the young lovers, but joins his wife and Lady Booby in trying to dissuade Joseph from marrying so far beneath the station of the Boobys. A real impediment turns up when an itinerant merchant proves that Fanny's hitherto unknown parents are the same as Pamela's! Mr. and Mrs. Andrews are called for, appear, and tell how Fanny has been stolen by gypsies when a baby, and exchanged for another, who was Joseph. But the latter bears the identifying strawberry-mark of the lost Wilson baby. Thus, at last, Joseph Wilson and Fanny Andrews are free to marry.

Fielding's next novel was the satirical *The Life of Mr. Jonathan Wild the Great*, written with much irony on the iniquity of human beings. Under the pretense of showing the hero to be a great man, Fielding follows Jonathan Wild from the days when he learned the arts of picking pockets and becoming a sharper, until he becomes more proficient than any of his teachers. He marries a loose woman, indulges in knavish plots, and finally ends on the gallows tree. In this book Fielding's legal studies proved useful. The novelist reveals himself thoroughly familiar with the habits of thieves, and even knows their slang.

The History of Tom Jones, A Foundling

This 1749 novel is Fielding's best novel, and the greatest of the century. There are critics who say that it has never yet been equalled. Here Fielding exhibits his genius for managing a large number of life-like characters and subplots, and weaving them all into a unified novel. Between the separation of Tom from his sweetheart at the beginning of the novel, and his being reunited with her at the end, we encounter an unending variety of incidents. Always in the background is the mystery of Tom's parentage. There is a wonderful feeling of everyday reality throughout the book, as we wander with Tom through the countryside, along roads, in taverns, and through the streets of London. The character studies of Tom, Allworthy, Partridge, Squire Western, and Sophia are all done with vivacity and humaneness.

The story tells how a kind gentleman, Allworthy, living in the country with his sister Bridget, returns one night from London to find an infant lying on his bed. He decides, against the advice of his household, to keep and provide for the child. Wishing to know its parents, he sends out his housekeeper to make inquiries. After a short investigation, one Jenny Jones, a young woman of the village, admits to being the mother but refuses to say who the father is. Allworthy, being of a generous disposition, arranges that Jenny be sent to a distant county, where she may make a fresh start and not be burdened with an evil reputation. Shortly after, his sister, Bridget, meets a captain Blifil, a brother to an old friend of the family. Soon the captain marries Bridget, not for love, but for the fortune that will be his on Allworthy's death. While waiting for his brother-in-law to die, Blifil has a child by Bridget, a boy. But not long thereafter Blifil himself dies. Young Blifil and Tom Jones are raised as brothers. Even as a boy, Tom Jones shows up to disadvantage in comparison with Blifil, and early earns the reputation of being less likely to become a man of virtue. Both the boys' teachers, Mr. Square and especially the Reverend Mr. Thwackum, favor Blifil and dislike Jones. Thwackum, an advocate of the power of the rod, uses it frequently, but always upon Tom; both pedants judge that Allworthy's fortune will fall to Blifil. Tom is caught in various misdeeds, such as robbing an orchard, stealing a duck, appropriating a ball, and even becomes suspect of ingratitude when he sells a horse given him by Squire Allworthy.

As it turns out later, Tom's misdeeds were indulged so that he might feed the family of Black George, a gamekeeper once employed by Allworthy, who, Tom believes, lost his job because of Tom. In time Tom has an affair with Molly Seagrim, a daughter of Black George, and she bears him a child. Such immoral conduct further lowers Allworthy's opinion of Tom. At about this time, Tom has become a good friend to a neighbor, Squire Western. After returning from a hunt with him, Tom saves his daughter Sophia from a serious fall from her horse. In the act of rescuing her, Tom breaks his arm and remains at the Westerns', with Sophia nursing him back to health. Sophia and Tom have been childhood friends, and soon realize that they have fallen in love with each other. Tom begins to worry about Molly and the promises he has made to her because of his obligations to her. Visiting Molly in an attempt to come to an understanding with her, he finds her in bed with his teacher, the philosopher Square, and thereupon loses all qualms of conscience concerning her future. He also has reason to doubt that the child is his after all, since Tom was not Molly's first lover. Still he promises to provide for her. When he hears the news that Allworthy is very ill, Tom hastens home. Allworthy recovers, and Tom is so delighted at his benefactor's return to health that he drinks too much in celebration. Blifil, annoyed at Tom's state, makes some slighting remarks about Tom's origins, and a fight ensues. A little while later, Tom is discovered in what appears to be a compromising situation by Blifil and Thwackum while strolling in the fields, and beats them soundly when they attempt forcibly, but unsuccessfully, to ascertain the identity of the girl. During the fight Molly slips away.

In the meantime, Western's sister, while visiting with her brother, discovers Sophia to be in love, but erroneously supposes Blifil to be the object of the girl's affections. She informs Squire Western of what she believes to be an authentic fact, and Western immediately proposes to Allworthy a match between Blifil and Sophia. Allworthy consents. Sophia, learning to whom she is to be wed, refuses to marry Blifil; Western now learns that it is Tom she loves, and becomes infuriated. Blifil, realizing that he must deal with Tom before he can have Sophia, relates to Allworthy the incident of his beating, and, more important, the drunkenness of Tom in a highly distorted version which Thwackum eagerly backs up. Allworthy becomes entirely embittered against Tom. Accused, Tom is too much overwhelmed to defend himself. Allworthy commands him to leave. In equally difficult straits, Sophia runs away from home to avoid marrying Blifil.

We now follow our hero, Tom Jones, through many adventures. First he decides to make his way to Bristol to try his fortunes at sea, but, upon encountering a group of soldiers going to fight against the forces of the returning Stuarts, he decides to join them. Before starting with the regiment, he receives a blow on the head in a quarrel, and is laid up for a few days. During this time Tom meets one Partridge (once thought to be his father) who follows Jones, still believing him to be in Allworthy's favor. They pass through several adventures together, the most notable being when Jones rescues a Mrs. Waters from assault. Sophia happens to arrive at the same inn where Tom is staying, and wishing to see him is put off by Partridge. Sophia discovers that Tom has been sleeping with Mrs. Waters, and she departs in a fit of indignation, leaving behind a muff which was dear to them both. Tom, discovering the muff, and hence that Sophia was there, abandons all idea of joining his regiment to fight for the Protestant cause, and instead pursues Sophia. At this time Sophia meets her cousin, Mrs. Fitzpatrick, who was running from her husband, and together they go to London. In London Sophia remains under the protection of a relative, Lady Bellastron. En route to London himself, Tom encounters a highwayman, manages to disarm him, and credits the robber's story that he wished to feed his starving family; finding the gun empty of bullets, he releases him and gives him some money. Arriving in London, Tom attempts to locate Sophia. Discovering that she has traveled with Mrs. Fitzpatrick, he luckily finds the latter's residence, procures audience with her, but finds her obdurate against supplying him with knowledge of Sophia's whereabouts. He stays at the inn of Mrs. Miller, often frequented by Squire Allworthy on his visits to town; he performs several good offices for Mrs. Miller. He saves the honor of her family by being instrumental in bringing about the marriage of her daughter to a man who has seduced the girl, Nancy, even though the groom's father objects to the match. Also, he aids a cousin of Mrs. Miller and his family from starving; this turns out to be the same man who tried to rob him on the road.

After a little while in London, Tom is invited to a masquerade ball by Lady Bellastron, who, having seen him at Mrs. Fitzpatrick's, was much taken by his aspect. Believing she can lead him to Sophia, he attempts to cultivate her friendship. She, however, wishes to have him as a lover, and presents him with various gifts, chiefly money, of which he is now in dire need. One evening, when calling at her house, Tom accidentally meets Sophia there. The lovers soon make up. Tom, wishing to break off all ties with Lady Bellastron, sends a letter, upon the advice of a friend, proposing marriage. The letter is a success; but Lady Bellastron, now indignant and very jealous, desires revenge, and attempts to marry Sophia to a young lord whom she dislikes. But the nobleman's suit is not encouraged; Bellastron urges him to rape Sophia, so that she will be willing to marry him. After a few qualms, he consents; the stage set, he stalks his victim. But as he is just beginning his first advances amid the screams of Sophia, Squire Western bursts in, having at last located his daughter. He takes her from her "protectress" and swears that she must marry Blifil. At this time Tom has a duel with Mrs. Fitzpatrick's husband, who thinks Tom his wife's lover. Tom seriously wounds his adversary, and is thrown in jail.

Sophia has her own troubles: Lady Bellastron and Sophia's aunt wish her to marry the nobleman, and her father is adamant about the marriage with Blifil. Allworthy and Blifil arrive in London at Western's request, who has promised a quick wedding; they take up residence at Mrs. Miller's. Mrs. Miller soon acquaints Allworthy with Tom's fate and with all the good he has done. But Allworthy does not change his opinion of Tom. Blifil, learning that Tom is in prison and could be charged with murder, attempts to forge the evidence and testimony against the man he hates. Mr. Square writes a letter to Allworthy telling him the true incidents of Tom's drunkenness. Allworthy receives, too, a call from Mrs. Waters, who turns out to be Jenny Jones, the supposed mother of Tom; but she informs Allworthy that Tom Jones is really the child of his sister Bridget, and that she was well rewarded for acknowledging the baby as hers. The father was a Mr. Summer, who died about the time the child was born. Allworthy now discovers that Blifil, on the night of Bridget's death, when Allworthy himself was ill, deliberately retained a letter sent him by his sister to unfold the truth about Tom's parentage. Fitzpatrick recovers from his wound, and is able to clear Tom of all guilt by admitting that the duel had been his own contriving. A reconciliation takes place between Allworthy and Tom. Allworthy is filled with the greatest delight to find that Tom is really his nephew, a close relative after all. Blifil is sent away to fend for himself. But all is not clear sailing for Tom and Sophia; Sophia has had his letter to Lady Bellastron called to her attention with the facts all distorted in the presentation of this damning evidence. Sophia feels disillusioned in her lover, and begins to view him with coldness. Mrs. Miller, however, proves to be a good friend to Tom. That good woman's untiring efforts make Sophia confront the real circumstances of the letter; Miss Western also learns that Tom has turned down a proposal of marriage offered him by a rich, young, and extremely attractive widow. All that he has done has been out of love for her, Sophia, even to the writing of that letter. Sophia begins to fall in love with her hero all over again. And now the Fates cease to be unkind to the union of the two lovers. Squire Western learns that Tom is All-worthy's nephew, and so far from holding out against the marriage, becomes as anxious as they to speed it. The wedding takes place on the next day, and everyone is happy at the end. "Whatever in the nature of Jones had a tendency to vice has been corrected . . . by his union with the lovely and virtuous Sophia."

Not the least attractive part of this breezy and engaging novel is the series of delightful essays which are interspersed throughout the pages of the story by Fielding—essays on all manner of subjects, and among the best ever written in English.

Fielding's last novel, *Amelia* (1751) is filled with propaganda against the English prison system and the corruption of the police. Fielding had been magistrate of a police court, and had become very conscious of the need for reform in dealing with crime. It is said that the heroine of this novel was a portrait of his first wife, whom he had adored. It is her constancy and self-sacrifice that preserve the hero from ruin, to which his love of pleasure seems almost inevitably to lead him. In this book Fielding comes near to falling into the sentimentalizing that was so fashionable. His pictures of London slums are very real, and prepare the way for the novels of Dickens.

TOBIAS SMOLLETT (1721–1771)

Tobias Smollett was the father of the nautical novel. For some time he served as a surgeon in the West Indies, while a very young man; he married a Creole whom he dearly loved. On his return to London he published his first novel, *The Adventures of Roderick Random* (1748), a coarse, almost brutal tale in the picaresque tradition. Many of its salty incidents were part of his own experience. The hero is followed on sea and land from Europe to South America. He is a rogue without scruples, and he is always getting into trouble. After attempting unsuccessfully to marry various heiresses, he finally marries a girl with whom he is in love.

The Adventures of Peregrine Pickle (1751) is conceived in the same racy manner. It contains Smollett's finest portrait, that of the old salt, Commodore Trunnion. The novel also contains some clever satire on contemporary politics and literary affairs. There are some wonderful pieces of grotesque humor throughout the book.

From 1756 to 1763, Smollett became the head of a kind of factory for turning out literary hack work on travel, geography, and history and making translations. He also edited the *Critical Review*, the *British Magazine*, and the *Briton*. During these busy years he wrote two more picaresque novels, *Ferdinand Count Fathom* (1753), a story whose plot is rather superior to Smollett's earlier novels, though written with less zest; and *Sir Launcelot Greaves* (1760), a poor imitation of *Don Quixote*.

His last novel, written while he was in very poor health, *The Expedition of Humphrey Clinker* (1771), is his best. It is cast in the epistolary style and is rather loosely strung together. But much of Smollett's indecency and brutality of mood is gone here. The tone is mellowed and mature, and the result is a wonderful picture of English life in town and at the fashionable resorts. The plot deals with the adventures of the bachelor Matthew Bramble, and his sister Tabitha, a spinster, who travel with their nephew and niece, Jerry and Lydia Melford. The company is at Bath, now at London, now in Edinburgh, and now in the Highlands of Scotland. Humphrey Clinker, who joins the group on his travels, is a quick-witted servant who marries the Bramble's maid, and later turns out to be Matthew Bramble's illegitimate son. In this novel we see to perfection Smollett's talent for recreating characters from low life, such as are not to be met with in the pages of his contemporaries.

LAURENCE STERNE (1713–1768)

Laurence Sterne is in a class by himself among English novelists. His two celebrated books can be called novels only because they defy any other kind of classification. Sterne spent his childhood in Ireland with the regiment in which his father served as a subaltern. He went to Cambridge, and there studied for the ministry. Through the aid of a relative, he became prebend of York, more because it assured him a livelihood than through any deep religious calling. York was a merry town in those days, and Sterne fell in happily with the fast life led there by society. Although married, he frequently was in love with other women. He went in for racing, hunting, and unearthed all kinds of rare books which he read with delight. He was temperamentally an eccentric, and indulged his tastes to the limit. Even his sermons took on all sorts of oddities of style and thought uncommon to ecclesiastical oratory.

The Life and Opinions of Tristan Shandy, Gentleman

When Sterne was forty-six the first two volumes of *The Life and Opinions of Tristram Shandy, Gentleman* appeared, and caused a sensation. This was in 1759. The succeeding volumes were issued in 1761, 1762, 1765 and 1767.

Fielding and Richardson were through as novelists, and Smollett was occupied with his hack work. The public was waiting for a new novel, and Sterne supplied them with one that belonged to a new species. His mind was a storehouse of quaint learning, and he was well-acquainted with the work of Rabelais and Burton, both of them masters of the quaint. No stranger book than *Tristram Shandy* has ever been written. The author himself admitted that when he had written a sentence he trusted to God for the next. Sterne followed his imagination wherever it led him—and it led him to fantastic places. The book has very little plot; it is almost all digression. There is a wonderful inebriated air of fantasy throughout. The digressions are amazing in kind and quantity. Some follow from the story, others are introduced for no apparent reason. The first volume opens with what is an attempt to tell of the birth of the hero. But at once associations spring up at every turn, and the second volume closes with the hero still unborn. In fact, Tristram Shandy is the one person who never really appears in the book. In Sterne's topsy turvy world there are many wonderful portraits, however, notably the cracked Mr. Shandy, Uncle Toby, Corporal Trim, and the Widow Wadman. Every kind of oddity is thrust into the book. We find fantastic punctuation, asterisks that mislead us, diagrams, and a long excommunication in Latin. In one place where a minor character is introduced, the author leaves a blank page for the reader to write in his own description. Sterne has many qualities in addition to his genius for being entertaining. His zest never tires, his fund of humor is inexhaustible and his dialogue has the very sound of actual speech.

"Pray, my Dear," quoth my mother, "have you not forgot to wind up the clock?" With this irrelevant and badly-timed question at the moment his parents are busy conceiving him, the mother of Tristram Shandy so disconcerts his father that our hero's entire career is destined to be affected by the crucial interruption. On the fifth day of November, 1718,—"as near nine calendar months" later "as any husband could in reason have expected," Tristram is born at Shandy Hall. That evening his father has been in the parlor with Mr. Shandy's brother, Uncle Toby, an old soldier, and they have been engaged, as ever, in argument. Uncle Toby dwells near his brother in a little house bequeathed to him; the retired hero is

> a gentleman who, with the virtues which usually constitute a man of honor and rectitude—possessed one in a very eminent degree . . ., and that was a most extreme and unparalleled modesty of nature;—though I correct the word nature, for this reason, that I may not prejudge a point . . ., and that is, Whether this modesty of his was natural or acquired.

Our author raises the question because the fact is that Uncle Toby was wounded in the groin during the battle of Namur. He has brought with him into retirement Corporal Trim, who has been disabled by a wound in the left knee, and who has been to Uncle Toby "a valet, groom, barber, cook, sempster, and nurse." It was Trim's inspired notion to construct on the wide lawn behind Uncle Toby's little house an elaborate series of model fortifications. Here Uncle Toby spends much of his time directing fanciful battles, and thus acquiring material for his discourses on military engagements. Mr. Shandy loves his gentle brother, but has little sympathy for that kind of talk. Not fond of listening to anyone else, Mr. Shandy is moved to irritation by his brother's disquisitions on matters military; himself a collector of all sorts of scraps of recondite information, Mr. Shandy constantly breaks in upon Uncle Toby's observations to indulge in long monologues during which he airs his own scatter-brained theories—chief among which are his convictions on the importance of names and long "noses." He has already decided that his son must be adorned with the name of Trismegistus. Hearing of the imminent appearance of his offspring, Mr. Shandy against his will sends for the midwife his spouse insists upon having; to run no risks he also summons Dr. Slop, an incapable quack. The medico is to earn his fee by sitting with Mr. Shandy and Uncle Toby in the parlor consuming a bottle of wine and much talk, while the midwife is to assist Mrs. Shandy in her labors. At the end of thirty-four chapters (!) Dr. Slop enters the back parlor where Mr. Shandy and Uncle Toby "were discoursing upon the nature of women." While they are waiting for word of the midwife (in the forty-second chapter!), Corporal Trim reads them a sermon. Presently there is a commotion overhead.

Many chapters later Dr. Slop goes upstairs to see if he can be of service. Bungling the job, Doctor Slop brings Tristram into the world with what the author euphemistically refers to as a crushed "nose." Mr. Shandy does not doubt that this catastrophe is a direct result of Mrs. Shandy's inopportune question at the moment of the child's conception. (Later on in life, a falling window-sash is to bring further anatomical disaster upon the boy Tristram as he is answering a call of nature through an open window.) Meanwhile, Mr. Shandy is so overcome with disappointment that he goes to his room and flings himself prostrate upon his bed; then he arises to go for a walk to the fishpond. Returning to the parlor, he finds Trim and Uncle Toby recreating a battle scene. Too much concerned with his misfortune to upbraid them for such an occupation at this crucial hour, Mr. Shandy embarks upon a long lamentation:

> "Unhappy . . . child of wrath! child of decrepitude! interruption! mistake! and discontent! . . . With all my precautions, how was my system turned topside-turvy in the womb with my child! his head exposed to the hand of violence . . . that at this hour 'tis ninety percent. insurance that the fine network of the intellectual web be not rent and torn into a thousand tatters!"

Willing to take no further chances with disaster, Mr. Shandy accedes to his brother's suggestion that the Rev. Mr. Yorick, the village pastor, be summoned at once to baptize the child. The desperate father, rushing off to dress, entrusts the maid Susannah with the information that the boy is to be christened "Trismegistus." The girl confuses the name, and Mr. Yorick bestows the name of Tristram upon the child—a name which in Mr. Shandy's philosophy is the most calamitous in its inevitable blighting of anyone's life. Thus the elder Shandy is cast down by the knowledge that Tristram has been three-fourths handicapped from the beginning: by the circumstances of his conception, his crushed "nose," and his tragic name. After a while, the reader is notified of the death of Mr. Shandy's first son, Bobby.

> When my father received the letter which brought him the melancholy account of my brother Bobby's death, he was busy calculating the expense of his riding post from Calais to Paris, and

so on to Lyons . . . When the letter was brought into the parlor . . .
my father had got forwards again upon his journey to within a
stride of the . . . stage of Nevers.—By your leave, Mons. Sanson,
cried my father, striking the point of his compasses through Nevers
into the table—and nodding to my uncle Toby to see what was in
the letter . . . He leaned forwards upon the table with both elbows
as my uncle Toby hummed over the letter . . .—he's gone! said my
uncle Toby.—Where—Who? cried my father.—My nephew, said
my uncle Toby.—What—without leave—without money—without
governor? cried my father in amazement. No: he is dead, my dear
brother, quoth my uncle Toby.—Without being ill? cried my father
again.

To meet this event Mr. Shandy summons up quotations on life and death
from the philosophers. As the book nears its last quarter, we begin to put
together the pieces of the story of Uncle Toby's romance with the Widow
Wadman. Anxious to marry again, the lady engages upon a campaign to win
Uncle Toby's hand. Gentle soul that he is, he has little idea of which way her
friendship is tending, until she begins to make queries into the nature of his
wound and its precise location. Uncle Toby agrees to gratify her curiosity by
promising to allow her to put her finger on the very spot where he has been
wounded. He brings her a map of the battlefield of Namur, where he was
struck, and bids her touch the spot he indicates. The widow is silenced by
Uncle Toby's innocence. It is Corporal Trim who finally explains to his master that the lady wishes to know the anatomical location of his wound, not
the geographical. Uncle Toby is so dumbfounded at the possibility of his
being exposed to the mortification of such an exposure that he ends at once
the incipient romance. In this madcap novel it is characteristic that the final
page finds Dr. Slop still present, and that the hero of *The Life and Opinions
of Tristram Shandy, Gentleman* has hardly managed to be born when the
work is over. The incidents herein related pursue a dizzying course; we are
often told the conclusion of an affair at first, and do not know its beginnings
until much later. We are tempted to ask with Mrs. Shandy at the end: "L - - d!
said my mother, what is this all this story about? A Clock and a Bull, said
Yorick."

Sterne came to London and was there lionized. His talk was enjoyed, even
though he was fond of making it quite naughty. Perhaps the fact that his
contemporaries made so great a virtue out of sanity and order is responsible
for the success of Sterne's raising confusion into a fine art. In his novel there
is also, however, a strong element of sentimentality. After a journey to the
continent, Sterne published, shortly before his death, *A Sentimental Journey
to France and Italy* (1768), in which his penchant for inspired lunacy was
combined with a heavier seasoning of sentimentality. The book even contains a rapturous apostrophe to "sensibility" as the means that lifts us up to
heaven. A famous line in this uncompleted novel is: "God tempers the wind
to the shorn lamb."

MINOR NOVELISTS

Henry Mackenzie (1745–1831)

A Scottish writer who became a disciple of Sterne, Mackenzie carried out Sterne's "sensibility" to the limits of the ridiculous. *The Man of Feeling* (1771) has as hero a man who goes about in search of things to weep over. Its sequel, *The Man of the World* (1773) is written in the same style. The books were enormously popular. Mackenzie was also the editor of two periodicals modeled on *The Spectator, The Mirror* (1779–1780) and *The Lounger* (1785–1789). It was in the latter that Mackenzie publicly recognized the greatness of his fellow countryman, Robert Burns.

Fanny Burney (1752–1840)

Fanny Burney became Madame D'Arblay when she married a refugee-nobleman from France. Her *Diaries* give us a very vivid picture of the inner life at Court, where she spent much of her life. She is the originator of the novel of home life. Her *Evelina* (1778), *Cecilia* (1782), and *Camilla* (1796) show her talent for recreating conversation and scenes familiar to her in the homes of people who move in the highest society. She has a delightful sense of caricature, but her novels are marred by sentimentality and moral pompousness. She prepared the way, however, for Jane Austen.

Horace Walpole (1717–1797)

Walpole is one of the best of our English letter writers. His friendship with the poet Gray proved very important in the latter's career. Walpole is the father of the "Gothic" novel—the novel of mystery and terror. *The Castle of Otranto* (1764) is an attempt to use the Middle Ages as a setting, and even pretended to be a translation from the early Italian. There is much paraphernalia of terror and villainy in it, but it started a vogue that was to be an important factor in the growth of the Romantic movement. The plot deals with the unexplained death of Conrad on the eve of his marriage to the daughter of the Marquis of Vincenza. The Prince of Otranto, Manfred, Conrad's father, thereupon decides to marry the girl himself. First, however, he will have to divorce his wife. Manfred's grandfather's portrait comes down from the wall to talk to him. The Marquis's daughter escapes from the danger of Manfred with the aid of a peasant. It is later revealed that this peasant is actually the rightful heir to the Kingdom of Otranto, and that Manfred had poisoned the heir's father. Walpole is also the author of a Gothic tragedy in blank verse dealing with the theme of incest, *The Mysterious Mother* (1768).

Ann Radcliffe (1764–1823)

Mrs. Radcliffe continued in the tradition established by Walpole. She is the author of a number of such novels. The best known is The *Mysteries of Udolpho* (1794), a book teeming with mysterious passages, disappearing walls, shrouded figures, unexplained groans and clanking of chains. It shows the school at its most extravagant. A better novel is her *The Italian, or The Confessional of the Black Penitents* (1797). Mrs. Radcliffe is able to make her terrors seem very real and to raise intense excitement of suspense over the possibilities of coming events. She is quite adept in chilling the spine. She also exhibits a tendency still common to horror stories in eventually explaining the apparently supernatural as being due, after all, to natural phenomena.

The popularity of Mrs. Radcliffe's novels did much to accelerate the success of the Romantic movement that was just beginning to come into its own when she wrote.

REVIEW QUESTIONS

THE EIGHTEENTH CENTURY

Multiple Choice

1. _____ Compared to the literature of the seventeenth century, the literature of the eighteenth century is
   a. calmer in tone
   b. more revolutionary and experimental
   c. more violent
   d. less social in its concerns

2. _____ The Industrial Revolution did all of the following except
   a. increase the wealth and power of the middle class
   b. increase the wealth and power of the aristocracy
   c. encourage the growth of towns
   d. force many of the poor off the land

3. _____ The Augustan Age is so called because
   a. Augustus ruled as a monarch during this period
   b. the literature was august in its tone
   c. the literature was at the end of a cycle
   d. it valued the kind of literary perfection once achieved under Augustus

4. _____ Eighteenth century comedy differs from Restoration comedy in that it
   a. is more sentimental
   b. satirizes social behavior
   c. concentrates on characters from the lower classes
   d. frequently relies on stock character types

5. _____ The *Essay on Criticism* is filled primarily with Pope's
   a. original critical propositions
   b. rephrasing of established critical propositions
   c. attacks on neoclassical criticism
   d. romantic analysis of individual poets

6. _____ Except for the poetry of Pope, the literature of the eighteenth century was notable primarily for its
   a. prose
   b. plays
   c. sonnets
   d. epics

7. _____ Addison and Steele are remembered primarily for their
   a. journalistic essays
   b. novels
   c. verse
   d. dislike for one another

8. _____ Locke's philosophy focused on
   a. the inherent qualities of mind present at birth
   b. the process by which the mind interprets sensory experience
   c. the divine spark within human cognition
   d. the transcendental truths beyond sensual experience

9. _____ Samuel Johnson began his literary career as a
   a. poet
   b. dictionary writer
   c. novelist
   d. journalist

10. _____ James Boswell achieved his literary fame primarily by writing a biography of
    a. Ben Jonson
    b. William Shakespeare
    c. William Congreve
    d. Samuel Johnson

True or False

11. _____ Scotland and England were united as Great Britain during most of the eighteenth century.
12. _____ In its form and content, the literature of the eighteenth century can best be described as experimental and nonconformist.
13. _____ Alexander Pope's two *Essays* (*On Criticism* and *On Man*) were written in poetic form.
14. _____ John Gay is best known as the author of popular opera, *The Beggar's Opera.*
15. _____ *The Battle of the Books* deals with the controversy of whether European literature is better than native English literature.
16. _____ In *Gulliver's Travels,* the horse figures represent supernatural beings.
17. _____ Addison and Steele's celebrated essays are exclusively devoted to political topics
18. _____ Samuel Johnson's work in poetry began with imitations of other writers.
19. _____ The greatest actor of tragedy in Johnson's day was his pupil, David Garrick.
20. _____ In Sheridan's *School for Scandal*, Mrs. Malaprop and Captain Absolute figure as key characters.

Fill-in

21. Chesterfield is remembered for the _____ he wrote.
22. Thomas Paine's writings greatly influenced the revolutionaries in _____ .

23. Gibbon blames the decline and fall of the Roman Empire on the triumph of _____ .
24. William Godwin was known as a "perfectionist" because he believed man to be innately _____ .
25. Defoe's works are more in the style of the _____ than that of the true novel.
26. The Licensing Act required plays to be read and approved before performance by agents of the _____ .
27. Henry Fielding wrote several plays, although his lasting reputation rests primarily on his _____ .
28. *Pamela*, one of the first novels, is structured as a series of _____ .
29. Henry Walpole and Ann Radcliffe wrote _____ novels.
30. *Tristram Shandy*, one of the most unusual novels ever written, is filled with _____ more than consistent plot.

Matching

31. _____ Richardson
32. _____ Pope
33. _____ Swift
34. _____ Fielding
35. _____ Sheridan
36. _____ Goldsmith
37. _____ Johnson
38. _____ Smollett
39. _____ Defoe
40. _____ Boswell

a. *The Life of Samuel Johnson*
b. *Tale of a Tub*
c. *The Vanity of Human Wishes*
d. *Moll Flanders*
e. *She Stoops to Conquer*
f. *The Rivals*
g. *Clarissa*
h. *Windsor Forest*
i. *Adventures of Peregrine Pickle*
j. *Joseph Andrews*

Answers

1. a	15. f	28. letters
2. b	16. f	29. gothic
3. d	17. f	30. digressions
4. a	18. t	31. g
5. b	19. t	32. h
6. a	20. f	33. b
7. a	21. letters	34. j
8. b	22. America	35. f
9. a	23. Christianity	36. e
10. d	24. good	37. c
11. t	25. picaresque novel	38. i
12. f	26. Lord Chamberlain	39. d
13. t	27. novels	40. a
14. t		

GLOSSARY

Allegory: A literary device, in prose or poetry, in which a literal character, event or object also possesses another level of meaning, usually philosophical, theological, or aesthetic. Thus an allegory may illustrate a philosophical idea or a moral or religious principle. (Examples: the *Romance of the Rose,* Spenser's *Faerie Queene,* Bunyan's *Pilgrim's Progress)*

Alliteration: The proximity of words beginning with the same sound. ("*Counsel* or *consolation* we may bring")

Allusion: An indirect or explicit reference to a well-known place, event, or person. Allusion in literature often takes the form of a figure of speech.

Anapest: A foot consisting of two unaccented syllables and one accented syllable (the first three syllables of "unreliable").

Archetype: In literature, archetypal criticism examines types of narrative, character, and image which occur in a large variety of texts. Literary archetypes, like the Jungian archetypes of the collective unconscious, are said to reflect a group of elemental and universal patterns, that trigger an immediate and profound response from the reader.

Assonance: The repetition, in a line of prose or poetry, of similar or identical vowel sounds. (Example: "maiden shaded by a glade")

Ballad: A narrative song, originally a folk song. (Example: *Edward)*

Ballade: A lyrical form borrowed from the French, consisting of three stanzas and an envoi. Each stanza and the envoi conclude with the same line as a refrain. (Example: *The Complaint of Chaucer To His Empty Purse)*

Blank Verse: Iambic pentameter unrhymed. (Example: Milton's *Paradise Lost)*

Caesura: A break in a line of verse. (Example: the versification of *Beowulf)*

Chivalric romance: A genre of narrative developed in twelfth-century France, similar to the epic in form but treating the themes of courtly love and chivalry. This form of romance was spread through the courts of France by troubadours and minstrels, eventually finding its way to England in the works of Malory, Chaucer, and others.

Conceit: An involved figure of speech. (Example: Shakespeare's sonnet No. 30)

Consonance: The repetition of consonant sounds, with a change in the vowel that follows the consonant. (Example: give, gave)

Couplet: Two consecutive lines of verse.

Dactyl: A foot consisting of one accented syllable and two unaccented syllables. ("Dóminant")

Dimeter: A line containing two feet. ("And nó birds sińg")

Elegy: A lyrical poem in memory of someone dead. (Example: Chaucer's *The Book of the Duchess*)

Enjambment: Verse the meaning of which runs on into the next line. (Example: most of Shakespeare's plays)

Epic: A long narrative poem. A folk epic, celebrates the exploits of a national hero or national heroes. A literary epic also follows the principles laid down by the classical epic tradition beginning with Homer. (Examples: folk epic—*Beowulf*; literary epic—*Paradise Lost*)

Epigram: A brief pointed observation.

Euphuism: An artificial style invented by Lyly, and characterized by the use of balanced and antithetical clauses, alliteration, and farfetched conceits.

Fabliau: A satiric or comic tale and a common literary form in the Middle Ages, the fabliaux both mocked and reveled in the obscene and vulgar elements in lives of both middle- and lower-class persons. Many of Chaucer's *Canterbury Tales* are perfect examples of the fabliau form, including the "Miller's Tale."

Foot: The fundamental unit of verse.

Free verse: Verse without any regular meter or foot.

Genre: A French word meaning type, kind, or form; in literature the term is used to designate different literary forms, such as *tragedy, satire, epic* and more recently *novel, biography*, and so on.

Heroic couplet: Two lines of iambic pentameter, rhyming and containing a complete unit of thought. (Example: Pope's *Rape of the Lock*)

Hexameter: A line containing six feet. (Fáir hárbor thát them seéms, so ín they éntered áre")

Invocation: An appeal for inspiration.

Irony: A figure of speech in which the explicit meaning of a statement or action differs drastically from its implicit meaning. Types of irony include dramatic irony, verbal irony, structural irony. (Example: a priest as a villain.)

Lamb: A foot consisting of one unaccented syllable and one accented syllable. (prefér)

Lyric: A short poem, usually nonnarrative, in which the text expresses the speaker's emotional or mental state. A lyric is often written in the first person, and is often associated with songs and other musical forms. (Example: Herrick's "Upon Julia's Clothes")

Lyrical poetry: Poetry expressing the personal feelings of the author. (Example: "Lycidas")

Metaphor: A figure of speech identifying an object or person with another object or person. ("It is the star to every wandering bark")

Meter: The recognizable and repeated rhythms and stresses created by verse form. Iambic pentameter is the most common meter of English poetry.

Metonomy: A figure of speech in which a literal term or attribute of one thing comes to represent another to which it has a contiguous relation. (Example: the use of "crown" to mean king or queen)

Mimesis: A Greek word meaning *imitation*, mimesis is the active or dynamic representation of a literal (sensual) or metaphysical (spiritual) reality in a work of art or literature.

Monometer: A line containing only one foot.

Motif: A thematic or structural element used and repeated in a single text, or in the whole of literature. A motif may be a literary device, an incident, a formula, or a reference. (Also "leitmotif" or guiding motif)

Octave (also called **Octet**): The first part of an Italian or Petrarchan sonnet, consisting of eight lines. (Example: Rossetti's *Sonnet on a Sonnet*)

Ode: A lyrical poem of high and formal style, usually rhymed, which often addresses itself to a praised person, object or quality. (Example: Wordsworth's "Ode: Intimations of Immortality")

Onomatopoeia: Sound imitative of sense ("*clanking* chains")

Pastoral: A poem in which the characters are shepherds and the setting is in the country. (Example: *Lycidas*)

Pentameter: A line containing five feet. (Nine tímes the spáce that meásures dáy and níght")

Personification: A figure of speech or rhetoric in which inanimate objects or abstractions are given human qualities, or represented as having human form. (Example: "that lazy old sun")

Petrarchan or **Italian sonnet:** A sonnet consisting of two sections, an octave and a sestet. The octave rhymes *abbaabba*; the sestet rhymes *cdecde*, or *cdeedc*, or *cdcdcd*. (Example: Rossetti's *Sonnet on a Sonnet*)

Pindaric ode: A lyrical poem of lofty mood written in groups of three stanzas: a strophe, an antistrophe, and an epode. The strophe and antistrophe are in the same meter and follow the same rhyme scheme. The epode is free. (Example: Gray's *The Bard*)

Quatrain: A stanza of four lines.

Rime royal: A stanza consisting of seven lines in iambic pentameter rhyming *ababbcc*. (Example: Chaucer's *Troilus and Criseyde*)

Satire: A work of literature that attacks society's vice and folly through irony and wit. (Example: Pope's *Dunciad*)

Scansion: The analysis of verse or poetry to uncover its meter and rhythmic patterns.

Sestet: The second part of a Petrarchan or Italian sonnet, consisting of six lines.

Shakespearean or **English sonnet:** A sonnet consisting of two sections; twelve lines and a couplet. The twelve lines rhyme *ababcdcdefef.* The couplet rhymes *gg.* (Example: Shakespeare's sonnets)

Sonnet: A lyrical poem in fourteen lines of iambic pentameter, written according to the Petrarchan or Shakespearean scheme, or some variation of either.

Spenserian stanza: A stanza consisting of nine lines, the first eight in iambic pentameter, the last in iambic hexameter, and rhyming *ababbcbcc.* (Example: *The Faerie Queene*)

Synecdoche: A figure in which a part of something is taken to represent the whole. (Example: "ten sails on the horizon," meaning ten ships)

Terza rima: Verse arranged to rhyme *aba bcb cdc* etc. (Example: Shelley's *The Triumph of Life*)

Tetrameter: A line containing four feet. (Ah, whát can áil thee, wrétched wíght")

Theme: An idea presented and expanded upon in a literary work. A theme can be explicit or implicit, and is usually suggested by the narrative action.

Trimeter: A line containing three feet. ("And yét is hére todáy")

Trochee: A foot consisting of one accented syllable and one unaccented syllable. ("Lísten")

SUGGESTED READINGS

The Old English Period

Alcock, Leslie. *Arthur's Britain, History and Archaeology.* Cambridge, 1956.

Blair, P. H. *An Introduction to Anglo-Saxon England.* Cambridge, 1956.

Bruce-Mitford, R. *The Sutton-Hoo Ship Burial: A Handbook.* 1972.

Higley, S. L. *Between Languages.* Philadelphia, 1993.

Matthew, D. J. A. *The Norman Conquest.* New York, 1966.

Newton, S. *The Origins of Beowulf and the Pre-Viking Kingdom of East Anglia.* London, 1993.

Page, R. I. *Life in Anglo-Saxon England.* London, 1970.

Scullard, H. H. *Roman Britain.* London, 1979.

Southern, R. W. *The Making of the Middle Ages 972-1204.* New York, 1959.

Wacher, John. *Roman Britain.* London, 1978.

The Middle English Period

Barnes, G. *Counsel and Strategy in Middle English Romance.* New York, 1993.

Bennett, H. S. *Six Medieval Men and Women.* Cambridge, 1955.

Cohn, Norman. *The Pursuit of the Millenium.* New York, 1961.

Galbraith, V. H. *The Making of Domesday Book.* Oxford, 1961.

Holt, J. C. *Magna Carta.* Cambridge, 1965.

Keen, M. *The Outlaws of Medieval Legend.* London, 1987.

Lander, J. R. *Conflict and Stability in Fifteenth Century England.* London, 1969.

Morgan, G. *Medieval Balladry and the Courtly Tradition.* New York, 1993.

Platt, Colin. *Medieval England.* New York, 1978.

Poole, A. L., ed. *Medieval England.* Oxford, 1958.

Runciman, S. *A History of the Crusades.* Cambridge, 1954.

Turville-Petre, T. *The Alliterative Revival.* Cambridge, 1977.

Weiss, Roberto. *Humanism in England during the Fifteenth Century.* Oxford, 1967.

Zbierkska-Sawala, A. *Early Middle English Word Formation.* New York, 1992.

Chaucer

Brewer, D. S. *Chaucer.* London, 1953.

Brown, P. *The Age of Saturn.* New York, 1991.

Buckler, P. *Love and Death in Chaucer's Book of the Duchess.* Bowling Green, 1991.

Coghill, N. *The Poet Chaucer.* Oxford, 1950.

Denley, M. *Middle English: Chaucer.* New York, 1989.

Fisher, S. *Chaucer's Poetic Alchemy.* New York, 1988.

Gerould, G. H. *Chaucerian Essays.* Princeton, 1952.

Malone, K. *Chapters on Chaucer.* Baltimore, 1951.

Muscatine, C. *Chaucer and the French Tradition.* Berkeley, 1957.

Root, R. K. *The Poetry of Chaucer.* New York, 1950.

Speirs, J. *Chaucer the Maker.* New York, 1951.

Tatlock, J. S. P. *The Mind and Art of Chaucer.* Syracuse, 1950.

Wiehe, R. *The Two Gardens of Sacred and Profane Love.* New York, 1992.

Malory

Vinaver, E., ed. *The Works of Sir Thomas Malory.* Oxford, 1954.

Gaines, B. *Sir Thomas Malory.* New York, 1990.

Kennedy, B. *Knighthood in the Morte d'Arthur.* New York, 1992.

The Ballads

Leach, M., ed. *English Medieval Ballads.* New York, 1955.

Medieval Drama

Anderson, Fleming. *Commonplace and Creativity.* London, 1985.

Craig, H. *English Drama of the Middle Ages.* London, 1955.

Harris, J. *Medieval Theater in Context.* New York, 1992.

Patern, S. *The Liturgical Context of Early European Drama.* New York, 1989.

Salter, F. M. *Medieval Drama in Chester.* Toronto, 1955.

The Renaissance, the Reformation, and the Elizabethans

Allison, R. F. *The Contemporary Printed Literature of the English Counter-Reformation, 1558–1640.* New York, 1989.

Alpers, Paul. *The Poetry of "The Faerie Queene."* Princeton, 1967.

Anglo, S. *Spectacle, Pageantry, and Early Tudor Policy.* Oxford, 1969.

Babb, L. *The Elizabethan Malady.* New York, 1951.

Bates, C. *The Rhetoric of Courtship in Elizabethan Language and Literature.* Cambridge, 1992.

Bennett, H. S. *English Books and Readers 1558–1603.* Cambridge, 1965.

Burke, Peter. *The Renaissance Sense of the Past.* London, 1969.

Byrne, M. S., ed. *Lisle Letters.* Chicago, 1981.

Dickens, A. G. *The English Reformation.* New York, 1964.

Eisenstein, Elizabeth. *The Printing Press as an Agent of Change.* Cambridge, 1979.

Elton, J. R. *Reform and Renewal.* Cambridge, 1973.

Holden, W. P. *Anti-Puritan Satire, 1572–1642.* New Haven, 1954.

Hurstfield, Joel. *Freedom, Corruption, and Government in Elizabethan England.* London, 1973.

Lewis, C. S. *English Literature in the 16th Century.* London, 1954.

Morey, A. *The Catholic Subjects of Elizabeth I.* New York, 1978.

Salomon, B. *Critical Analyses in English Renaissance Drama.* New York, 1991.

Starnes, W. T. *Classical Myth and Legend in Renaissance Dictionaries.* Chapel Hill, 1955.

Thomas, Keith. *Religion and the Decline of Magic.* London, 1971.

Tillyard, E. M. W. *The English Renaissance.* Baltimore, 1952.

Williams, Penry. *The Tudor Regime.* Oxford, 1979.

Marlowe

Dabbs, T. *Reforming Marlowe.* New York, 1991.

Greg, W. W. *Dr. Faustus.* London, 1950.

Henderson, P. *Christopher Marlowe.* London, 1952.

Levin, H. *The Overreacher.* Cambridge, 1952.

Sales, R. *Christopher Marlowe.* New York, 1991.

Tydeman, W. *Christopher Marlowe.* London, 1989.

Wilson, F. P. *Marlowe and the Early Shakespeare.* London, 1953.

Shakespeare

Bamber, L. *Comic Women, Tragic Men: A Study of Gender and Genre in Shakespeare.* Stanford, 1982.

Bullough, G., ed. *Narrative and Dramatic Sources of Shakespeare.* New York, 1973.

Danby, J. F. *Poets on Fortune's Hill.* New York, 1952.

Dean, L. F. *Shakespeare.* Oxford, 1957.

Doran, M. *Shakespeare's Dramatic Language.* Madison, 1976.

Drakakis, J., ed. *Alternative Shakespeares.* New York, 1985.

Fluchere, H. *Shakespeare.* London, 1953.

Garrett, J. *Talking of Shakespeare.* London, 1954.

Greene, G., ed. *The Women's Part: Feminist Criticism of Shakespeare.* Urbana, 1980.

Gregg, W. W. *The Shakespeare First Folio.* London, 1955.

Halliday, F. E. *The Enjoyment of Shakespeare.* London, 1952.

Harbage, A. *Shakespeare and the Rival Traditions.* New York, 1952.

Huhner, M. *Shakespearean Studies.* New York, 1952.

Knight, G. W. *The Wheel of Fire.* London, 1954.

McCurdy, H. G. *The Personality of Shakespeare.* New Haven, 1953.

Meader, W. G. *Courtship in Shakespeare.* New York, 1954.

Simpson, P. *Studies in Elizabethan Drama.* London, 1955.

Stirling, B. *Unity in Shakespearean Tragedy.* New York, 1956.

Watkins, W. B. C. *Shakespeare and Spenser.* Princeton, 1950.

Woodbridge, L. *Shakespeare: A Selected Bibliography of Modern Criticism.* New York, 1988.

Elizabethan Dramatists and Poets

Boas, F. S. *Queen Elizabeth in Drama.* New York, 1950.

Bowers, F. T. *On Editing Shakespeare and the Elizabethan Dramatists.* Philadelphia, 1955.

Bradbrook, M. C. *The Growth and Structure of Elizabethan Comedy.* London, 1955.

Curry, J. V. *Deception in Elizabethan Comedy.* New York, 1955.

Hodges, C. *The Recovery of the Elizabethan and Jacobean Playhouse.* New York, 1989.

Marcus, L. *Recent Studies in Elizabethan and Jacobean Literature.* New York, 1992.

Reed, R. R. *Bedlam on the Jacobean Stage.* Cambridge, 1952.

Simpson, P. *Studies in Elizabethan Drama.* London, 1955.

Beaumont and Fletcher

Appleton, W. W. *Beaumont and Fletcher.* New York, 1956.

Bliss, L. *Francis Beaumont.* New York, 1987.

Danby, J. F. *Poets on Fortune's Hill.* New York, 1952.

Findelpearl, P. *Court and Country Politics in the Plays of Beaumont and Fletcher.* Princeton, 1990.

Gossett, S. *The Influence of the Jacobean Masque on the Plays of Beaumont and Fletcher.* New York, 1988.

Waith, E. M. *The Pattern of Tragicomedy in Beaumont and Fletcher.* New Haven, 1952.

Campion

Davis, W. *Thomas Campion.* New York, 1987.

Lindley, D. *Thomas Campion.* New York, 1986.

Wilson, C. *Words and Notes Coupled Lovingly Together.* New York, 1989.

Chapman

Braunmuller, A. R. *Natural Fictions.* New York, 1991.

Lord, G. *Homeric Renaissance.* New Haven, 1956.

Sanre, G. *The Mystification of George Chapman.* Chapel Hill, 1989.

Dekker

Bowers, F. *Thomas Dekker, the Dramatic Works.* Cambridge, 1955.

Champion, L. *Thomas Dekker and the Traditions of English Drama.* New York, 1985.

Gasper, J. *The Dragon and the Dove.* London, 1990.

Thornton, G. E. *The Social and Moral Philosophy of Thomas Dekker.* New York, 1955.

Drayton

Brink, J. R. *Michael Drayton Revisited.* New York, 1990.

Dyer

Barrel, J. *English Literature in History.* New York, 1983.

Ford

Oliver, H. J. *The Problem of John Ford.* Melbourne, 1955.

Greene

Crupi, Charles. *Robert Greene.* New York, 1986.

Dean, J. S. *Robert Greene.* London, 1984.

Heywood

Baines, Barbara. *Thomas Heywood.* New York, 1984.

Jonson

Butler, M. *Late Jonson.* London, 1992.

Chute, M.G. *Ben Jonson of Westminster.* New York, 1953.

Evans, R. *Jonson, Lipsius, and the Politics of Renaissance Stoicism.* New York, 1992.

Patridge, A. *The Accidence of Ben Jonson's Plays.* London, 1953.
Potter, L. *Seeing and Believing.* Edinburgh, 1991.

Lyly
Feinberg, N. *Elizabeth, Her Poets, and the Creation of the Courtly Manner.* New York, 1988.

Marston
Tucker, K. *John Marston.* London, 1985.

Massinger
Clark, I. *The Moral Art of Philip Massinger.* New York, 1993.

Middleton
Schoenbaum, S. *Middleton's Tragedies.* New York, 1955.
Steen, S. *Ambrosia in the Earthly Vessel.* New York, 1993.

Peele
Braunmuller, R. *George Peele.* New York, 1983.
Horne, D. H. *Minor Works of George Peele.* New Haven, 1952.

Raleigh
Strathmann, E. A. *Sir Walter Raleigh.* New York, 1951.
May, S. *Sir Walter Raleigh.* New York, 1989.

Shirley
Clark, I. *Professional Playwrights.* Lexington, 1992.
Lucow, B. *James Shirley.* New York, 1981.

Sidney
Buxton, J. *Sir Philip Sidney and the English Renaissance.* New York, 1954.
Danby, J. F. *Poets on Fortune's Hill.* New York, 1952.
Gibbons, B. *Amorous Fictions and As You Like It.* London, 1987.
Hager, A. *Dazzling Images.* New York, 1991.
Miller, N. *Rewriting Lyric Fictions.* Amherst, 1990.

Spenser
Arthos, J. *On the Poetry of Spenser.* London, 1956.
Bernard, J. *Ceremonies of Innocence.* Cambridge, 1989.
Chang, S. *Allegory and Courtesy in Spenser.* Edinburgh, 1955.
Hardin, R. *Civil Idolatry: Desacralizing and Monarchy in Spenser, Shakespeare, and Milton.* Ottawa, 1992.
Heninger, S. K. *Sidney and Spenser.* Philadelphia, 1989.
King, J. *Spenser's Poetry and the Reformation Tradition.* Princeton, 1990.
Rooks, J. *Love's Courtly Ethic in The Faerie Queene.* New York, 1992.
Watkins, W. B. C. *Shakespeare and Spenser.* Princeton, 1950.
Whitaker, V. K. *The Religious Basis of Spenser's Thought.* Stanford, 1950.

Surrey
Sessions, W. *Henry Howard, Earl of Surrey.* New York, 1986.

Tourneur
Schuman, S. *Cyril Tourneur.* New York, 1977.

Webster
Bogard, T. *The Tragic Satire of John Webster.* Berkeley, 1955.
Callaghan, D. *Women and Gender in Renaissance Tragedy.* New York, 1989.
Leech, C. *John Webster.* London, 1951.
Ronald, M. S. *John Webster.* New York, 1989.

Wyatt
Foley, S. M. *Sir Thomas Wyatt.* New York, 1990.

The Seventeenth Century
Bethell, S. L. *The Cultural Revolution of the 17th Century.* New York, 1951.
Boyce, B. *The Polemic Character.* New York, 1955.
Everitt, A. *Change in the Provinces: The Seventeenth Century.* Leicester, 1969.
Kenyon, J. *The Popish Plot.* London, 1972.
King, B. *Seventeenth Century English Literature.* New York, 1982.

Nardo, A. *The Ludic Self in Seventeenth Century Literature.* New York, 1991.

Parry, G. *The Seventeenth Century.* London, 1989.

Stone, L. *The Crisis of Aristocracy 1558–1641.* New York, 1965.

Wedgwood, C. V. *Seventeenth-Century English Literature.* Oxford, 1950.

Wiley, M. L. *The Subtle Knot.* Cambridge, 1952.

Wilson, C. *England's Apprenticeship 1603–1673.* New York, 1965.

The Bible

Finy, T. *The Lion and the Lamb.* New York, 1992.

Frye, N. *Words with Power.* New York, 1990.

Nida, E. A. *God's Word in Man's Language.* New York, 1952.

Rypins, S. *The Book of Thirty Centuries.* New York, 1951.

Bacon

Case, T. *The Advancement of Learning and the New Atlantis.* London, 1956.

Cocquevillette, D. *Francis Bacon.* Stanford, 1992.

Dick, H. G., ed. *Selected Writing of Sir Francis Bacon.* New York, 1955.

Dodd, A. *Francis Bacon's Personal Life Story.* New York, 1986.

Green, A. W. *Sir Francis Bacon, His Life and Works.* London, 1952.

Jameson, T. H. *Francis Bacon.* New York, 1954.

Wybrow, C. *The Bible, Baconism, and Mastery over Nature.* New York, 1991.

Cavalier Poets

Summers, C., ed. *Classic and Cavalier.* Pittsburgh, 1982.

Walton, G. *The Cavalier Poets.* London, 1982.

Carew

Selig, E. *The Flourishing Wreath.* New Haven, 1958.

Cowley

Trotter, D. *The Poetry of Abraham Cowley.* New York, 1979.

Crashaw

Roberts, J. R. *Richard Crashaw.* St. Louis, 1985.

Donne

Carey, J. *John Donne's Life, Mind, and Art.* New York, 1990.

Fish, S. *Masculine Persuasive Force: Donne and Verbal Power.* Chicago, 1990.

Gransden, K. *John Donne.* London, 1954.

Louthan, D. *The Poetry of John Donne.* New York, 1951.

Patrides, C. *The Complete English Poems of John Donne.* London, 1990.

Taylor, E. *Donne's Idea of a Woman.* New York, 1991.

G. and P. Fletcher

Kastor, F. *Giles and Phineas Fletcher.* New York, 1978.

Herbert

Flesch, W. *Generosity and the Limits of Authority.* Cornell, 1992.

Hodgkins, C. *Authority, Church, and Society in George Herbert.* St. Louis, 1993.

Lull, J. *The Poem in Time.* New York, 1990.

Herrick

Gertzman, J. *Fantasy, Fashion, and Affection.* New York, 1986.

Hageman, E. *Robert Herrick.* London, 1983.

Martin, L. C., ed. *The Poetic Works of Robert Herrick.* London, 1956.

Lovelace

Weidhorn, M. *Richard Lovelace.* New York, 1970.

Marvell

Bloom, H. *Andrew Marvell.* New York, 1989.

Condran, C., ed. *The Political Identity of Andrew Marvell.* New York, 1990.

Wallerstein, R. C. *Studies in Seventeenth Century Poetics.* Madison, 1950.

Suckling

Squier, C. *Sir John Suckling.* New York, 1978.

Traherne

DeNeef, A. L. *Traherne in Dialogue.* Chapel Hill, 1988.

Dowell, G. *Enjoying the World.* London, 1990.

Willy, M. E. *Life Was Their Cry.* New York, 1950.

Vaughan

Bethell, S. L. *The Cultural Revolution of the Seventeenth Century.* New York, 1951.

Clements, A. *Poetry of Contemplation.* New York, 1990.

Waller

Hillyer, R. "Better Read than Dead: Waller's 'Of English Verse,'" *Restoration* (Spring, 1990): 33ff.

Wither

Hensley, C. S. *The Later Career of George Wither.* London, 1969.

Browne

Finch, J. S. *Sir Thomas Browne.* New York, 1950.

Post, J. *Sir Thomas Browne.* New York, 1987.

Taylor

Porter, H. B. *Jeremy Taylor, Liturgist 1613–1667.* London, 1979.

Walton

Anderson, J. *Biographical Truth.* New Haven, 1984.

Epstein, W. *Recognizing Biography.* Philadelphia, 1987.

Milton

Arthos, J. *On a Mask Presented at Ludlow Castle.* Madison, 1954.

Cawley, R. R. *Milton's Literary Craftsmanship.* Oxford, 1951.

Darbishire, H., ed. *Poetical Work of John Milton.* London, 1955.

Dorian, D. *The English Diodatis.* Rutgers, 1950.

Gregory, E. R. *Milton and the Muses.* New York, 1989.

Hanford, J. H., ed. *Poems of John Milton.* New York, 1953.

Hardin, R. *Civil Idolatry: Desacralizing and Monarchy in Spenser, Shakespeare, and Milton.* Ottawa, 1992.

Kinney, C. R. *Strategies of Poetic Narrative.* Cambridge, 1989.

Kirkonnel, W. *The Celestial Cycle.* Toronto, 1952.

Le Comte, E. S. *Yet Once More.* New York, 1953.

Marjara, H. *Contemplation of Created Things: Science in Paradise Lost.* Toronto, 1991.

Musacchio, G. *Milton's Adam and Eve: Fallible Perfection.* New York, 1991.

Pommer, H. F. *Milton and Melville.* Pittsburgh, 1950.

Schultz, H. *Milton and Forbidden Knowledge.* New York, 1955.

Sprott, S. E. *Milton's Art of Prosody.* London, 1953.

Wofford, S. *The Choice of Achilles: The Ideology of Figure in the Epic.* Stanford, 1992.

Wolfe, D. M., ed. *The Complete Prose Works of John Milton.* New Haven, 1960.

The Restoration

Jose, N. *Ideas of the Restoration in English Literature 1660–1671.* Cambridge, 1984.

Lund, R. D. *Restoration and Early Eighteenth Century English Literature 1660–1740.* New York, 1980.

Spector, R. D. *Backgrounds to Restoration and Eighteenth Century Literature.* New York, 1989.

Restoration Drama

Bevis, R. W. *English Drama.* London, 1988.

Leggatt, A. *English Drama.* London, 1989.

Etherege

Markley, R. *Two-Edg'd Weapons.* London, 1988.

Wycherley

Marshall, W. *A Great Stage of Fools.* New York, 1993.

Congreve

Ewald, A. C., ed. *Complete Plays of William Congreve.* New York, 1956.

Lynch, K. M. *A Congreve Gallery.* Cambridge, 1951.

Thomas, D. *William Congreve*. New York, 1992.

Otway
Derrick, S. *The Dramatic Censor*. New York, 1985.
Taylor, A. M. *Next to Shakespeare*. Chapel Hill, 1950.

Pepys
Delaforce, P. *Pepys in Love*. London, 1986.
Heath, H. T. *Letters of Samuel Pepys*. London, 1955.
Taylor, I. *Samuel Pepys*. New York, 1989.

Dryden
Frost, W. *Dryden and the Art of Translation*. New Haven, 1955.
Harth, P. *Pen for a Party*. Princeton, 1993.
Hooker, E. N. and Swedenbourg, H. T., ed. *The Works of John Dryden*. Berkeley, 1960.
Larson, M. *Translation: Theory and Practice*. New York, 1991.
Myerson, G. *The Argumentative Imagination*. Manchester, 1992.

Defoe
Allen, W. E. *Six Great Novelists*. New York, 1955.
Backsheider, P. *Daniel Defoe*. Baltimore, 1989.
Fitzgerald, B. *Daniel Defoe*. London, 1955.
Flynn, C. *The Body in Swift and Defoe*. Cambridge, 1990.
Watson, F. *Daniel Defoe*. London, 1952.

The Eighteenth Century
Baxter, Stephen. *William III and the Defense of European Liberty*. New York, 1966.
Bosker, A. *Literary Criticism in the Age of Johnson*. London, 1953.
Boys, R. C. *Studies in the Augustan Age*. New York, 1952.
Chambers, J. D. and Mingay, G.E. *The Agricultural Revolution 1750–1880*. New York, 1966.
Deane, Phyllis. *The First Industrial Revolution*. Cambridge, 1979.

Humphreys, A. R. *The Augustan World*. London, 1954.
Mingay, G. E. *English Landed Society in the Eighteenth Century*. London, 1963.
Moore, C. A. *Backgrounds of English Literature 1700–1760*. St. Paul, 1953.
Mucke, D. E. von. *Virtue and the Veil of Illusion*. Stanford, 1991.
Plumb, J. H. *The Origins of Political Stability in England 1675–1724*. Boston, 1967.
Rogers, Pat. *Grub Street*. London, 1972.
Rude, George. *Hanoverian London*. London, 1971.
Spector, R. D. *Backgrounds to Restoration and Eighteenth Century English Literature*. New York, 1989.
Waldroper, John. *Kings, Lords, and Wicked Libellers: Satire and Protest 1760–1837*. London, 1973.
Watt, Ian. *The Rise of the Novel*. Berkeley, 1971.

Pope
Dobree, B. *Alexander Pope*. New York, 1952.
Fairer, D. *The Poetry of Alexander Pope*. London, 1989.
Knight, D. *Pope and the Heroic Tradition*. New Haven, 1951.
Knight, G. W. *Laureate of Peace*. Oxford, 1955.
Mack, M. ed. *Essay on Man*. London, 1951.
Quintero, R. *Literate Culture: Pope's Rhetorical Art*. Newark, 1992.
Richardson, J. A. *Falling Towers*. Newark, 1992.
Tillotson, G., ed. *The Rape of the Lock*. New Haven, 1955.
Williams, A. L. *Pope's Dunciad*. New York, 1955.

Gay
Wilton, C. *John Gay and the London Theater*. Lexington, 1993.

Swift
Bullitt, J. M. *Jonathan Swift and the Anatomy of Satire*. Cambridge, 1953.
Ewald, W. B. *The Masks of Jonathan Swift*. Cambridge, 1954.
Forster, J. P. *Jonathan Swift*. London, 1991.

Greenacre, P. *Swift and Carroll.* New York, 1955.

Hammer, S. B. *Satirizing the Satirists.* New York, 1990.

Hunting, R. *Jonathan Swift.* New York, 1989.

Murray, J. M. *Jonathan Swift.* New York, 1954.

Price, M. *Swift: an Introduction.* Oxford, 1955.

Addison and Steele

Ketcham, M. G. *Transparent Designs.* Atlanta, 1985.

Loftis, J. C. *Steele at Drury Lane.* Berkeley, 1952.

Johnson

Bate, W. J. *The Achievement of Samuel Johnson.* Oxford, 1955.

Cafarelli, A. *Prose in the Age of Poets.* Philadelphia, 1990.

Clifford, J. L. *Young Sam Johnson.* 1955.

Greene, D. J. *Samuel Johnson.* New York, 1989.

Hinnant, C. H. *Samuel Johnson.* New York, 1988.

Ralegh, W. *Johnson on Shakespeare.* Oxford, 1952.

Boswell

Clingham, G. *James Boswell.* Cambridge, 1992.

Cochrane, H. E. *Boswell's Literary Art.* New York, 1992.

Pottle, F. A. *Boswell on the Grand Tour.* New York, 1953.

Goldsmith

Dixon, P. *Oliver Goldsmith Revisited.* New York, 1991.

Burke

Ayling, S. *Edmund Burke.* New York, 1988.

Ferguson, F. *Solitude and the Sublime.* London, 1992.

Stanlis, P. J. *Edmund Burke.* New York, 1991.

Sheridan

Worth, K. *Sheridan and Goldsmith.* New York, 1992.

Gibbon

Craddock, P. *Edward Gibbon.* Baltimore, 1989.

Joyce, M. *Edward Gibbon.* London, 1953.

Porte, R. *Gibbon.* New York, 1988.

Paine

Ayer, A. J. *Thomas Paine.* London, 1988.

Philip, M. *Thomas Paine.* Oxford, 1989.

Wilson, J. *Thomas Paine.* New York, 1989.

Godwin

Clemit, P. *The Godwinian Novel.* London, 1993.

Monro, D. H. *Godwin's Moral Philosophy.* Oxford, 1953.

Rodway, A. E. *Godwin and the Age of Transition.* London, 1952.

The Novel

Kahn, Madeline. *Narrative Transvestism.* New York, 1991.

McKillop, A. D. *The Early Masters of English Fiction.* New York, 1956.

Scheick, W. J. *Fictional Structure and Ethics.* Atlanta, 1990.

Burney

Epstein, J. *The Icon Pen.* Ann Arbor, 1989.

Fielding

Allen, W. E. *Six Great Novelists.* New York, 1955.

Dudden, F. H. *Henry Fielding.* London, 1952.

Hume, R. *Henry Fielding and the London Theatre.* London, 1988.

Pringle, P. *Hue and Cry.* New York, 1955.

Rivero, A. J. *The Plays of Henry Fielding.* New York, 1989.

Radcliffe

Cotton, D. *The Civilized Imagination.* Cambridge, 1985.

Richardson

Gwilliam, T. *Samuel Richardson's Fictions of Gender.* Stanford, 1993.

Mullan, J. *Sentiment and Sociability.* London, 1988.

Sale, W. M. *Samuel Richardson*. New York, 1950.

Smollett

McNeil, D. *The Grotesque Depiction of War and the Military in Eighteenth Century English Fiction*. Newark, 1990.

Preston, T. *The Expedition of Humphrey Clinker*. Athens, 1990.

Wagner, P. *The Life and Adventures of Sir Launcelot Greaves*. London, 1988.

Sterne

Fredman, A.G. *Diderot and Sterne*. New York, 1955.

Lamb, J. *Sterne's Fiction and the Double Principle*. Cambridge, 1989.

Traugott, J. *Tristram Shandy's World*. Berkeley, 1954.

Walpole

Lewis, W. W., ed. *The Correspondence of Horace Walpole*. New Haven, 1955.

Miller, N. *Strawberry Hill*. New York, 1986.

INDEX